SECOND LANGUAGE WRITING
Series Editor, Paul Kei Matsuda

Second language writing emerged in the late twentieth century as an interdisciplinary field of inquiry, and an increasing number of researchers from various related fields—including applied linguistics, communication, composition studies, and education—have come to identify themselves as second language writing specialists. The Second Language Writing series aims to facilitate the advancement of knowledge in the field of second language writing by publishing scholarly and research-based monographs and edited collections that provide significant new insights into central topics and issues in the field.

Books in the Series

The Politics of Second Language Writing: In Search of the Promised Land, edited by Paul Kei Matsuda, Christina Ortmeier-Hooper, and Xiaoye You (2006)
Building Genre Knowledge, Christine M. Tardy (2009)
Practicing Theory in Second Language Writing, edited by Tony Silva and Paul Kei Matsuda (2010)
Foreign Language Writing Instruction: Principles and Practices, edited by Tony Cimasko and Melinda Reichelt (2011)

Foreign Language Writing Instruction

Principles and Practices

Edited by
Tony Cimasko and Melinda Reichelt

Parlor Press
Anderson, South Carolina
www.parlorpress.com

Parlor Press LLC, Anderson, South Carolina 29621

© 2011 by Parlor Press
All rights reserved.
Printed in the United States of America

SAN: 254-8879

Library of Congress Cataloging-in-Publication Data

Foreign language writing instruction : principles and practices / edited by Tony Cimasko and Melinda Reichelt.
   p. cm. -- (Second language writing)
 Includes bibliographical references and index.
 ISBN 978-1-60235-224-7 (pbk. : alk. paper) -- ISBN 978-1-60235-225-4 (alk. paper) -- ISBN 978-1-60235-226-1 (adobe ebook) -- ISBN 978-1-60235-227-8 (epub)
  1. English language--Study and teaching--Foreign speakers. 2. English language--Composition and exercises--Study and teaching--Foreign speakers. 3. Second language acquisition. I. Cimasko, Tony, 1969- II. Reichelt, Melinda.
 PE1128.A2F596 2011
 418.0071--dc22
                                  2011011272

Cover design by Paul Kei Matsuda and David Blakesley
Printed on acid-free paper.

Parlor Press, LLC is an independent publisher of scholarly and trade titles in print and multimedia formats. This book is available in paper, hardcover, and Adobe eBook formats from Parlor Press on the World Wide Web at http://www.parlorpress.com or through online and brick-and mortar bookstores. For submission information or to find out about Parlor Press publications, write to Parlor Press, 3015 Brackenberry Drive, Anderson, SC, 29621, or email editor@parlorpress.com.

Contents

Introduction *vii*

Part I: The State of Foreign Language Studies

1 Foreign Language Writing: An Overview *3*
   Melinda Reichelt

2 Reading to Write in a Foreign Language: Cognition and Task Representation *22*
   Marcela Ruiz-Funes

3 The Language Learning Potential of Writing in Foreign Language Contexts: Lessons from Research *44*
   Rosa M. Manchón

4 Foreign Language Writing in the Era of Globalization *65*
   Jean Marie Schultz

Part II: National and Regional Profiles of Foreign Language Writing Instruction

5 EFL Class in Morocco: The Role of Writing *83*
   Rachida Elqobai

6 L2 Writing Instruction in Japanese as a Foreign Language *98*
   Yukiko Abe Hatasa

7 Issues and Challenges in Teaching and Learning EFL Writing: The Case of Hong Kong *118*
   Icy Lee

Part III: Foreign Language Programs

8 Ideas into Words: Narrowing the Gap in Doctoral Candidates' Academic Writing in EFL   *138*
   Hadara Perpignan

9 Foreign Language Writing Instruction: A Principled Eclectic Approach in Taiwan   *159*
   Hui-Tzu Min

10 Teaching English Writing in Ukraine: Principles and Practices   *183*
   Oleg Tarnopolsky

11 Developing Spanish FL Writing Skills at a Netherlands University: In Search of Balance   *201*
   Marly Nas and Kees van Esch

Part IV: Pedagogical Concerns

12 The Quest for Grammatical Accuracy: Writing Instruction among Foreign and Heritage Language Educators   *225*
   Natalie Lefkowitz

13 Student Perceptions of Writing as a Tool for Increasing Oral Proficiency in German   *255*
   Helga Thorson

14 Teaching Academic Writing to Advanced EFL Learners in China: Principles and Challenges   *285*
   Wenyu Wang

Afterword   *311*

Contributors   *323*

Index   *329*

About the Editors   *347*

Introduction

In the last several decades, research into second language (L2) writing has grown from an adjunct of L2 speaking and listening, to a fully formed field with its own theories and interests, one that recognizes the importance of L2 writing on its own terms. However, most L2 writing research has focused primarily on writing in English as a second language (ESL), that is, writing in English in English-dominant contexts. This is despite the fact that a great deal of foreign language (FL) writing occurs around the world in a broad diversity of languages and contexts.

The purpose of this volume is to take a significant step forward in addressing this imbalance in the literature. While addressing the lack of balance between second language (primarily ESL) and FL writing literature is worthwhile in its own right, devoting greater attention to FL writing is important for reasons that have a direct bearing upon future research and pedagogy. As is noted in greater detail in the Afterword, both SL and FL writing literature can complement and enhance one another in significant ways. For example, a number of important themes, necessarily in the foreground in discussions of FL writing, are sometimes neglected in the ESL writing literature, and we hope the attention paid in this volume to these topics will stimulate further exploration of these topics in the ESL writing literature. These topics include the status of English and its relationship with other languages; the effects of broader national, economic, and social contexts on learning and practice; and institutional influences from teachers, administrators, available resources, educational goals, curriculum guidelines, organizational regulations, and other contextual circumstances. Additionally, attention to similarities and differences between principles and practices involved in teaching ESL and FL writing can help fill gaps in the FL writing literature, including but not limited to FL-specific theoretical work and exploration of multilingual/multicultural identity construction.

Both teachers and researchers in the field of foreign language writing will find this collection useful. We believe the field of L2 writing will benefit from recognizing the continuing importance of issues related to writing in English as a foreign language—as well as other foreign languages being taught around the world. Likewise, we hope this book will also be helpful for those who are focused on second language studies, rather than foreign language studies, bringing them new perspectives on L2 writing and thus providing insights beyond those that have already been provided by the research and other literature on ESL writing.

Overview

This book is divided into four main sections. Foreign language writing in the real world does not organize itself into such neat and discrete categories, however; the reader will see significant overlaps between the interests and methodologies of the individual writers. In part, this represents the shared resources of instructors and researchers working across different languages. It also represents the influence research has on contemporary pedagogy, and the dependence of research upon findings in individual learning experiences.

The State of Foreign Language Writing Studies: Part I provides a portrait of the state of current FL writing literature. Like second language writing and mainstream rhetoric and composition, contemporary interests in FL writing are diverse, taking multiple, complementary perspectives that provide a richer view of FL learning and teaching. This section explores the contextual factors that influence FL writing around the world. Additionally, it describes the cognitive dimensions of FL writing, the instrumental role of writing in FL learning, and the implications of globalization for FL writing and pedagogy.

As Melinda Reichelt notes in chapter 1, pedagogical approaches to FL writing are shaped to a significant degree by a range of local, contextual factors. These include the role and status of the target language in the broader teaching environment; students' purposes for learning the language; economic, historical, and political factors; and local educational practices, including practices related to FL teaching and first language (L1) literacy instruction. In addition to presenting FL writing instruction from this context-based perspective, Part I of this volume explores the role of cognition in FL writing. In chapter 2, Marcela Ruiz-Funes provides an overview of the work on cognition in reading-to-write in foreign languages, drawing on research from L1 and L2 studies as a framework for her own research into US-based Spanish student writers. Part I of this volume also examines the ppotential of FL writing to foster target language learning. As Rosa Manchón argues in chapter 3, empirical evidence suggests FL writing provides several important functions related to overall target language learning. These include a noticing function that allows learners to monitor their own output and to focus their attention on input; a hypothesis testing function that allows learners to judge their own production; and a metalinguistic function that Manchón says, quoting Swain, "forces the learner to pay attention to the means of expression needed in order to successfully convey his or her own intended meaning." In chapter 4, Jean Marie Schultz also praises FL writing for its potential to facilitate overall target language development and delineates further benefits of FL writing, including increasing the writer's self-awareness, cross-cultural sensitivity, and ability to write in the L1. Schultz argues that a key phenomenon influencing foreign language writing in today's world is the trend towards globalization, noting that the role of English as lingua franca around the world problematizes the teaching of other foreign languages. She argues persuasively that, because of this trend, the need to teach FL writing is more urgent than ever.

National and Regional Profiles of Foreign Language Writing Instruction: Part II explores the role of FL writing in various sociocultural contexts. As the authors of the chapters in Part II note, FL writing instruction is impacted by a range of sociolinguistic considerations, including the role the FL plays in the overall linguistic ecology of the teaching environment; local attitudes toward the FL; L1 traditions of teaching writing in the target language; and learners' needs, motivations, and challenges regarding writing in the target language. The authors in this section describe how pedagogy in their local contexts addresses—or fails to address—these sociocultural considerations.

Rachida Elqobai discusses the sociolinguistic situation in Morocco, describing in chapter 5 the complex roles played in Morocco by Berber, English, Arabic, Spanish, and French, especially in the educational system. Elqobai explains that this intricate sociolinguistic milieu complicates the teaching of EFL writing in Morocco. If they are to be effective, she argues, "imported" approaches to EFL writing instruction must be adapted to suit the particular contingencies of the Moroccan context. Yukiko Abe Hatasa also describes the impact of contextual factors on the teaching of FL writing. In chapter 6, she delineates how writing instruction in Japanese is impacted by the particular characteristics and needs of US learners of Japanese, along with the difficulties posed for native English speakers by the Japanese language and writing system. In chapter 7, Icy Lee examines how one important aspect of context—political factors—impact English language writing instruction in Hong Kong. She argues that the transition from British to Chinese rule is progressively transforming English from a second language into a foreign language, and that because of this change, English writing is coming to be seen by many as less meaningful and as a mechanical chore.

Foreign Language Programs: Part III examines the influence of whole programs on FL pedagogy, including attempts by FL instructors to create pedagogy that balances program- and department level stresses with individual learner needs; whether and how successfully new macrostrategic frameworks for teaching can be integrated into the mainstream practices that dominate a department; and the strategies FL writing instructors are free to pursue in balancing local and global writing considerations. These chapters indicate a strong awareness in current FL writing literature for not only the need to plan around program and department forces—rather than treating instructors as autonomous—but also to encourage more mutual contributions.

The relationships between programmatic context and instruction are varied, and are viewed in a variety of ways. In chapter 8, Hadara Perpignan discusses her EFL teaching for PhD students as being situated in the context of her department and university, and also within the dominant view in Israeli academics of English as important but clearly secondary. Within this system, EFL writing instruction must come to terms with the motivation for learning as "extrinsic and nonintegrative." In response, the writing curriculum for PhD students is informed by a strong process orientation that allows for students' own particular goals. Hui-Tzu Min, in chapter 9, outlines a "principled eclectic approach" that, like the example in Israel, combines basic post-process principles with more local requirements. However, curriculum design relies more on teachers' understanding of writing than on students' own input, and the program aims to "equip students with the prerequisite knowledge of the sociocultural conventions of the dis-

Introduction											xi

course community in Anglophone countries." The incorporation of foreign/western elements of writing instruction into the tertiary English writing program at a Ukrainian university described in chapter 10 by Oleg Tarnopolsky illustrates another kind of FL writing program, one that is required to be more responsive to a much broader range of FL writing needs than the particularly academic ones of the previous two chapters. Finally, in chapter 11, Marly Nas and Kees van Esch describe a Spanish foreign language writing program that confronts not only immediate issues, but historical pressures as well—a program and pedagogy that have grown despite the lack of a "great tradition in teaching writing in a FL" in the Netherlands.

Pedagogical Concerns: The fourth and final part of the book focuses squarely on the classroom, the beliefs and specific principles that inform pedagogical practices and how they impact students, and instrumental uses of writing to aid FL oral production and their influence on students' opinions. Like the issues described in the section before it, issues surrounding FL pedagogy are diverse, and the literature does not hesitate to call attention to serious criticisms of teachers and curricula alike.

In chapter 12, Natalie Lefkowitz examines activities and attitudes among FL and heritage language (HL) university level instructors, and finds that despite the importance of process and post-process in mainstream and ESL writing, accuracy remains a top priority, even to the possible detriment and discouragement of students. Just as instructor behavior is crucial to consider, instructor attitudes play an important role in students' own attitudes about themselves, indicating another area of interest in FL writing literature today. Helga Thorson, in chapter 13, notes that many instructors continue to use FL writing not for its own sake, but as an adjunct to the teaching and learning of oral language. Student attitudes toward FL writing in this capacity (as described in Thorson's chapter, about learners of German) vary considerably, but tend toward a positive correlation between familiarity and perceived usefulness of writing. Finally, personal perspectives have an important function in understanding FL writing pedagogy, as in Wenyu Wang's detailed and systematic reflection on her own practices in chapter 14.

This volume aims to take stock of the current, evolving understanding of pedagogical practices among experts in the field of FL writing, while developing a fuller appreciation for the rich institutional and sociocultural forces that shape and are shaped by FL instruction. In doing so, it takes an important step toward creating a more comprehensive, accurate theory of L2 writing, one that takes into consideration the many contexts and languages in which L2 writing occurs.

Acknowledgments

Our first appreciation must go to Tony Silva and Paul Kei Matsuda for creating the Symposium on Second Language Writing, for editing a series of volumes based on the Symposium, and for initiating and providing support throughout the authoring and editing of the book. As the collection began to take shape, David Blakesley served as a helpful source of guidance as it moved through the cogs of Parlor Press. The individual authors and the reviewers all deserve particular praise, as they were more than anyone else the patient and thorough heart and soul of the book. Much of the credit for bringing final, polished perfection to the book goes to our copyeditor, Terra Williams. Any book is the culmination of a very long creative and collective process, and *Foreign Language Writing Instruction: Principles and Practices* is no different. Even before the book began to take shape, there was the Symposium, and we would be remiss if we neglected to give particular recognition to Beril Tezeller Arik and Jihyun Im, the co-chairs of the Symposium's Graduate Student Conference, and thanks to all the volunteers who made the Symposium—and through a very long causal chain, this book—happen. We would like to make a special note in honor of the memory of Hadara Perpignan, who passed away shortly before publication. Her contributions to foreign language writing research and pedagogy have been considerable, and we are honored to have her scholarship in these pages. Finally, we would like to extend our warmest appreciation to our spouses, Dong-shin and Jay. Dong-shin, you have been an inspiration during the creation of this collection, as you always have been. And Jay, thank you for your unwavering support and willingness to provide me with time to work on this project.

Foreign Language Writing Instruction

1 Foreign Language Writing: An Overview

Melinda Reichelt

Foreign language writing, or FL writing, is the phenomenon of writers composing in a language that is neither the writer's native language nor the dominant language in the surrounding context. For example, when native speakers of Chinese write in English in Taiwan (see Min, chapter 9), or when native Dutch speakers compose in Spanish in the Netherlands (see Nas and van Esch, chapter 11), they are writing in a foreign language, as are American students writing in Spanish in the US (see Ruiz-Funes, chapter 2). In contrast, of course, the term *second language* writing is often used to refer to situations where writers are composing in a language that is not their native language, but *is* the dominant surrounding language—such as when non-native English speakers in the US or Australia, for example, write in English. For clarity's sake, the term "L2 writing" is used in this chapter as an umbrella term to cover both second and foreign language writing.

In most instances, determining whether a person is writing in a second versus a foreign language is fairly straightforward. However, there are some cases where, often as a by-product of colonization, a language has had and continues to have a special status in a given region, and it is difficult to determine whether individual writers of that language should be considered to be writing in a second or foreign language. Kachru (1992) describes the differing statuses of English in various countries, using the terms Inner Circle, Outer Circle, and Expanding Circle. Inner Circle countries are those in which English is traditionally considered the dominant language, that is, the US, UK, Canada, Australia, and New Zealand. Non-native English speakers writing in English in these contexts are generally considered to be writing in a second language, not a foreign language. Expanding Circle countries are those where English is considered a foreign language, such as China, Japan, and Saudi Arabia. Non-native English speakers writing in English in these contexts are considered to be writing in English as a foreign language.

Countries in the in-between category, the Outer Circle countries, are countries affected by what Phillipson (1992) calls "linguistic imperialism." According to Kachru (1992), these are contexts in which non-native varieties of English have been institutionalized because of extended periods of colonization, such as India, Singapore, Kenya, and Hong Kong. Kachru calls these ESL countries, but he estimates that perhaps only 10% of the population may actually be English users. Thus, in this chapter, I include writing in English in Kachru's Outer Circle countries in my discussion of FL writing. I also include writing done in languages other than English that may have official status in multilingual countries but are not necessarily the dominant languages for learners engaged in writing. (For further discussion of the difficulty in determining whether a given environment should be labeled a second or foreign language context, see Lee's discussion in chapter 7 of the case of Hong Kong. See also Elqobai, chapter 5, for a discussion of the complexities of FL writing instruction in a post-colonial, multilingual environment.)

Foreign Language Writing: The "Other" L2 Writing

In the last several decades, research into L2 writing has increased exponentially. However, most of this research has focused on writing in English as a second language rather than on writing in foreign languages. This is despite the fact that a great deal of FL writing occurs around the world in various contexts. The purpose of this volume is to begin to address this imbalance in the literature. The chapters in this volume are based on presentations given at the seventh Symposium on Second Language Writing (Purdue University, W. Lafayette, Indiana, June 5–7, 2008). The conference theme was "Foreign Language Writing: Principles and Practices."

My own interest in FL writing began in 1994 when, as part of my dissertation research, I spent a year investigating writing instruction at the *Gymnasium Kronshagen,* a secondary school in Germany, where I later conducted several other research projects (Reichelt, 1997a, 1997b, 2003). I collaborated later with a colleague to investigate the role of writing in her university level German language class in the US (Reichelt & Bryant, 2001), and I investigated EFL writing instruction in Poland (Reichelt, 2005). Additionally, I conducted an analysis of the literature about FL writing instruction in the US (Reichelt, 1999, 2001) and examined the literature on FL writing instruction in various contexts around the world (Reichelt, 2009).

In this chapter, I present some of the findings of my research. I overview the scope and nature of the literature on foreign language writing, confining myself primarily to sources published in English, due to my own linguistic limitation. I then describe some of the contextual factors that shape foreign language writing instruction in contexts around the globe, noting how authors of subsequent chapters in this volume expand on such themes.

NATURE AND SCOPE OF THE FL WRITING LITERATURE

Languages and Institutional/Geographical Contexts in the FL Writing Literature

The FL writing literature published in English stems from a broad range of geographical contexts. Much of it focuses on North America and Asia, with some focusing on Europe and only a small amount on South America, Africa, and the Middle East. Much of this FL writing literature focuses on writing done at the tertiary level. For example, Haneda (2005) investigated university level Japanese writing in Canada; Hedgcock and Lefkowitz (1996) focused on university level learners writing in French, Spanish, and German in the US; Ruiz-Funes (1999, 2001) researched university level Spanish writing in the US; and Thorson (2000) investigated university level German writing in the US.

A great deal of the FL writing literature focuses on EFL writing, also often at the tertiary level. For example, Aliakbari (2002) researched EFL writing in Iran, and Leibowitz (2004, 2005) investigated English language writing in South Africa. EFL writing research focusing on levels besides tertiary education includes Lee (2004), who investigated English language writing instruction at the secondary level in Hong Kong, and Simpson (2004), who researched elementary EFL writing in Ecuador.

Topics Addressed in the FL Writing Literature

The topics addressed in the FL writing literature can be classified under three categories: pedagogical works, empirical research, and works that are primarily theoretical in nature. The pedagogical literature on FL writing consists mostly of discussions of pedagogical issues such as the role of grammar instruction (Muncie, 2002) or reading-writing connections (Ruiz-Funes, 1999, 2001), along with descriptions of classroom procedures the authors have implemented and are recommending to their readers, such as portfolio writing (Coombe & Barlow, 2004; Paesani, 2006) and use of email (Conroy, 2004).

Within the research literature, publications focus on a range of topics, including FL writers' texts; FL writers' perceptions, processes, and strategies; the effects on FL writing on various classroom procedures; individual differences among writers; and contexts in which FL writing is undertaken. (See Reichelt, 2009 for a selected bibliography of works on FL writing.) For example, de Haan and van Esch (2005) analyze the FL writing of Dutch university students, using holistic, syntactic, and lexical analyses to measure development over time; Kuiken and Vedder (2008) examine the linguistic performance of Dutch learners of Italian and French who responded to writing tasks of differing cognitive complexity; Hatasa and Soeda (2000) examine strategy use and L1 use among university level native English speakers writing in Japanese; Wang and Wen (2002) investigate Chinese EFL learners' use of L1; Armengol-Castells (2001) looks at FL writers' text-generating strategies in Catalán, Spanish, and English; Min (2006) investigates the effects of trained peer review in EFL writing; Cheng (2002) investigates FL writing anxiety, noting differences that correlated with writing competence, gender, and length of study; and Kobayashi and Rinnert (2008) examine the effects of intensive training at the secondary level for writing essays for university entrance essay exams in Japan.

There also exist works related to FL writing that are primarily theoretical in nature (O'Brien, 2004), many of which are overtly political in approach. For example, Canagarajah (1999) adopts a critical pedagogical perspective, investigating within the Sri Lankan Tamil community the attitudes and classroom life of teachers and students in relation to center-based methods and materials for developing literacy skills in English. Ramanathan (2003) describes how unequal access to literacy in a post-colonial context perpetuates inequalities produced by colonization, and Gui (2008) argues that EFL writing instruction in China reflects the institutional imposition of English in China for national, social, and economic advancement.

Research Methods Used in the FL Writing Research Literature

A range of research methods are employed in FL writing research, including text analysis; think-aloud protocols; interviews and questionnaires; participant-observation; reflection; analysis of video-taped writing sessions; use of software programs that track composing and revision; and examination of reading and writing logs.

Venues for Publication of FL Writing Literature

Published sources about FL writing appear mostly in the form of journal articles or dissertations, although books and book chapters on FL writing also exist. The *Journal of Second Language Writing* publishes the most articles on FL writing, but *Foreign Language Annals*, *The Modern Language Journal*, and *System* also publish significant numbers of FL writing articles.

Otherwise, FL writing articles are scattered in a broad range of journals. Some are published in journals that focus on English as an L2, including *ELT Journal*, *English Teaching Forum*, *TESOL Quarterly*, the *International Journal of English Studies*, the *Journal of English for Academic Purposes*, *ESP Journal*, and *the Internet TESL Journal*. Other FL writing articles are published in journals that publish work related to a range of languages; these journals include *Language Learning*; *Language Awareness*; *RELC Journal*; *Language and Education*; *Language Teaching Research*; *Language, Culture, and Curriculum*; *JALT*; *French Review*; *Hispania*; *Die Unterrichtspraxis*; and *Deutsch als Fremdsprache*. In addition, FL writing articles appear in journals focusing on applied linguistics, including the *ITL Review of Applied Linguistics*, the *Indian Journal of Applied Linguistics*, and the *Canadian Journal of Applied Linguistics*. Additionally, some FL writing articles are published in educational journals, including *Learning and Instruction*, *Asia Pacific Educational Review*, *Educational Action Research*, and *Educational Review*.

This list of journals is not intended to be exhaustive, but instead to illustrate how widely scattered the literature on FL writing is. Because of this, it is not possible to keep up with the body of literature in this area by simply paying attention to the articles in a handful of journals. However, the annotated bibliographies appearing at the end of each issue of the *Journal of Second Language Writing* provide a convenient way of tracking the FL writing literature published in English.

Contextual Factors Influencing FL Writing Instruction

Leki (2001) delineates a number of contextual factors that particularly impact writing instruction in EFL environments. These include practical factors such as large class sizes, time constraints, the need to accommodate local circumstances, a lack of instructor experience in teaching EFL writing, and a lack of student experience and training in L1 writing. Additionally, she explains several important ideological factors that influence EFL writing instruction, including the necessity of justifying the large investments required for teaching EFL writing, especially considering that devoting resources to writing can detract from other areas. Leki also argues for the rights of participants to resist "center imposed" materials and teaching methods from English-dominant countries, and she posits a need for discussions with students about how writing instruction can expand rather than limit their options. Based on my own research, I have also identified factors that influence FL writing instruction. These include the following: linguistic considerations, including the role and status of the FL in the broader teaching environment; economic, historical, and political factors; and educational considerations, including practices related to FL teaching and L1 literacy instruction.

Below, I draw on various published sources as well as my own research to provide descriptions of FL writing instruction in several contexts. These descriptions are intended to illustrate the ways in which FL writing instruction in a range of environments is shaped by various linguistic, historical, political, economic, and educational factors.

Germany

According to Berns (1992), in Germany, knowledge and use of English serves as a status symbol for Germans of all ages. English is by far the most-commonly-learned second language in Germany, and almost all secondary students study English (Bliesener, 1988). Given the important role of English in Germany, it is not surprising that English language writing is an important aspect of secondary education, especially at the *Gymnasium,* the most rigorous type of German secondary school. By the time *Gymnasium* students reach grade eleven, they are expected to be able to complete demanding reading and writing tasks in English and are held to high standards of linguistic correctness and stylistic appropriateness (*Lehrplan für die Sekundarstufe II,* 2002). Students are also expected, of course, to complete similar, demanding written work in their German classes. In fact, many of the writing tasks assigned in English classes are drawn from the German language curriculum.

Gymnasium education places a strong emphasis on critical, close reading of texts, and this emphasis influences EFL writing instruction. *Gymnasium* students in grades six through nine complete text-based creative writing designed to help students engage with the texts and thus better understand them (Beile, 1996; Holtwisch, 1996; and Piepho, 1998). These tasks serve as preparation for the careful reading needed for writing the literary interpretations and other text analyses emphasized in the upper grades of the *Gymnasium.*

The German tradition of *Bildung,* education, significantly impacts the types of tasks assigned in upper level *Gymnasium* English classes. More than just the passing on of knowledge and skills, *Bildung* emphasizes the overall formation of the individual and includes development of attitudes, views, and values (Bliesener 1988). The *Gymnasium* English curriculum for older students reflects this notion of *Bildung* by requiring students to read and write about a broad range of texts, ones chosen by their teachers to deepen their understanding of the cultures and important texts of English-dominant countries. Students in the upper grades of the *Gymnasium* are expected to be able to discuss, read, and write about complex social, cultural, and political issues in English.

The curricular emphasis in EFL instruction on undertaking writing that is based on close, critical reading of texts stems at least in part from Germany's history and a concomitant quest for objective thinking. Students in grades eleven and above are typically assigned three-part writing tasks with questions requiring summary of a text, then analysis, and finally, a personal commentary. Such tasks are intentionally designed to move students from objectivity to subjectivity. As one teacher told me, this task structure is partly in response to past problematic experiences with the *Besinnungsaufsatz,* an essay form in which students were required to respond to a moral issue; during the Third Reich, students were assigned this type of essay and were expected to write answers consistent with the Nazi party's beliefs.

Poland

In Poland, motivation for learning English, including learning to write in English, is high because of the prestige English enjoys in Poland, and because of Poles' perceptions that to function competitively in the European Union, they need to increase their levels of FL proficiency. Additionally, there is a growing sense of need in Poland for written FL skills, especially in English, primarily for making and maintaining foreign business contacts, particularly within Europe (Reichelt, 2005).

In light of these perceived needs for FL writing, the Polish government has begun requiring graduating secondary school students to select a FL as one of their subjects for the written portion of the school-leaving exam; the majority choose English (Reichelt, 2005). Pressure to prepare for the written portions of the school-leaving exam has led to a greater focus on writing instruction in FL classrooms, especially on short, communicative tasks like writing postcards or notes, since these are typical exam tasks. Additionally, writing is employed in FL classrooms because it is considered useful in supporting overall language learning by reinforcing grammar and vocabulary. Because of heavy teacher workloads, it is difficult for teachers to provide individual feedback on writing to students. In order to reduce the number of papers a teacher must look at, students often work in groups to write a collaborative text and respond to each other's writing (Reichelt, 2005).

At the university level in Poland, hiring practices significantly influence EFL writing instruction: instructors from English-dominant countries are often employed to teach writing, and they typically bring with them teaching materials and practices from home, including the use of process writing and peer feedback (Reichelt, 2005).

United States

As Schultz notes in chapter 4 of this volume, the effects of globalization and the dominance of English influence the roles of foreign languages in the US and thus impact FL writing research and pedagogy. Because of the role of English as a world language, as well as geographical and political factors, there is often less motivation and emphasis on FLs in the US than in many other countries.

One result is that FL instruction in the US often occurs at beginner or near beginner levels, even in colleges and universities. Common writing activities include guided composition and work at the sentence or paragraph level. Because of the difficulty of identifying specific writing needs beyond the classroom, FL writing instruction in the US sometimes also includes dialog journal writing (Peyton & Reed, 1990) and creative and expressive writing tasks (Bräuer, 1997) designed to foster students' interest and motivation. Additionally, FL curricula often employ writing as a means of supporting overall target language, including oral skills and grammar. In this volume, Thorson (chapter 13) reports on her investigation of the perception of US university students of German regarding writing as a means of increasing oral proficiency, and Lefkowitz (chapter 12) describes how, in her university's foreign language department, instructors' pursuit of grammatical accuracy in their students' writing often overshadows other writing-related concerns.

For the relatively few US university students who take higher level foreign language courses, writing is also used in analysis of literature (Hadley, 2000). However, as Ruiz-Funes indicates in chapter 2 of this volume, many US university students struggle with completing the demanding writing assignments of their upper level FL classes, despite having succeeded in their intermediate level courses. Ruiz-Funes describes reading-writing connections in foreign languages, noting the complex relationship between reading comprehension, writing skills, task representation, and overall linguistic proficiency.

Recently, literature about FL writing instruction has emphasized the development of integrated literacy skills. Kern (2004) describes literacy as focusing on "relationships between readers, writers, texts, culture, and language learning" (p. 3) and argues that literacy can be used as an "organizing principle" (p. 4) for teaching academic language. Byrnes (2002) describes implementation of a content-oriented, genre-based literacy approach to language teaching in the German program at Georgetown University, including in her discussion a description of her program's development of task-based writing assessment. Kern & Schultz (2005) call for context-sensitive research into literacy practices that takes social factors into consideration, advocating FL pedagogy that fosters development of interpretive skills and better understandings of "the culturally embedded intellectual processes behind specific types of writing" (p. 385). To illustrate such an approach, they provide a detailed description of the curriculum for a third year French reading and composition course at the University of California at Santa Barbara. In chapter 4 of this volume, Schultz describes another third year French course, this one within a global studies curriculum. The course involves reading and writing about texts related to the French presence in Africa; literary texts written by authors grappling with multicultural and multilingual issues; and texts related to France's status as a member of the European Union.

FL writing instruction in the US has been influenced to some degree by practices common in US ESL writing instruction (Hadley, 2000; Krug, 2004; Reichelt, 1999), which has itself been shaped by L1 writing instruction in the US (Silva, 1990). While approaches to teaching L1 composition vary widely, one especially influential aspect has been the process approach to writing, involving use of planning activities, multiple drafts, teacher and peer feedback, and revision (Ferris & Hedgcock, 2005; Hadley, 2000; Lee & VanPatten, 2003).

FL writing instruction in the US is also shaped by the widespread availability of technology, especially at the university level. Many university FL programs provide students with opportunities to visit language labs outfitted with computers and other media to engage in such activities as using email (Conroy, 2004) and the Web (Pooser, 2004). Additionally, FL writing instruction in the US is impacted by increasing numbers of heritage language (HL) learners in FL classrooms, especially Spanish language classrooms, as described by Lefkowitz in chapter 12 of this volume. Because their writing does not always conform to their instructors' expectations, it elicits a range of teacher responses. Finally, as Schultz indicates in chapter 4 of this volume, FL writing in the US is often affected by lack of teacher preparation for teaching writing.

People's Republic of China (PRC)

You (2004, 2005) argues that EFL writing instruction in China reflects the quest for Chinese modernization. With the implementation of China's "Open Door" policy in 1978, he writes, the study of English was encouraged, although students were to avoid in their writing the use of western ideas (unless criticizing them). Because of the needs of the emerging market economy, English classes were offered in the areas of trade, journalism, and international relations, and these courses provided students with opportunities to undertake writing related to these fields. As manufacturing increased in China, students began to see English writing ability as vital to their professional development. You (2004) notes that English language writing instruction in China is heavily influenced by the nationally unified syllabus and the related standardized exams. English teachers usually focus their writing instruction on preparing students to write for the College English Test (CET), which typically requires students to write a 100–120-word essay in thirty minutes on a topic related to general knowledge or daily life (Li, 2007).

Because of large class sizes in China, small group work is difficult to implement (Sapp, 2001). Additionally, due to very heavy workloads, university instructors in China are rarely able to provide individual feedback on students' writing. Instructors often employ model essays in class, encouraging students to memorize as many model essays from their exercise books as they can (You, 2004, 2005). However, Yang, Badger, and Yu (2006) report that some instructors are experimenting with process approaches to writing instruction, including instructor feedback on intermediary drafts.

In chapter 14 of this volume, Wang describes an approach to teaching EFL writing to English majors in a Chinese university, providing a picture of writing instruction that looks somewhat different from You's. This is perhaps due to the fact that the writing course she has developed is for English majors rather than non-English majors. She discusses the adaptation to her particular context of various approaches described in the L2 writing, including product-, process-, and genre-based practices.

Ukraine

Tarnopolsky (2000) writes that English is in great demand in Ukraine. Based on over five hundred interviews with potential students over several years, he found that students expressed an increased desire to learn not only business writing skills, but also beginning level writing skills that they could later develop for their own specific purposes. Based on interviews with students in his English courses, Tarnopolsky found that a crucial element for the course's success related to motivation. Students indicated that because they had no urgent, immediate needs for writing in English, course assignments needed to be "fun" in order to hold their interest. In chapter 7 of this volume, Tarnopolsky notes that English language writing in Ukraine was neglected in past years because the Communist regime discouraged contact outside of the Soviet Union. After the downfall of Communism, however, people needed English language writing skills to develop outside contacts. Tarnopolsky notes that large class sizes and heavy teaching loads impact FL writing instruction in Ukraine, and that English language writing pedagogy needs to be suited to the particular characteristics of the Ukrainian context.

Turkey

Clachar (2000) delineates local contextual factors that can affect university level EFL writing instruction in Turkey, focusing on "institutional, societal, and cultural pressures" (p. 84) related to teachers' attitudes toward western writing instruction, including process and rhetorical approaches. In her ethnographic study, Clachar found that some of the teachers she studied adopted an oppositional stance toward western approaches to writing instruction, while others expressed "accommodative ambivalence" (p. 76). Teachers who adopted an oppositional stance argued that imposition of western rhetorical forms overshadowed students' own cultural styles of writing. They indicated that within Turkish culture, knowledge is to be understood, respected, and preserved, while western writing pedagogy encourages students to tear apart and criticize texts. Additionally, these teachers argued, Turkish writing is writer-based rather than reader-based, there is a tolerance for contradictions in a text, and subtlety, digression, and indirection are valued. These teachers indicated that their students therefore had difficulty mastering such traditional western forms as argumentation, comparison/contrast, and cause/effect. These teachers also argued that poor grammar and spelling were more likely to reflect negatively on their students' perceived literacy than would an inability to master these western forms.

In contrast, other teachers who were part of Clachar's (2000) study displayed an "accommodative ambivalence" toward western approaches to teaching writing. These teachers viewed exposure to western pedagogies and rhetorical forms as a source of "enrichment" for students rather than an "imposition" upon them (79). Although these teachers exhibited some apprehension about the mismatch between traditional Turkish attitudes toward knowledge versus those reflected in western approaches to teaching writing, overall, these teachers found it important to expose students to western rhetorical styles as a means of fostering "international communication and socioeconomic mobility" for their students (p. 80).

Italy

Hargan (1995) discusses EFL writing instruction in the Law, Politics and Economics faculties of a small Italian university, focusing on problems related to the models of English language academic writing used by instructors in this Italian-medium instructional environment. In addition to their subject studies, students in this faculty take EFL courses that require, in the fourth year, a written academic research project. Students had recently been given the option of using this English language research paper to also fulfill a small thesis-like project required for their subject-area studies, in effect killing two birds with one stone. Students submit this paper to both their English teacher and a subject-area supervisor. The EFL teachers involved, who are typically native English speakers, complain that their students' projects are difficult to read, characterized by plagiarism or over-use of summarizing, and lacking in explicit argument structures, supporting evidence, originality, and a sense of the writer's opinion or point of view.

Hargan (1995) argues that EFL instructors' expectations of their students' written projects are in conflict with local practices and thus their students' educational experiences. Essay writing, she notes, is not a key feature of the Italian educational system, where oral examinations and oral reports are much more common. When students write their research projects in English, it is their first academic research writing experience in *any* language. However, students do have experience with the summarize-and-comment format, which the EFL instructors criticize in their students' work. Hargan argues that, given these factors, along with the fact that students have limited English proficiency and have had very little time to acquire proficiency in academic writing, EFL writing teachers should re-examine their expectations. They should, she writes, avoid imposing their ethnocentric and counterproductive norms that are based on an idealized view of the nature of English language academic writing. Instead, they should value students' summarizing and commenting skills, acknowledging the important, complex task that summarizing presents, as well as its value for student learning. She urges incorporation of an oral presentation component to the research project and, when appropriate, discussion with students about the norms of Anglophone and international writing so that students can decide for themselves what norms to adopt.

The Impact of Contextual Factors on Other Environments Addressed in This Volume

The purpose of this volume is not to focus solely on contextual factors impacting FL writing instruction; the volume is much broader in scope. Nonetheless, authors in this volume do describe a broad range of linguistic, historical, political, economic, and educational factors impinging upon FL writing in the contexts in which they work. For example, several authors describe how the role of the target language impacts FL writing instruction in their own contexts. For example, Lee (chapter 7) discusses how the changing language policies in Hong Kong have affected the status of English and influenced English language writing instruction; Elqobai (chapter 5) describes how the complex multilingual situation in Morocco shapes English language writing instruction; Nas and van Esch (chapter 11) assert that because of the relatively insignificant role of Spanish in the Netherlands, university level students usually bring no previous Spanish language instruction to the classroom, which means that Spanish language writing instruction must start at a beginning level; and Perpignan (chapter 8) describes the effects on writing instruction for PhD students in Israel who need to write in English for publication and for communicating with foreign colleagues via email.

Another linguistic factor affecting FL writing instruction described by several authors in this volume is the difficulty of writing in a FL. Hatasa (chapter 6) emphasizes that for native English speakers, writing in Japanese is very difficult, due to various linguistic and orthographic factors. This difficulty must be taken into consideration when designing writing instruction in Japanese and setting expectations for students' writing achievements. Perpignan notes that, despite their well-developed disciplinary skills and knowledge, some of her PhD students in Israel struggle with the writing they must do to publish their work in English or communicate with foreign colleagues.

The authors of subsequent chapters also describe the influence of economic factors in FL instruction: Min (chapter 9), for example, notes that foreign trade in Taiwan led to an increase in the number of years of required English language instruction in schools; Lee (chapter 7) notes that English in Hong Kong is used as "a tool for maintaining the status of Hong Kong as a first-class financial and commercial center"; Hatasa (chapter 6) notes the increase in interest in Japanese instruction in the US when Japan became a strong economic power in the 1980s; and Elqobai (chapter 5) notes that in Morocco, economic development and expanding trade have helped English to be seen as an important developmental tool, to such an extent that English is taking over some of the functions once associated with French, a language with a strong foothold due to its role in the colonization of Morocco.

Educational factors also significantly influence FL writing instruction, as described by many of the authors in this volume. Practical factors such as large class sizes and heavy teaching loads impact FL writing instruction in Hong Kong (Lee, chapter 7) and Morocco (Elqobai, chapter 5). Lack of teacher preparation in FL writing can limit writing instruction, as indicated by Lee (Hong Kong). Additionally, in FL contexts, writing in the target language may not be valued for its own sake, possibly because students may lack an immediate need for writing. Thus, FL writing is often assigned as a means of supporting target language proficiency rather than for its own sake. Manchón (chapter 3) analyzes the results of published empirical studies that investigate the role of FL writing in language learning.

Other educational factors that influence FL writing instruction in various contexts are the need for teaching methods and materials that are developed for various local contexts (see Elqobai, chapter 5, and Min, chapter 9, this volume) and cross-cultural conflicts, sometimes related to differences in written conventions between the target language culture and the students' own cultures (see Hatasa, chapter 6, Min, chapter 9, and Wang, chapter 14, this volume).

Conclusion

Although the majority of the L2 writing literature has focused on ESL environments, L2 writing is a much broader phenomenon than writing in English as a second language. Around the world, people grapple with writing and teaching writing in various non-native languages in a wide variety of contexts, including many FL contexts. Although each of these settings possesses unique features and influences, L2 writing of every sort, including but not limited to ESL writing, exhibits commonalities. In every context, linguistic, historical, political, economic, and educational factors exert their influences on the daily realities of teaching L2 writing. Awareness of how these influences impact L2 writing instruction—including ESL writing instruction—in a very broad range of contexts is an important precursor to development of an accurate and inclusive theory of L2 writing.

REFERENCES

Aliakbari, M. (2002). Writing in a foreign language: A writing problem or a language problem? *Pan-Pacific Association of Applied Linguistics, 6,* 157–68.

Armengol-Castells, L. (2001). Text-generating strategies of three multilingual writers: A protocol-based study. *Language Awareness, 10,* 91–106.

Beile, W. (1996). Kreatives Schreiben in der fremden Sprache. *Der Fremdsprachliche Unterricht, 30,* 4–11.

Berns, M. (1992). Sociolinguistics and the teaching of English in Europe beyond the 1990s. *World Englishes, 11,* 3–14.

Bliesener, U. (1998). Foreign language teaching in Germany. *Bildung und Wissenschaft, 4,* 2–32. (ERIC Document Reproduction Service No. ED436098)

Bräuer, G. (1997). Schreiben im Fremdsprachenunterricht? *Die Unterrichtspraxis: teaching German, 30,* 1–7.

Byrnes, H. (2002). The role of task and task-based assessment in a content-oriented collegiate foreign language curriculum. *Language Testing, 19,* 419–37.

Canagarajah, A. S. (1999). *Resisting linguistic imperialism in English teaching.* New York: Oxford University Press.

Cheng, Y.-S. (2002). Factors associated with foreign language writing anxiety. *Foreign Language Annals, 35,* 647–656.

Clachar, A. (2000). Opposition and accommodation: An examination of Turkish teachers' attitudes toward western approaches to the teaching of writing. *Research in the Teaching of English, 35,* 67–100.

Conroy, P. V. (2004). Email or blackboard: Teaching advanced French composition. *The French Review, 77,* 550–559.

Coombe, C., & Barlow, L. (2004). The reflective portfolio: Two case studies from the United Arab Emirates. *English Teaching Forum, 42,* 18–23.

de Haan, P., & van Esch, K. (2005). The development of writing in English and Spanish as foreign languages. *Assessing Writing, 10,* 100–16.

Ferris, D., & Hedgcock, J. S. (2005). *Teaching ESL composition: Purpose, process, and practice.* Mahwah, NJ: Lawrence Erlbaum.

Gui, L. (2008). Critical pedagogy in EFL college writing instruction in China: An untested feasibility. PhD Dissertation, University of Toledo.

Hadley, A. O. (2000). *Teaching language in context.* Boston, MA: Heinle.

Haneda, M. (2005). Investing in foreign-language writing: A study of two multicultural learners. *Journal of Language, Identity, and Education, 4,* 269–90.

Hargan, N. (1995). Misguided expectations: ESL teachers' attitudes towards Italian university students' written work. *Language and Education, 9,* 223–232.

Hatasa, Y., & Soeda, E. (2000). Writing strategies revisited: A case of non-cognate L2 writers. In B. Swierzbin, F. Morris, M. Anderson, C. Klee, & E. Tarone (Eds.), *Social and cognitive factors in second language acquisition: Selected proceedings of the 1999 second language research forum* (pp. 375–96). Sommerville, MA: Cascadilla Press.

Hedgcock, J. S., & Lefkowitz, N. (1996). Some input on input: Two analyses of student response to expert feedback in L2 writing. *The Modern Language Journal, 80,* 287–308.

Holtwisch, H. (1996). Kreative Klassenarbeiten und ihre Bewertung im Englischunterricht der Sekundarstufe I. *Praxis des Neusprachlichen Unterrichts, 43,* 237–245.

Kachru, B. B. (1992). Teaching world Englishes. In Kachru, B. B. (Ed.), *The other tongue: English across cultures* (pp. 355–365). Urbana: University of Illinois Press.

Kern, R. (2004). Literacy and advanced foreign language learning: Rethinking the curriculum. In H. Byrnes and H. H. Maxim (Eds.), *Advanced foreign language learning: A challenge to college programs* (pp. 2–18). Boston, MA: Thomson Heinle.

Kern, R., & Schultz, J. M. (2005). Beyond orality: Investigating literacy and the literary in second and foreign language instruction. *The Modern Language Journal, 89,* 381–92.

Kobayashi, H., & Rinnert, C. (2008). Task response and text construction across L1 and L2 writing. *Journal of Second Language Writing, 17,* 7–29.

Kuiken, F., & Vedder, I. (2008). Cognitive task complexity and written output in Italian and French as a foreign language. *Journal of Second Language Writing, 17,* 48–60.

Krug, C. (2004). Realistic composition assignments for our students. *The French Review, 78,* 76–92.

Lee, I. (2004). Error correction in L2 secondary classrooms: The case of Hong Kong. *Journal of Second Language Writing, 13,* 285–312.

Lee, J. F., & VanPatten, B. (2003). *Making communicative language teaching happen.* Boston, MA: McGraw-Hill.

Lehrplan für die Sekundarstufe II: Gymnasium, Gesamtschule, Fachgymnasium: Englisch. (2002). Kiel: Ministerium für Bildung, Wissenschaft, Forschung und Kultur des Landes Schleswig-Holstein.

Leibowitz, B. (2004). Becoming academically literate in South Africa: Lessons from student accounts for policymakers and educators. *Language and Education, 18,* 35–52.

Leibowitz, B. (2005). Learning in an additional language in a multilingual society: A South African case study on university-level writing. *TESOL Quarterly, 39*, 661–681.

Leki, I. (2001). Material, educational, and ideological challenges of teaching EFL writing at the turn of the century. *International Journal of English Studies, 1*, 197–209.

Li, Y. (2007). Apprentice scholarly writing in a community of practice: An intraview of an NNES graduate student writing a research article. *TESOL Quarterly, 41*, 55–79.

Min, H.-T. (2006). The effect of trained peer review on EFL students' revision types and writing quality. *Journal of Second Language Writing, 15*, 118–41.

Muncie, J. (2002). Finding a place for grammar in EFL composition classes. *ELT Journal, 56*, 180–86.

O'Brien, T. (2004). Writing in a foreign language: Teaching and learning. *Language Teaching, 37*, 1–28.

Paesani, K. (2006). *Exercices de style:* Developing multiple competencies through a writing portfolio. *Foreign Language Annals, 39*, 618–39.

Peyton, J. K., & Reed, L. (1990). *Dialogue journal writing with nonnative English speakers: A handbook for teachers.* Alexandria, VA: TESOL.

Phillipson, R. (1992). *Linguistic imperialism.* Oxford: Oxford UP.

Piepho, H. (1998). Schreiben: Eine Kulturtechnik zwischen Konvention und Kreativität. *Der Fremdsprachenunterricht, 42*, 8–10.

Pooser, C. (2004). Bringing the web to the foreign language writing class. *French Review, 78*, 94–102.

Ramanathan, V. (2003). Written textual production and consumption (WTPC) in vernacular and English-medium settings in Gujarat, India. *Journal of Second Language Writing, 12*, 125–150.

Reichelt, M. (1997a). An investigation of first language and second language (English) composition theory and instruction at the secondary level in Germany. *Dissertation Abstracts International, 57(11)*, 4726.

Reichelt, M. (1997b). L2 writing instruction at the German 'Gymnasium': A 13th-grade English class writes the 'Abitur.' *Journal of Second Language Writing, 6*, 265–291.

Reichelt, M. (1999). Toward a more comprehensive view of L2 writing: Foreign language writing in the US. *Journal of Second Language Writing, 8*, 181–204.

Reichelt, M. (2001). A critical review of research on FL writing classroom practices. *The Modern Language Journal, 85*, 578–598.

Reichelt, M. (2003). Defining "good writing": A cross-cultural perspective. *Composition Studies, 31*, 99–126.

Reichelt, M. (2005). English language writing instruction in Poland. *Journal of Second Language Writing, 14*, 215–232.

Reichelt, M. (2009). A critical evaluation of writing teaching programmes in different language settings. In R. Manchón (Ed.), *Learning, teaching, and researching writing in foreign language contexts* (183–206). Clevedon, England: Multilingual Matters.

Reichelt, M. (2009). Bibliography of sources on foreign language writing. In R. Manchón (Ed.), *Learning, teaching, and researching writing in foreign language contexts.* Clevedon, England: Multilingual Matters.

Reichelt, M., & Bryant, K. (2001). Writing in a second-year German class. *Foreign Language Annals, 34,* 235–243.

Ruiz-Funes, M. (1999). The process of reading-to-write used by a skilled Spanish-as-a-foreign-language student: A case study. *Foreign Language Annals, 32,* 45–62.

Ruiz-Funes, M. (2001). Task representation in foreign language reading-to-write. *Foreign Language Annals, 34,* 226–34.

Sapp, D. A. (2001). Globalization and "just" pedagogy: A description, interpretation, and critique of English composition pedagogy in China, Brazil, and Spain. PhD Thesis, New Mexico State University.

Silva, T. (1990). Second language composition instruction: Developments, issues, and directions in ESL. In B. Kroll (Ed.), *Second language writing: Research insights for the classroom* (11–23). New York: Cambridge UP.

Simpson, J. M. (2004). A look at early childhood writing in English and Spanish in a bilingual school in Ecuador. *International Journal of Bilingual Education and Bilingualism, 7,* 432–48.

Tarnopolsky, O. (2000). Writing English as a foreign language: A report from Ukraine. *Journal of Second Language Writing, 9,* 209–26.

Thorson, H. (2000). Using the computer to compare foreign and native language writing processes: A statistical and case study approach. *The Modern Language Journal, 82,* 155–70.

Wang,W., & Wen, Q. (2002). L1 use in the L2 composing process: An exploratory study of 16 Chinese EFL writers. *Journal of Second Language Writing, 11,* 225–46.

Yang, M., Badger, R., & Yu, Z. (2006). A comparative study of peer and teacher feedback in a Chinese EFL writing class. *Journal of Second Language Writing, 15,* 179–200.

You, X. (2004). "The choice made from no choice": English writing instruction in a Chinese university. *Journal of Second Language Writing, 13,* 97–110.

You, X. (2005). Writing in the "devil's" tongue: A history of English writing instruction in Chinese colleges, 1862–2004. PhD dissertation, Purdue University, AAT 318553.

2 Reading to Write in a Foreign Language: Cognition and Task Representation

Marcela Ruiz-Funes

The development of reading and writing skills has a central role in the FL curriculum.[1] The importance of these abilities is even stronger in upper level courses where reading and writing are assigned in combination, as in the case of reading-to-write tasks. In these tasks students are asked "to read articles or literary selections and to react and respond to them in an insightful and critical manner" (Kern & Schultz, 1992, p. 2). The complexity involved in these skills as well as the web of processes that readers/writers orchestrate have been unveiled by researchers in first language (L1) and to some extent by those in second/foreign languages (L2/FL) who seek an understanding of the cognition of reading-to-write acts.

This chapter provides an overview of the cognition of reading to write in a foreign language and explains the processes that are orchestrated when students participate in such a complex intellectual activity. It highlights the major studies done in L2/FL writing process research and their implications for teaching, the notion of reading as an interactive process, and the importance of *task representation* in reading to write. The theoretical framework of this work is based on the investigations conducted by Flower (1990) on reading to write in English as a L1 and those of Carson (1993) in English as a second language (ESL).

THE SIGNIFICANCE OF RESEARCH ON THE WRITING PROCESS

Research on the process of writing has brought a new dimension in understanding and dealing with writing in our classes. This work is important because it opened the way to the exploration of complex cognitive acts. As Zamel (1982) remarks, research on the process of writing started because we needed to understand how we could help our students become better writers. Research on writing as product was not offering the answers educators needed.

The most significant conclusion drawn from the work in both L1 and L2/FL writing is that the ability to write effectively not only requires knowledge of linguistic features, but also, involves the activation of a series of thinking processes the integration of which constitutes what is known as the writing process (Zamel, 1982; Connor, 1984; Dvorak, 1986; Scott, 1996). Among these processes, the following have been most frequently identified: task conceptualization, brainstorming or generating ideas, planning, formulation (converting thoughts and ideas into language), problem solving, evaluation, restructuring, revision, editing, and use of metacognitive strategies (Roca de Larios, Manchón, Murphy, & Marín, 2008; Leki, Cumming, & Silva, 2008) that are recursive, dynamic, and temporal in nature (Roca de Larios et al., 2008). FL writing researchers and practitioners have widely acclaimed the writing process approach, yet they still see the need to strengthen its implementation in the FL curriculum, especially in writing complex tasks:

> The strategies that make up the composing process are most valuable when writing involves complex issues and difficult problems. There is less need for planning, rereading, and revision when writing simple descriptions and summaries, and more need for these strategies when writing requires the integration of a great deal of diverse information, when a complex analysis is called for, or when data can be interpreted in different ways. (Krashen & Lee, 2004, p. 11)

Research on L2 writing process has provided us with valuable insights mainly into the differences in the composing processes used by more skilled versus less skilled writers (Krashen, 1984; Kroll, 1990; Raimes, 1987; Zamel, 1982, 1983), the relationship between L2 proficiency and revision and planning (Kobayashi & Rinnert, 2001; Yasuda, 2004; Akyel, 1994), the relationship between L2 proficiency and processing time dedicated to writing processes (Roca et al., 2008), the use and dependency of L1 in L2 writing (Wang & Wen, 2002; Hirose and Sasaki, 1994), and the transferability of composing strategies from the L1 to the L2/FL (Krashen & Lee, 2004).

Research on the differences in the composing processes used by more skilled versus less skilled writers shows that good writers "have better and more sound procedures for getting their ideas down on paper" (Krashen, 1984, p. 12) than less skilled ones do. In particular, good writers differ from less proficient ones in two major aspects: planning and revising (Krashen, 1984; Zamel, 1983). Both groups of writers spend time planning before they write, but good writers do more general planning, have more flexible plans, and are more willing to modify them to meet the requirements of the assigned task depending on its topic, characteristics of the task, audience, and purpose (Hirose & Sasaki, 1994; Victori, 1999; Sasaki, 2000). On the other hand, less skilled writers tend either to be disturbed if they cannot develop a complete plan since they view their planning as a final framework onto which they build and expand their writing (Zamel, 1983); or they do very little planning, thus missing a general guide to organize and start their writing.

Clear differences have also been observed between skilled and less skilled writers in their revision strategies. Skilled writers tend to regard revision as a means of discovering ideas and revise at all levels: from secondary, structural elements to important and more complex changes in content and organization (Krashen, 1984; Sommers, 1978; Zamel, 1983; Raimes, 1987). Less skilled writers, on the other hand, are mostly concerned with "local problems from the very beginning, changing words and phrases but rarely making changes that affect meaning" (Zamel, 1983, p. 174). Such excessive concern with surface correction hinders all possible ability to compose as the "overall relationship between ideas suffers" (Zamel, 1983, p. 173).

A number of studies have explored the relationship between L2 proficiency and revision and planning. In regards to the former, findings show that L2 proficiency is significantly related to revision at the intersentential rather than the essay level (Kobayashi & Rinnert, 2001) and that previous writing experience has a stronger impact in the revision strategies than L2 proficiency level (Yasuda, 2004). As to planning, results suggest that more proficient L2 students write better plans in their L2 that result in better quality compositions than those written by less proficient L2 writers when planning in their L1 or L2 (Akyel, 1994). Research on the relationship between L2 proficiency and processing time dedicated to writing processes indicates that regardless of L2 proficiency level, L2 writers dedicate most of their time to formulation, and as L2 proficiency increases, so does the amount of time applied to planning, evaluation, and revision, and the allocation of time to different composing processes tend to be more balanced (Roca de Larios et al., 2008).

Studies on the use and dependency of L1 in L2 writing also led to some relevant results. Findings reveal that L1 dependency declines with higher levels of L2 proficiency of the writer and his/her writing experience. However, the L1 is heavily used during the idea-generating and idea-organizing processes (Wang & Wen, 2002), particularly by less skilled writers who tend to generate their ideas in their L1 and then translate them into the L2 (Hirose and Sasaki, 1994).

Other investigations have considered the transferability of composing strategies from the L1 to the L2/FL. According to Krashen and Lee (2004), findings indicate that some aspects of the composing process transfer, especially in the planning and revision stages. Most studies present results that are merely suggestive, and, therefore, additional work on the transfer of strategies from the L1 to L2/FL is needed.

The Process of Reading

Since the early 1970s, researchers studying reading comprehension in both L1 and L2/FL started to view reading as an active, interactive process that involves not only understanding of words and sentences, but also the creation of a model within the mind of the reader (Barnett, 1986; Carrell & Eisterhold, 1983; Goodman, 1968; Hammadou, 1991), as reading is "less a matter of extracting sound from print than of bringing meaning to print" (Smith, 1983). This conceptualization of reading has become the foundation for interactive models of comprehension that attempt to describe features of language (lexical items, syntax, topic, etc.), features of the reader (purpose, prior knowledge, proficiency, etc.), and the manner in which these features interact in the reading comprehension process (Phillips, 1984; Hammadou, 1991).

Among the major factors that affect the construction of meaning from a given text, L2/FL reading researchers have explored the effect of the reader's prior knowledge and context (Carrell & Eisterhold, 1983), the reader's ability to make inferences, and elaboration (Hammadou, 1991; Reder, 1980). Findings reveal that both prior knowledge (the reader's general knowledge of, or cultural familiarity with a given topic) and context (as for example, the title of a text, illustrations, etc.) have a significant impact on comprehension, stronger than the teaching of vocabulary or other lexical features, especially for beginning and intermediate L2/FL students (Carrell & Eisterhold, 1983; Hammadou, 1991; Levine & Haus, 1985; Lee, 1986a, 1986b). On the other hand, lack of relevant prior knowledge as well as gaps in cultural background information inhibit or distort comprehension (Melendez, 1985). The importance of prior knowledge in the comprehension process has suggested that "what is understood depends [more] on the reader rather than on the linguistic difficulty of the text" (Swaffar, Arens, & Byrnes, 1991). In addition, results show that the activation of prior knowledge is an important factor in the reader's ability to make inferences. Inferring, "a thinking process that involves reasoning a step beyond the text, using generalizations and explanations" (Hammadou, 1991, p. 28), has proved to be crucial for accurate comprehension and for the construction of meaning. In relation to elaboration, studies show that it plays a central role in the comprehension and retention processes, as elaboration provides redundancy in the memory structure, which in turn helps the reader avoid forgetting the information read and contributes to its fast retrieval (Reder, 1980). This notion implies that the more extra processing a reader does, the better the material will be retained.

The Cognition of Reading to Write

Most of what we know about reading to write and the relationship between reading and writing in L2/FL derives mainly from research in L1. Of crucial value is the research done by Flower (1990), Stein (1990a), Kennedy (1985), and Kantz (1990a, 1990b). These studies provide a theoretical framework for the cognition of reading to write and a categorization of reading-to-write tasks as *Summary, Summary and Comment, Free Response to the Topic, Synthesis,* and *Interpretation with a Rhetorical Purpose.*

Stein (1990a) proposes a model of the cognition of reading to write that includes monitoring, elaborating, structuring, and planning. These processes occur in a recursive, non-linear manner, allowing the reader/writer to move back and forth from one process to another at any time during his/her performance of the task. The processes are defined as follows: *Monitoring* is the process through which readers and writers check back on the source text and the progress of their own text to identify problems with processing (Baker & Brown, 1984a, 1984b; Newell & Simon, 1972). *Structuring* is the process through which readers/writers reorganize and shape the information from the source text to create a new text. *Planning* is a central process in moving from reading to creating a new text (Stein, 1990a). And *Elaborating* is the process through which readers/writers activate their prior knowledge into the reading and writing task. The process of elaboration makes it possible to see how reading and writing interact as "prior knowledge combines with source text propositions to create new ideas and critical perspectives" (Stein, 1990b, p. 122). According to Stein (1990b) *elaboration* serves three distinct purposes: (1) *To generate ideas.* The importation of prior knowledge not only helps students to comprehend source text propositions, but also to decide what is important about those propositions. Such a selection, in turn, leads students to create their own ideas and opinions on the topic. (2) *To develop a critical perspective.* The use of prior knowledge serves to compare and test the validity of the ideas on the source text, leading students to develop a critical attitude on the topic: "[elaboration] enables [students] to draw inferences and analogies, to see ideas from a variety of perspectives, which may well influence the perspective they choose when they write" (1990b, p. 154). Lastly (3) *to build a representation of the source text.* The representation the students build of the source text contains information derived from the text itself and from memory. In the process of representation building, part of the information is common to many readers, as it may refer to shared experiences in the world at large, but part is individual, "containing each student's unique ideas, perspectives, beliefs, values, personality traits, interests and style" (1990b, p. 154). Students select material from this personalized representation and use it as the basis for their own text.

The major insight gained from Stein's studies is the value and potential of elaboration in transforming information from the source text to create a new text. However, Stein found that students tended to overlook or did not exploit the potential of elaboration, devaluing their own ideas. This, in turn, prevented them from being creative and critical. Further, students were often unaware of the value of the process of elaboration itself, and appeared to engage in it automatically, "without conscious control of the process" (1990b, p. 155). According to Stein, this finding shows that students may benefit from formal instruction on the process of elaboration and its outcomes. Students can be taught metacognitive skills, that is, the functions of elaboration, the value of elaborative material they generate, and the impact it has, directly and indirectly, on the writing they produce. This awareness may help students value their own ideas and experiences and use them more critically in performing academic tasks.

The Process of Reading to Write in L2/FL

In L2/FL, few studies in this area have been conducted (Campbell, 1987, 1990; Carson, 1993; Ruiz-Funes, 1994, 1996). They have granted valuable insight to the field by exploring an often neglected aspect of L2/FL academic writing and by yielding information necessary to guide future research and to improve pedagogy in the reading/writing classrooms. Of significant value is the work done by Campbell (1987) and Carson (1993) in ESL who pointed out the concept of "authority" in the reading-to-write process and the importance of developing critical literacy skills in the ESL classes. From a FL perspective, Ruiz-Funes (1994, 1996, 1999a, 1999b, 2001) studied the process of reading to write of skilled FL writers and highlighted the significance of task representation in this process.

Campbell (1987) explored the process of writing from sources used by native and non- native speakers of English at the undergraduate level. Analysis of the data was based primarily on Kirby and Kantor's (1983) concept of "authority," defined as "a good understanding and confidence of that understanding of both the background text and his/her emerging text" (Campbell, 1987). She notes that good readers and writers have "authority" that allows them to produce better quality academic papers. On the contrary, less skillful readers and writers lack authority and, consequently, they try to simplify the task as much as possible "by avoiding the text, copying the text, or simplifying the structure of the merging text to accommodate repetitious patterns of use of the background text" (p. 113). As a result, the texts produced are of low quality for academic standards. She proposes three hypotheses on writing from source texts that may be of use for future research: (1) There is a positive relationship between comprehension of the background text and overall writing quality of the student paper: as comprehension of the background text increases, so does overall writing quality (p. 128). (2) There is a negative relationship between authority over the background text (as measured by a reading comprehension rating plus a rating of self-confidence in understanding of the text) and simplification of the use of information from the background text (e.g., avoidance, copying, repetition of the structure in the emerging text): as authority over the background text increases, simplification of the use of information from the background text decreases (1987, p. 129). (3) There is a positive relationship between overall writing quality and backgrounding of information from the source text: as writing quality increases, information from the source text functions more often as background than as foreground (as defined by Hopper & Thompson, 1980).

Carson and Leki (1993) present a compilation of studies on reading and writing in ESL. Their work discusses issues that range from the importance of developing critical literacy in ESL classes (Gajdusek & van Dommelen, 1993), the need for ESL students to develop metacognitive knowledge of the processes involved in reading and writing (Devine, 1993), the relationship between reading and writing skills (Flahive & Bailey, 1993), and task representation (Connor & Carrell, 1993). In addition, pedagogical implications are discussed that emphasize the use of a sequential recursive syllabus using reading and writing (Spack, 1988).

Within a FL context, Ruiz-Funes (1994, 1996, 1999a, 1999b) explored the process of reading to write used by skilled learners of Spanish in an upper level Spanish composition course. The analysis was based on Stein's (1990a) model of the cognition of reading to write. The major processes identified in addition to the composing processes themselves (planning, writing, revising, editing) were *synthesizing, monitoring, structuring,* and *elaborating*. These processes served specific functions in the performance of the reading-to-write task: (1) the process of *synthesizing* served primarily to design a framework or plan, to organize ideas, compile information from the source text and from the reaction around which the students developed their essays; (2) the process of *monitoring* served to check for accuracy of information and to collect relevant information from the source text; (3) the process of *structuring* served the function of selecting relevant information and restructuring it according to the intended purpose of the writer; and (4) the process of *elaborating* seemed to be the most important one and served the functions of generating new ideas, evaluating, and judging. In addition, the findings indicate the high level of awareness and control the subjects had of the processes they used. In particular, they were aware of the process of elaboration and of the important role it played in integrating information from the source text with their own ideas.

Ruiz-Funes (1994) points out a number of related issues that need to be addressed in future research to reach a more comprehensive understanding of the cognition of reading to write in a FL. Of special significance is the relationship between processes used and *task representation*—the manner in which students interpret an assigned task and, therefore, the type of paper they produce. Task representation determines whether individual papers fulfill the teacher's expectations and how they are evaluated (Flower, 1990; Kantz, 1990a, 1990b); however, it is often taken for granted and, as such, considered of no interest for research. In the next section a review of the work done on task representation in L1 and L2/FL writing is presented and its implications for future research are highlighted.

Task Representation

The most significant studies conducted on task representation are those by Flower (1990) and Kantz (1990a), both with L1 college students. Flower's findings revealed that students interpreted the "same college writing assignment in strikingly different ways" (p. 35). She explains this phenomenon as the result of the students' awareness, or lack of it, of the conventions of academic discourse and of the instructors' expectations, which to a certain extent students are supposed to infer. Along these lines Flower remarks: "[T]o represent a task is to imagine a rhetorical situation—to conjure up teachers past and present, their expectations and responses, texts one has read and written, conventions, schemas, possible language—as well as one's own knowledge, needs, and desires" (p. 54).

The students in her study were given a typical college level assignment that required reading, synthesizing, interpreting, using relevant data, and writing one's own statement (p. 42). The students' task representations differed in three major areas: major source of information; text format and features; and organizing plans, strategies, and goals (p. 42). The tasks they produced were categorized as: *summary, response, review, synthesis,* and *synthesis with a rhetorical purpose.* Each of these tasks offered advantages and disadvantages while demanding more or less effort from the writer. Of the five tasks, synthesis with a rhetorical purpose is considered the most difficult but offering the most benefits;

it is the most intellectually sophisticated of all because "it asks the writer to reorganize and integrate information around a controlling concept" (p. 50). Only a few students, however, interpreted the task in this manner.

Flower (1990) formulates a tentative theory of task representation as a constructive process organized around three principles:

1. Writers do not 'choose' a representation; they 'construct' one, integrating elements from a large set of options and schemas (p. 54).

2. Because the process of constructing a task representation depends on noticing cues from the context and evoking relevant memories, it can extend over the course of composing (p. 56).

3. Developments and changes in a writer's representation can lead to problems in constructing an integrated task and text (p. 58).

Similar conclusions are drawn by Kantz (1990b), who discusses problems that L1 college students have with writing from source texts, in particular, with writing persuasive research papers. The major problem identified was in creating original arguments by transforming the material from the source text so as to fulfill the expectations of academic written discourse. Kantz found that students interpreted the assignment in different ways, which, in turn, required different demands and led to papers of different quality. To this, Kantz states:

> A writing-from-sources task can be as simple as collating a body of facts from a few short texts on a familiar topic into a new text that reproduces the structure, tone, and purpose of the originals, but it can also involve applying abstract concepts from one area to an original problem in a different area, a task that involves examining the relationships among material. ... (p. 76)

Task Representation in L2/FL Writing

Research on L2/FL task representation is scant. In analyzing the ways L2/FL students interpret a reading-to-write task, we may ask ourselves if task representation is linked to the motivation the task arouses in the students, to the clarity of the assignment itself, to standard "academic discourse" being a new phenomenon to the students, to the degree to which students think about the assignment, or to their ability as writers and readers. Or else L2/FL task representation may be linked to other factors such as the students' proficiency level in the L2/FL. Within an ESL context, Connor and Kramer (1995) studied the task representation of three ESL and two American Business graduate students. They compared the task representation of each group of students, examining the differences in task representation of the ESL students in relation to both their language skills and their professional training and background. The subjects completed the reading of a business case and wrote a policy report as part of one of their course assignments and participated in a series of retrospective interviews.

Findings from this study indicate that the task representation of the two ESL students with the lowest language proficiency levels as indicated by the TOEFL scores differed markedly from that of the American students. These two students merely summarized the information in the source case and did not reveal a rhetorical purpose in their report. Likewise, the task representation of the three ESL students was also affected by their language proficiency and professional training and background. The task representation of the ESL student with the highest TOEFL score was very similar to the one produced by the American students and showed the evaluative and interpretive goals as he engaged in the reading-to-write task. The authors conclude that "when differences in task representation exist between L1 and L2 writers, the source of these differences may be cultural and educational as well as language-oriented" (p. 172).

From a FL perspective, Ruiz-Funes (2001) explored: (1) how third year students of Spanish represented an assigned reading-to-write task as indicated by the type of papers they produced, and (2) the relationship between the linguistic quality of those papers and the type of task representation. The students wrote a paper based on the reading of the literary selection, *Kike* by Hilda Perera (1994), a Hispanic juvenile short novel rich in cultural references. They wrote the first draft in class and completed it over the period of a week in class as well. The final version was typed in the language laboratory. Students were allowed to use the text, class notes, dictionaries, and other references. The task was as follows (no further directions or explanations were given to the students):

Analice los cambios que vive Kike y cómo éstos afectan su identidad cultural. ¿Logra Kike encontrar una solución a su problema de identidad? Use ejemplos del texto para ilustrar/apoyar sus ideas. Escriba como mínimo 2 páginas a máquina y a doble espacio.

(Analyze the changes Kike experiences and how they affect his own cultural identity. Is he able to find a solution to his identity problem? Use examples from the text to support your ideas. Write at least two pages typed and double spaced.

The most revealing findings from this investigation are: (1) given the same reading-to-write assignment, FL students interpreted the task in different ways, and therefore, produced different types of papers; (2) the ability to write syntactically complex sentences did not lead to cognitively sophisticated composing; (3) the ability to write with grammatical accuracy was not an indicator of the students' ability to express elaborated ideas; and (4) the ability to write with grammatical accuracy might lead to the students' ability to write more syntactically complex sentences.

For 1 above (given the same reading-to-write assignment, FL students interpret the task in different ways, and therefore, produce different types of papers) the following categories identified by Kantz (1990) were used as the basis to analyze the papers the students produced: *Summary:* States the gist or selected ideas from the source text; *Summary And Comment:* Combines a summary of selected review of material from the source text with commentary or additions by the writer; *Free Response to the Topic:* Discusses the topic with little reference to information from the source text; *Synthesis:* Organizes a discussion (which draws on source materials) around a unique (nonobvious) controlling concept; *Interpretation with a Rhetorical Purpose:* Organizes a discussion (which draws on source materials) around a unique and apparent rhetorical purpose (beyond summary, comment, or synthesis).

The papers the students produced were categorized as follows: *Summary* (3), *Summary and Comment* (6), and *Interpretation with a Rhetorical Purpose* (5).

Summary

The students who used this category took a chronological approach, stating all the events from the beginning to the end and seldom making personal references to the impact of the events on the development of the protagonist's personality. These personal references, moreover, were brief, vague, and superficial. The analysis requested in the assignment was absent.

Summary and Comment

The majority of the students adopted this approach. The summary followed a chronological order that governed the structure of the papers. Unlike the *Summary* category, this approach incorporated the main ideas from the source text with more attempts to interpret the events that affected the main character's search for his cultural identity. The attempts to interpret these changes were somewhat insightful, yet the writers quickly moved to narrate or describe the next event. The students alternated between reviewing or summarizing the ideas in the source text and adding their own comments or associations. Typically, in this category students summarized the source text and added an "opinion paragraph" at the beginning or the end (Flower, 1990). As Flower remarks, this plan allows writers to express their own ideas in an easy and natural way, yet it does not encourage writers to find connections or resolve conflicts: " . . . the writer could simply walk through the source text, reviewing the main points in the order found in the notes, adding occasional comments when he or she has something to say" (Flower, 1990, p. 46).

Interpretation with a Rhetorical Purpose

Papers written by the second largest group fell into this category. These papers contained a synthesis of the crucial events that affected the protagonist's search for his own cultural identity, but most importantly, they included an analysis of those events that served the writers as a means of building a case of their own. The writers in this category were able to transform, adapt, and reconstruct the information from the source text to serve their own purpose. Such purpose governed the selection of information and the organization of the entire text. Papers in this category combined the ideas of their writers with those in the source text in an analytical and elaborated fashion.

The linguistic quality of the students' papers was measured by their syntactic complexity as well as their grammatical accuracy. For the former, the author used T-Unit Analysis. T-unit (minimal terminable unit) was coined by Hunt (1965) who describes it as "one main clause plus the subordinate clauses attached to or embedded within it" (p. 49). For the latter, an error coding system was adapted from Lalande's (1984) Essay Correction Code (ECCO). In order to determine the syntactic complexity of the papers, the researcher calculated the number of T-units and the mean length of T-units (MLTU). The MLTU was calculated by dividing the total number of words in each paper by the total number of T-units (MLTU=Nw/Ntu). In addition to T-Unit analysis, the quality of the students' papers was measured in relation to their grammatical accuracy. Each grammatical mistake was coded and tallied on each paper. The total number of errors and the ratio of number of errors per T-unit was calculated per paper (individual students) and per paper category (groups).

It was assumed that the papers within the more cognitively complex categories such as *Synthesis* and *Interpretation with a Rhetorical Purpose* would be more syntactically complex (higher mean length of T-Units), and would have fewer grammatical errors compared to the papers in the other categories. The author followed Hunt's (1965) and Mills's (1990) findings to make this assumption. Contrary to this initial assumption, the data indicates that the MLTU of the papers within the more cognitively elaborated category—*Interpretation*—was not higher than that of the other paper types. In fact, it was slightly higher than the MLTU of the simplest category (*Summary*) and lower than that for the *Summary and Comment* papers; however, the difference in MLTU among the three paper categories was not significant. In addition, the *Interpretation* papers had the highest ratio of grammatical errors per T-unit (1:1.5) compared to the other paper types. The *Summary and Comment* papers received the best scores in both syntactic complexity and grammatical accuracy. The results from 2 and 3 above indicate that grammatical accuracy does not correlate with a more elaborated and sophisticated writing style. Students may choose to keep their sentence length and complexity very simple and safe in order to receive a higher grade if they perceive that grammatical accuracy is the entire basis for their grade. As a result, the sentences may be perfect grammatically, yet dull in style and content.

These findings suggest that the ability to read insightfully and write critically in a FL is linked to other more complex thinking and cognitive processes rather than to the language skills of the writer as measured by syntactic complexity and grammatical accuracy. In the same way, the ability to interpret a reading-to-write task appropriately and therefore, to produce the required type of paper is not directly dependent upon such linguistic measures either, but instead, upon other more cognitively complex factors that need to be explored. As Schultz (1991b) stated:

> Upper-division instructors may well react to student writing difficulties by prescribing additional grammar instruction, but ironically, research has repeatedly shown that grammar instruction has little if any impact on composition skills [. . . grammatical accuracy] is not necessarily an indicator of student ability to express personal meaning in the target language. (p. 412)

Future research on task representation in FL reading to write should explore the factors that lead students to interpret a task in different ways. Some of these factors include the level of students' awareness of the conventions of academic writing, the students' experience as writers and readers in their L1 and L2, or their level of literary interpretation skills. These factors, in turn, have important pedagogical and curricular implications as has been suggested by the work done on FL reading to write from a pedagogical perspective. Of special interest are the studies conducted by Schultz (1991b), Schofer (1990, 1991), Barnett (1991), and Henning (1992), which are presented below.

Pedagogical and Curricular Issues

Most of the work related to FL reading to write deals with pedagogical and curricular issues. Some studies point to the lack of adequate transition from intermediate to advanced FL classes and propose ways to narrow the gap between the two levels. Students move from one level to the next without the necessary preparation in reading and writing processes and strategy use that would allow them to succeed in the advanced courses. Schultz (1991b) acknowledges this problem and remarks that "students who apparently do well in language classes often seem to be at a loss when faced with the demands of upper-division courses" (p. 411). The author criticizes the lack of appropriate composition skill preparation at the intermediate level, as it is seen in many of today's major institutions, in terms of upper-division expectations. Intermediate level students are generally taught to write in the simplest modes, such as description and narration, and sometimes exposition. Very seldom is there consideration given to the writing modes students are expected to produce in advanced courses.

Schultz (1991b) proposes a comprehensive program that focuses on writing tasks based on the reading of literary texts. The program is based primarily on the following principles: (1) "it targets . . . the mode of essay students will be expected to write at the next level of study . . ."; (2) "[it] disperses grading criteria for compositions over categories other than grammar alone"; (3) it incorporates a variety of response mechanisms, from teacher response to student response-group work; and (4) "[it] is fundamentally process-oriented" (p. 414-15). One of the major goals of the program is to prepare students to think critically about the texts they read in order to respond to and write about them insightfully and argumentatively.

The gap between intermediate and advanced level classes is also criticized by language and literature experts who point out the lack of adequate preparation students have to process literary texts in the target language. This problem is found to be rooted in the supplementary role literature often plays in lower level foreign language classes (Schofer, 1990). Researchers (Schofer, 1990, 1991; Barnett, 1991) propose the integration of literature in the core of language teaching from the elementary level so that "students have a better preparation in reading and writing as they go from [the so-called] language to literature courses" (Schofer 1990, p. 326). Along with this, Henning (1992) proposes the use of a literary interpretation scale that goes from Novice to Superior and that is linked to the ACTFL Reading Proficiency Guidelines at the Advanced and Superior levels. According to Henning, students would move from recognizing events of an uncomplicated short story and retelling it simply by repeating, paraphrasing, or translating segments of the text (Novice) to comprehending factual elements of the text almost completely and summarizing plot accurately (Intermediate) to moving outside the text to engage its sociocultural and historical contexts (Advanced) to doing critical literary analysis (Superior). She further suggests that students are going to compose according to their level of interpretation ability. The possibility of a correlation between task representation and literary interpretive skills needs to be further explored as it may provide important information on the cognition of reading-to-write in a FL.

Conclusions

In reviewing the major work done on the process of reading to write, the following conclusions are drawn: First, the exploration of the process of reading to write in L2/FL is still in its initial stages. A preliminary identification has been provided of the processes L2/FL students orchestrate when they perform reading-to-write tasks. However, the relationship between process use and certain contextual factors such as students' task representation and students' level of proficiency, among others, need to be further investigated. Exploration of these factors within subject comparisons of L1 and L2 reading and writing may allow us to see more clearly the complex interaction between reading comprehension, composing skills and task representation, and the students' linguistic abilities. Second, the research suggests that not only is it important to explore the processes that L2/FL readers and writers activate, but also to study the degree of awareness students have of such processes. Identification of reading and writing processes as well as metacognitive knowledge seem to be intrinsically interrelated. Third, there is indication that some progress has been made in bringing theory into the classroom; however, there is still an urgent need to implement such theory into the practices of L2/FL classrooms, particularly in upper level courses where reading and writing tasks become more complex and students orchestrate multiple processes (Krashen & Lee, 2004). And finally, the review indicates the need for articulating the FL curriculum to narrow the gap between intermediate and upper level courses, as pointed out by Schultz (1991b), Schofer (1990, 1991), and Henning (1992) above, to ensure the continuous development of students' reading and writing as well as critical literary skills.

Notes

1. This manuscript contains sections that appear in articles written by the author and previously published in *Foreign Language Annals* (1999b and 2001). Permission to republish such sections was granted by ACTFL as publisher in May 2008.

References

Akyel, A. (1994). First language use in EFL writing: Planning in Turkish vs. planning in English. *International Journal of Applied Linguistics, 4,* 169–96.

Baker, L., & Brown, A. L. (1984a). Cognitive monitoring in reading. In J. Flood. (Ed.), *Understanding reading comprehension* (pp. 21–44). Newark, DE: International Reading Association.

Baker, L., & Brown, A. L. (1984b). Metacognitive skills in reading. In P. D. Pearson, R. Barr, M. L. Kamil, & P. Mosenthal. (Eds.), *Handbook of reading research* (pp. 353–94). NY: Longman.

Barnett, M. A. (1986). Syntactic and lexical/semantic skill in foreign language reading: importance and interaction. *The Modem Language Journal, 70*(4), 34–49.

Barnett, M. A. (1991). Language and literature: False dichotomies, real allies. *ADFL Bulletin, 22*(3), 7–11.

Campbell, C. C. (1987). Writing with others' words: The use of information from a background reading text in the writing of native and non- native university composition students. Unpublished dissertation. ProQuest document ID: 749180241.

Campbell, C. C. (1990). Writing with others' words: Using background reading text in academic composition. In B. Kroll. (Ed.), *Second language writing: Research issues for the classroom* (pp. 211–30). New York: Cambridge University Press.

Carrell, P. L., & Eisterhold, J. C. (1983). Schema theory and ESL reading pedagogy. *TESOL Quarterly, 17*(4), 553–74.

Carson, J. G. (1993). Reading for writing: Cognitive perspectives. In J. G. Carson, & I. Leki (Eds.), *Reading in the composition classroom* (pp. 85–104). Boston, MA: Heinle and Heinle.

Carson, J. G., & Leki, I. (Eds.). (1993). *Reading in the composition classroom.* Boston, MA: Heinle & Heinle.

Connor, U. M. (1984). Recall of text: Differences between first and second language readers. *TESOL Quarterly, 18*(2), 239–56.

Connor, U. & Carrell, P. (1993). The interpretation of tasks by writers and readers in holistically rated direct assessment of writing. In J. G. Carson & I. Leki (Eds.), *Reading in the composition classroom* (pp. 141–160). Boston, MA: Heinle & Heinle.

Connor, U. M. & Kramer, M. G. (1995). Writing from sources: Case studies of graduate students in business management. In D. Belcher & G. Braire (Eds.), *Academic writing in a second language: Essays on research and pedagogy* (pp. 155–182). Norwood, NJ: Ablex.

Devine, J. (1993). The role of metacognition in second language reading and writing. In J. G. Carson & I. Leki (Eds.), *Reading in the composition classroom* (pp. 105–127). Boston, MA: Heinle & Heinle.

Dvorak, T. (1986). Writing in the foreign language. In B. H. Wing (Ed.), *Listening, reading and writing: Analysis and application* (pp. 145–67). Middlebury, VT: Northeast Conference.

Flahive, D. E., & Bailey, N. H. (1993). Exploring reading/writing relationships in adult second language learners. In J. G. Carson & I. Leki (Eds.), *Reading in the composition classroom* (pp. 128–140). Boston, MA: Heinle & Heinle.

Flower, L. (1990). The role of task representation in reading-to-rite. In L. Flower, V. Stein, J. Ackerman, M. J. Kantz, K. McCormick, & W. C. Peck, (Eds.), *Reading-to-write: Exploring a cognitive and social process* (pp. 35–75). New York: Oxford University Press.

Gajdusek, L., & van Dommelen, D. (1993). Literature and critical thinking in the composition classroom. In J. G. Carson & I. Leki (Eds.), *Reading in the composition classroom* (pp. 197–218). Boston, MA: Heinle & Heinle.

Goodman, K. S. (Ed.). (1968). *Reading in the composition classroom*. Detroit, MI: Wayne State University Press.

Hammadou, J. (1991). Interrelationships among prior knowledge, inference, and language proficiency in foreign language reading. *The Modem Language Journal, 75*(1), 27–38.

Henning, S. D. (1992). Assessing literary interpretation skills. *Foreign Language Annals, 25*(4), 339–355.

Hirose, K., & Sasaki, M. (1994). Explanatory variables for Japanese students' expository writing in English: An exploratory study. *Journal of Second Language Writing, 3*, 203–29.

Hopper, P. J., &. Thompson, S. A. (1980). Transitivity in grammar and discourse. *Language 56*(2), 251–299.

Hunt, K. W. (1965). *Grammatical structures written at three grade levels*. Champaign, IL: National Council of Teachers of English, Research Report No. 3.

Kantz, M. (1990a). Helping students use textual sources persuasively. *College English, 52*, 74–91.

Kantz, M. J. (1990b). Promises of coherence, weak content, and strong organization: An analysis of the students' texts. In L. Flower, V. Stein, J. Ackerman, M. J. Kantz, K. McCormick, & W. C. Peck, (Eds.), *Reading-to-write: Exploring a cognitive and social process* (pp. 76–95). New York: Oxford University Press.

Kennedy, M. L. (1985). The composing process of college students writing from sources. *Written Communication, 2*, 434–56.

Kern, R. G., & Schultz, J. M. (1992). The effects of composition instruction on intermediate level French students' writing performance: Some preliminary findings. *The Modern Language Journal, 76*, 1–13.

Kirby, D. R., & Kantor, K. L. (1983). Towards a theory of developmental rhetoric. In A. Freeman, I. Pringle, & J. Yalden (Eds.), *Learning to write: First language/second language* (pp. 87–97). London: Longman.

Kobayashi, H., & Rinnert, C. (2001). Factors relating to EFL writers' discourse level revision skills. In R. M. Manchón (Ed.), *Writing in the L2 classroom: Issues in research and pedagogy* (71–102.). Special Issue of *International Journal of English Studies, 1*(2).

Krashen, S. (1984). *Writing: Research, theory, and application.* Oxford, UK: Pergamon Press.

Krashen, S., & Lee, S-Y. (2004). Competence in foreign language writing: Progress and lacunae. *Literacy across Cultures, 12*(2), 10–14.

Kroll, B. (Ed.). (1990). *Second language writing: Research insights for the classroom.* New York: Cambridge University Press.

Lalande, J. F. II. (1984). Reducing composition errors: An experiment. *Foreign Language Annals, 17*(2), 109–117.

Lee, J. F. (1986a). Background knowledge and L2 reading. *The Modern Language Journal, 70,* 350–54.

Lee, J. F. (1986b). On the use of recall task to measure L2 reading comprehension. *Studies in Second Language Acquisition, 8,* 83–93.

Leki, I., Cumming, A., & Silva, T. (2008). *A synthesis of research on second language writing in English.* New York: Routledge.

Levine, M. G., & Haus, G. J. (1985). The effect of background knowledge on the reading comprehension of second-language learners. *Foreign Language Annals, 18*(5), 391–97.

Melendez, J. E. (1985). Applying schema theory to foreign language reading. *Foreign Language Annals, 18*(5), 399–403.

Mills, C. (1990). Syntax and the evaluation of college writing: A blind alley. In L. Arena (Ed.), *Language proficiency: Defining teaching and testing* (pp. 107–119). New York: Plenum Press.

Newell A., & Simon, H. A. (1972). *Human problem solving.* Englewood Cliffs, NJ: Prentice-Hall.

Perera, H. (1994). *Kike.* Madrid: Ediciones SM.

Phillips, J. K. (1984). Practical implications of recent research in reading. *Foreign Language Annals, 17*(4), 285–96.

Raimes, A. (1987). Language proficiency, writing ability, and composing strategies: A study of ESL college student writers. *Language Learning, 37*(3), 439–68.

Reder, L. M. T. (1980). The role of elaboration in the comprehension and retention of prose: A critical review. *Review of Educational Research, 50,* 5–53.

Roca de Larios, J., Manchón, R., Murphy, L., & Marín, J. (2008). The foreign language writer's strategic behaviour in the allocation of time to writing processes. *Journal of Applied Linguistics, 17*(1), 30–47.

Ruiz-Funes, M. (1994). *An exploration of the process of reading-to-write used by skilled Spanish-as-a-foreign-language students.* Unpublished dissertation. ProQuest document ID: 741993121.

Ruiz-Funes, M. (1996). The process of reading-to-write used by a learner of Spanish: A case study. Paper presented at MIFLIC Conference.

Ruiz-Funes, M. (1999a). The process of reading to write used by a skilled Spanish-as-a foreign language student: A case study. *Foreign Language Annals, 32*(1), 45–62.

Ruiz-Funes, M. (1999b). Writing, reading, and reading-to-write in a foreign language: A critical review. *Foreign Language Annals, 32*(4), 514–526.

Ruiz-Funes, M. (2001). Task representation in foreign language reading-to-write. *Foreign Language Annals, 34,* 226–234.

Sasaki, M. (2000). Toward an empirical model of EFL writing processes: An exploratory study. *Journal of Second Language Writing, 9,* 259–91.

Schofer, P. (1990). Literature and communicative competence: A springboard for the development of critical thinking and aesthetic appreciation of literature in the land of language. *Foreign Language Annals, 23*(4), 325–34.

Schofer, P. (1991). Writing mode in the articulation of language and literature classes: Theory and practice. *The Modern Language Journal, 75*(4), 411–17.

Schultz, J. M. (1991b). Writing mode in the articulation of language and literature classes: Theory and practice. *The Modem Language Journal, 75(4),* 411–17.

Scott, V. M. (1996). *Rethinking foreign language writing.* Boston, MA: Heinle & Heinle.

Smith, F. (1983). Reading like a writer. *Language Arts, 60,* 558–67.

Sommers, N. I. (1978). *Revision in the composing process: A case study of college freshmen and experienced adult writers.* Doctoral dissertation, Boston University.

Spack, R. (1988). Initiating ESL students into the academic discourse community: How far should we go? *TESOL Quarterly, 22*(1), 29–51.

Stein, V. (1990a). Exploring the cognition of reading-to-write. In L. Flower, V. Stein, J. Ackerman, M. J. Kantz, K. McCormick, & W. C. Peck, (Eds.), *Exploring a cognitive and social process* (pp. 119–43). New York: Oxford University Press.

Stein, V. (1990b). Elaboration: Using what you know. In L. Flower, V. Stein, J. Ackerman, M. J. Kantz, K. McCormick, & W. C. Peck, (Eds.), *Reading-to-write: Exploring a cognitive and social process* (pp. 144–54). New York: Oxford University Press.

Swaffar, J. K., Arens, K. M., and Byrnes, H. (1991). *Reading for meaning: An integrated approach to language learning.* New Jersey: Prentice Hall.

Victori, M. (1999). An analysis of writing knowledge in EFL composing: A case study of two effective and two less effective writers. *System, 27,* 537–55.

Wang, W., & Wen, Q. (2002). L1 use in the L2 composing process: An exploratory study of 16 Chinese EFL writers. *Journal of Second Language Writing, 11,* 225–46.

Yasuda, S. (2004). Revising strategies in ESL academic writing: A cases study of Japanese postgraduate student writers. *Journal of Asian Pacific Communication, 14,* 91–112.

Zamel, V. (1982). Writing: The process of discovering meaning. *TESOL Quarterly, 16,* 195–209.

Zamel, V. (1983). The composing processes of advanced ESL students: Six case studies. *TESOL Quarterly, 17,* 165–87.

3 The Language Learning Potential of Writing in Foreign Language Contexts: Lessons from Research

Rosa M. Manchón

Introduction

This chapter looks into the connections between writing and language learning, an issue clearly at the interface between second language acquisition (SLA) and second language (L2) writing research, and one whose relevance in discussions of foreign language (FL) writing is particularly salient. Concerning SLA-L2 writing interfaces, Ortega and Carson (2010: 49) suggest:

> At the broadest level [. . .] L2 writing SLA interfaces revolve around the fundamental question of how linguistic expertise in the L2 may constrain the development of L2 composing abilities and, conversely, the less pondered question of how L2 writing may foster overall second language development.

My focus of concern is the "less pondered question" mentioned in the quotation as I shall revisit the empirical literature on the instrumental role that writing can have in the language learning experience of foreign language (FL) learners. Seen from a SLA perspective, the exploration of the potential language learning of writing can be linked to current theorizing in the field. For instance, in their recent account of SLA theories, VanPatten and Williams (2007) suggest that one of the ten issues any comprehensive theory of SLA must account for is: "There are limits on the effect of output (learner production) on language acquisition" (p. 12). The investigation into these limits and effects would require gathering empirical evidence to either support or refute Lee and VanPatten's (1995, p. 95) contention that "while output practice may help fluency and accuracy in production, it is not responsible for getting the grammar into the learner's head." This differential effect of output practice is still an empirical question, and thus the relevance of putting these tenets to empirical test as far as written output is concerned. In addition, as noted by Shehadeh (2002), investigating the role of output practice in SLA is also relevant from a pedagogical angle because any advancement in this domain "may provide insights that help educators and language teachers make language learning more effective" (p. 641).

From the perspective of L2 writing research, the exploration of the language learning potential of writing is in part related to the purported second language bias of L2 writing scholarship (see Manchón, 2009; Manchón and de Haan, 2008; Ortega, 2004) and, as a consequence, to the recognition that any comprehensive theory or model of L2 writing must account for the variety of contexts and situations in which people write and learn to write. In this respect, and in contrast to what may be the norm in most second language contexts, the role writing can play in certain FL contexts may be partially or totally instrumental in nature given that many FL learners may not have immediate needs to "learn to write" for personal, academic, and/ or professional reasons. Rather, their learning aims might be more in line with "writing to learn" purposes, i.e. writing as a means to learn the L2. The implication would be that, as noted by Harklau (2002), our research agenda must include the exploration of "how L2 learners learn how to write," as well as the not less important question of "the instrumental role that writing can play in the acquisition of a second language in educational settings" (Harklau 2002, p. 345).

The chapter is organized as follows: I start by summarizing the theoretical underpinnings of the role of output practice in SLA as the necessary background to understanding the research on the language learning potential of writing. I then present a summary overview of some strands of research that have either directly or indirectly shed light on the issue. The main part of the chapter is devoted to the analysis of selected empirical findings in this body of literature and to the assessment of the implications that may derive from them in terms of instructional interventions and routes to pursue in future research.

Two issues ought to be clarified at this point. First, throughout the chapter I talk about FL contexts in general, which should not be interpreted as a lack of recognition on my part of the complexity and variability that characterize foreign language contexts in terms of human, educational, social, and material conditions. As Ortega (2009) warns us, "we should take great care to avoid the pitfall of treating teachers, writers, and writing contexts across studies as belonging to an undifferentiated, homogeneous contextual class of 'FL' or 'EFL'" (p. 250). Second, my focus on the learning potential of literacy experiences should not be interpreted to mean that I consider language learning to be the only or even the main aim of teaching writing in FL contexts. Yet, I do believe that, as mentioned earlier, there are some FL contexts in which, in addition to other possible purposes and values, it is theoretically and educationally relevant to exploit the language learning potential afforded by literacy practices if only because of the crucial role the printed word may play in the language learning experience of many FL classroom learners.

The Language Learning Potential of Writing: Theoretical Underpinnings

The rationale for the language learning potential of writing derives from various influential theoretical strands of SLA research. The first of these is Skill Learning Theory (cf. DeKeyser, 1998, 2001, 2007; Segalowitz, 2003), particularly regarding the role the theory attributes to language practice (which would include oral and written uses of language) in consolidating and automatizing linguistic knowledge as a necessary condition to improve task performance. In one of the most recent accounts of the theory, DeKeyser (2007) explains that "a large amount of practice is needed to decrease the time required to execute the task (reaction time), the percentage of errors (error rate), and the amount of attention required (and hence interference with/from other tasks). This practice leads to gradual automatization of knowledge" (pp. 88–89). An empirical question would be the investigation of whether or not these outcomes may derive from written output practice.

Focus on Form (FonF) research is another relevant area within SLA studies (cf. Doughty, 2001; Doughty & Williams, 1998; Norris & Ortega, 2000); its main tenet is that attention to language as an object while engaged in communication is beneficial for L2 development, a condition afforded by certain forms of written communication. This explains the abundant and growing body of literature framed in this paradigm that has explored L2 learning via writing, with an important line of research being the one devoted to the investigation of the type and amount of attention to language matters fostered by various FonF writing tasks, as will be seen in a later section.

The language learning potential of writing can also be linked to the Noticing Hypothesis (cf. Schmidt, 1990, 1993,, 2001; Izumi, 2003), with its emphasis on the crucial role of attention in SLA and the need for learners to notice gaps in their interlanguages (IL) as well as the gap between their language resources and the L2 rules for SLA to proceed. Schmidt (2001) has suggested that

> attention to input is seen as essential for storage and a necessary precursor of hypothesis formulation and testing. [. . .] Attention is what allows speakers to become aware of a mismatch or gap between what they can produce and what they need to produce, as well as between what they produce and what proficient target language speakers produce. (p. 6)

Again, this noticing activity may naturally derive from the problem-solving activity involved in composing (see Manchón & Roca de Larios, 2007), a task that, particularly when performed in an L2, entails a continuous search to find the linguistic resources with which to express one's intended meaning.

Finally, and very importantly, the language learning potential of writing can be viewed in relation to the Output Hypothesis (cf. Swain, 1985, 1995, 1998, 2000, 2005), which posits that language output, in addition to being the end result of the language learning process, can have an important role in promoting language development because producing language (either orally or in writing) pushes learners into making their output more precise, more coherent, and more appropriate. In the original formulation of the Hypothesis, Swain argued that the production of this "pushed" output leads learners to engage in processes thought to be conducive to language development, including noticing processes (in line with the Noticing Hypothesis mentioned above), hypothesis testing, and metalinguistic awareness.

As far as the *noticing function* of output is concerned, the argument is that "it is while attempting to produce the target language [. . .] that learners may notice that they do not know how to say (or write) precisely the meaning they wished to convey" (Swain, 1998, p. 67). Very important for present purposes is the suggestion that this noticing activity has a consciousness-raising function that may lead learners to look for ways to fill their noticed gaps, and/or to engage in more focused attention to incoming input (which, in the case of writing, would mean paying focused attention to the feedback received on their own output). As we shall see in later sections, plenty of research efforts have gone into the investigation of the noticing function of writing practice (both when producing texts and when processing the feedback obtained on one's own productions), although its impact on learning (particularly in the long-term) is still an empirical question.

Regarding the *hypothesis-testing function* of output, it is argued that the search for an optimal match between intentions and their expression that lies at the heart of writing may trigger internal feedback in the form of self-evaluation of one's own choices or, alternatively, L2 writers may test their hypotheses about the L2 via the feedback obtained on their own writing. This could mean the temporal dimension of writing (in contrast to the on-line production of speech) would in principle allow for "cognitive comparison" (cf. Doughty, 2001), a process whereby learners compare what they have noticed in the input (in this case the feedback on their writing) with their own representation of the L2.

Finally, with respect to the *metalinguistic function* of output, Swain (1985) suggested the production of output is "the trigger that forces the learner to pay attention to the means of expression needed in order to successfully convey his or her own intended meaning" (p. 249). This reflection on language may help students develop their L2 knowledge as it "may deepen the learner's awareness of forms, rules, and form-function relationship if the context of production is communicative in nature" (Izumi, 2003, p. 170). This is an expanding line of research and, therefore, whether or not this awareness has a long-term impact on learning is still an empirical question, as should be evident in the review of the literature presented in a later section.

The Language Learning Potential of Writing: An Overview of Research

The empirical research that has shed light on the language learning potential of written output encompasses two main groups of studies: "descriptive" and "interventionist" investigations. In the first case researchers have described the manner in which the production of written output (both in individual and collaborative writing) fosters the processes of focus on form, noticing, hypothesis testing, and metalinguistic awareness (cf. Alegría de la Colina & García Mayo, 2007; Cumming, 1990; Fortune, 2005; Fortune & Thorp, 2001; García Mayo, 2002a, 2002b; Kuiken & Vedder, 2002a, 2002b; Leeser, 2004; Lindgren & Sullivan, 2003; Manchón, Roca de Larios, & Murphy, 2009; Qi & Lapkin, 2001; Storch, 1998a, 1998b, 1999, 2001, 2005; Storch & Wigglesworth, 2007). Interventionist studies, in contrast, have gone one step further and have explored the effects of this linguistic processing activity upon learning, with some experimental intervention mediating the process. This mediation has taken two main forms. The participants in some studies have been asked to produce some writing, and they were then provided with some type of input or feedback whose effects on the participants' subsequent writing was investigated. This input/feedback has included the reformulation of the students' original texts (cf. Adams, 2003; Lapkin, Swain, & Smith, 2002; Qi & Lapkin, 2001; Swain & Lapkin, 2002; Tocalli-Beller & Swain, 2005; Watanabe & Swain, 2007); a comparison of various forms of feedback, for instance, reformulation and editing/error correction (cf. Sachs & Polio, 2007; Storch, 2008; Wigglesworth, 2008); the provision of models (Hanaoka, 2007); feedback on the students' writing and reflection (languaging) on it (Suzuki, 2008); peer reflection while writing followed by FonF (Lindgren & Sullivan, 2003); or tutorial sessions (Nassaji & Swain, 2000). The other type of intervention corresponds to studies that have looked into the potential of output practice by comparing output learning conditions with input learning conditions, particularly input enhancement and input processing (cf. Benati, 2005; Izumi, 2002; Izumi & Bigelow, 2000; Izumi, Bigelow, Fujiwara, & Fearnow, 1999; Qin, 2008).

In terms of research methodology, researchers have investigated the effects of learner-related variables (mainly L2 proficiency and writing expertise) as well as task-related variables (including individual and collaborative writing, output/input learning tasks, or a range of tasks that varied along a language-meaning continuum) upon the attention paid to language matters during writing (as measured by a unit of analysis known as "language-related episodes," Swain & Lakpin, 1995). In other studies (mainly interventionist in nature) the language processing activity engaged in while writing or processing feedback was the independent variable of the research, and its impact upon learning (always short-term effects) the dependent variable, such learning being measured by performance on language tests, characteristics of the texts produced, or the incorporations of forms that were the focus of the instruction or experimental intervention in the participants' subsequent written production. Both product data (i.e. essays, text reconstruction tasks, test scores, note taking, and underlining) and process data (i.e. think-aloud protocols, retrospective protocols, and retrospective questionnaires) have been employed. Some interventionist studies have made use of the pre-test/treatment/post-test design.

Taken as a whole, this research has been framed in both cognitive theories of language and language learning (basically the ones mentioned in the previous section), as well as more socio-cognitive and sociocultural approaches. For instance, many descriptive and interventionist studies of collaborative writing adopt sociocultural views of the role of interaction in language acquisition (cf. Donato, 1994; Swain, 2000), which assume both that social interactions result in the appropriation of linguistic knowledge by the individual, and that individual knowledge is socially constructed during collaborative problem-solving tasks.

The Language Learning Potential of Writing: Research Findings

Four main findings in this body of research collectively considered are relevant from the perspectives of research and pedagogy. Taken together, they shed light on the range of individual and social variables that appear to mediate the language learning potential writing may have in the learning experience of FL writers.

FL writers devote much attention to decisions about language both when writing individually and while engaged in collaborative writing.

There is ample empirical evidence to posit an active linguistic processing taking place while writing. These findings derive from studies that have investigated L2 writing processes, both in individual writing (cf. Roca de Larios, Manchón, Murphy, & Marín, 2008; Wang & Wen, 2002) and when working in pairs (cf. Storch & Wigglesworth, 2007). A common finding in this body of literature is that L2 writers devote between 60% and 80% of their composing time to text generating activity, which means language-related concerns are particularly relevant in L2 writing (cf. Cumming, 2001; Manchón, 2009). For instance, in Roca de Larios et al. (2008) we investigated the allocation of composing time to different writing activities during the process of creating a text in a FL. We gave the same writing task (an argumentative essay) to three groups of Spanish FL writers who varied in their L2 proficiency (ranging from pre-intermediate to advanced). They wrote under time-compressed conditions (they had one hour to complete the task) and were asked to think aloud while composing. The analyses conducted on these think-aloud protocols revealed that these EFL writers, regardless of their proficiency level, devoted most of their attentional resources to generating their texts, although clear proficiency-related differences were observed: the less proficient EFL writers in this study devoted almost all of their attentional resources to converting their ideas into language (81%), whereas more proficient learners, in addition to devoting a substantial amount of their composing time to generating their texts (around 60%), were also able to reflect on their linguistic choices via the processes of revision and evaluation (which ranged from 6% in the case of the less proficient learners to 20% of composition time in the case of the most proficient participants). Further confirmation of these proficiency-related differences was obtained in other studies conducted with the same participants and the same data (see Manchón, Roca de Larios, & Murphy, 2009). It was found that the lower the L2 proficiency level, the more time these EFL writers devoted to compensating for linguistic deficits, and the higher the level, the more they tried to tackle more sophisticated problems related to ideational or textual preoccupations. This problem-solving activity on the part of the more proficient writers led them, for instance, to look for ways to upgrade and refine their lexical choices. Seen in the light of the Output Hypothesis, these findings can lead us to the conclusion that it was only the more proficient writers in this research who appeared to have enough time and attentional resources available to attempt to produce the type of pushed output thought to be relevant for language learning.

To my mind, a clear pedagogical implication of these findings is the consideration of the importance of the temporal dimension of writing: FL writers need to be allowed sufficient time on the completion of their writing tasks as a necessary requirement (albeit not the only one) to be able to engage in the type of deep problem-solving behaviour thought to lead to the production of comprehensible output and, consequently, to L2 development (see Hayes & Nash, 1996; Manchón & Roca de Larios, 2007; Shehadeh, 2002, for further arguments along these lines). Not having access to this extra time would be particularly detrimental for lower proficiency FL writers who might (strategically) approach writing tasks in a such a way that their main or only preoccupation may be to find a way to get a text on the page, a text that would not necessarily represent an instance of the type of pushed output thought to be relevant for either the consolidation or the expansion of their linguistic resources.

The importance of time in writing and what time buys is very clearly expressed in the following extract from one of the EFL university students in our current project on the learning potential of writing. When asked to reflect on her language learning experience, she stated:

> [1] I think that writing is one of the best ways to learn a foreign language [. . .] When you speak, you do not have much time to think about what you are saying and to reflect [. . .]. On the contrary, when you write, you have much time to think and to apply all the rules you have studied and to make the right arrangement of the sentence. Moreover, in writing you have the choice to read again what you wrote, so that you can [. . .] correct your mistakes. As writing gives you the chance to think and reflect, it also helps you in deepening [your knowledge of the] language. (Unpublished data from Manchón, Roca de Larios, & Murphy)

As we shall see in the next sections, plenty of research evidence exists on the thinking and reflection processes mentioned by the EFL writer in this excerpt.

Writing enhances linguistic processing.

In line with the tenets of the theoretical strands reviewed in earlier sections, there is empirical evidence to support the view that the attention paid to language matters while writing fosters the writers' engagement in a type of linguistic processing deemed to be conducive to language learning. These findings derive from studies that have explored both individual writing (cf. Cumming, 1990; Swain & Lapkin, 1995) and collaborative writing, in this case including both descriptive studies framed in the FonF paradigm (Alegría de la Colina & García Mayo, 2007; Fortune, 2005; García Mayo, 2002a, 2002b; Fortune & Thorp, 2001; Kuiken & Vedder, 2002a, 2002b; Leeser, 2004; Stprch, 1998a, 1998b, 1999, 2001, 2002a, 2002b, 2005, 2007; Suzuki & Itagaki, 2007; Swain, 1998; Swain & Lapkin, 1998), and interventionist studies, particularly the research on reformulation (Adams, 2003; Lapkin, Swain, & Smith, 2002; Qi & Lapkin, 2001; Swain & Lapkin, 2002; Tocalli-Beller & Swain, 2005; Watanabe & Swain, 2007).

In terms of individual writing, two pioneer studies by Cumming (1990) and by Swain and Lapkin (1995) offered strong empirical evidence of the attention paid to form-meaning connections while composing. Cumming, for instance, found that 30% of his participants' decision making episodes focused on metalinguistic and ideational concerns concurrently, a behaviour he interpreted as a "plausible (though still hypothetical) process of language learning" (p. 500). Similarly, Swain and Lapkin's (1995) analysis of the think-aloud protocols of eight immersion students composing in French provided further evidence of the linguistic processing fostered by trying to express meaning in writing. They argued that when solving their linguistic problems, these ESL writers "engaged in mental processing that may have generated linguistic knowledge that is new for the learner, or consolidating existing knowledge" (p. 384). Similar conclusions have been reached in studies of collaborative writing. For instance, Storch and Wigglesworth (2007) concluded that the collaboration engaged in by their participants resulted not only in more accurate texts, but also in opportunities for these writers "to engage with and about language," from which the authors conclude that collaborative writing tasks "provide a site for language learning" (p. 172).

Regarding collaborative writing, research has also shown that the language learning afforded by collaborative writing is partially dependent on the nature of the interaction engaged in by the writing partners. The suggestion is that the most useful pattern is "collaboration" (see Storch, 2002a, 2002b, 2007), as mutual collaboration would guarantee the engagement in what Donato (1994) called "collective scaffolding" and Swain (2000) "collaborative dialogue," two terms that refer to mutual scaffolding during the dialogic resolution of the language-related problems encountered while expressing meaning in writing. However, given that research has shown that interaction does not necessarily result in collaboration (Kuiken & Vedder, 2002a; Storch, 2007; Watanabe & Swain, 2007), it has been suggested that some form of instructional intervention is required to guarantee mutual involvement in the decision making and problem solving process posed by writing tasks. In this respect, Storch (2007, p. 156) suggests that "careful monitoring of the nature of pair work to ensure collaboration is important if pair work is to be beneficial for language learning."

In addition to the nature of collaboration among peers, research has also drawn our attention to the crucial role played by individual differences in collaborative writing (cf. Fortune, 2005; Hanaoka, 2007; Leeser, 2004; Qi & Lapkin, 2001; Swain & Lapkin, 1998). For instance, Leeser' s (2004) research has provided clear evidence of the mediating role played by the writer's L2 proficiency in bringing about learning during collaborative writing. Leeser found that the proficiency of each dyad member affected how much the writers in the study focused on form while writing, the types of forms they focused on, and how well they resolved the language problems they encountered. This speaks to the pedagogical relevance of taking principled decisions regarding the pairing of students during collaborative writing tasks. For instance, it is pedagogically relevant to ask whether low proficiency learners benefit at all from being paired with higher proficiency learners in terms of what Leeser calls "developmental readiness" (p.73): the author asks if lower proficiency learners can "actually appropriate and internalize" the linguistic knowledge focused on by the higher proficiency member of the dyad.

Finally, another research finding with clear pedagogical implications is that, as might be expected, the uptake in collaborative writing tasks includes both correct and incorrect solutions to problems. This is why Storch (1998b, 2002b) suggests that it is important "for teachers to monitor the deliberations and decisions learners make as they work in groups or pairs and do follow-up class work if necessary" (Storch, 2002b, p. 147) or "follow up such collaborative tasks with teacher feedback" (Storch, 1988b, p. 299). However, we may wonder whether the material conditions of many FL classrooms would permit this instructional guidance, monitoring, and scaffolding, as well as whether or not the tight time schedule many FL teachers have to deal with would make the whole sequence of group work, monitoring of the interaction, and follow up activities a viable and practical way of helping FL learners learn in some FL classrooms.

Linguistic processing while writing is task-dependent.

Two groups of studies within the descriptive strand have shed light on this issue. In the first case, researchers have investigated L2 learners performing more or less meaning-based or language-based writing tasks in order to investigate which tasks promote more focus on form (cf. Alegría de la Colina & García Mayo, 2007; Kuiken & Vedder, 2002a; Fortune & Thorp, 2001; García Mayo, 2002a, 2002b; Storch,1998a, 1998b, 2001). Meaning-based tasks include, for instance, composition and dictogloss tasks (writers jointly reconstruct a text previously read out to them), whereas language-focused tasks include controlled grammar tasks and writing editing tasks. In the second group of studies, researchers have compared individual and collaborative writing in terms of writing processes and products (cf. Kuiken & Vedder, 2002b; Storch, 1998b, 1999, 2005, 2007; Storch & Wigglesworth, 2007).

Not too surprisingly, it has been found that the attention paid to language while writing is task-dependent. Various studies have shown that while engaged in composition and dictogloss tasks (both being meaning-based tasks as defined above) students produced fewer language related episodes than when completing more language-based tasks, a finding that, interestingly, once again seems to be related to time on task issues: the writers in the collaborative writing studies mentioned above appeared to need a substantial amount of their task time to agree on the meaning of their jointly written texts, or to plan text and procedures. As a consequence, less task time was available to focus on language. This time variable might also explain some of the findings obtained in studies that have compared individual and collaborative writing (cf. Kuiken & Vedder, 2002b; Storch, 1998b, 1999, 2005, 2007; Storch & Wigglesworth, 2007). In terms of products, texts written in collaboration appear to be shorter (perhaps because of the extra time needed to agree on meaning when engaged in collaborative writing), more accurate, at times more linguistically complex, and more succinct. It has been suggested (cf. Storch, 2005) that these characteristics might be the outcome of the type of linguistic processing afforded by the mutual feedback provided and received in collaborative writing.

Several implications derive from these findings. In terms of time on task requirements, it looks as if the payoff of the extra time required in collaborative writing is accuracy in production, which might point to a possible link between collaborative writing and consolidation of linguistic knowledge. Incidentally, the speculation about the possible link between writing and the consolidation of linguistic knowledge is a constant in the research in the field. For instance, in one of the pioneering studies in the area, Cumming (1990) suggested that "writing may help students develop better control over their processes of producing a second language without necessarily affecting their knowledge of the language" (p. 504). Similarly, in his review of the empirical research on the role of output (both oral and written) in SLA, Shehadeh (2002) argues that one of the key issues future research must answer relates to whether the production of comprehensible output leads to "the internalization of new linguistic knowledge or the consolidation of existing knowledge or whether it constitutes some sort of language development" (p. 613). In a more recent publication Sachs and Polio (2007) offer suggestions as to the manner in which this language development may be conceptualized and operationalized in empirical research. Referring to Norris and Ortega (2003), these scholars remind us that it might be relevant to view L2 acquisition as consisting of "gradual and non-linear changes in both linguistic and metalinguistic behaviour," thus including not only "the appropriate use of linguistic forms but also, for example, the constructs of emergence, detection, restructuring, and awareness" (Sachs and Polio, 2007, p. 75). Following from here, Sachs and Polio contend that "a range of psycholinguistic processes might be seen as constituting steps towards L2 development" (p. 75). Future research must continue to search for answers regarding the manner in which writing can contribute to this range of psycholinguistic learning processes. Until then, any claims regarding the relationship between engagement in writing and long-term development in SLA remain purely speculative.

The potential learning outcomes of written output practice appear to be mediated by the nature of the linguistic processing engaged in while writing.

Another piece of the puzzle has been provided by several studies within the interventionist strand: there are very telling indications in this research that the learning effects of output practice are closely linked to the depth of processing engaged in while writing. It should be remembered that in all these cases we are concerned with learning conditions in which students write; they then receive some sort of input (various forms of feedback, models to analyze, or reflection on language), and then the effect of this input on subsequent language production is measured. What this research has uncovered is that the final intake of the learner's processing of this input is dependent upon whether or not learners engage in deeper processing than just noticing differences between their own writing and the input they receive on it at the level of simple detection. For instance, Adams (2003) analyzed Spanish FL learners' noticing processes while comparing their own texts with a reformulated version in two different conditions: with or without stimulated recall on the participants' noticing activity. She reports that the deeper processing fostered by the meta-reflection in the stimulated recall condition resulted in more intake and more learning. Similarly, Bitchener (2008) found that the provision of feedback with either oral or written metalinguistic explanations resulted in greater learning gains than feedback that did not engage learners' attention in this further processing. Finally, in studies comparing input and output learning conditions (Izumi, 2002; Izumi & Bigelow, 2000; Izumi et al., 1999) the greater learning gains in the output condition were attributed to, first, the iterative process of successive waves of input and output students had to deal with, as well as the deeper processing engaged in by the participants in the output condition. Regarding the latter, Izumi (2002) has argued that "the greater learning evidenced by the output subjects suggests that output triggered deeper and more elaborate processing of the form, which led them to establish a more durable memory trace" (p. 570).

Taken together, these findings shed further light on some of the pedagogical decision making that must go into promoting language learning via writing. One such area would be related to feedback purposes and options. I would like to suggest that in writing to learn conditions, it makes pedagogical sense to distinguish between "feedback for accuracy" from "feedback for acquisition," a distinction hardly at all debated or explored in the otherwise abundant research on feedback in L2 writing, but nevertheless a crucial distinction when it comes to FL learning settings. When viewed from the perspective of development in language learning, the relevant type of feedback should be feedback for acquisition, i.e. feedback aimed at promoting learning understood as either the consolidation or the expansion of linguistics resources, or along the continuum of psycholinguistic processes mentioned above. It might be the case that the provision of feedback for acquisition might require a kind of pedagogical intervention whereby L2 writers are encouraged to engage in the type of deep processing behaviour fostered by explicit learning conditions in the processing of feedback, conditions that could include various levels of awareness with understanding, meta-reflection on one's noticing activity and, very importantly, an iterative process of writing, input/feedback, noticing/reflection, and new output. Whether these conditions can be better rendered by various types of individual or collaborative writing, or by the various feedback options discussed in the literature are further open questions for further research.

Summary and Conclusions

There are lessons to be learned from the empirical research on the language learning potential of L2 writing reviewed in this chapter. First, from the perspective of pedagogy, we have empirical evidence in support of the view that writing engages learners in processes that are thought to be conducive to language learning, particularly noticing and metalinguistic reflection. Many more open questions exist regarding whether or not this linguistic processing leads to learning, and what type of learning this would be. However, one lesson to be learned from research is that the possible learning outcomes of the linguistic processing engaged in while writing appear to depend at least on the following:

- Whether or not L2 writers are given sufficient time to complete their writing tasks;
- Whether or not the interaction engaged in while writing with another partner results in collaboration and mutual scaffolding;
- Whether or not the pedagogical intervention requires students to engage in explicit, deep processing learning conditions;
- Whether or not these learning conditions entail an iterative process of output + input + noticing/reflection + output.

There are also lessons for future research. Despite the abundant body of knowledge accumulated, it seems that, in line with the claims made by Shehadeh (2002) some years ago, a much more encompassing acquisitional research agenda still needs to be set up. Because of their possible pedagogical relevance, relevant items in this research agenda would be the exploration of the levels and types of language learning deriving from feedback for accuracy and feedback for acquisition, as well as the type of pedagogical intervention most conducive to fostering the purported "gap filling" and focused attention to incoming input that in theory derives from the linguistic processing inherent to the act of writing, an issue hardly at all researched in the available literature. This research agenda also needs to make room for the longitudinal investigation of the language learning potential of output practice given that the results regarding acquisition refer only to short-term impact on learning. Finally, I also suggest that this future research agenda, in addition to further controlled laboratory type of research similar to the ones now available, also needs to include research conducted in real classrooms, with real teachers, and real students. Only then will we be able to assess which pedagogical options aimed at promoting language learning effectively work in which FL classrooms and with which students.

Author's Note: This chapter is part of a research program on the language learning potential of writing funded by Fundación Séneca (Agency of Science and Technology, Murcia Autonomous Government) via Research Grant 05668/PHCS/07.

References

Adams, R. (2003). L2 output, reformulation, and noticing: Implications for interlanguage development. *Language Teaching Research, 7*(3), 347–376.

Alegría de la Colina, A., & García Mayo, M. P. (2007). Attention to form across collaborative tasks by low-proficiency learners in an EFL setting. In M. P. García Mayo (Ed.), *Investigating tasks in foreign language learning* (pp. 91–116). Clevedon, UK: Multilingual Matters.

Benati, A. (2005). The effects of processing instruction, traditional instruction and meaning-output instruction on the acquisition of the English past simple tense. *Language Teaching Research, 9*(1), 67–93.

Bitchener, J. (2008). Evidence in support of written corrective feedback. *Journal of Second Language Writing, 17*(2), 102–118.

Cumming, A. (1990). Metalinguistic and ideational thinking in second language composing. *Written Communication, 7,* 482–511.

Cumming, A. (2001). Learning to write in a second language: Two decades of research. *International Journal of English Studies, 1*(2), 1–23.

DeKeyser, R. (1998). Beyond focus on form: Cognitive perspectives on learning and practising second language grammar. In C. Doughty & J. Williams (Eds.), *Focus on form in classroom second language acquisition* (pp. 42–63). Cambridge: Cambridge University Press.

DeKeyser, R. (2001). Automaticity and automatization. In P. Robinson (Ed.), *Cognition and second language instruction* (pp. 125–151). Cambridge: Cambridge University Press.

DeKeyser, R. (2007). Skill acquisition theory. In B. VanPatten & J. Williams (Eds.), *Theories in second language acquisition* (pp. 97–113). Mahwah, NJ: Lawrence Erlbaum.

Donato, R. (1994). Collective scaffolding in second language learning. In J. P. Lantolf & G. Appel (Eds.), *Vygotskian approaches to second language research* (pp. 33–56). Norwood, NJ: Ablex.

Doughty, C. (2001). Cognitive underpinnings of focus on form. In P. Robinson (Ed.), *Cognition and second language instruction* (pp. 206–257). New York: Cambridge University Press.

Doughty, C., & Williams, J. (Eds.) (1998). *Focus on form in classroom second language Acquisition*. Cambridge: Cambridge University Press.

Fortune, A. (2005). Learners' use of metalanguage in collaborative form-focused L2 output tasks. *Language Awareness, 14*, 21–38.

Fortune, A., & Thorp, D. (2001). Knotted and entangled: New light on the identification, classification and value of language related episodes in collaborative output tasks. *Language Awareness, 10*, 143–160.

García Mayo, M. P. (2002a). The effectiveness of two form-focused tasks in advanced EFL pedagogy. *International Journal of Applied Linguistics, 12*(2), 156–175.

García Mayo, M. P. (2002b). Interaction in advanced EFL pedagogy: A comparison of form-focused activities. *International Journal of Educational Research, 37*, 323–341.

Hanaoka, O. (2007). Output, noticing, and learning: An investigation into the role of spontaneous attention to form in a four-stage writing task. *Language Teaching Research, 11*(4), 459–479.

Harklau, L. (2002). The role of writing in classroom second language acquisition. *Journal of Second Language Writing, 11*, 329–350.

Hayes, J. R. & Nash, J. G. (1996). On the nature of planning in writing. In M. Levy & S. Ransdell (Eds.), *The science of writing* (pp. 29–55). Mahwah, NJ: Lawrence Erlbaum.

Izumi, S. (2002). Output, input enhancement, and the noticing hypothesis: An experimental study of ESL relativization. *Studies in Second Language Acquisition, 24*, 541–577.

Izumi, S. (2003). Comprehension and production processes in second language learning: In search of the psycholinguistic rationale of the output hypothesis. *Applied Linguistics, 24*(2), 168–196.

Izumi, S., & Bigelow, M. (2000). Does output promote noticing and second language acquisition? *TESOL Quarterly, 34*(2), 239–278.

Izumi, S., Bigelow, M., Fujiwara, M., & Fearnow, S. (1999). Testing the output hypothesis: Effects of output on noticing and second language acquisition. *Studies in Second Language Acquisition, 21*(3), 421–452.

Kuiken, F., & Vedder, I. (2002a). Collaborative writing in L2: The effect of group interaction on text quality. In S. Ransdell & M. Barbier (Eds.), *New directions for research in L2 writing* (pp. 169–188). Dordrecht: Kluwer.

Kuiken, F., & Vedder, I. (2002b). The effect of interaction in acquiring the grammar of a second language. *International Journal of Educational Research, 37,* 343–358.

Lapkin, S., Swain, M. & Smith, M. (2002). Reformulation and the learning of French pronominal verbs in a Canadian French immersion context. *The Modern Language Journal, 86*(4), 485–507.

Lee, J. F. & VanPatten, B. (1995). *Making communicative language teaching happen.* New York: McGraw-Hill.

Leeser, M. J. (2004). Learner proficiency and focus on form during collaborative dialogue. *Language Teaching Research, 8*(1), 55–81.

Lindgren, E. & Sullivan, K. P. H. (2003). Stimulated recall as a trigger for increasing noticing and language awareness in the L2 writing classroom: A case study of two young female writers. *Language Awareness, 12*(3&4), 172–186.

Manchón, R. M. (2009). Broadening the perspective of L2 writing scholarship: The contribution of research on foreign language writing. In R. M. Manchón (Ed.), *Foreign language writing. Learning, teaching, and research* (pp. 1–19). Clevedon: Multilingual Matters.

Manchón, R. M., & de Haan, P. (2008). Writing in foreign language contexts: An introduction. *The Journal of Second Language Writing, 17*(1), 1–6.

Manchón, R. M. & Roca de Larios, J. (2007). Writing-to-learn in instructed language contexts. In E. Alcón & P. Safont (Eds.), *The intercultural speaker. Using and acquiring English in instructed language contexts* (pp. 101–121). Dordrecht: Springer-Verlag.

Manchón, R. M., Roca de Larios, J., & Murphy, L. (2009). The temporal dimension and problem-solving nature of foreign language composing. Implications for theory. In R. M. Manchón (Ed.), *Foreign language writing. Learning, teaching, and research* (pp. 102–129). Clevedon: Multilingual Matters.

Nassaji, H. & Swain, M. (2000). A Vygotskian perspective on corrective feedback in L2: The effect of random versus negotiated help on the learning of English articles. *Language Awareness, 9*(1), 34–51.

Norris, J. M., & Ortega, L. (2000). Effectiveness of L2 instruction: A research synthesis and quantitative meta-analysis. *Language Learning, 50,* 417–528.

Norris, J. M., & Ortega, L. (2003). Defining and measuring L2 acquisition. In C. Doughty & M. H. Long (Eds.), *The handbook of second language acquisition* (pp. 717–761). Oxford: Blackwell.

Ortega, L. (2004). L2 writing research in EFL contexts. Some challenges and opportunities for EFL researchers. *ALAK Newsletter.* Spring.

Ortega, L. (2009). Studying writing across English as a foreign language contexts: Looking back and moving forward. In R. M. Manchón (Ed.), *Foreign language writing. Learning, teaching, and research* (pp. 232–255). Clevedon: Multilingual Matters.

Ortega, L., & Carson, J. (2010). Multicompetence, social context, and L2 writing research praxis. In T. Silva and P. K. Matsuda (Eds.), *Practicing theory in second language writing* (pp. 48-71). West Lafayette, IN: Parlor Press.

Qi, D. S., & Lapkin, S. (2001). Exploring the role of noticing in a three-stage second language writing task. *Journal of Second Language Writing, 10*(4), 277–303.

Qin, J. (2008). The effects of processing instruction and dictogloss tasks on the acquisition of the English passive voice. *Language Teaching Research, 12*(1), 61–82.

Roca de Larios, J., Manchón, R. M., Murphy, L., & Marín, J. (2008). The foreign language writer's strategic behaviour in the allocation of time to writing processes. *Journal of Second Language Writing, 17*(1), 30–47.

Sachs, R., & Polio, C. (2007). Learners' uses of two types of written feedback on an L2 writing revision task. *Studies in Second Language Acquisition, 29,* 67–100.

Schmidt, R. W. (1990). The role of consciousness in second language learning. *Applied Linguistics, 11,* 206–226.

Schmidt, R. W. (1993). Awareness and second language acquisition. *Annual Review of Applied Linguistics, 13,* 11–26.

Schmidt, R. W. (2001). Attention. In Robinson, P. (Ed.), *Cognition and second language instruction* (pp. 3–32). Cambridge: Cambridge University Press.

Segalowitz, N. (2003). Automaticity and second languages. In C. Doughty & M. Long (Eds.), *The handbook of second language acquisition* (pp. 382–408). Oxford, Blackwell.

Shehadeh, A. (2002). Comprehensible Output, from occurrence to acquisition: An agenda for acquisitional research. *Language Learning, 52*(3), 597–647.
Storch, N. (1998a). Comparing second language learners' attention to form across tasks. *Language Awareness, 7*(4), 176–191.
Storch, N. (1998b). A classroom-based study: Insights from a collaborative test reconstruction task. *ELT Journal, 52*(4), 291–300.
Storch, N. (1999). Are two heads better than one? Pair work and grammatical accuracy. *System, 27,* 363–374.
Storch, N. (2001). Comparing ESL learners' attention to grammar on three different classroom tasks. *RELC Journal, 32*(2), 104–124.
Storch, N. (2002a). Relationships formed in dyadic interaction and opportunity for learning. *International Journal of Educational Research, 37,* 305–322.
Storch, N. (2002b). Patterns of interaction in ESL pair work. *Language Learning,* 52(1), 119–158.
Storch, N. (2005). Collaborative writing: product, process, and students' reflections. *Journal of Second Language Writing, 14,* 153–173.
Storch, N. (2007). Investigating the merits of pair work on a text editing task in ESL classes. *Language Teaching Research, 11*(2), 143–159.
Storch, N. (2008). Students' engagement with feedback on writing: The role of memorization and learner agency. Paper presented at the AAAL 2008 Annual Conference, Washington, DC, March.
Storch, N., & Wigglesworth, G. (2007). Writing tasks: The effect of collaboration. In M. P. García Mayo (Ed.), *Investigating tasks in foreign language learning* (pp. 157–177). Clevedon, UK: Multilingual Matters.
Suzuki, W. (2008). The effect of written languaging combined with feedback on second language writing. Paper presented at the AAAL 2008 Annual Conference, Washington, DC, March.
Suzuki, W., & Itagaki, N. (2007). Learner metalinguistic reflections following output-oriented and reflective activities. *Language Awareness, 16*(2), 131–146.
Swain, M. (1985). Communicative competence: Some roles of comprehensible input and comprehensible output in its development. In S. Gass & C. Madden (Eds.), *Input in second language acquisition* (pp.235–153). Rowley, MA: Newbury House.
Swain, M. (1995). Three functions of output in second language learning. In Cook, G. & Seidlhofer, B. (Eds.), *Applied linguistics. Studies in honour of H. G. Widdowson* (pp. 125–144). Oxford: Oxford University Press.
Swain, M. (1998). Focus on form through conscious reflection. In C. Doughty & J. Williams (Eds.), *Focus on form in classroom second language acquisition* (pp. 64–81). Cambridge: CUP.

Swain, M. (2000). The output hypotheses and beyond: Mediating acquisition through collaborative dialogue. In J. Lantolf (Ed.), *Sociocultural theory and second language learning* (pp. 97–114). Oxford: Oxford University Press.

Swain, M. (2005). The output hypothesis: Theory and research. In E. Hinkel (Ed.), *Handbook of research in second language teaching and learning* (pp.471–181). Mahwah, NJ: Lawrence Erlbaum.

Swain, M., & Lapkin, S. (1995). Problems in output and the cognitive processes they generate: A step toward second language learning. *Applied Linguistics, 16,* 371–391.

Swain, M., & Lapkin, S. (1998). Interaction and second language learning: Two adolescent French immersion students working together. *The Modern Language Journal, 82*(3), 329–337.

Swain, M., & Lapkin, S. (2002). Talking it through: Two French immersion learners' response to reformulation. *International Journal of Educational Research, 37,* 285–304.

Tocalli-Beller, A., & Swain. M. (2005). Reformulation: The cognitive conflict and L2 learning it generates. *International Journal of Applied Linguistics, 15*(1), 5–28.

VanPatten, B., & Williams, J. (2007). Introduction: The nature of theories. In B. VanPatten & J. Williams (Eds.), *Theories in second language acquisition* (pp. 1–16). Mahwah, NJ: Lawrence Erlbaum.

Wang, W., & Wen, Q. (2002). L1 use in the L2 composing process: An exploratory study of 16 Chinese EFL writers. *Journal of Second Language Writing, 11,* 225-246.

Watanabe, Y., & Swain, M. (2007). Effect of proficiency differences and patterns of pair interaction on second language learning: collaborative dialogue between adult ESL learners. *Language Teaching Research, 11*(2), 121–142.

Wigglesworth, G. (2008). The effect of different modes of feedback on intermediate and advanced learners' writing. Paper presented at the AAAL 2008 Annual Conference, Washington, DC.

4 Foreign Language Writing in the Era of Globalization

Jean Marie Schultz

The effects of globalization have become a common subject of discussion, and it is therefore not surprising that the topic is also having a significant impact on higher education. Since the late 1990s a variety of disciplines have, in fact, been reconfiguring their curricula in response to globalization and to the popularity of the relatively new field of global studies. In 2001, for instance, the *PMLA* devoted an entire issue to the impact of globalization on the study of English, with contributors offering often very different views on the direction the study of literature should take. In terms of foreign language education there has likewise been a decided increase in attention to the teaching of culture from a global perspective (Tonkin, 2001; Edwards, 2001; Robinson, 2001). The lead article in the *PMLA* volume has had a significant impact on my own thinking about the teaching of language in general and of writing in particular in light of the rise of globalization and the popularity of global studies; the author of the lead article, Professor Giles Gunn, is one of the primary founders of the Global Studies major at my university (see Gunn, 2001). The major, which is one of the first of its kind in the United States, serves as a model for numerous other such programs nation-wide[1]. With over nine-hundred students, Global Studies is currently the most popular interdisciplinary major on the University of California Santa Barbara campus, with students taking a wide range of courses in foreign language, anthropology, geography, sociology, economics, political science, and literature. In response to the number of global studies students in their courses, these departments, as well as others, have in turn refined the curricula of certain courses in order better to meet the needs of the many global studies students enrolled. As the *PMLA* volume, as well as the 2007 MLA Ad Hoc Committee on Foreign Languages report (MLA, 2007), indicates, the reconfiguration of majors to account for globalization is not endemic to UCSB alone, but represents rather a national trend in education, where departments of English and of foreign language in particular see the reshaping of their curricula as essential for responding to shifting educational needs and student interests, as well as, in some cases, for their very survival in an increasingly global economy. Although the impact of global studies on a variety of disciplines is an important topic in education in general, its influence on the teaching of foreign languages is potentially dramatic, given that global studies programs often require extensive language study[2]. Moreover, under the influence of globalization and the need to produce highly literate second language learners, the literacy components of foreign language curricula are drawing increased attention (Kern & Schultz, 2005). Globalization and the emergence of global studies as an important academic field thus conjoin to put into question both the underlying premises upon which foreign language composition studies are built and the methodologies currently implemented in the classroom.

Globalization and the Teaching of Literature: Historical and Political Grounding and Issues of Cultural Identity

The teaching of foreign language writing in the United States has long been significantly influenced by approaches within English and ESL composition programs. Because these programs in turn are often influenced by contemporary critical and pedagogical trends in English literature, it is worth exploring the impact globalization is currently having on this discipline in order to understand better the globally-oriented contexts that may well come to shape the teaching of foreign language writing.

In his 2001 article "Beyond Discipline? Globalization and the Future of English," Paul Jay examines the development of the concept of globalization from its initiation by economists and social scientists, as a way of analyzing the expansion of western capitalism and the growth of world economies that traverse international borders, to its impact on academic disciplines. He pays particular attention to the role of literature as a facilitator of cultural globalization and as an important contributor to global studies. Jay sees essentially two trends that bear directly upon the way in which the study of literature is evolving. On the one hand, the fact that globalization can be seen exclusively in post-modern terms as "a set of explosive forces" (p. 36) suggests that a reconfigured study of literature should concentrate on things global primarily from the nineteenth century through the present. For Jay, the implications of this position are clear in terms of curtailing and possibly undermining the importance of studying literature written prior to the age of empire building. However, drawing upon Frederic Jameson's work in the *Political Unconscious,* Jay makes a strong case for an historical view of globalization as it manifests itself in literary texts: "Globalization can certainly help us map the future of literary studies, but it also provides an important way to rethink our approach to the study of literature across a range of historical periods" (p. 36). For Jay, the reconfiguration of the study of literature should entail a historically grounded, political approach that recognizes the central role of the concept of the nation-state in terms of colonialism and its aftermath and the dissolution of this concept in light of cultural and economic intersections. Jay proposes a comprehensive and historicized reconfiguration of literary studies within the context of globalization as crucial to the future of the field. This historical grounding becomes all the more crucial in light of the multiculturalism that globalization entails.

The impact on personal national identity that transnational economic and cultural trends, immigration, and the need for multilingualism bring to bear also implicitly refocuses the study of literature along lines of ethnic identity for which the seemingly clear lines of the past have now blurred. During the rise of the nation-state, identification with the official language of one's nationality was an integral part of one's concept of self. As Humphrey Tonkin (2001) points out, "One of the legacies of the European conception of the nation-state, in which the notion of a unified and unifying national language plays such an important role, is a kind of language loyalty that devalues bilingualism and assumes that the ideal condition is one in which an individual speaks a single language and everyone else does the same" (p. 8). Within this context, the study of a foreign language was considered beneficial as long as it had a clearly defined purpose—for business, travel, or personal interest—apart from any effects of language learning on personal self-definition. Now, however, globalization has refocused concepts of linguistic, ethnic, and religious identity in ways that are as likely to lead to conflict as are the issues of historicism. Stephen Greenblatt (2001) writes compellingly about the inauthentic nature of analyzing literature according to neat, self-contained categories and the violence of imposing ethnic or religious stereotypes upon literature or its readers and researchers. He reacts strongly to the assumption that Hispanics will automatically focus on things Hispanic, and he cites his own case, where once during an interview he was asked why he specialized in English literature of the sixteenth-century, a period with virtually no Jewish writers. He notes that nineteenth and early twentieth century academic institutions, together with an intensification of ethnocentrism, racism, and nationalism, are largely responsible for such pigeonholing of literary studies and the consequent neglect of the cultural cross-fertilization that has, in fact, always been a hallmark of literature. According to Greenblatt (2001), "Literary critics, busily making claims for cultural authenticity, have been far too prone to ignore the overwhelming evidence of cultural *métissage,* a global circulation, mutual influence, and cross-breeding deriving from the very substance of the objects we study" (p. 59). For Greenblatt, as well as for Wai Chee Dimock, who posits the extraterritorial nature of literature which should be understood "[. . .] as [. . .] random radii linking a text to an ever more dispersed readership" (2001, p. 178), globalization refocuses the way in which we must come to understand cultural identity as manifested in literary texts. With the dissolution of the nation-state, concepts of national and ethnic identity have become very complex indeed.

Globalization, the Rise of English, and the Situation of Foreign Languages

The dual trends of historical and political groundedness and attention to cultural identity that inform the teaching of English in an era of globalization apply as well to the teaching of foreign languages, and particularly to foreign language writing, as we shall see. However, different from its effect on the teaching of English, the rise of globalization has had a problematic and often paradoxical effect on language learning in the United States. Despite increased transnational interaction, particularly in economic and technological domains, which might seem to entail a parallel increased interest in language learning, we see rather an increased status accorded to English as the international language of communication. With the increasing domination of the American economy worldwide during the 1990s, the mastery of English was prerequisite to success in the new global marketplace. Moreover, the trend toward English as the language of business, scientific research, and technology, particularly with the world wide web and the Internet, has spread the use of English in unprecedented ways. The predominance of English as the new *lingua franca* in a sense represents an exaggerated evolution in the politics of monolingual supremacy that dominated the concept of the nation-state in the age of empire building. According to Tonkin (2001), "[. . .] English is the Microsoft of languages—the linguistic medium that has acquired such a dominant role in the marketplace that it seems to have become self-perpetuating" (p. 6). For foreign language specialists, this trend toward universal English has proven alarming; and some cannot help but express their concern that learning languages other than English will fall away and that the cultural differences that are so valued in the field will be reduced and over time irrevocably lost to the lure of American materialism and economic forces.

American beliefs in their linguistic self-sufficiency have long colored attitudes toward the need to learn foreign languages, marking them with a certain complacency, with noted blips characterized by a flurry of attention to language learning generally initiated by political concern over national security or American technological or economic competitiveness. Currently Mandarin and Arabic are the focus of national attention. The subordination of some languages to others deemed more critical to national security or economic advancement (or at times simply to fashion) represents, however, a pervasive and troubling view toward language study in general, namely that it is justified only if there is a practical, that is, economic or national security, reason for doing so. For educational policy setters, languages deemed less important can easily become dispensable and ultimately eliminated. Language choice is therefore reduced and options are offered on the basis of practicality and popularity. The impact of this view on the advancement of second language research cannot help but be deleterious. Writing in out-of-favor languages becomes systematically less important and consequently less research is devoted to it.

This attitude toward language learning coupled with the predominance of English raises the question of learning to write in a foreign language at all, particularly if language learners most likely will never be asked to do so in any context other than an academic one. The question has plagued the teaching of foreign language long before the concept of globalization existed. Attention to writing in foreign language education has always held, and continues to hold, an ambivalent position in the foreign language curriculum (Leki, 2000; O'Donnell, 2007). Prior to the development of the audio-lingual method, the direct method, the proficiency movement, and communicative approaches, writing under grammar translation largely involved translation from the L1 to the L2 or the completion of focused, often discrete point type exercises. With the emphasis on speaking skills all of the above-named methods generated, writing declined still further (Harklau, 2002; Kern, 2000). Beginning in the early eighties, however, in response to a crisis within foreign language departments regarding students' abilities to write effectively in their upper division advanced literature and culture courses (Barnett, 1991; Byrnes, 1998; Schultz, 1991), foreign language writing received more attention, with writing now redefined more realistically and dynamically as the ability to communicate individual content in a compelling manner. This increased attention led in turn to research focused on best methods for teaching foreign language writing, research that inevitably drew upon the far better developed body of research in composition studies and second language writing in English (Manchón and de Haan, 2008; Ortega, 2004; Scott, 1996). Although foreign language writing research continues to lag behind the work done in English and ESL, it has made tremendous strides over the past thirty years, as the 2008 volume of the *Journal of Second Language Writing* as well as the 2008 Symposium on Second Language Writing clearly attest.

Despite these strides, the need to justify writing in the foreign language curriculum continues to plague the field. As Leki (2000) notes, "Although the role and importance of L2 writing in language teaching has increased substantially over the last 20 years, in many FL environments, L2 writing continues to be neglected in favor of speaking, listening, and reading" (p. 104), an assessment echoed by Linda Harklau (Harklau, 2002). Mary O'Donnell's 2007 survey of college level foreign language writing practices and policies produced mixed results on the current state of writing instruction in the foreign language curriculum. Although instructors surveyed tended to implement process approaches to writing, they did not apply these practices systematically nor did they go beyond them in terms of incorporating new research into their curricula. Moreover, instructors tended to require few and relatively short writing assignments (O'Donnell, 2007, pp. 658–663). Finally, in addressing the need to revitalize foreign language curricula in light of a troubling decline in student numbers for some languages, a decline attributed precisely to the privileging of English that globalization has entailed (Edwards, 2001, p. 13), some foreign language specialists have recommended an increased emphasis on oral communication and a decreased emphasis on grammatical accuracy in writing (Swaffar, 1999).

There are, however, other reasons for a current trend toward the subordination of writing to other skills in the foreign language curriculum in the United States. Some of these stem from the lack of confidence many language teachers have in terms of their own writing ability, their lack of knowledge in the field of composition studies, and their subsequent feelings of doubt in their ability to teach their students to write well (O'Donnell, 2007). Moreover, the sheer difficulty and stress of the endeavor of correcting student work effectively and of offering constructive feedback, which continues to be an area of conflicting research findings, also explains in part the reluctance of some teachers to take on the teaching of writing, particularly when it involves additional work in the form of research into best practices (O'Donnell, 2007). All these factors combine to make the teaching of foreign language writing perhaps the most problematic of the four skills, although none of these is insurmountable. More troubling, however, is the trend toward globalization with its privileging of English as the common medium for written communication, which subtly undermines the place of foreign language writing, making it seem more problematic than previously and even possibly irrelevant. Perhaps echoing their teachers' reservations, many motivated American students of foreign language nevertheless wonder why they should write at all when from a practical standpoint their own English will continue to serve them well. In his discussion of monolingualism in America, John Edwards (2001) comments that "[. . .] monolingualism is not a paradox, and to say that Americans 'want' to be monolingual would seem to miss the point—it is simply that English serves them across domains" (p. 14).

The Case for Foreign Language Writing

Whereas the case for learning to write in English within the context of globalization seems self-evident, the justification for writing in a foreign language is now slippery indeed. However, in addressing the monolingualism that one side of globalization seems to imply, Tonkin (2001) makes a strong general statement for the learning of foreign languages, and he calls on foreign language faculty to make a concerted contribution to educational efforts within the context of globalization. He writes,

> [. . .] if those of us who are native-English speakers confuse our professional self-sufficiency in English with a belief that all we need to understand the world is the English language, we will be quite wrong. Our colleagues need languages to gain a perspective on themselves and to move beyond the comfortable and mobile milieu in which they live. (p. 8)

The case for the teaching of writing in the foreign language curriculum has perhaps become more subtle than previously, but precisely because of globalization, it has become more urgent.

For language teachers, one of the primary concerns is quite simply the acquisition of the language; and from this perspective, a large body of research reveals that writing can play a significant role (Chandler, 2004; Fathman & Whalley, 1990; Frantzen, 1995; Manchón and de Haan, 2008; O'Donnell, 2007; Pavlenko, 2007; Schultz, 1991; Scott, 1996). O'Donnell (2007) summarizes her extensive review of foreign language writing research, noting, "Researchers claim that the more students write, the more their ability to write fluently and accurately improves" (p. 651; see also Schultz, 1991). In a recent talk, Pavlenko (2007) noted that one of the best methods for fostering the acquisition of grammar was through the use of writing. Research by Kuiken and Vedder (2008) suggests that assigning cognitively complex writing tasks in a foreign language may well help students attend more closely to their grammatical accuracy and thereby consolidate their linguistic knowledge.

The impact of foreign language writing on literacy skills extends beyond the realm of the grammatically accurate, however. The potential reverberations of L2 writing on the L1 not only in terms of grammar and syntax but also in terms of genre conventions and cultural sensitivity figures among the more recent and more provocative areas of research. The transference effect of L1 writing skills to the L2 has long been substantiated (Leki, 2000; Scott, 1996; Zamel, 1983).

Far less attention has been paid to the possible impact of the L2 on the L1. Noting, in fact, that research into language interaction has focused almost exclusively on the effect of the L1 on the L2, Hands and Cossé (2004) carried out a study on native Spanish speakers of English and native English speakers of Spanish in order to determine whether or not language transference processes in writing were bi-directional. They further set out to determine what kinds of changes occurred in both the L1 and L2 as a result of language learning. Their research reveals that bilingual writers generate proportionately more complex sentences than do monolingual writers. Moreover, they seem to be more culturally sensitive than their monolingual counterparts, modifying their writing according to the cultural orientation of their projected readers. Although Hands and Cossé make a strong case for further study of bi-directional transference, their research strongly suggests bilingualism enriches both the L1 and L2. Kobayashi's and Rinnert's (2008) study of bi-directional linguistic and rhetorical transference for Japanese students writing in English is equally provocative. The results of their study lead them to conclude that "the interaction between intensive L1 and L2 training [in writing] led to greater effects than either of the separate kinds of training alone would have allowed [them] to predict" (Kobayashi & Rinnert, 2008, p. 20). Within the context of globalization, these research results make a strong case for the teaching of writing in the foreign language classroom in order to enrich our students linguistically and culturally in both their L1 and L2 and thereby to prepare them better for the challenges of an increasingly globalized world.

Given the pervasive effect of globalization and multiculturalism on language learning in general and on second language writing in particular, the potential bi-directional effect of writing instruction in both the L1 and the L2 holds exciting potential for significant linguistic and rhetorical cross-fertilization in terms of richer expressive possibilities. Certainly the choice of writers as diverse as Eva Hoffman, Nancy Huston, André Makine, and Hector Bianciotti to write in their L2 speaks to the creative potential of second language writing[3]. For our students, then, the very process of having to grapple with the grammar and syntax of the L2 and of having to tap into and come to terms with written genres that perhaps do not exist in the L1, has the potential to foster linguistic interactions that take students beyond a superficial experience of language learning for practical purposes. These linguistic findings may well apply equally to genre issues. Consequently, an enticing area of foreign language research is to determine the extent to which the understanding of genres that do not exist in one's native language has the potential to provide language learners insight into the thought processes of the cultures that practice them. Recent research by Pavlenko (2007) points to the possibility that we think differently in different languages. If this is indeed so, then language learning bears directly upon questions of self-identity or the possibility of multiple cultural and linguistic identities, questions that seem all the more urgent within the context of globalization.

In their 2005 article, Kern and Schultz target specifically the ways in which second language literacy must be redefined to take into account the trend toward globalization. They propose an integrative and culturally-embedded approach to the teaching of literacy skills that accounts for cognitive, social, and linguistic practices, one that situates foreign language writing within its sociopolitical and larger historical contexts. Although the teaching of English can and should go further in exploring how such approaches might realize themselves in the curriculum, the field of English language composition studies has gone further in this direction than its foreign language counterpart, which, as O'Donnell's (2007) study reveals, has largely stagnated. Referring to the cognitively simple composition assignments removed from their cultural context and based largely on plot summary or experiential responses to texts that predominate in foreign language writing tasks, Kern and Schultz (2005) state that

> these practices do not go far enough toward fostering the development of interpretative abilities to the extent necessary to grapple with the dynamics of the finely differentiated meaning of the literary as repository of the multicultural. Nor do they take into account the need to recognize the conventions of academic and other institutional forms of writing. . . . (p. 385)

Within the context of globalization, which should make the contributions of foreign language education so compelling within environments of higher learning, it seems to me ironic and disheartening that the teaching of writing within foreign language departments in the United States should still lag in terms of incorporating into the curriculum the growing body of L2 research. I suggest, therefore, that just as globalization reconfigures the teaching of literature and other disciplines, so, too, must the teaching of foreign language writing be reconfigured. Foreign language writing needs to be situated with an outward focus, taking into account the sociopolitical underpinnings of literacy within a global context. This outward focus needs to be counterbalanced, however, with an inward focus on the questions of personal identity that globalization has made more complex. In other words, the teaching of writing needs also to draw students' attention to issues of their emerging bilingual identity co-construction.

Foreign Language Writing in a Global Studies Curriculum

Heidi Byrnes (1998) makes a strong case for the teaching of foreign language within a content-rich arena that conjoins with other disciplines to foster students' literacy skills. She says, "Foreign language departments must learn to play a crucial role in enhancing students' literacy, students' ability to interpret and produce texts, orally and in writing, in a fashion that shows a rich awareness of the relation among the sociocultural contexts of use, meaning, and significance." (p. 283)

More recently, within the context of globalization, the 2007 MLA Ad Hoc Committee on Foreign Languages report (MLA, 2007) emphasizes the importance of encouraging learners to become deeply transcultural and translingual through the study of a foreign language. Given the potential effects that focused writing instruction can play in this process, it is crucial to situate approaches to writing within historical, political, and cultural contexts. In 2006, the French language program at UCSB made just such an effort by creating a special focus section of their French 6 course (last trimester of second year French) tailored to the interests of UCSB's Global Studies majors. Although not closed to students from other disciplines, the course embeds language instruction within three distinct units designed to capitalize upon the effects of globalization outlined above and thereby to respond to the literacy needs of Global Studies majors.[4]

Addressing the historical and sociopolitical issues of immigration and racial discrimination, the first unit of the course, entitled "The French Presence in Africa" ("La présence française en Afrique"), focuses on Senegal in order to examine French and African relations from their origins under colonialism to the present day, and focusing in particular on evolving notions of slavery and its eventual abolition. Students study not only the history of Senegal, but also the original 1685 document legislating the treatment of slaves ("Le Code noir"), the encyclopedia article of 1766 on slavery, the 1848 decree abolishing slavery, and finally the 2005 speech by the French ambassador to Senegal in which he emphasizes the close historical and economic ties between the two countries. Discussion questions developed for the unit target the development of students' critical reading skills by encouraging them to interpret the cultural and political views implicitly expressed in each document, thus providing an overview of evolving attitudes toward slavery. The approach to writing is both process- and genre-based, and in one iteration of the course, students are encouraged to produce the French genre of "notes de synthèse" or policy brief. The policy brief focuses on a specific problem in a country for the purpose of formulating foreign policy. It begins by tracing the history of the problem, analyzes the current situation, and finally proposes a solution. Students in the Global Studies French course, the majority of which are already familiar with the policy brief from their Global Studies courses, study the French version of this genre. They pay attention to organizational differences, tone and voice, vocabulary, and of course content. For their own follow-up writing assignment, students select a Francophone country other than Senegal for their own research, which feeds into both oral and written activities. For their papers, they target a specific problem that the country faces, and they write their own policy briefs.

The second unit of the course is overtly literary in orientation but focuses directly on multicultural identity and multilingual issues. It is organized around the reading of texts written by Francophone authors who grapple directly with issues of bilingualism, more specifically with their own relationship to French as a second language. The section includes works by Nancy Huston (English, French), Assia Djebar (Arabic, French, English), Mohammed Dib (Arabic, French), Marjane Satrapi (Farsi, French, German), Andrée Chédid (Arabic, French), and MC Solaar (French, Arabic, English, French), all of who exemplify different and politicized relationships to French. Huston, for example, made a conscious choice to embrace French language and culture, in a sense rejecting her native Anglophone Canadian and American experiences. For Djebar, French was the language of her father's school in Algeria. Its study represented the family's livelihood, offered the possibility of broader choices in life, but symbolized also the language of the colonizing nation ultimately responsible for emigration and dislocation. Satrapi studied French in a *lycée* (French high school) in Tehran. For her, her second language provides a means by which to analyze more objectively Iranian culture and to introduce it to the French world. The rapper MC Solaar's parents immigrated to Paris from Chad when he was very young. His music, which is marked by code switching, uses language as a vehicle for political and social critique. All of the above authors characterize their relationship to French as fraught with multiple struggles—linguistic struggles in trying to master the language, identity struggles in trying to redefine themselves bilingually and biculturally, artistic struggles as they contend with a linguistic medium in which they are not quite entirely at home and yet through which they have chosen to express their ideas. Despite the difficulty of these authors' struggles, it is precisely through them that their creativity manifests itself. By working with these authors, then, the students enrolled in the Global Studies French course find themselves in similar relationships to French. They must come to terms with texts they cannot read as automatically as texts in their native language; and it is through striving to read and to analyze these texts that they then, too, appropriate more of the language and make it their own. In terms of writing activities, students have the choice of writing a more standard analytical, academic essay on the author's work of their choice or of writing a self-reflective essay on their own struggles with French and the ways in which their identity shifts and develops as they conceive of themselves as bilingual speakers and writers. As Kern and Schultz (2005) note, in developing their literacy skills, "language learners can borrow, adapt, and appropriate elements from a range of discourses to develop their own unique voices in a second language" (p. 383).

The final section of the Global Studies French course is overtly political and deals with France's relationship to the European Union and the legal implications of France's status as a member of the European Council. Here students examine excerpts from original legal documents on human rights, as well as a specific legal case in which French law is subordinated to European Council law. The case involves the inheritance of two sons, one legitimate and one illegitimate. In the case of legitimate children in both France and within the European Union, inheritances are divided in equal shares. French law differs from European Union law, however, in the case of illegitimate children. French law dictates that they receive only half of what would be the normal portion, with the rest going to the legitimate children. In the particular case used in the Global Studies French course, the illegitimate son appeals before the European Council the decision of the French court that deprives him of part of his inheritance. Students review both sets of law and some of the legal arguments made by both sides in court. In terms of writing, they produce argumentative essays justifying their own decisions in the case, using the principles expressed in the legal documents to support their positions, which also serve as models for the legal review genre.

The Global Studies French course has so far proven to be very popular among students at UCSB. The majority of students interested in taking French 6, even those who are not Global Studies majors, opt for the Global Studies version over the regular, more traditional, primarily literature-based French course. The choice seems to be indicative of students' more international orientation in the wake of globalization. Moreover, the practice in written genres that have a practical application—the policy brief and the legal analysis—speaks for the professional sensitivity of students who are looking for ways to use their developing language skills in their future careers. Nevertheless, the more experiential and literature-based writing assignment encourages students to reflect on themselves and the modifications to their own self-concept that bilingualism and biculturalism entail. In terms of writing, the Global Studies French course affords us the opportunity to expand writing instruction beyond the experiential essays of most intermediate French programs, or even beyond the academic essay on a literature topic[5], and to embrace cognitively challenging modes of writing in non-traditional venues. Hopefully over time, the effects of these modes on students' skills and language acquisition will contribute further to our research base in foreign language writing.

Conclusion

As is the case for many disciplines, the implications of globalization and the academic field of Global Studies for the teaching of second and foreign language writing are complex, far-reaching, and at times contradictory. The trend toward globalization would seem to call for approaches to curricula and writing pedagogies that are grounded within sociopolitical, historical, and culturally rich contexts in which interdisciplinarity plays a significant role. Such broadening of our approaches to the teaching of writing are crucial in order to prepare our students better for the demands of the international arena in which we now live. Moreover, such approaches draw increased attention to the potential positive role in foreign language writing curricula of genre-based pedagogies. Culturally determined genres should not, of course, be imposed upon learners as representative of the values and ideologies of the dominant culture to be emulated but rather, according to Ken Hyland (2007), as "a necessary basis for critical engagement with cultural and textual practices" (p. 152). Both the policy brief and the legal analysis completed in the French 6 Global Studies course represent such an effort. Moreover, these writing tasks draw on research findings on potential bi-directional, bilingual writing transference effects, an area that offers rich possibilities for further investigation.

Situating the teaching of second and foreign language writing within historically embedded and sociopolitical cultural contexts should not, however, ignore issues of individual identity co-construction. Our students need to learn to conceive of themselves as bi- and/or multilingual and multicultural speakers and writers. Virtually all bi- and multilingual writers, from André Makine to Alice Kaplan, from Eva Hoffman to Nancy Huston, speak of their struggle to write in their L2 and of the crucial role this struggle plays in helping them to redefine themselves as members of at least two distinct cultures. Our students, too, face the very same struggles, struggles that are necessary if they are to develop their fluency in the language and their sensitivity to other cultures and points of view, in short, in order to become "translingual" and "transcultural." By encouraging students to attend to language, to its cultural differentiation, and to struggle themselves with expressing new meanings, foreign language writing can play a crucial role in this process. Foreign language writing provides students with new tools of self-discovery and creativity within the new cultural contexts globalization entails. As Stephen Greenblatt notes (2001), "Language is the slipperiest of human creations; like its speakers, it does not respect borders, and, like the imagination, it cannot ultimately be predicted or controlled" (p. 62).

Despite the potential benefits of foreign language writing and the polyvalent roles it can play within the context of globally constructed curricula, we as teachers need nevertheless to be constantly vigilant and to evaluate the effects and implications of any new movement. For the trend toward globalization, which on the one hand does much to support the teaching of foreign language in the United States, at the same time risks doing much to undermine that very endeavor. I have already noted the way in which the privileging of English as the medium of expression in a globalized world subtly undermines the justification for rigor in foreign language teaching, particularly in regard to writing, which requires attentive and focused multi-pronged efforts on the part of teachers. As Lourdes Ortega (2004) very aptly notes, the ESL-oriented research base of foreign language writing "diminishes the capacity of L2 writing education across diverse settings" (p. 8) and her subsequent call for language specific research efforts is well placed. The tendency of a shortsighted interpretation of globalization to popularize some languages considered critical at the expense of others thus further risks eroding the research base of foreign language writing. In the United States, the languages that have generated the most research in terms of foreign language writing are Spanish, French, and German. Although the number of students taking Spanish should continue to keep their research base strong, certainly the situation in German, and to a lesser extent in French, may well prove problematic for furthering foreign language writing research. Rather than privileging one language over the other on the basis of popularity or political trends, we need language policies that will support the continuing research and pedagogical efforts of well established languages, research that may well bear upon the less well developed pedagogies for critical needs and less-commonly-taught languages, which also in turn need more focused support for developing their writing research base. Globalization, the very definition of which suggests intersecting efforts of cooperation among countries, needs to be extended as well to first, second, and foreign language writing research.

Notes

1. The Global Studies major was founded in 1999 and was one of the first of its kind in the United States.

2. The global studies major at UCSB has recently revised its language requirement from two to three years of study.

3. The effects of working with French on students' bilingual identity co-construction have been noted in Schultz, 2004.

4. I would like to thank the Office of Educational Development for providing funding for the creation of the French 6 Global Studies focus section. I would also like to thank Dean David Marshall for providing additional funding for the teaching of French 6 GS. Finally, I would also like to

thank Dr. Pierre Bras for his tireless work in creating the course reader, as well as Maryam Emami for her supporting role.

5. I have worked extensively with literature in the language classroom. See Schultz, 2001.

REFERENCES

Barnett, M. (1991). Language and literature: False dichotomies, Real Allies. ADFL *Bulletin 22*(3), 7–11.

Byrnes, H. (1998). Constructing curricula in collegiate foreign language departments. In H. Byrnes (Ed.) *Learning foreign and second languages* (pp. 262–295). New York: The Modern Language Association of America.

Chandler, J. (2004). A response to Truscott. *Journal of Second Language Writing, 13*, 345–348.

Dimock, W. C. (2001). Literature for the planet. *PMLA, 116,* 173–188.

Edwards, J. (2001). Languages and language learning in the face of world English. A*DFL Bulletin, 32,* 10–15.

Fathman, A., & Whalley, E. (1990). Teacher response to student writing: Focus on form versus content. In B. Kroll (Ed.), *Research insight in the foreign language classroom* (pp. 178–190). Cambridge, MA: Cambridge University Press.

Frantzen, D. (1995). The effects of grammar supplementation on written accuracy in an intermediate Spanish content course. *The Modern Language Journal, 70,* 329–344.

Greenblatt, S. (2001). Racial memory and literary history. *PMLA, 116,* 48–63.

Gunn, G. (2001). Introduction: globalizing literary studies. *PMLA, 116,* 16–31.

Jay, P. (2001). Beyond discipline? Globalization and the future of English. *PMLA, 116*(1), 32–47.

Hands, E. A., & Cossé, L. (2004). Academic biliteracy and the mother tongue. In C. L. Moder & A. Martinovic-Zic (Eds.), *Discourse Across Languages and Cultures* (pp. 285–300). Amsterdam: John Benjamins.

Harklau, L. (2002). The role of writing in classroom second language acquisition. *Journal of Second Language Writing, 11,* 329–350.

Hyland, K. (2007). Genre pedagogy: Language, literacy and L2 writing instruction. *Journal of Second Language Writing, 16,* 148–164.

Kern, R. (2000). *Literacy and language teaching.* New York: Oxford University Press.

Kern, R., & Schultz, J. M. (2005). Beyond orality: Investigating literacy and the literary in second and foreign language instruction. *The Modern Language Journal, 89,* 381–393.

Kobayashi, H., & Rinnert, C. (2008). Task response and text construction across L1 and L2 writing. *Journal of Second Language Writing, 17,* 7–29.

Kuiken, F., & Vedder, I. (2008). Cognitive task complexity and written output in Italian and French as a foreign language. *Journal of Second Language Writing, 17,* 48–60.

Leki, I. (2000). L2 writing: A commentary. *Learning and Instruction, 10,* 101–105.

Manchón, R., & de Haan, P. (2008). Writing in foreign language contexts: An introduction. *Journal of Second Language Writing, 17,* 1–6.

MLA Ad Hoc Committee on Foreign Languages. (2007). Foreign languages and higher education: New structures for a changed world. Retrieved November 29, 2008 from http://www.mla.org/pdf/forlang_news_pdf.pdf.

O'Donnell, M. E. (2007). Policies and practices in foreign language writing at the college level: Survey results and implications. *Foreign Language Annals, 40,* 650–671.

Ortega, L. (2004). L2 writing research in EFL contexts: Some challenges and opportunities for EFL researchers. *Applied Linguistic Association of Korea Newsletter.*

Pavlenko, A. (2007). Learning to think for speaking in a second language. Lectured delivered at the *Applied Linguistics Lecture Series,* University of California at Santa Barbara, April 20, 2007.

Robinson, B. (2001). Tactical humanists: Foreign cultural literacy in the postexcellent institution. *ADFL Bulletin, 32*(2), 19–23.

Schultz, J. M. (1991). The role of writing mode in the articulation of language and literature classes: Theory and practice. *The Modern Language Journal, 75,* 411–416.

Schultz, J. M. (2001). The Gordian knot: Language, literature, and critical thinking. In V. M. Scott & H. Tucker (Eds.). *SLA and the literature classroom: Fostering dialogues* (pp. 35–74). Boston, MA: Heinle & Heinle.

Schultz, J. M. (2004). Toward a pedagogy of the Francophone text in intermediate language courses. *The French Review 78,* 260–277.

Scott, V. M. (1996). *Rethinking foreign language writing.* Boston, MA: Heinle & Heinle.

Swaffar, J. (1999). The case for foreign languages as a discipline. *ADFL Bulletin, 30,* 6–12.

Tonkin, H. (2001). Language learning, globalism, and the role of English. *ADFL Bulletin, 32*(2), 5–9.

Zamel, V. (1983). The composing processes of advanced ESL students: Six case studies. *TESOL Quarterly, 17,* 167–187.

5 EFL Class in Morocco: The Role of Writing

Rachida Elqobai

Abu-Rabia (1996) defined learning a language as a "social phenomenon" emphasizing that it is "like any other phenomenon in life and is affected by social practice and social context" (p. 82). Since effective and efficient approaches and techniques are essential tools for achieving the goals of the language class, language teaching approaches must be adjusted to the social context where learning takes place. In other words, even the newest and most efficient "adopted" (Melouk, 2007) approaches should be "adapted" to the context where they are to be implemented (You, 2004a, 2004b) in order for these methods to be effective. Additionally, for any language teaching/learning to be accomplished efficiently, there is a need for the practices to match the stated underlying principles.

Teaching/learning English is no exception. Although English has always been an important component of the Moroccan sociolinguistic tissue, little is known internationally about the status of English and its functions in Morocco's key domains of politics, education, and the economy. It is, however, important to praise the important role of the national annual conference of the Moroccan Association of Teachers of English (MATE) in bringing together scholars to discuss different issues related to EFL teaching in Morocco, and in keeping EFL teachers updated on the most recent theories and methods in the field.

The aim of the present chapter is, first, to overview the Moroccan linguistic landscape. The status and uses of the English language, especially in the educational system, are described, spotlighting the gap between the whys and the hows in the EFL classroom in the intricate Moroccan sociolinguistic context. The second part of this chapter describes the role of writing in the EFL classroom, bringing to light the gap between writing to learn and learning to write. EFL pedagogy in the Moroccan educational system focuses more on teaching students how to write in English rather than teaching them how to use writing to learn English. Besides, the educational context makes correct and efficient implementation of the approaches, such as process writing, difficult, and in some areas almost impossible, especially in rural areas. The writing strategies of some Moroccan students are also described. Finally, this chapter ends with a strong call for Moroccan education agents, including decision makers and practitioners, to work together toward bridging these gaps in order to improve EFL teaching in particular and foreign language teaching in general.

Moroccan Linguistic Landscape

Morocco's geographical situation and history have greatly contributed to shaping the kingdom's linguistic landscape. As a multilingual country, Morocco is viewed as a meeting place for many different and distant languages, including Berber, the language of the indigenous population of Morocco, and English, nowadays the language of technology and scientific knowledge. The Moroccan multilingual milieu can be presented as follows:

Arabic: Also called standard or classical Arabic, it is the national/official language of the kingdom. Being the language of instruction, children start learning it in first grade. Arabic or, more appropriately, "academic Arabic," is not the Moroccan pupils' mother tongue but is rather their "academic L1" (Elqobai, 2004, 2006b).

Moroccan Arabic/dialect (darija): The Moroccan dialect, one of the spoken versions of classical Arabic, is the mother tongue and tool of daily communication for most of the Moroccan population, including a large portion of Berbers. It is spoken throughout the country in various but still similar regional varieties.

Berber/Amazigh: As a second national language, Berber is currently taught in some schools throughout the country. It is the mother tongue and, in some areas, the only communication tool for a large part of the population, especially in the mountains. Its three regional varieties, *Tamazight, Tachelhit,* and *Tarifit,* are spoken by a large number of Moroccans, including non-Berber people.

French: Because of its colonial history, its socioeconomic status and function, and its use in many key domains, such as administration, media, and instruction, French has, for a long time and until recent years, enjoyed the privileged rank of "semi-official status" (Melouk, 2007). Up until the eighties and before the implementation of Arabization (discussed below), it was the language of instruction. Arabization and globalization account to a great degree for the decline of French and the spread of English in Morocco.

Spanish: Along with French, Spanish is still viewed as the language of the colonizer. It is used in the north and the south, even though its use is decreasing dramatically. It is offered as a second foreign language for high school students, along with English and other languages such as Italian and German.

English: Compared to French and Spanish, English has the privilege of having no "colonial connotation" (Sadiqi, 1991). As for the schooling system, while French is imposed, students in high school can choose English among other languages as their second foreign language, even though the large majority of students choose English for many reasons to be explained below. As in many non-English-speaking areas worldwide, English is used extensively among Moroccan youth, mainly "to access English language movies and music" (Reichelt, 2005), and for the connotation of prestige (Sadiqi, 1991; Buckner, 2007).

All these languages co-exist and contribute to the Moroccan linguistic landscape. They are all in use to some extent, depending on their different statuses and diverse functions (Boukous, 1995). Besides, many other languages enrich the linguistic landscape due to growth in tourism since Morocco is a world-famous tourist destination. These other languages are occasionally used and are therefore in contact with the ones described above, especially in areas where tourism is very developed, such as Marrakech and Agadir.

Arabic French "Conflict"

Although Arabic is the official national language, French has always overtaken this role because of its status and function, relegating Arabic to second place. To address this unbalanced situation, Arabization at school was decreed in the eighties, to initiate linguistic and cultural independence and to reinforce the national status of Arabic. Hence, the scientific subjects usually taught in French were switched to Arabic, while French continues to be taught as the first foreign language.

Arabization was applied in the secondary schools with no coordination between the secondary and tertiary education, where sciences continue to be taught in French. The absence of coordination was significant at all levels and affected all educational aspects, including students' academic learning, their linguistic competence, and consequently their communicative ability. This lack of planning, in addition to the lack of adequate logistical coordination and, more importantly, lack of adequate human resources, made the implementation of Arabization a disaster from which the whole educational system still suffers. The whys and hows of Arabization and its consequences are beyond the scope of the present chapter, yet it is worth mentioning here that its effects are reflected not only in students' skills in French but also in English, because of their increasing lack of motivation in learning languages, including Arabic. The failure of Arabization is to a great extent responsible for the proliferation of private schools, including an increasing number of language centers.

It is important to emphasize the disparity between public and private schooling systems. Students in the public system struggle with foreign language incompetence, and this inequitable situation affects their chances in the job market: public school students are less competitive, and their chances of getting into good schools or getting good jobs, especially with big companies, are dramatically reduced locally, regionally, and internationally.

To sum up, the Arabic/French conflict does not reinforce either language; on the other hand, the international context is reinforcing the status of the English language, and Morocco is no exception (Buckner, 2007). All the stated factors, including global and local circumstances, contribute dramatically to the spread of English in Morocco.

The Status of English

The quickly growing interest in English in Morocco can be explained by the phenomenon of globalization. Since socioeconomic status is always relevant to both individual and professional language choices (Messaoudi, 2007), the worldwide spread of English "is at once the product of and pathway to globalization" (Buckner, 2007, p.135). Growing economic needs and rapid development in various vital sectors, entailing the enlargement of the circle of Morocco's partners, is making English a development tool for both individuals and companies, making it "a powerful language and the language of power" (Zughul, 2002, p.140). As a result of this fast growing spread, English is not only competing with French (Sadiqi, 1991), but "French is giving way to English" (Zughol, 2002, p.140). In other words, English is taking over territory from French.

English in the Moroccan Educational System

The reinforced status of English is reflected in the recent reform of the Moroccan educational system, including the new governmental language policy and orientation toward English. The national charter of education attributes to English a privileged position in the foreign language curriculum by prescribing its introduction in middle school (although widespread implementation is still far from being achieved) and by planning to introduce it in the last year of elementary school.

Yet EFL pedagogy in Morocco encounters many obstacles that keep it from being as successful as it should be. These impediments are mainly related to the gap between the whys and the hows of foreign language policy in general and EFL pedagogy in particular. While the pedagogical principles appear to be up-to-date and relevant to both the international context and national needs, actual practices are far behind. The teaching/learning environment is undeniably an important impediment to synchronization of practices with principles, mainly the crowded classroom where, in some areas, there are always more than forty students in a class. The time devoted to EFL instruction is another constraint: the reduced number of hours per week has a significant impact both on teachers' performance and students' learning. In addition to this, the teaching material is most of the time inappropriate for the teaching context, and there is a total absence of technological support. Working with such large groups and in such a poor context makes it almost impossible for teachers to achieve the activities' objectives and to implement the approaches and methods recommended by the official guidelines for teaching English.

An example of these imported approaches is the standards-based approach adopted by the national charter for education and recommended by the official EFL teaching guidelines. This standards-based approach is very appealing to administrators; however, for practitioners, including teachers and supervisors, this approach is setting high expectations (Chaibi, 2006) that are most likely not achievable in the Moroccan context. Therefore, if new approaches and methods such as standards-based or competency-based approaches are to be implemented in Morocco without creating the necessary conditions to meet the challenge, they will be implemented ineffectively and can have adverse effects. As Cheddoudi (2006) writes,

> In our school curriculum, emphasis has now been shifted to the competency-based approach in second and foreign language teaching. But a lot of the concepts associated with the new currently advocated methodology are still beyond the teacher's understanding . . . Pessimistically, adverse effects are also probable since the teaching-learning setting (overcrowded traditional classes) is widely different from the setting from where the Standards originated. (p.8)

Hence, the lack of teacher training, so emphasized by the education charter, is a crucial obstacle to EFL class efficacy. There is no question of the teachers' goodwill nor of the effectiveness of the approaches, but when one observes the rudimentary means provided to achieve the ambitious classroom objectives, it can easily be concluded that very few EFL teachers are likely to take up the challenge.

This situation brings to light the gap between principles and practices in the Moroccan EFL classroom. Yet, to briefly recapitulate this gap, it is necessary to point out that the hows of EFL classes should be understood at two levels:

Official hows: recommended by the official guidelines based on the most recent theories and adopting the most recent teaching approaches and techniques.

Implemented how: reflected in the daily classroom's reality and practices. Some teachers do not hesitate to admit that the poor infrastructure of the learning/teaching environment, including a total absence of technological tools and the overcrowded classroom, in addition to the students' lack of motivation in high school, constrain them to rely in many cases on audio-lingual methods to accomplish their task.

The large gap between the whys and the hows in the EFL classroom in Morocco's multilingual sociolinguistic context is a significant impediment to classroom success; the existence of this gap negatively affects both teachers' performance and students' linguistic skills, including writing skills.

The Role of Writing in the EFL Class

Writing in a second or foreign language is not viewed only as one of the competences that any program aims to provide. Rather, L2 writing is defined as "a multidimensional intellectual endeavor" (Kaufer & Dunmire, 1995), where diverse competences are mobilized, because students use all their skills and competences, including cultural competence, to accomplish any writing task. Therefore, writing is an integrative activity that requires not only linguistic knowledge, but also sociocultural awareness, especially in a multilingual context such as Morocco. Yet, in Morocco, there is still a long way to go before EFL writing rises to the privileged role it should be playing in foreign language classes.

As a component of EFL classes, writing is also affected by the gap between principles and practices in the Moroccan system. This gap is, at least partly, related to the role of writing in learning the language. While the official hows in teaching writing, recommended by the official guidelines, embrace the most recent approaches (such as process writing, endorsed by the standards-based framework at the secondary level), daily classroom practices still relegate writing to the position it held in traditional methods that viewed writing as the least important skill. Leki (2003) pointed out that "the argument for a privileged role for writing classes in L2 learning had to be specifically made in the 1960 and 1970's as a challenge to audio-lingual methods" (p. 315). It is argued here that in Morocco, the claim for this privileged role needs to be made by abolishing "the assumptions that under privilege[d] the written language" (Matsuda, 2001, p. 84) in order for writing to play an effective role in learning the language.

Except for students who choose to specialize in French or English literature, there is no writing class at any educational level. Even in English departments where composition classes are offered, "students have a very limited ability to communicate their ideas effectively in writing" (Bellout, 2000, pp. 25–26). Bellout stresses that timing and most especially "the lack of principled framework" hinder the achievement of the objectives of these composition classes, limiting students' opportunities to learn to effectively and appropriately make use of written discourse, and argues that "a principled eclectic approach has to underlie the syllabus design of the composition course in Moroccan departments" (p. 28). Bellout highlights the great differences among various students' needs and concludes that some students may benefit from training, while others may benefit from linguistic-oriented instruction, and that process writing may not be the solution for all writers.

Moroccan EFL writers' needs relate to their linguistic proficiency, their writing skills, and most importantly their sociolinguistic background. While relating students' problems in EFL writing to their linguistic proficiency, and while noting how some students contrive "to put their ideas into paper due to their limited linguistic knowledge" (Bouziane, 1999, p.13), Bouziane warns that "exposing students with different needs to one approach may not be fruitful" (p. 13). Thus, these new approaches need to undergo some changes and modifications to be suitable to the Moroccan context and to achieve the expected goals: "This may entail necessary changes so that a method will accommodate the specificities of the Moroccan classroom" (Bouziane, 1996, p. 25).

Because learning to write is more than just learning to "write things down" in the target language (Omaggio, 2000, p. 280), there is a need to rethink the role of writing in learning the language. Many scholars, in fact, call for more focus on the role of writing in language learning. Harklau (2002), for example, argued that L2 writing research is focused more on teaching students how to write in the target language, noting that "few L2 writing researchers seem to explicitly relate their work to the question of how students use writing to learn a second language, tending instead to address the issue of how students learn to write in a second language" (p. 12). For Moroccan EFL classes to be effective, and for Moroccan students to efficiently communicate in English using both oral and written discourse to meet the challenges imposed by globalization, there is an urgent need for important changes, such as shifting the focus from teaching to learning and from knowledge to skills (Buckner, 2008), including communicative skills. These shifts and their objectives need to be considered before determining which approaches or methods to implement. It is argued here that there is also a need for shifting the focus from learning to write to writing to learn. This will happen primarily through reviewing the status of writing in EFL classes, because writing is still relegated to a position of lesser importance, which is reflected both in time allotted (less than 25% of weekly class time) and its share of the class grades. In the baccalaureate final exam, for example, the writing section accounts for about a quarter of the grade, while the grammar and reading comprehension parts are graded equally. Therefore, examining the hows of writing and the role attributed to writing in learning the language in EFL class in the Moroccan educational system illuminates a great deal of the students' struggle with writing in high school and later during their higher education, as well as in their professional lives.

Students' Struggle with Writing

The preliminary results of one study (Elqobai, in progress) show students' awareness of their lack of writing skills and their apprehension towards writing resumes, cover letters, applications for training, scholarships, jobs, training reports, final projects, and so on, as well as their expressed need for composition classes. This study involves a group of graduate students asked about their difficulties in foreign languages, namely French as a first foreign language and English as a second foreign language. A high percentage of the students' answers demonstrate their struggle with administrative and professional writing in foreign languages. Although the gaps in their French are slightly less important than in English because of language experience, students expressed their wish for a composition class in the senior year of high school. They believe this class should be mandatory in freshman year in college. It is worth noting here that no writing labs exist at the university level to assist students; they are on their own in this struggle with writing. To remedy this problematical situation and to overcome their English inefficiency at all education levels, most Moroccan students rely on their L1 in different steps of their writing processes and for different purposes.

This commonly used practice among second language writers has been confirmed over the years by many studies (i.e., Arndt, 1987; Berman, 1994; Cohen & Brooks-Carson, 2001; Cumming, 1989; Edelsky, 1982; Elqobai, 2006a, 2006b; Friedlander, 1990; Hall, 1990; Kobayashi & Rinnert, 1992; Qi, 1998; Raimes, 1985; Silva et al., 2003; Uzawa, 1996; Wang, 2003; Wang & Wen, 2002; Woodall, 2002). Relying on L1 while writing in L2 makes the writing process very exhausting for second language writers. Additionally, Moroccan students rely on more than one language when writing in English, further complicating this cross-language task. Therefore, while seeking help in their L1s (Elqobai, 2006b), as will be explained later, students employ one of the following strategies to keep up their productivity in the writing process.

The first writing strategy is word-for-word translation; bearing in mind interference problems its use engenders (Elqobai, 2006a), one can easily imagine how demanding accomplishing the writing task can be. Having been a French high school teacher myself for many years, and based on my current experience teaching English at a school of science and technology, I can state that word-for-word translation is widely used among students as a primary writing strategy. In fact, grading students' composition has always been, and still is, a challenging task for me because this writing strategy makes it hard for me to better understand my students' texts and to provide them with appropriate feedback (Elqobai, 2006a).

It is necessary to clarify that this word-for-word translation is just a "relexification" of another translated product from Arabic, rather than an actual translation. Indeed, while accomplishing the writing task in English, students have at least three languages at hand, mainly their Arabic dialect, classical Arabic, and French. Therefore, they typically first translate their sentences from Arabic to French and then from French to English. Considering that French is the most recent language learned, and that students are writing in English as a third academic language, some scholars explain students' use of French chronologically (Cenoz, 2001). That is, third language writers rely on the last acquired language. Although this issue is beyond the present chapter's purpose, it is argued here that in the Moroccan students' situation, it is more about cognition between French and English than about chronology. In any case, the use of word-for-word translation does not make students' writing task any easier. Moreover, because of students' low proficiency in both French and English, their limited vocabulary, and their insufficient spelling skills, they end up transcribing many "lexical inventions" (Dewalae, 1998).

To make their word-for-word translation less time consuming, students rely on free online translation websites that they use as a shortcut to accomplish their writing tasks and make them as non-painful and undemanding as possible. Needless to say, the products of these emergency resources are meaningless and sometimes very ironic. Because of differences between Arabic and English, and given that students go from Arabic to English through French most of the time, writing a paper is for them a very complicated task. A graduate student who relied on free online translation for a research paper on "ground water" ended up using "water tablecloths" instead, demonstrating how dangerous the use of this strategy can be.

The second strategy is plagiarism. Aware of their shortcomings, students, especially at the university level, realize how important English is for their higher education as well as for their professional lives. At the same time, they find themselves on their own with no tutors and no writing labs, unlike many international universities. Some students do not hesitate to use plagiarism as a mean of masking their English inefficiency. A number of them fail to obtain good work or study opportunities, not because of their disciplinary incompetence, but because of their linguistic inabilities. Some students, those who can afford it, find themselves limited to seeking help at private language centers so they can at least partly address their weaknesses and improve their communication and writing skills in order to increase their chances of getting into well-known science and engineering schools or to be competitive enough on the job market. It is important to note that educational administrators are trying to remedy the situation by introducing English language modules to the university curriculum in science schools.

One can easily imagine how complicated and demanding the completion of a writing task can be for Moroccan EFL students. In EFL classes in Morocco, where teachers are still struggling with teaching students how to write in English, writing still has a long way to go before rising to a privileged role in language learning. Bearing that in mind, even learning how to write as an objective does not seem achievable, at least for the time being and given current circumstances, no matter which approaches are imported and how recent and efficient they are in other parts of the world. In others words, using writing to learn the target language in EFL classes in the Moroccan educational system is certainly not something that can seriously be thought about any time soon.

Conclusion

Because of the gap between the principles and the practices, in the Moroccan public educational system in general and in EFL classes in particular, imported approaches to writing instruction can not be implemented in an effective way. Moreover, even when teachers try hard to do so, the results, especially the students' performance in English, do not demonstrate the success these same approaches provide in other teaching contexts worldwide, mainly in Europe and the US. That is to say, in the Moroccan foreign languages teaching context, in order to bridge the gap, there is a need for the practices to be improved, so they can match the principles, in order for the objectives to be reached. In my opinion, many changes and improvements are necessary, such as reinforcing the role of writing in EFL classes, adjusting the imported approaches to the specific multilingual Moroccan context, taking into consideration the students' linguistic background as well as their proficiency and motivation, and helping them to understand their goals so they can develop their own effective strategies. According to Benson & Nunan (2005), "understanding your aims or goals is one of the bases in developing an effective set of language learning strategies" (p. 80). In essence, motivation and the goals underlying English learning could dramatically affect learners' strategies. The role of writing in learning the language should be privileged, and students should be encouraged to write more in terms of quantity and quality with a variety of appropriate tools for developing their writing strategies and working process. As noted by Silva et al. (2003), " . . . how important it is for teachers to present a variety of perspectives, approaches, and strategies to their students so that eventually each writer can develop a process that works for her or him in a given writing situation" (p. 110).

Reinforcing the role of writing in EFL classes also implies reinforcement of teachers' training and motivation. Indeed, improvement of EFL classes cannot be achieved without English teachers' development. This development, according to many Moroccan scholars such as Cheddoudi (2006), involves providing proper training as well as the appropriate logistical equipment, supervising, guiding and counseling, but also "rewarding teachers for their achievements" (p. 11).

To sum up, Moroccan educational system administrators need to be more aware of the importance of foreign language classes in general and of EFL class in particular for students' education and careers, not only in principle but most especially in practice. They should take into account the specificities of the Moroccan teaching/learning context in order to develop the appropriate teaching material and to adapt imported teaching approaches and methods. They must consider that what works in Europe or in the US will not necessarily work in Morocco because of contextual realities, including sociolinguistic factors. This is not meant to question the effectiveness of the imported methods, but to stress that these attractive and very appealing approaches and methods require significant adjustments to fit the reality of the Moroccan EFL context. This will certainly involve a tremendous amount of attention, willingness, and effort from all the agents of the educational system in order for the principles to match the practices, for the whys to match up to the hows, for the objectives to be realistic and realizable, for writing to fully play its pertinent role in learning the target language, and ultimately for the approaches to be effectively implemented and successfully optimized.

References

Abu-Rabia, S. (1996). Attitudes and cultural background and their relationship to reading comprehension in second language: A comparison of three different social contexts. *International Journal of Applied Linguistics, 6,* 81–107.

Arndt, V. (1987). Six writers in search of texts: A protocol-based study of L1 and L2 writing. *ELT Journal, 41*(4), 257–267.

Benson, P., & Nunan, D. (2005). *Learners' stories: Difference and diversity in language Learning.* Cambridge: Cambridge University Press.

Bellout, Z. (2000). Syllabus design for the course of composition in Moroccan English departments. Proceedings of the 20th MATE annual Conference. In A. Zaki (Ed.), *The new education reform in Morocco: The role of English* (pp: 25-30). Kenitra: MATE.Berman, R. (1994). Learners' transfer of writing skills between languages. *TESL Canada Journal, 12,* 29–46.

Boukous, A. (1995). *Société, langues et culture au Maroc: Enjeux et symboliques.* Publications de la Faculté des Lettres et des Sciences Humaines, Rabat.

Bouziane, A. (1996). Preparing teachers for the third millennium. Proceedings of the 16th MATE Annual Conference. In E. El Haddad & M. Najbi (Eds.), *ELT in Morocco: Perspectives for the 21st Century* (pp: 19-26). Mohammadia: MATE.

Bouziane, A. (1999). Towards a curriculum of EFL writing in Morocco. Proceedings of the 19th MATE Annual Conference. In M. Ahllal; O. Marzouki & M. Najbi (Eds.), *ELT Curriculum: New challenges, new solutions* (pp: 6-18). Marrakech: MATE

Buckner, L. (2007). Students' motivations for studying English. *Attarbya wa ttakewin, Education Moroccan Journal, 3,* 133–150.

Buckner, E. (2008). English language learning in the context of globalization: Insights from Morocco. Proceedings of the 28th MATE Annual Conference. In M. Hassim, M. Hammani, A. Chaibi & M. Najbi (Eds.), *Assessing quality in language education: Focus on Teacher competencies, Educationnal Materials and Learner performances* (pp: 115-158). Eljadida: MATE

Cenoz, J. (2001). The effect of linguistic distance, L2 status and age on crosslinguistic influence in third language acquisition. In J. Cenoz, B. Hufeisen,

& U. Jessner (Eds.), *Cross-linguistic influence in third language acquisition: Psycholinguistic perspectives* (pp. 8–20). Clevedon, UK: Multilingual Matters.

Chaibi, A. (2006). Competency-based & standards-based education. *MATE Newsletter, 26*(3–4), 4–7.

Cheddoudi, A. (2006). Teaching EFL through the competency-based. *MATE Newsletter, 26*(3–4), 7–13.

Cohen, A. D, & Brooks-Carson, A. (2001). Research on direct versus translated writing: Students' strategies and their results. *The Modern Language Journal, 85,* 169–188.

Cumming, A. (1989). Writing expertise and second language proficiency. *Learning Language, 39*(1), 1–72.

Dewaele, J. (1998). Lexical inventions: French interlanguage as L2 versus L3. *Applied Linguistics, 19*(4), 471–490.

Edelsky, C. (1982). Writing in a bilingual program: The relation of L1 and L2 texts. *TESOL Quarterly, 16,* 211–228.

Elqobai, R. (2004). *The L1 effect on the L2 writing: Which L1?* Paper presented at the fourth Symposium on Second Language Writing. Purdue University, IN.

Elqobai, R. (2006a). Writing in cognate vs. non cognate languages: A comparative study of two groups of American students writing in Arabic and French as L2. *Dissertation Abstracts International.* AAI 3232171.

Elqobai, R. (2006b). *The L1S effect on the L2 writing: A case study of a Moroccan Berber writing in Arabic and French.* Paper presented at Petite et Grandes Langues Colloque. Sorbone University, France.

Friedlander, A. (1990). Composing in English: Effects of a first language on writing in English as a second language. In B. Kroll (Ed.), *Second language writing: Research insights for the classroom* (pp. 109–125). New York: Cambridge University Press.

Hall, C. (1990). Managing the complexity of revising across languages. *TESOL Quarterly, 24*(1), 43–60.

Harklau, L. (2002). The role of writing in classroom second language acquisition. *Journal of Second Language Writing, 11*(4), 329–350.

Kaufer, D., & Dunmire, L. (1995). Integrating cultural reflection and production in college writing curricula. In J. Petraglia (Ed), *Reconceiving writing, rethinking writing instruction* (217–238). Mahwah, NJ: Lawrence Erlbaum.

Kobayashi, H., & Rinnert, C. (1992). Effects of first language on second language writing: Translation versus direct composition. *Language Learning, 42*(2), 183–215.

Leki, I. (2003). Pushing L2 Writing Research. *Journal of Second Language Writing, 12*(1), 103–105.

Matsuda, P. K. (2001). Reexamining audiolingualism: On the genesis of reading and writing in L2 studies. In D. Belcher & A. Hirvela (Eds.). *Linking literacies: Perspectives on L2 reading-writing connections* (pp. 84–105). Ann Arbor: University of Michigan Press.

Melouk, M. (2007). La langue d'enseignement et l'enseignement des langues. *Attarbya wa ttakewin, Education Moroccan Journal, 3,* 101–111.

Messaoudi, L. (2007). L'économie des langues. *Attarbya wa ttakewin, Education Moroccan Journal, 3,* 112–124.

Omaggio, A. (2000). *Teaching language in context.* Boston, MA: Heinle & Heinle.

Qi, D. S. (1998). An inquiry into language–switching in second language composing processes. *Canadian Modern Language Review, 54*(3), 413–435.

Raimes, A. (1985). What unskilled ESL students do as they write. *TESOL Quarterly, 19,* 535–552.

Reichelt, M. (2005). English language writing instruction in Poland. *Journal of Second Language Writing, 14*(4), 215–232.

Sadiqi, F. (1991). The spread of English in Morocco. *International journal of the sociology of language. 87,* 99–114.

Silva, T., Reichelt, M., Chikuma, Y., Duval-Couetil, N., Mo, R, P., Velez-Rendon, G., & Wood, S. (2003). Second language up close and personal: Some success stories. In B. Kroll (Ed), *Exploring the dynamic of second language writing* (pp. 93–114). NY: Cambridge University Press.

Uzawa, K. (1996). Second language learners' processes of L1 writing, L2 writing, and translation from L1 to L2. *Journal of Second Language Writing, 5*(3), 271- 294.

Wang, L. (2003). Switching to first language among writers with differing second language proficiency. *Journal of Second Language Writing, 12*(4), 347–357.

Wang, W., & Wen, Q. (2002). L1 use in the L2 composing process: An exploratory study of 16 Chinese EFL writers. *Journal of Second Language Writing, 11*(3), 225–246.

Woodall, B. (2002). Language–switching: Using the first language while writing in a second language. *Journal of Second Language Writing, 11*(1), 7–28.

You, X. (2004a). "The choices made from no choice": English writing instruction in a Chinese University. *Journal of Second Language Writing, 13,* 97–110.

You, X. (2004b). New directions in EFL writing: A report from China. *Journal of Second Language Writing, 13,* 253–256.

Zughol, M. (2002). The language of power and the power of language in higher education in the Arab world: Conflict, dominance and shift. *Proceedings of the 22nd MATE Annual Conference.*

6 L2 Writing Instruction in Japanese as a Foreign Language

Yukiko Abe Hatasa

INTRODUCTION

Japanese language instruction in the US began as heritage language instruction in the late nineteenth century (Asato, 2005), but it was essentially terminated during World War II when Japanese Americans were sent to concentration camps (Morimoto, 1997). Thereafter, Japanese was taught as a foreign language for a very limited group of people such as military officers and academics, and it was categorized as a less commonly taught language (LCTL). This picture changed drastically during the 1980s when Japan became a major economic power in the world. During this period, learners who studied Japanese expanded to include members of the general public, and Japanese became the first Asian language to be taught in American high schools. Accordingly, learner interests have changed from academic to career and general interests in Japan and Japanese culture. The shift in learner population has affected approaches to Japanese language instruction, from grammar translation and/or audiolingual approaches to more communicative and functional approaches. Today, Japanese is no longer considered a LCTL. Indeed, according to the *ADFL Bulletin* (Welles, 2002), Japanese is the sixth most enrolled language among US college students, and it is the most popular among Asian languages.

Writing instruction has been affected by these historical changes as well. Systematic writing instruction was rarely conducted in Japanese as a foreign language (JFL) programs during the grammar translation period. Even under the audiolingual method, some scholars actively discouraged writing instruction at the beginning level because mastering the Japanese writing system was deemed to be too cognitively demanding for learners at this level (Jorden & Walton, 1987; Unger et al., 1993). Although writing instruction still remains a part of language arts exercises in many JFL programs, the advancement of communicative approaches has introduced realistic writing tasks that simulate writing activities outside of language classrooms.

This chapter first provides an overview of Japanese language instruction in the US. It then reports on current views about the place of writing instruction in JFL programs in US colleges and universities. Then, writing planning and instruction in these programs, as well as issues concerning such instruction, is discussed. In addition, instructional practices in JFL are compared with those in JSL, and issues that may need to be considered in JFL curricula are discussed.

CHARACTERISTICS OF FL WRITING INSTRUCTION IN JAPANESE

Unlike ESL writing programs, writing instruction in Japanese as a foreign language programs in the US do not necessarily focus on academic writing or composition. Writing activities are conducted for purposes of language practice, or to focus on practical daily activities such as letters, memos, diaries, and email. This is in part due to the fact that institutional goals and learner needs of FL programs are very different from those of ESL programs, and culturally distant languages like Japanese present very different needs and goals compared to cognate languages. Also, as Japanese is one of the most difficult languages for native speakers of English to acquire, extensive writing may not be a realistic objective. In addition, educational practices in Japan affect the way Japanese language instructors approach writing instruction in JFL programs.

Difficulty of Japanese language and expected proficiency

Japanese is one of the most difficult languages for native English speakers to acquire. For instance, in the mid 1980s, the Foreign Service Institute (FSI) of the US Department of State compiled approximate learning expectations for a number of languages based on the length of time it takes to achieve intermediate level proficiency (Higgs, 1984). According to this classification, Japanese is noted as a Category 4 language along with Arabic, Chinese, and Korean. Languages in this category require approximately 720 hours of formal instruction, while

Category 1 languages such as Spanish, French, and Italian take only 240 hours to achieve the same level of proficiency. German, which is categorized as a Category 2 language, requires 480 hours. If we assume that a learner receives one hour of instruction every day for five hours a week for two semesters, it would take 4.8 years to reach an intermediate level in Japanese, but 2.6 years in German, and only 1.6 years in Spanish and French.

In 2007, the FSI revised the above categorization (National Virtual Translation Center, 2007). The new version, shown in Table 1, is based on the length of time it takes to achieve general professional level proficiency, instead of the intermediate level proficiency adopted in the 1984 categorization. Again, Japanese is classified in the most difficult category, Category III, which would take approximately 2,200 instructional hours—four times more than Category I languages like Spanish. Moreover, Japanese is marked as the most difficult language within Category III, as shown in Table 1.

Table 1. Language difficulty and approximate learning time estimate by the Foreign Service Institute.

Category I: Languages closely related to English
23-24 weeks (575-600 class hours)

Afrikaans Danish Dutch French	Italian Norwegian	Portuguese Romanian	Spanish Swedish

Category II: Languages with significant linguistic and/or cultural differences from English
44 weeks (1100 class hours)

Albanian	*Finnish	Macedonian	Slovenian
Amharic	*Georgian	*Mongolian	Tagalog
Armenian	Greek	Nepali	*Thai
Azerbaijani	Hebrew	Pashto	Turkish
Bengali	Hindi	Persian (Dari,	Ukrainian
Bosnian	*Hungarian	Farsi, Tajik)	Urdu
Bulgarian	Icelandic	Polish	Uzbek
Burmese	Khmer	Russian	*Vietnamese
Croatian Czech	Lao	Serbian	Xhosa
*Estonian	Latvian	Sinhalese	Zulu
	Lithuanian	Slovak	

Category III: Languages which are exceptionally difficult for native English speakers 88 weeks (second year of study in-country) (2200 class hours)			
Arabic Cantonese	Mandarin	*Japanese	Korean
Other languages			
German	30 weeks (750 class hours)		
Indonesian, Malaysian, Swahili	36 weeks (900 class hours)		

Languages preceded by asterisks are typically somewhat more difficult for native English speakers to learn than other languages in the same category (National Virtual Translation Center, 2007).

The difficulty levels are based on instruction offered at the FSI, in which pre-selected learners receive highly intensive language instruction. Therefore, it would take even longer for regular college students to achieve the same level of proficiency. In the case of Japanese, then, it would be reasonable to say English-speaking learners of Japanese barely achieve intermediate level proficiency in Japanese after four years of daily instruction (Higgs, 1984), and it would take more than twenty years of formal instruction to achieve a professional level proficiency (National Virtual Translation Center, 2007).

In terms of proficiency standards in Japan, US students are not expected to obtain a high level of proficiency outside of Japan. According to the Japanese-Language Proficiency Test content specifications (Japan Foundation and Association of International Education, Japan, 2007), proficiency is categorized into the following four levels. Level 1 is generally required for a non-native speaker of Japanese to be admitted to college in Japan, and learners at this level are expected to have received nine hundred hours of formal instruction, and know two thousand kanji characters (Chinese characters used in Japanese texts) and ten thousand words; Level 2 assumes six hundred hours of instruction, and a knowledge of one thousand Chinese characters and six thousand words; Level 3 students are expected to have received three hundred hours of instruction and know three hundred Chinese characters and fifteen hundred words; finally, Level 4 requires 150 hours of instruction, and knowledge of one hundred Chinese characters and eight hundred words. Since most US college Japanese programs offer three to five hours of instruction a week for thirty weeks for lower division language courses, and the number of instructional hours tend to be reduced in upper division courses, it is reasonable to assume some learners who have completed two years of Japanese would pass Level 3, and most learners do not pass beyond Level 2 after four years of instruction unless they participate in a study abroad program in Japan. In other words, English-speaking JFL learners are not likely to progress beyond the intermediate level upon completing college level instruction.

Learner population and learner needs

Learner characteristics and their needs provide important considerations in any curriculum development. Types of skills to be taught are often shaped by balancing learner needs and institutional goals. In JFL programs, characteristics of learner population and learner needs seem very different between Asian countries and the US. Although Japanese is taught in 133 countries with a global learner population of approximately three million, a majority of learners come from East Asian countries (Japan Foundation, 2008). Among these, 30.6% of learners (910,957 people) come from South Korea, 23% come from China, followed by Australia (12.3%), Indonesia (9.2%), and Taiwan (6.4%). Many of these learners seek to study in Japan either to obtain an academic degree or to go on to a short-term study abroad program. This is reflected by the fact that over 90% of Japanese-Language Proficiency Test (JLPT) takers are East Asian students. As such, their motivation and need for writing in Japanese is high because virtually all Japanese institutions require composition in entrance examinations.

On the other hand, only 4.8% of learners come from North America, 4% of which are from the US. According to a survey conducted by the Japan Foundation (2008), American students' reasons for studying Japanese are very different from those of Asian students (see Figure 1). The strongest motivation for Japanese study is a general interest in Japanese culture, which is followed by communication in Japanese, studying in Japan, improvement of job prospects, and general interest in language. These reasons seem to reflect that American students consider Japan different or exotic compared to European countries. Also, the recent popularity of Japanese pop culture—particularly Japanese anime, films, and computer games (Hatasa, 2008)—may be a driving reason for Japanese language study. Although the respondents of the survey stated study abroad as one reason for studying Japanese, they seem to be primarily interested in short-term study abroad programs. Only 6% of college students take the JPLT, and only 17% of them take the Level 1 examination (Japan Foundation, 2008; Japan Foundation and Japan Educational Exchanges and Services, 2007).

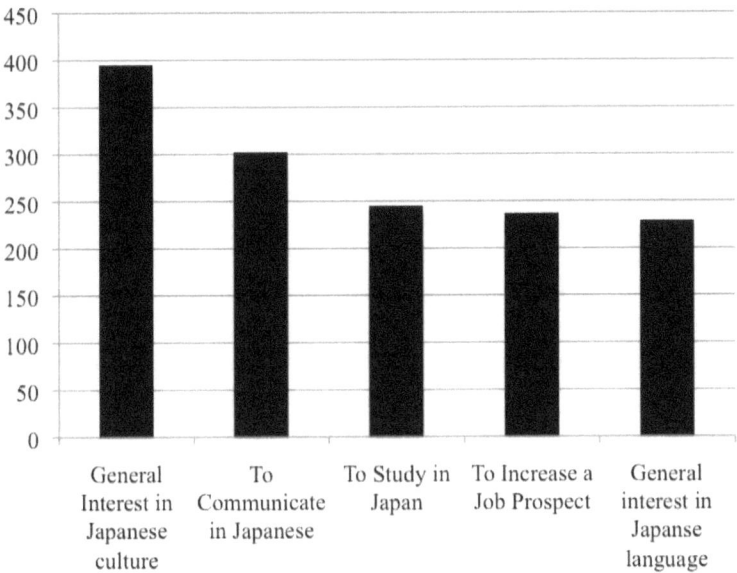

Figure 1: US college students' reasons for studying Japanese.

Curriculum objectives of US institutions

Just like learner needs, institutional goals or the goals of educational programs strongly influence how language is taught. For example, grammar translation was the predominant method in the nineteenth century because the purpose of teaching foreign language was to read scholarly materials rather than oral communication (Richards & Rogers, 2001).

Traditionally, Japanese language programs in the US belong to Japanese Language and Literature, Japanese Language and Culture, or Japanese Studies programs, and this structure has not changed much since the end of World War II (Hatasa, 2008). In these types of programs, an ability to read authentic text is essential, and for some disciplines such as anthropology and sociology, oral communication is also important. However, writing in Japanese is not as important as other skill sets. A majority of scholars in these disciplines write papers in English rather than Japanese. Given that Japanese is a difficult language for English speakers, much emphasis is placed upon the development of reading proficiency.

Characteristics of foreign language instructional settings

Unlike ESL programs, students in foreign language (FL) programs do not have to use the language outside of the classroom or to survive in society. This lack of necessity also brings about different levels of motivation (Dörnyei, 1994). Some learners take foreign language courses only to satisfy institution language requirements, while others have a strong drive to learn the language regardless of environmental limitations. Motivation is particularly important for languages like Japanese (Samimy & Tabuse, 1992; Kondo, 1999). In JFL, learning takes place at a much slower rate than other FL programs such as Spanish, French, and German. Students are often unable to understand Japanese TV programs or read Japanese newspapers even after three years of learning the language. Also, the target language input is highly limited in FL programs, and for alphabetic learners like American students, authentic Japanese texts, which consist of complex non-alphabetic writing systems, present considerable challenges to the learner. For these reasons, instruction must be designed to maintain motivation, and remain sensitive to learner needs. Because these needs rest primarily on culture and on oral communication, these aspects are much more emphasized in Japanese language instruction. Conversely, writing, which neither learners nor institutions consider to be a critical skill, tends to be subordinated to a secondary role.

Japanese writing instruction in Japan

In addition to the above factors, JFL composition instruction may be affected by the lack of training in writing Japanese among Japanese language instructors. This is because composition and rhetoric do not receive much attention in the Japanese educational system for the following reasons. First, the Japanese language education for native speakers focuses primarily on the development of reading skills rather than composition skills (Sato, 2006). According to the Japanese governments' guidelines for elementary, junior high, and high school education, the development of kanji and vocabulary knowledge is the focus of elementary education, and the emphasis gradually shifts towards reading comprehension of modern and classical literature (Ministry of Education, Culture, Sports, Science and Technology, 2008a, 2008b). Writing activities are usually included as a follow-up activity for reading activities, but systematic instruction in composition is not widely conducted (Ishihara, 2005; Ishihara and Saito, 2006). This is because college admissions in Japan are based on scores from a national examination that does not include writing (National Center for Test Administration, 2008). Only a limited number of institutions offer a composition test either for further screening or for Honors candidates. For these students, systematic writing instruction may be offered (Kobayashi & Rinnert, 2008). However, this type of instruction is not widely available for most students (Morishima, 2000).

Even after entrance into a secondary institution, a freshman rhetoric course is rarely required in Japanese colleges and universities, and lengthy term papers are rarely assigned in college classroom. Kobayashi and Rinnert (2001) report that their Japanese students write fewer and shorter papers than American students and receive very little feedback. As a result, Japanese students are poor at composition organizations in Japanese. For example, Nishigaki and Leishman (2000) find that their Japanese students' compositions tend to consist of one or more extended or "body" paragraphs without any introduction or conclusion. Also, a number of researchers have found that Japanese students, especially those who do not major in English, tend to start a text with specific details followed by a general statement, while American students write a general statement first and then provide specific details (Kobayashi, 1984; Takagi, 2000). Since the general-to-specific pattern of organization in English is also the preferred organizational pattern in Japanese (Kubota, 1998), Japanese college students are often unaware of how to organize a text.

Since the majority of Japanese language instructors in the US are native speakers of Japanese, their lack of writing experience and formal training in L1 writing puts a limitation on their ability to teach composition in Japanese. This may be another reason writing is rarely explicitly taught in Japanese language classrooms.

Characteristics of Written Japanese and Consideration for Writing Instruction

The previous section illustrates possible reasons writing instruction in JFL programs remains a part of language arts instead of composition or rhetoric instruction. This section considers how writing is taught in JFL programs by focusing on characteristics of the Japanese writing system.

Japanese is a verb final language with an extensive agglutination. Lexical overlap between Japanese and English is only about 10%, so the majority of vocabulary must be newly learned. In addition, Japanese written lexicon and spoken lexicon are very different, necessitating the memorization of a large number of vocabulary items in order to read and write. Another difference between Japanese and English text is the use of cohesive devices. In Japanese, pronouns are rarely used to create cohesion. Instead, repetitions and deletion of nouns are heavily used as cohesive devices. Learning to use these devices tends to be very difficult, as neither deletion nor repetition is commonly used in English.

Some organizational patterns such as *Ki-Sho-Ten-Ketsu* organization can present a difficult obstacle for learners. This format was originally developed for Chinese poetry, and it typically comprises four units: opening, development, shifts of a topic, and an element unrelated to the previous paragraphs. It is a popular format used in writing essays and stories in Japanese, and is often seen in newspaper articles and short essays. However, American students have problems understanding text organized within this format (Tateoka, 1996) because it does not have any thesis statement, and paragraph development is not as straightforward as it is in English.

Perhaps the most difficult aspect of written Japanese is Japanese orthography. A typical Japanese text does not have any word boundaries and consists of three types of scripts: hiragana, katakana, and kanji, as shown in Figure 2.

私はこれからの中国におけるファーストフード市場で、既存の中国語のファースト

フード企業が生き残っていくために四つの提案をしました。一つ目は、企業の

「ブランド化」とフランチャイズ店の拡大、二つ目は、スピードを追求しつつ、

品質を確保すること、三つ目は、低価格商品の開発、四つ目は、良いサービスの

提供です。

Figure 2. A typical Japanese text.

Hiragana and katakana are syllabaries in which one letter represents a moraic unit, and thus they are phonetic systems like alphabetic orthography. Hiragana is used for function words and inflectional endings, as well as for some content words. If we extract hiragana from the text in Figure 2 it would look like the text in Figure 3. Because hiragana represents primarily function words, it is virtually impossible for Japanese readers to guess the content of this text.

はこれからの　　における　　　　　　で、　の　の

　　が　き　っていくために　つの　　をしました。つ は、　　の

「　　　」と　　　　　の　、つ は、　　　を　　しつつ、

　を　　すること、つ は、　　　の　、つ は、い　　の

です

Figure 3. Hiragana extracted from the original Japanese text.

Katakana is used for loan words, onomatopoeic expressions, and scientific terms. Hiragana consists of forty-six characters and two diacritic marks to represent 113 simple morae. Similarly, katakana, with forty-seven characters (including a symbol for a long vowel) and two diacritic marks, represents more than 130 morae. Figure 4 shows the katakana that appears in Figure 2, and it shows the following loan words: ファーストフード (fast food), ブランド (bland), フランチャイズ (franchise), スピード (speed), and サービス (service). Based on these lists, it is possible to deduce that the text has something to do with fast food, but the list of items are not nearly enough to understand the content.

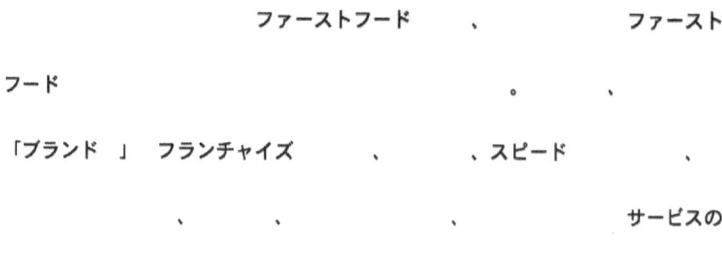

Figure 4. Katagana extracted from the original Japanese text.

The third type of script, kanji, is a logographic system in which one character represents a morpheme, or a word, and is used for content words. Figure 5 shows extracted kanji from Figure 2, and it shows over twenty content words and verbal stems. Compared to katakana, which only indicated five content words, it is much easier to guess the meaning of the text from kanji.

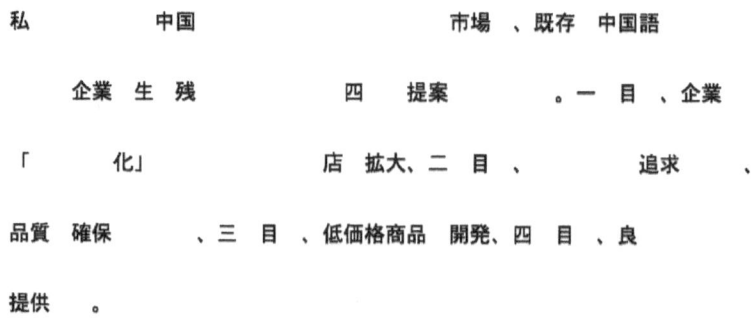

Figure 5. Kanji extracted from the original Japanese text.

The number of kanji words used for daily purposes (*joyo kanji*) is limited to 1,945 by the Ministry of Education, but the majority of Japanese texts contain more than three thousand letters (National Language Research Institute, 1994). For example, the number of kanji letters used is about 5,100 in Japanese literary texts, 3,328 in magazines, and 3,213 in newspapers.

While hiragana and katakana show a highly regular and transparent sound-grapheme correspondence, most kanji have multiple readings, and their pronunciation depends on the words in which they appear. Having no writing of their own, the Japanese began importing Chinese characters to write their own language around the late fourth or early fifth century (Taylor & Taylor, 1995). In so doing, they employed two adaptation strategies, one based on meaning and the other based on sound. According to the meaning-based strategy, kanji was used to write a Japanese word, which was synonymous with the Chinese word written with it. For example, the Japanese word for "wave" was used alongside the Chinese character with the same meaning, 波, but its pronunciation in Chinese [pua] was replaced by the corresponding Japanese word, *nami*. In contrast, according to the sound-based strategy, kanji was used to represent Japanese sound. For instance, the character 波 was used to represent the syllable [ha][1] because of its close resemblance to [pua] in middle Chinese (Yamada, 1983). In this usage, the character 波 was used as a grammatical morpheme, a topicalization marker, and its meaning was completely ignored (Coulmas, 1991, 1999). The pronunciation derived from the meaning-based strategy is called *kun*-reading, and the pronunciation derived from the sound-based strategy is called *on*-reading.

The adaptation of Chinese characters continued for almost one thousand years, and many characters were introduced into Japanese writing with more than one different Chinese dialect pronunciation and meaning. As a result, most kanji characters used today have multiple pronunciations. For example, the character 行 can be pronounced as [gyo], [koo], [an], [kun], [i(ku)], [yu(ku)], and [okona(u)] and express the meanings "walk," "drive," "do," "line," "sequence," and "travel." In order to determine which reading is intended in a given case, the reader has to rely on contextual information and certain general principles (Taylor & Taylor, 1983, 1995). Hiragana and katakana are visually simple, consisting of a maximum of six strokes. In contrast, kanji tends to be visually complex, as in 鬱. In fact, most kanji characters consist of more than ten strokes (National Language Research Institute, 1994).

Needless to say, mastery of the writing system is difficult for both native speakers and learners of Japanese. Hatasa and Soeda (2000) report that even advanced learners of Japanese who have close to ten years of learning experience still need to rely on Japanese dictionaries in writing. For this reason, writing instruction in Japanese involves a long-term teaching of the Japanese orthography.

EXAMPLE OF WRITING INSTRUCTION IN A JAPANESE AS A FOREIGN LANGUAGE PROGRAM

Given the complexity of written Japanese, writing provides a unique challenge to JFL programs. Keeping learners motivated and addressing their needs, all while satisfying institutional goals, is essential to assist JFL students in overcoming the difficulty of and slow progress in learning Japanese. This section describes one attempt to teach writing in a JFL program and illustrates the challenges involved in teaching writing in this context.

The example program is in one of the Big Ten universities in the midwestern US. The majority of the students are Caucasian American. Less than 10% of students come from other ethnic backgrounds. Most non-Caucasian students are Chinese and Korean. Students take these courses because of interest in Japanese culture. Approximately one-third of them are majors in Japanese. There are virtually no opportunities to practice Japanese outside of class, so instructors and students organize conversation hours approximately three times a week outside of class.

The university offers four years of Japanese language courses and one review course for high school graduates. In general, four skills are emphasized in all of the courses, though there is a gradual shift in emphasis from speaking/listening to reading/writing over the four years. The first two years of instruction are based on a combination of topic and structural syllabi, and emphasize strategic instruction. In the third year, a conversation course that is based on a functional syllabus and a reading and writing course that employs a topic syllabus are offered. Both courses emphasize cultural aspects of Japanese, and a variety of materials such as textbooks, authentic materials, and computers are used. The fourth year Japanese course adopts a content-based instructional approach. It is a repeatable course, so instructional contents change every year, covering a variety of aspects of Japanese culture, economy, society, and politics.

Writing instruction is conducted throughout the course. In the first and second years, writing is a part of language arts. It is usually tied with reading or conversational activities. Vocabulary development is emphasized in the first two years of instruction, though focused instruction on written vocabulary items does not start until the third year. Hiragana and katakana are taught in the first year, and hiragana is used as a transcription device throughout the four-year period. Kanji is taught gradually, starting with simple and concrete symbols (e.g., pictographs and ideographs). In the first two years, kanji writing is practiced in class so that students develop a kinetic memory for basic shapes and stroke order. Handwriting in kanji also helps students to understand that many kanji characters consist of a combination of a set of recursive shapes. Kanji compounds are the most typical of Japanese written vocabulary, so they are introduced starting in the second year. Extensive practice with kanji compounds is done in the third and fourth years.

In terms of discourse organization, the first two years introduce some cohesive devices such as the deletion of topic nouns, repetition, demonstrative pronouns and adjectives, and transition devices. Additionally, simple narrative and descriptive texts are included in the first and second years. Rhetorical organization for expository and argumentative texts is introduced in the third and fourth years. At the upper level, writing is tied to cultural materials and discussions, so students practice outlining, summarizing, and note-taking as they view Japanese TV programs and read newspapers and editorials. Because one Japanese program regularly hosts an essay contest for high school and college students in the area, the students in the university also practice "speech text" writing (composing essays that are later read publicly) at all levels..

Computer technology is used from the beginning, to practice orthography, email, and composition, but it is not used as extensively as it is in European languages. This is because Japanese word processing software, including MS Word, is tolerant of errors, and lexical and syntactic errors are not marked. As such, students must be absolutely accurate to produce correct kanji. This forces students to focus more on low level language processing rather than content and discourse organization. Therefore, writing practice with word processors tend to be limited to short texts.

Course	Instructional hours	Contents	Writing instruction
First year	5 hours a week (150 hours a year)	• 4 skills, • Topic & structure syllabus. • Strategic instruction • Text *(Nakama: Communication, culture, context, vol. 1)* • JLPT : Level 4	• Hiragana & Katakana • About100 kanji, • About 700 basic vocabulary items • Mechanics, Punctuation • Deletions, demonstrative words Simple description (houses, rooms, family members etc) • Post cards, simple memos, email messages, speech text
Second year	5 hours a week (150 hours a year)	• 4 skills, • Topic & structure syllabus • Text *(Nakama: Communication, culture, context, vol. 2)* • JLPT : Level 3	• About 250 kanji, • About 750 basic vocabulary items Transition devices (Demonstrative words, Connectives) • Repetitions • Letters, recipes, simple narratives CV, speech text (1-2 page)
Third year conversation	3 hours a week (90 hours a year)	• Listening and conversation • Functional syllabus • Self-made materials, authentic materials	• Kanji review • About 300 spoken vocabulary items
Third year reading/ writing	3 hours a week (90 hours a year)	• Reading and writing • Topic syllabus • Self-made materials & authentic materials	• 300+ kanji • About 500 written vocabulary, two kanji compounds, etc. • Word processing, • On-line & electronic dictionaries • Outlining, summarizing • Expository writing • Blog, short opinion paper (1-2 pages), speech text

Course	Instructional hours	Contents	Writing instruction
Fourth year	3 hours a week (90 hours a year)	• 4 skills • Content based instruction • Self-made materials & authentic materials	• 300+ kanji • 500+ vocabulary items • Kanji compounds, four kanji compounds compound verbs, etc • Summarizing, outlining note-taking • Argumentative text & opinion paper • Blogs, speech text

Table 2: Japanese Language program and writing instruction.

Students' evaluations in all of the courses are very high, showing a high rate of satisfaction. Also, the attrition rate is rather low in this university. These facts show that the program is working reasonably well. However, the effectiveness of writing instruction in terms of proficiency level has yet to be examined.

Conclusion

This chapter discussed current views about writing instruction in Japanese as a foreign language programs in US colleges and universities, and examined the reasons behind such views from the following perspectives: difficulty of Japanese in comparison with other foreign languages; learner needs and instructional goals; and characteristics of Japanese language and backgrounds. Additionally, how writing is planned and taught in these programs and issues involved in writing instruction in such contexts were discussed.

Writing has not played a major part in JFL instruction; therefore, not much research on L2 writing has been conducted. However, given the context of instruction, studies on L2 writing in Japanese cannot simply simulate English studies, thus requiring different types of research. One possible research area may be the development of productive orthographic knowledge. Previous research on Japanese orthography has focused on recognition (Koda, 2005), and little is known about how learners learn to acquire productive orthographic knowledge, or what factors cause learning difficulty in producing kanji. Such research should help us find both short-term and long-term strategies for teaching kanji for production. In addition, it can enable learners to focus more on idea development and organization as well as raising awareness of their composing processes.

Another topic that may help Japanese writing instruction is how to provide feedback when learners tend to focus on low level skills like kanji production (Hatasa & Soeda, 2000). L2 feedback studies in Japanese have started only recently. Almost all studies have been conducted with subjects who had considerable knowledge of kanji because they were either advanced students, or they used Chinese characters in their L1 (Ikeda, 2001; Hirose, 2000; Kageyama, 2000). However, no studies on either teacher feedback or peer feedback have ever been conducted for JFL learners in the US. Since JFL learners tend to be lower in proficiency and have not developed a high level of orthographic or lexical knowledge, they may not benefit from the types of feedback that have been found to be useful for JSL or ESL learners. Therefore, further research is essential to see whether findings from previous feedback research are applicable to JSL learners.

These are just a few of the research areas that may be fruitful for improving JFL writing instruction. Since JFL writing studies is in its infancy, many more studies need to be done to improve instructional quality to assist JFL learners in acquiring writing skills.

Note

1. [ha] is the current pronunciation of this character. In classical Japanese, it was [pa], which is more similar to the pronunciation of the same character in middle Chinese [pua].

References

Asato, N. (2005). *Teaching Mikadoism: The attack on Japanese language schools in Hawaii, California, and Washington, 1919–1927.* Honolulu: University of Hawaii.

Coulmas, F. (1991). *The writing systems of the world.* Oxford, UK: Blackwell Publishers.

Coulmas, F. (1999). *The Blackwell encyclopedia of writing systems.* Oxford, UK: Blackwell Publishers.

Dörnyei, Z. (1994). Motivation and motivating in the foreign language classroom. *The Modern Language Journal, 78,* 273–284.

Hatasa, Y. (2008). Beioku ni okeru gaikokugo to shite no nhongo kyooiku. [Japanese as a foreign language education in the United States]. In Y. Hatasa (Ed.), *Gaikokugo to shite no nhongo kyooiku: Takakuteki shiya ni motozuku kokoromi* [*Japanese as a foreign language education: Multiple perspectives*] (pp. 1–16). Tokyo: Kurosio Shuppan.

Hatasa, Y. A., & Soeda, E. (2000). Writing strategies revisited: A case of non-cognate L2 writers. In B. Swierzbin, F. Morris, M. E. Anderson, C. A. Klee, & E. Tarone (Eds.), *Social and cognitive factors in second language acquisition: Selected proceedings of the 1999 second language research forum* (pp. 375–396). Somerville, MA: Cascadilla Press.

Higgs, T. (Ed.). (1984). *Teaching for proficiency, the organizing principle.* Lincolnwood, IL: National Textbook Company.

Hirose, W. (2000). Bogo ni yoru peer response ga suikoo sakubun ni oyobosu kooka: Kankokujin chuukyuugakushuusha o taishoo to shita sankagetukan no jugyoo katsudoo o tooshite [Effects of L1 peer feedback editing: Findings from a three-month classroom study of Korean-speaking intermediate learners]. *Gengo Bunka to Nihongo Kyooiku* [*Language Culture and Japanese Language Education*], *19,* 24–37.

Ikeda, R. (2001). Nihongo sakubun kyooiku ni okeru pia resuponsu no kenkyuu [Research on peer response in Japanese writing instruction]. Unpublished doctoral dissertation, Ochanomizu University.

Ishihara, T., & Saito, M. (2006). Dootoku yori mo ritereshii o: Kokugo kyooiku wa nani o oshiteieu no ka [Literacy over morality: What Japanese language education teaches now]. *Eureka, 9,* 37-65.

Ishihara, C. (2005). *Kokugo kyooiku no shisoo* [*Philosophy of Japanese language education*]. Tokyo: Chikuma Shoboo.

Japan Foundation. (2008). *Kaigai no nihongo kyooiku no genjoo: Nihongo kyooiku kikan chosa 2006* [*Status of Japanese language instruction in overseas: 2006 survey of Japanese language educational institutions*]. Tokyo: Bonjinsha.

Japan Foundation and Association of International Education, Japan. (2007). *Nihongo nooryoku shken shutsudai kijun* [*Japanese-Language Proficiency Test: Test content specifications*]. Tokyo: Japan Foundation.

Japan Foundation and Japan Educational Exchanges and Services. (2007). *Nihongo nooryoku shaken: Kekka no gaiyoo* [*The Japanese-Language Proficiency Test: Summary of results*] Retrieved from http://www.jees.or.jp/jlpt/jlpt_result.html.

Jorden, E. H., & Walton, A. R. (1987). Truly foreign languages: Instructional challenges. *The Analysis of the American Academy, 490,* 110–124.

Kageyama, Y. (2000). Jookyuu gakushuusha ni yoru suikoo katsudoo no jittai: pia resuponsu to kyooshi fiidobakku [Advanced learners' editing activities: Peer response and teacher feedback]. *Oyanomizu Joshi Daigaku Jinbun Kagaku Kiyoo* [*Journal of Ochanomizu Women's University Humanities Department*], *54,* 107–119.

Kobayashi, H. (1984). Rhetorical patterns in English and Japanese. *TESOL Quarterly, 18*(4), 737–738.

Kobayashi, H., & Rinnert, C. (2001). *The role of academic writing in higher education in Japan: Current status and future perspectives* (Report for the Japanese Ministry of Education, Science and Culture, Research Grant No. 11680263). Hiroshima: Hiroshima University, Faculty of Integrated Arts and Sciences.

Kobayashi, H., & Rinnert, C. (2008). Task response and text construction across L1 and L2 writing. *Journal of Second Language Writing, 17,* 7–29.

Koda, K. (2005). *Insights into second language reading: A cross-linguistic approach.* New York: Cambridge University Press.

Kondo, K. (1999). Motivating bilingual and semibilingual university students of Japanese: An analysis of language learning persistence and intensity among students from immigrant backgrounds. *Foreign Language Annals, 32,* 77–88.

Kubota, R. (1998). An investigation of L1-L2 transfer in writing among Japanese university students: Implications for Contrastive Rhetoric. *Journal of Second Language Writing, 7,* 69-100.

Ministry of Education, Culture, Sports, Science and Technology. (2008a). *Shoogakkoo gakushuu shidoo yooryoo kaisetsu: Kokugo-hen* [*Commentaries on the guidelines for elementary school education*]. Tokyo: Tooyookan.

Ministry of Education, Culture, Sports, Science and Technology. (2008b). *Chuugakkoo gakushuu shidoo yooryoo kaisetsu: Kokugo-hen* [*Commentaries on the guidelines for Junior high school education: Japanese Language*]. Tokyo: Tooyookan.

Morimoto, T. (1997). *Japanese Americans and cultural continuity: Maintaining language through heritage* (*Garland Reference Library of Social Science*). United Kingdom: Routledge.

Morishima, H. (2000). *Atarashii kokugojugyoo no soozoo: Konnichiteki kadai to sono hoohoo* [*Inventing a new method of teaching Japanese: Current issues and solutions*]. Tokyo: Kyooiku Shuppan.

National Center for Test Administration. (2008). *Daigaku nyuusi sentaa shiken riyoo daigaku kokkooshiritudaigaku gaido bukku (nyuugakusha senbatuhoohoo ichiran)* [*A guidebook for national, state and private universities and colleges on the national college entrance examination: A list of methods of making admission decision*]. Tokyo: Nikkei Insatsu.

National Language Research Institute. (1994). *Joyo kanji no shutoku to shidou* [*Acquisition and teaching of* Joyo kanji]. National Language Research Institute, Research Report, 106.

National Virtual Translation Center. (2007). *Language learning difficulty for English speakers.* Retrieved from http://www.nvtc.gov/lotw/months/november/ learningExpectations.html.

Nishigaki, C., & Leishman, S. (2000). An analysis of composition of Japanese college students. *Chiba daigaku kyouikugakubu kiyo* [*Bulletin of the Faculty of Education, Chiba University*], *48,* 87–99.

Richards, J., & Rogers, T. (2001). *Approaches and methods in language teaching.* Cambridge: Cambridge University Press.

Samimy, K. K., & Tabuse, M. (1992). Affective variables and a less commonly taught language: A study in beginning Japanese classes. *Language Learning, 42,* 377–398.

Sato, I. (2006*). Kokugokyookasho no sengoshi* [*Post-war history of Japanese language textbooks*]. Tokyo: Keiso Shobo.

Takagi, A. (2000). Contrastive rhetoric: Language transfer from Japanese to English writing. *Kantokoshinetsu eigo kyoiku gakkai kenkyu kiyo* [*KATE Bulletin*]*, 14,* 21–33.

Tateoka, Y. (1996) Bunshoo koozoo no chigai ga dokkai ni oyobosu eikyoo: Eigobogowasha ni yoru nihongo hyooronbun no dokkai [The effects of text organization on reading comprehension: English speaking learner's readings of Japanese editorial essays]. *Nihongo Kyooiku* [*Journal of Japanese Language Teaching*]*, 88,* 74–90.

Taylor, I, & Taylor, M. (1983). *Psychology of reading.* New York: Academic Press.

Taylor, I., & Taylor, M. (1995). *Writing and literacy in Chinese, Korean, and Japanese.* Amsterdam: John Benjamins.

Unger, J. M., Lorish, F. C., Noda, M., & Wada, Y. (1993). *A framework for introductory Japanese language curricula in American high schools and colleges.* Washington, D.C.: National Foreign Language Center.

Yamada, K. (1983). *Kanji no gogen* [*Etymology of kanji*]. Tokyo: Kadokawa Shoten.

Welles, E. (2002). Foreign language enrollments in United States institutions of higher education, fall 2002. *ADFL Bulletin, 35*(2–3), 7–25.

7 Issues and Challenges in Teaching and Learning EFL Writing: The Case of Hong Kong

Icy Lee

Introduction

When I first began publishing about writing in Hong Kong, one question that always puzzled me was whether I should refer to writing in Hong Kong as ESL (English as a second language) or EFL (English as a foreign language). In my earlier publications, I used ESL rather than EFL, though I knew English was not bona fide ESL in Hong Kong (but neither did I perceive it as entirely EFL). Looking back, one unspoken reason for my choice of ESL was possibly that with heavily ESL-oriented research in L2 (second language) writing (see, e.g., Manchón & de Hann, 2008), describing my work as ESL could have made it more mainstream and more worthy of publication. In recent years, however, I have started referring to writing in Hong Kong as EFL (e.g., Lee, 2008). In fact, the changing status of English in Hong Kong has been reflected in other published works in the field. In O'Brien's (2004) extensive review of FL (foreign language) writing published in *Language Teaching*, English in Hong Kong is referred to as a foreign rather than a second language (SL). In Ortega's (2004) summary of EFL studies published in the *Journal of Second Language Writing*, works from Hong Kong are cited as examples of EFL studies. Within Hong Kong itself, a decade ago, Falvey (1998) had already argued for the role of English as a FL rather than a SL. In Lin's (2008) recent plenary presentation at a local international language in education conference, English was referred to categorically as a FL in Hong Kong.

Despite the perceived FL status of English, there is still some ambivalence regarding the role of English in Hong Kong. Officially foreign languages in Hong Kong refer to, instead of English, languages like Spanish, French, and German. While English is said to play a non-dominant role in EFL contexts (such as China and Taiwan), it is both politically incorrect and practically inapt to say that English has a non-dominant role to play in Hong Kong (with English being an official language in the territory, apart from Chinese). It is also simplistic to think that because Hong Kong is now part of China, the challenges writing teachers and students face are the same as those in China. The position I take, at the outset of this chapter, is that in order to fully understand the issues and challenges teachers and students face in Hong Kong, it would be useful to temporarily forego the ESL and EFL labels and examine more closely the teaching and learning of writing against the backdrop of the changing status of English in Hong Kong, especially after the handover in 1997.

In post-colonial Hong Kong, English continues to have an important role. However, complaints about falling English standards have been escalating, and there is a general perception that people with a good command of written English are at a premium. Why have years of English language education in Hong Kong failed to produce students whose writing measures up to society's expectations? This question provides the point of departure for the chapter, which attempts to examine the problems students and teachers face in the Hong Kong writing classroom.

The chapter begins by situating English language writing within the Hong Kong context with reference to the status of English and the role of English writing in Hong Kong. It then examines writing from the vantage point of learning and teaching, uncovering the myriad of issues and challenges that may confront EFL learners and teachers in similar contexts. Then the chapter puts forward a number of recommendations, with likely relevance for other EFL contexts. Finally, it revisits the status of writing in Hong Kong and concludes that the issues and challenges raised in the chapter are likely to have pertinence for both EFL and ESL contexts.

Changing Role of English in Hong Kong

Hong Kong had been a British colony for 155 years until the handover in 1997. English was then (and is still) one of the two official languages in Hong Kong, apart from Chinese, and second language education was understood as English language education. Even then, English was referred to as an auxiliary language with restricted functions (Luke & Richards, 1982) (i.e., neither a second nor foreign language). In pre- and post-colonial Hong Kong, the large majority of people in Hong Kong are ethnic Chinese and speak Cantonese as their mother tongue, which is "the language of the home, the street and the entertainment media" (Education Commission, 1994, p.15). After the handover in 1997, Hong Kong has witnessed the increasing importance of Putonghua (i.e., standard Mandarin based on the Beijing dialect, also the official spoken language of the Peoples' Republic of China), with the government keen on promoting the development of biliteracy (in Chinese and English) and trilingualism (in Cantonese, Putonghua, and English)[1]. To this end, the mandatory mother tongue-medium of instruction policy was implemented in 1998, requiring all secondary schools in Hong Kong to shift to Chinese-medium instruction (which is Cantonese rather than Putonghua), whereas before 1998 about 90% of secondary schools were English-medium (though mixed-code teaching—i.e., mixture of Cantonese and English, existed in many schools). Under the mother tongue policy, a total of 114 schools (about 30%) were allowed to teach in the medium of English, as they were able to demonstrate over a three-year period, based on an academic aptitude test administered in grades five to six, that at least 85% of their first-year intake were able to learn effectively in either Chinese (i.e., Cantonese as the spoken language and standard written Chinese as the written language) or English. Another measure to promote biliteracy and trilingualism, announced in 1998, was that Putonghua would be offered as a subject as part of the core curriculum in all local schools in Hong Kong. Despite the rising importance of Chinese, the official language of instruction in universities is English, and a pass in English in the university entrance exam is a prerequisite for university admission. It can be perfectly understood then that parents want their children to be educated in English-medium schools in order to increase their chance of success in life. Since the mother tongue policy has been in place, a lot of dissenting voices have been heard. For one thing, the majority of secondary students in Hong Kong (i.e., those studying in

Chinese medium schools) have had less exposure to English, as they learn English only as a subject rather than use it as a tool for learning (the majority of primary schools teach in the Chinese-medium). There is a general perception that English standards are falling as a result of the mother tongue policy. In May 2009, the government, after reviewing the medium of instruction policy, finalized on its new fine-tuning policy[2] to give secondary schools flexibility to supplement mother-tongue teaching by allowing them to adopt English as the medium of instruction in up to 25% of total time across subjects. In spite of divided opinions about the best direction to take regarding medium of instruction for secondary students, Hong Kong is unanimous in its view on the urgency to upgrade English standards to maintain the city as an international center in the world.

In domains such as the civil service, legislature, and judiciary, the language situation has also changed in post-colonial Hong Kong. In Legislative Council meetings, there has been "a marked shift from English to Cantonese" (Bolton, 2002, p.8). In the civil service, the localization policy has resulted in a reduction of expatriates and a concomitant increased emphasis on Chinese. Meetings are more commonly held in Cantonese than English, except with the presence of foreigners. English, however, remains the dominant language of written records in the civil service. In judiciary, while court records and legal documents are in English, Cantonese is increasingly used in legal courts (before 1997 English was the chief language). The change in the language situation in Hong Kong has inevitably given an impression that English is used less frequently in public domains, and hence there is in general a less English-rich environment in the territory. A case in point is the limited circulation of English language newspapers and print media. Presently, the *South China Morning Post* remains the leading voice of English language journalism. *Asiaweek,* which was established in 1975 and based in Hong Kong, closed in 2001 due to "dwindling profitability" (Bolton, 2002, p.11).

In personal domains, although English is not the main tool of social communication and has been perceived as increasingly foreign after 1997, its infrequent use by people may have been overstated. As suggested by Bolton (2000), English has intruded into the personal domain rather unnoticeably. With over 200,000 Filipina domestic helpers in the territory, English is used in families with Filipina domestic helpers, and small children are seen speaking to their helpers in English. With more local students going to international schools in Hong Kong, and with returnees from overseas countries, Hong Kong has emerged as a truly multicultural city. In addition, more and more young people surf the Internet in their leisure (in both English and Chinese). Among university students, English emails are preferred to Chinese "not least because of the relative ease of communication in typing English emails, compared with inputting Chinese characters" (Bolton, 2002, p.11). With the growing popularity of online activities like MSN, Facebook, and blogging, English, though not necessarily accurate/standard English, is increasingly used as a tool of written communication among people in Hong Kong.

In business and commerce, English remains a *lingua franca* for communication. It is a tool for maintaining the status of Hong Kong as a first class financial and commercial center in the world. Against such a background of the changing status of English is the government's perpetual emphasis on the importance of English and its commitment to raising English language standards in Hong Kong. The community in general has high expectations of people's English proficiency, and the hope of the government is to nurture the English abilities of the community so that Hong Kong can become a truly biliterate and trilingual city and maintain its position as the most cosmopolitan and international city in Asia. As a result, considerable resources have been devoted to upgrading English standards. The workplace English campaign, for example, was set up in 2000 with a view to improving English skills of relatively junior staff in businesses. Substantial resources have also been put into English language teacher education to upgrade English standards of English teachers—e.g., the government-subsidized overseas immersion programs for pre-service English teachers enrolled in bachelor of education and full-time postgraduate diploma in education programs. Schools are endowed with funds to improve English language teaching, aside from the native-speaking English Teacher (NET) scheme, which was launched in 1998 to upgrade English standards in Hong Kong schools.

In post-colonial Hong Kong, therefore, English continues to play a crucial role. Despite the continual complaints about falling English standards, what remains clear is that Hong Kong needs people with strong English abilities, including writing abilities, to help the city thrive as an international center in the world.

Learning and Teaching Writing in Hong Kong

Despite years of investment in English language education, annual reports about students' writing performance in public examinations, released by the Hong Kong Examinations and Assessment Authority, have continued to puzzle the public as to why common problems persist in student writing. For example, in the examiners' report for the 2007 Hong Kong Certificate of Education Examination (public exam for grade ten students), students' compositions were said to exhibit common problems like memorized essays (and hence irrelevant content), miscomprehension of essay topics (e.g., essay topic requiring students to write about ways to prevent cruelty to pets was misinterpreted as why people should keep pets), and common spelling mistakes (e.g., *principle* for *principal, drogan* for *dragon*). The perception of low writing standards in Hong Kong is much aggravated by the unsatisfactory results English teachers themselves have obtained in the writing paper of the language benchmarking test mandated for English teachers. Since its inception in 2001, there has been annual coverage of teachers' unacceptably high failing rate in the writing paper (worst among all language skills) in the media, the lowest being 29% in 2002 and the best only 45.9% in 2006. Common mistakes found in teachers' writing reportedly include the following: *balance life* instead of *balanced life, detail plan* instead of *detailed plan,* and *colleges* instead of *colleagues.*

What is amiss with the way writing is learned and taught in Hong Kong? What issues and challenges do students and teachers face in the writing classroom? This section attempts to answer these important questions by examining writing from the learning and teaching perspectives, with a specific focus on the school context (primary one to secondary seven, i.e., grades one to thirteen). Since the majority of work on EFL writing relates to tertiary education, I hope this chapter can redress the current imbalance.

Writing as a chore

In Hong Kong, given the limited roles of English outside the classroom, learning English is primarily driven by extrinsic and utilitarian motives (i.e., educational, vocational, and/or socioeconomic advancement) (Lo & Hyland, 2007). In writing, such pragmatism is manifested in an approach that places emphasis on decontextualized sentence writing practice and writing as a vehicle for language reinforcement at the expense of self-expression, creativity, and originality. For students, writing typically refers to compositions they submit to their teachers on a regular basis as part of continuous assessment. Writing is rarely a pleasure but instead a tremendous source of pressure for students. Few students in Hong Kong experience the joy of writing, with the majority seeing writing as a chore with little relevance to their everyday lives.

Primacy of written accuracy

The utilitarian approach to writing translates into a practice that emphasizes grammar and vocabulary above all else, making students believe the ability to produce grammatically accurate texts is the most important goal of writing. In Fan's (1993) study, it was found that students relied on strategies like memorization of model texts, for fear that expressing their own ideas in writing would cause them more grammatical errors. Students consider their lack of linguistic competence to be their major stumbling block in learning to write. They are afraid of making mistakes and reluctant to take risks in writing. Teachers' written feedback is primarily error-focused, reinforcing students' belief that to produce error-free writing is the most important goal in learning to write (Lee, 2004).

Writing without reading

Research on reading-writing connections has demonstrated that reading experience is likely to improve writing ability (Grabe & Kaplan, 1996; Hirvela, 2004; Stotsky, 1983). However, in Hong Kong, students are known for their lack of interest in reading in general, and particularly reading in English. With the mandatory mother tongue policy in 1998 and the declining use of English in secondary schools, students in general have less exposure to English print materials. Despite the government's earlier attempt to promote extensive reading through the extensive reading scheme (set up in 1991), the initiative has yielded disappointing results (Green, 2005). In post-colonial Hong Kong, students are generally exposed to less English reading material (as aftermath of the mother tongue policy), and it is unlikely that students' writing development can benefit from their impoverished reading experience[3]. Such a lack of exposure to reading may further throw light on the writing difficulties students face.

Assessment culture

The strong assessment culture in Hong Kong schools has posed further obstacles to students' writing development. While schools concentrate their efforts on improving exam performance (Davison, 2004), students' motivation for learning writing is largely driven by a desire to get good scores in examinations, which are very high-stakes in Hong Kong. In fact, such an assessment culture in Hong Kong is well-documented in earlier local research, and seen as the major culprit for impeding the implementation of process pedagogy (Brock, 1995; Curtis, 2001; Curtis & Heron, 1998; Hamp-Lyons, 2006; Pennington, Brock, & Yue, 1996). The entrenched exam-oriented system in Hong Kong has made it very difficult for teachers to help students develop intrinsic motivation for writing.

The problem is also that within the assessment culture, Hong Kong teachers are spending much more time responding to student writing than teaching writing or thinking about ways to improve their writing instruction—in a real sense burning their midnight oil to mark student writing (Lee, 2005). They are exhausted and yet find little improvement in student writing as a result of their drudgery. For students, teachers' continuous assessment (that focuses heavily on language form) demotivates them further, making them dread writing (for fear of making mistakes) and lose confidence in themselves as writers.

Teachers' instructional practice

A decade ago, Lee's (1998) survey showed that teachers focused mainly on grammar and vocabulary in the writing classroom. More recently, Lo and Hyland (2007) have referred to the prevalent writing program as one that focuses on testing of students' writing, with writing topics drawn from coursebooks, teacher-led instruction that addresses grammar and vocabulary students need for the writing, as well as in-class timed writing requiring single drafts. Instruction is still primarily conceived in terms of the vocabulary and grammatical structures required for the writing with much less attention paid to discourse level concerns. Audience is not specified, and no one except the teacher reads student writing. Writing is conceived as a cognitive activity that has little relevance to students' lives. In spite of the espoused aims laid out in Hong Kong curriculum documents regarding the implementation of process writing, teacher-student conferences, peer evaluation, and portfolio assessment (Curriculum Development Council, 2002, 2006), conventional teaching methods prevail in Hong Kong schools, which are often attributed to the traditional school culture, aside from domination of an exam culture (Evans, 1996; Davison, 2007; Hamp-Lyons, 2006). Students play the role of passive recipients and are not made to take responsibility for their own learning. It is unlikely that existing writing instructional practices are able to enhance students' motivation for writing.

A recent writing lesson I have observed confirms the traditional, grammar-focused orientation to writing instruction. In the lesson, the teacher focused on the teaching of passives and toward the end of the lesson asked the grade eight students to practice using the target language in a recipe, "How to make a dish of fried shrimps." A number of verbs/phrases were provided (e.g., *peel, mix with sauce, fry, wash*) to help the students write the recipe. What made the lesson worse than a typical form-focused writing lesson is that the writing was devoid of audience and a relevant context, and the teacher, with little idea about the language features of a recipe, asked students to use passives instead of imperatives in a recipe genre.

Teacher competence

Earlier studies by Hirvela and Law (1991) and Lee (1996) have found that Hong Kong teachers rate writing their weakest competency in terms of proficiency and teaching. In recent years, teachers' writing abilities have been put to the most stringent test in Hong Kong since the government implemented the language proficiency requirement in 2001 (often referred to as the language benchmarking test for speaking, listening, reading, writing, and classroom language). The writing paper requiring teachers to (1) write an essay of 400 words and (2) correct and explain written errors, has had the lowest passing rate since 2001 (compared with speaking, reading, and listening). The results showed that teachers failed the writing paper mostly because of their poor performance in correcting and explaining written errors.

What is most ironic is that when Hong Kong writing classrooms put so much emphasis on testing student writing and teachers spend a massive amount of time marking student writing, the language benchmarking test results have disclosed that teachers are weak in correcting and explaining student errors. In Lee's (2004) study on the accuracy of teacher error corrections, the findings indicate that half of her participating teachers correct errors inaccurately. When teachers themselves cannot correct errors (and explain errors) accurately, the effectiveness of their written feedback is called into question.

Although teacher incompetence in writing may have been overstated by the low passing rates of the language benchmarking tests, whose results are probably skewed by teachers' under-performance in correcting and explaining errors (and there are teachers exempt from the benchmark requirements who may fare better in writing), the language benchmarking tests have raised public concern about teacher professionalism as a whole, and in particular teachers' competence as writers and teachers of writing.

Material and sociopolitical challenges

Exacerbating the problem teachers face is their excessive workload (e.g., secondary teachers teach an average of 25–30 English lessons per week/cycle, with each lesson lasting about forty minutes), not only from their day-to-day teaching and the onerous task of error correction, but also from a host of non-teaching duties, demands of education reform, and professional development activities they undertake to fulfill the government's requirement of life-long learning. There are other material challenges such as large class sizes, tight teaching schedules, and strict deadlines for returning marked compositions to students.

Worse still, teachers lack the autonomy to change conventional practices, as they are held accountable to school administrators, students and parents, who are all concerned about school performance as manifested in public exam results. Even though some teachers are keen on exploring innovative ideas in teaching writing, their efforts are often thwarted by unsupportive school leaders. The experience of Hamp-Lyons, Chen, and Mok (2001), in their attempt to develop materials to support secondary teachers' use of process pedagogy, has shown that it is the lack of support from school leaders, apart from the dominant exam culture, that poses obstacles to innovative pedagogy. Some teachers in the study admitted they had to revert to the more traditional approach to protect themselves from criticism by department heads or principals, for fear they might be blamed for students' less satisfactory results due to their involvement in innovative practices.

Meeting the Challenges

Given the issues and challenges discussed in the preceding section, it is important to put writing in perspective, rethink the writing needs of students, and reprioritize emphases in teaching, learning, and assessment of writing. The recommendations that follow, which are by no means exhaustive, are likely to have relevance for EFL contexts that share similar concerns.

Building motivation and confidence in writing

Motivation plays a pivotal role in language acquisition (see Dornyei, 2003). The first challenge for writing teachers, irrespective of students' writing purposes and needs (whether writing is for grammar practice, creative expression, or discovery of meaning), is to find ways to enhance students' motivation for writing. Given this, it is crucial to establish a writing environment that provides incentives so that students develop a real interest in writing, engage in writing at a more personal and meaningful level, experience writing as a vehicle for personal expression, creativity, and self-discovery, and discover the joy of writing—in spite of the heavy emphasis on grammatical accuracy. Practices that ruin students' motivation must be stopped.

Using the recipe writing lesson mentioned above, a more interesting writing lesson may consist of one or more of the following elements: the teacher going through the actual cooking activity with students (or playing a video clip about the cooking activity); showing students samples of the recipe genre and teaching the language features and structure explicitly; asking students to choose a dish they like; and writing a recipe in groups (and even making students do the cooking and take photos of the selected dish afterwards). If writing can be integrated with other skills and made relevant to students' daily life experience, it will be a much more rewarding and enjoyable experience for students.

To build students' confidence in writing, it is important to immerse them in writing, provide opportunities for writing practice on a regular basis, and help them build a good writing habit. Writing should not be mainly in the form of timed and/or assessed writing that Hong Kong students submit for scores/grades. Instead, writing can take alternative forms. It could be something students put down at the beginning of a lesson—about their expectations of the lesson. It could also be something they write at the end of the lesson, where they reflect on the learning. It could also be a riddle, a creative poem, a caption, an advertisement, a flyer, a notice, etc.—not subjected to assessment. While helping students develop written accuracy is, inter alia, a legitimate concern for writing teachers, it would help if teachers could de-emphasize their focus on form in feedback, encourage students to take risks by exploring ideas in writing, acknowledge students' effort, and boost their self-confidence through a great deal of fluency practice. Given that students in Hong Kong do not have a lot of opportunities to engage in writing in English outside the classroom (perhaps except for electronic communication), maximizing opportunities for writing both inside and outside the classroom could help students build a good writing habit and develop confidence in writing.

Language-in-use and genre approach to writing instruction

Coxhead and Byrd (2007) propose a language-in-use approach to teaching grammar and vocabulary in writing that is highly pertinent to the grammar-focused writing classroom in Hong Kong. In the recipe example cited above, the passives used in students' recipes serve to reinforce the target language without preparing students for real language use. To make the learning of writing more relevant and more interesting, a language-in-use approach, in combination with a genre approach, is useful. The focus is on "grammaring" rather than grammar (Larsen-Freeman, 2003), and how grammar is used to make meaning. In so doing, teachers tie in grammar teaching with writing instruction. In preparing students to write a recipe, for example, teachers can demonstrate the use of imperatives in some sample recipes and show students that writing is a tool for meaning making, rather than a mechanical way to regurgitate language structures and display linguistic knowledge.

One challenge, therefore, is for writing teachers to reconceptualize the place of grammar teaching and how it can be taught in conjunction with writing. In this regard, genre pedagogy is recommended (Hyland, 2007). Through learning explicitly about genres, generic structures, and lexico-grammatical features typical of specific genres, students learn to master grammar in connection with genres. When genres are used to provide an organizational principle for the writing syllabus, and when students are asked to write the genres they need to use and especially those they come across in daily life, students not only find the learning of writing much more relevant to their experience, but they also develop reading (since they are provided with sample texts to read) and other language skills as they participate in the explicit instruction cycle that characterizes genre pedagogy (see Hyland, 2007).

Attention to both process and product of writing

Writing is a painstaking task. For L2 learners, the writing product needs to be broken down into manageable steps so that they learn to write in stages and develop their composing competence. More attention, therefore, has to be paid to the process of writing. As for the writing product, a greater emphasis on discourse and genre is essential to help students understand the place of purpose, context, audience, and register in the production of written texts. As process and product are equally important, writing teachers can explore how a process-genre approach (see Badger & White, 2000) can be used to benefit students' learning of writing.

Interweaving assessment and teaching

Within the assessment culture in Hong Kong writing classrooms, there is a great need for teachers to balance their teaching and assessment efforts and bring assessment in alignment with teaching so that assessment serves the purpose of improving learning and teaching of writing. Hong Kong, as in other similar contexts, may need a revolution of some kind to overhaul the current assessment-oriented system in writing so that teachers can be freed up to engage in more meaningful teaching activities. By working smarter (but not necessarily harder)—e.g., by de-emphasizing error correction but laying a greater stress on content and organizational issues, by sharing responsibility with students through peer evaluation, and by assessing what is taught (e.g., responding to selected error patterns that tie in with grammar instruction, or assessing aspects of genre covered in explicit instruction), teachers can foster a closer connection between assessment and teaching.

In the UK, the Assessment Reform Group set up in 1989 has conducted research on assessment for learning and attested its benefits (Black & Wiliam, 1998; Black & Wiliam, 2003). In Hong Kong and other EFL contexts, where more attention is still paid to assessment of learning and summative assessment than the formative potential of assessment in writing (see Lee, 2007), much more work needs to be done to help teachers de-emphasize assessment of learning and engage in more productive practices that interweave teaching, learning, and assessment of writing (Colby-Kelly & Turner, 2007).

Technology in writing

Since most students in Hong Kong (as in some EFL contexts) use the computer and connect to the internet as a daily habit, writing teachers can make greater use of technology to help students see the relevance of writing, build a writing habit, and develop a stronger motivation for writing. For example, blogs can be used to enable students to document individual experiences, to keep in touch with friends (Lenhart & Fox, 2006), and more importantly to discover meaning, which is seen by Scott (1996) as particularly relevant for FL contexts. Teachers can share their own blogs with students and encourage them to post comments. Students can also start blogs, post personal writings, and engage in learning through interactions in a "community of practice" (O'Brien, 2004), e.g., by responding to one another's posts. Facebook, a social networking website, can be used to arouse students' interest in the use of written English for social communication. These activities, which are relevant to students' daily lives, are more likely to arouse their intrinsic motivation for writing. Aside from leisure writing, technology can be exploited as a pedagogical tool for different purposes. For instance, collaborative writing can be carried out using wikis (Sze, 2008), feedback can be delivered online (Milton, 2006), and computer software can be used to help students improve grammar and vocabulary in writing (e.g. Milton, 2008). With the growth of computer literacy in Hong Kong (and other EFL contexts), the potential of technology for enriching the writing classroom should definitely be explored.

Writing teacher education

In L2 writing, much more attention has been paid to the needs of those learning to write rather than those learning to teach writing (Hirvela & Belcher, 2007) and, as a result, the role of writing instruction still remains unclear for many writing teachers (Coxhead & Byrd, 2007). As pointed out by O'Brien (2004), writing teacher expertise is an area that warrants attention, specifically the relationship between writing teachers' expertise and students' writing development. In Hong

Kong, as in similar EFL contexts, much more attention is needed to help writing teachers understand their own theoretical orientations in teaching writing, and the ways in which a principled way of teaching and assessing writing can move students along in their writing development. How writing teachers learn to teach and develop their expertise in their specific contexts also provides interesting avenues for further research.

Research in school contexts

In Hong Kong and other EFL contexts, there is a bias toward writing research in tertiary contexts (Ortega, 2004). For instance, eight out of eleven articles about writing research in Hong Kong published in the *Journal of Second Language Writing* (since 1992) are about higher education. Research on school writing, particularly primary, is warranted. Specifically, ethnographic research that elucidates the teaching and learning of writing and how it is influenced by the overall context and the circumstances that govern teachers' work will be a welcome addition to the currently under-researched school writing in Hong Kong and EFL contexts in general.

CONCLUSION

Writing has an important role to play in students' language development. In Hong Kong, as in similar L2 contexts, students need to develop writing skills to succeed in work and study, and to stay competitive. Leki (2003), however, cautions that the importance of L2 writing (particularly EFL) may have been overrated. For some students in Hong Kong, English writing has a minimal role to play in their lives once they leave school. After all, writing is a means not an end itself. In a cosmopolitan and multicultural society like Hong Kong, the ability to write in English provides people with an option and an extra tool to engage in communication. Even though some students do not end up in a workplace that requires good written English, it is important that we help them acquire the ability to write in another language and give them an additional tool to communicate in English—e.g., online communication. Such an option is particularly powerful given the strategic importance of English in Hong Kong.

Before I conclude, let me return to the earlier question I raised but put aside at the beginning of the chapter regarding the status of writing in Hong Kong—is it EFL or ESL? As we compare EFL with ESL writers, the former have less exposure to English outside formal learning environments and may have more instrumental motivation for learning writing. They tend to pay more attention to written accuracy and are faced with greater material challenges like large class sizes as well as sociopolitical challenges like high-stakes testing (Leki, 2001; Ortega, 2004). Given these distinctions, writing in Hong Kong is much more EFL than ESL. This, in a way, is a foregone conclusion because in recent literature, writing in Hong Kong is almost always referred to as EFL rather than ESL (see O' Brien, 2004; Ortega, 2004). While it is important, as this chapter has demonstrated, to examine the contexts, purposes, and motivations for writing, and design writing instruction that meets the needs of specific contexts (regardless of the EFL or ESL label), the case of Hong Kong has perhaps shown that it is not easy to distinguish the needs of EFL and ESL writers. Take Hong Kong and Singapore as examples. Although there are differences between writing in these two contexts, there are also vast similarities between the needs of learners and how pedagogy should be designed to take care of these needs. In the US context, though significant differences exist between FL and ESL writing, there are also a great many commonalties between the two (Reichelt, 1999, 2001). Whereas ESL writers need "more of everything" (Raimes, 1985, p. 250), EFL writers also need more of everything, perhaps *a lot* more of everything, including more

- **Explicit instruction**—such as explicit instruction in genres; more
- **Fluency practice**—to counterbalance the currently lopsided emphasis on language accuracy; and more
- **Long-term investment**—investment on the part of student writers, writing teachers, and writing teacher educators.

In that sense, the issues and challenges in teaching and learning writing are comparable across L2 contexts (EFL and ESL). It is important for writing practitioners to recognize and accommodate local needs while drawing upon insights gained from works in other contexts so as to bring greater benefits to their writing classrooms.

Notes

1. Before the handover in 1997, Chinese in Hong Kong was often used to refer to Cantonese as the language for spoken communication and Standard Modern Chinese as the written language. After the handover, "Chinese" has been used to refer to Putonghua as well.

2. The fine-tuning medium-of-instruction policy, which started with grade seven from the 2010/11 academic year onwards, allows secondary schools to introduce different medium-of-instruction arrangements to suit different needs of their students.

3. In 2007, school-based assessment was introduced for the English subject (contributing 15% to the total score of the public exam at the end of grade eleven/secondary five), requiring students to read English texts and then give oral presentations or participate in group interactions. School-based assessment aims to expose students to a greater variety of reading materials in English.

References

Badger, R., & White, G. (2000). A process genre approach to teaching writing. *ELT Journal, 54*(2), 153–160.

Black, P., & Wiliam, D. (1998). Assessment and classroom learning. *Assessment in Education, 5*(1), 7–74.

Black, P., & William, D. (2003). In praise of educational research: Formative assessment. *British Educational Research Journal, 29*(5), 623–637.

Bolton, K. (2000). The sociolinguistics of Hong Kong and the space for Hong Kong English. *World Englishes, 19*(3), 265–285.

Bolton, K. (2002). *Hong Kong English: Autonomy and creativity.* Hong Kong: Hong Kong University Press.

Brock, M. (1995). Resistance and change: Hong Kong students and the process approach. *Perspectives, 7*(2), 53–69.

Colby-Kelly, C., & Turner, C. E. (2007). AFL research in the L2 classroom and evidence of usefulness: Taking formative assessment to the next level. *Canadian Modern Language Review, 64*(1), 9–37.

Coxhead, A., & Byrd, P. (2007). Preparing writing teachers to teach vocabulary and grammar of academic prose. *Journal of Second Language Writing, 16,* 129–147.

Curriculum Development Council. (2002). *English language education: Key learning area curriculum guide (Primary 1—Secondary 3).* Hong Kong: Hong Kong Government Printer.

Curriculum Development Council. (2006). *English language education key learning area: New senior secondary curriculum and assessment guide (Secondary 4–6).* Hong Kong: Hong Kong Government Printer.

Curtis, A. (2001). Hong Kong student teachers' responses to peer group process writing. *Asian Journal of English Language Teaching, 11,* 129–143.

Curtis, A., & Heron, A. (1998). On being less innovative: Peer groups and process writing in Hong Kong. *Asia Pacific Journal of Language in Education, 8,* 99–117.

Davison, C. (2004). The contradictory nature of teacher-based assessment: ESL teacher assessment practices in Australian and Hong Kong secondary schools. *Language Testing, 21*(3), 305–334.

Davison, C. (2007). Views from the chalkface: English language school-based assessment in Hong Kong. *Language Assessment Quarterly, 4*(1), 37–68.

Dornyei, Z. (2003). Attitudes, orientations, and motivations in language learning: Advances in theory, research, and applications. *Language Learning, 53,* 3–32.

Education Commission. (1994). *Report of the working group on language proficiency.* Hong Kong: Hong Kong Government Printer.

Evans, S. (1996). The context of English language education: The case of Hong Kong. *RELC Journal, 27,* 30–55.

Falvey, P. (1998). ESL, EFL and language acquisition in the context of Hong Kong. In B. Asker (Ed.), *Teaching language and culture: Building Hong Kong education* (pp. 73-85). Hong Kong: Addison Wesley Longman.

Fan, F. H. K. (1993). How examinations affect students' approach to writing. In J.B. Biggs & D.A. Watkins (Eds.), *Learning and teaching in Hong Kong: What is and what might be* (pp.67–76). Hong Kong: Faculty of Education, The University of Hong Kong.

Grabe, W., & Kaplan, R. B. (1996). *Theory and practice of writing.* London: Longman.

Green, C. (2005). Integrating extensive reading in the task-based curriculum. *ELT Journal, 59*(4), 306–311.

Hamp-Lyons, L. (2006). The impact of testing practices on teaching: Ideologies and alternatives. In J. Cummins & C. Davison (Eds.), *International handbook of English language teaching* (Vol. 1) (pp.487–504). Norwell, MA: Springer.

Hamp-Lyons, L., Chen, J., & Mok, J. (2001). Introducing innovation incrementally: Teacher feedback on student writing. *ThaiTESOL Bulletin: Selected papers from the 21st Annual ThaiTESOL International Conference, 14*(2), 59–66.

Hirvela, A. (2004). *Connecting reading and writing in second language writing instruction.* Ann Arbor: University of Michigan Press.

Hirvela, A., & Belcher, D. (2007). Writing scholars as teacher educators: Exploring writing teacher education. *Journal of Second Language Writing, 16,* 125–128.

Hirvela, A., & Law, E. (1991). A survey of local English teachers' attitudes toward English and ELT. *Institute of Language in Education Journal, 8,* 25–38.

Hyland, K. (2007). Genre pedagogy: Language, literacy and L2 writing instruction. *Journal of Second Language Writing, 16,* 148–164.

Larsen-Freeman, D. (2003). *Teaching language: From grammar to grammaring.* Boston: Heinle & Heinle.

Lee, I. (1996). Hong Kong primary teachers' perspectives on ELT. *RELC Journal, 27*(2), 100–117.

Lee, I. (1998). Writing in the Hong Kong secondary classroom: Teachers' beliefs and practice. *Hong Kong Journal of Applied Linguistics, 3*(1), 61–76.

Lee, I. (2004). Error correction in L2 secondary writing classrooms: The case of Hong Kong. *Journal of Second Language Writing, 13*(4), 285–312.

Lee, I. (2005). Why burn the midnight oil marking student essays? *Modern English Teachers, 14*(1), 33–40.

Lee, I. (2007). Assessment for learning: Integrating assessment, teaching, and learning in the ESL/EFL writing classroom. *Canadian Modern Language Review, 64*(1), 199–214.

Lee, I. (2008). Understanding teachers' written feedback practices in Hong Kong secondary classrooms. *Journal of Second Language Writing, 17*(2), 69–85.

Leki, I. (2001). Material, educational, and ideological challenges of teaching EFL writing at the turn of the century. *International Journal of English Studies, 1*(2), 197–209.

Leki, I. (2003). A challenge to second language teaching professionals: Is writing overrated? In B. Kroll (Ed.), *Exploring the dynamics of second language writing* (pp.315–328). Cambridge: Cambridge University Press.

Lenhart, A., & Fox, S. (2006). Bloggers: A portrait of the Internet's new storytellers report for pew Internet and American Life Project. Retrieved from http://www.pewinternet.org/PPF/r/186/report_display.asp.

Lin, A. (2008, January). *Teaching English in the 21ˢᵗ century: Critical perspectives.* Paper presented at the International Conference on Responding to Change: Flexibility in the Delivery of language Programs. Hong Kong University of Science and Technology, Hong Kong.

Lo, J., & Hyland, F. (2007). Enhancing students' engagement and motivation in writing: The case of primary students in Hong Kong. *Journal of Second Language Writing, 16*(4), 219–237.

Luke, K. K., & Richards, J.C. (1982). English in Hong Kong: Functions and status. *English World-Wide, 3*(1), 47–64.

Manchón, R. M., & de Haan, P. (2008). Writing in foreign language contexts: An introduction. *Journal of Second Language Writing, 17*(1), 1–6.

Milton, J. (2006). Resource-rich web-based feedback: Helping learners become independent writers. In K. Hyland & F. Hyland (Eds.), *Feedback in second language writing: Contexts and issues* (pp.123–137). Cambridge: Cambridge University Press.

Milton, J. (2008, January). *Providing just-in-time resources for second language learners*. Paper presented at the International Conference on Responding to Change: Flexibility in the Delivery of Language Programs. Hong Kong University of Science and Technology, Hong Kong.

O'Brien, T. (2004). Writing in a foreign language: Teaching and learning. *Language Teaching, 37,* 1–28.

Ortega, L. (2004). Feature article: L2 writing research in EFL contexts: Some challenges and opportunities for EFL researchers. *Applied Linguistics Association of Korea Newsletter.*

Pennington, M., Brock, M. C., & Yue, F. (1996). Implementing process writing in Hong Kong secondary schools: What the students' responses tell us. *Perspectives, 8*(1), 150–217.

Raimes, A. (1985). What unskilled ESL students do as they write: A classroom study of composing. *TESOL Quarterly, 19*(2), 229–59.

Reichelt, M. (1999). Toward a more comprehensive view of L2 writing: Foreign language writing in the U.S. *Journal of Second Language Writing, 8*(2), 181–204.

Reichelt, M. (2001). A critical review of foreign language writing research on pedagogical approaches. *The Modern Language Journal, 85*(4), 578–598

Scott, V. M. (1996). *Rethinking foreign language writing.* Boston, MA: Heinle & Heinle.

Stotsky, S. (1983). Research on reading/writing relationships: A synthesis and suggested directions. *Language Arts, 60,* 627–642.

Sze, P. (2008). Online collaborative writing using wikis. *The Internet TESL Journal, 14(1).* Retrieved from http://iteslj.org/Techniques/Sze-Wikis.html.

8 Ideas into Words: Narrowing the Gap in Doctoral Candidates' Academic Writing in EFL

Hadara Perpignan

I write a research about the influnese of Nitche's filosofy of the poetry of Zvi Grinberg. In this research I want to ask, how it's imposible that the man killed the Gud can influence on a belives people [sic].

—Eva (pseudonym), 2007

Introduction

Teaching the elite of a university can be an awe-inspiring experience: PhD candidates in Israel are often at an advanced stage in their professional lives; they are mature in years and in life experiences; their academic research is cutting-edge and foreign, at least to me. Yet there is an enormous discrepancy between their preparedness in these aspects of their lives and their relative lack of preparedness regarding use of English. The very first class contact in the context of a course in Academic Writing for PhD candidates reveals their deep frustration at being asked to express highly complex ideas, of which they are rightfully proud, in language that one student referred to as *baby talk* or, worse still, at being unable to express them at all. The quotation above is meant to dramatize this issue. The challenge is that there is little time in which to turn this situation around, and I cannot give students the assurance that they will, within one semester, be able to communicate in English at a level to be proud of as well.

Indeed, for many of the students I teach, this is the most I can hope for: not that they be transformed into near-native users of a second language for all purposes, including the academic, but that they grow into people who can adopt a new identity (Ivanič, 1997), an academic persona in a foreign language under certain well-defined and limited circumstances. In what follows I describe the institutional context in which these goals are set and the many-faceted pedagogical principles that inspire teaching and learning toward these goals. Then I present the design of the course and illustrate its implementation through pedagogical tasks.

INSTITUTIONAL CONTEXT

Hebrew is the language of communication within universities in Israel. Academic writing in Israeli universities has not been systematically taught, although there is currently a movement toward filling this gap. Therefore, our academic EFL writers today have been exposed to little formal teaching of writing in any language beyond their secondary studies. However, all Israeli university candidates take a psychometric exam that includes a component that measures reading comprehension in English. Unless they have scored an exemption level on this exam, they are required to enroll in one of six levels of an English reading comprehension program. Thus, most do receive some English instruction during their BA studies, aimed at enabling them to cope with the bibliographies in English required in their content courses. In addition, at Bar-Ilan University, the second largest university in Israel, with 24,500 students and three hundred degree programs, an additional English course at the MA level is required. This course, although officially described as focusing on writing, recognizes the students' still-present needs for reading comprehension and oral presentation as well, which encourages a multi-skill, integrative approach, de-emphasizing writing. The university also offers an independent academic writing course for PhD students, with the declared purpose of publicizing internationally the research done at the university; this course is the focus of this chapter. The home to all of these English courses is a department or unit that is rightfully called the EFL department. This department offers academic writing in English services to all departments in the university, except, perhaps ironically, to the English literature and linguistics department.

Academic writing in English for Israeli PhD students has its origins in a project founded in 1987 and was funded by the Wolfson Charitable Trust for five years. When the funding dried up, some departments in some universities were able to maintain the courses themselves, although with great financial struggle. Even though the Wolfson project was not long-lived, it provided the vital kick-off to academic writing at the graduate level in Israel, and left a very valuable heritage of pedagogical principles (Zuckerman & Rubin, 2007).

At Bar-Ilan University, between thirty and forty students are enrolled each year in the course entitled Academic Writing for PhD Candidates. Its population consists of students of mixed disciplines (from Brain Research to Bible Studies), involved in various types of research (from the most empirical to the most theoretical), who are of mixed English proficiency levels and diverse L1 writing experience (from published authors to struggling first year thesis writers), and of various native language backgrounds (Russian, Arabic, Hebrew, and others).

This is a one-semester course with open admission and no exit exam. The meetings are weekly, totaling twenty-six academic hours, a dire reality of 19.5 hours of face-to-face contact in the best of times; conference hours are not scheduled as an integral part of the course. The course is required for some students and optional for others, depending on individual department regulations. These conditions, however distressing they may be, are not negotiable. It is therefore up to the teacher to use his/her judgment in making pedagogical choices that can compensate for them. Fortunately, the university and the EFL department provide the faculty, myself and others, with sufficient academic freedom to guarantee these choices.

One other favorable condition conceded to the faculty is the very small class size: twelve participants in each group. The distribution of students into groups is made roughly according to discipline and research type, rather than English language proficiency. This allows for the building of a core syllabus content of interest to most, within which each student can strive to perform to the best of his/her individual ability.

Due to the diversity in the circumstances described above, the goals of the course are defined differently by the different parties involved. The institutional definition is to enable the student to write flawless academic prose for the purpose of publication and conference presentation. The teaching staff's definition is for each individual student to achieve some degree of this ability, according to his/her initial English proficiency level, and progress in PhD research and Hebrew writing expertise. To complicate matters, student aspirations do not always match these goals, since many declare a still more urgent need to function in day-to-day situations, such as presenting their work orally and writing emails in English to foreign colleagues or consultants, as well as writing up research, which is the course's *raison d'etre*.

The Special Status of EFL Academic Writers

ESL students and their teachers were once called strangers in academia (Zamel, 1995) due to the cultural and linguistic distance between them and the requirements of the real world of academia in which the students were expected to write. I would like to suggest that in EFL we are *foreigners* in Academia. Academia is not a strange land, since PhD students already peripherally belong to it in one language. However, it is foreign in the sense that culturally, linguistically, and geographically, the land of their destination is physically removed from their point of departure: the incentive may be weaker, the road is even steeper, and the means of getting there frailer.

The wide recognition of the distinction between writing in L1 and writing in L2 (Johns, 1994; Silva, 1993) has perhaps obscured the differences between writing in EFL and writing in ESL and the processes involved in their acquisition. No research, to my knowledge, has investigated these differences systematically, in spite of the growing interest in foreign language writing reported in the timely editorial of the March 2008 issue of the *Journal of Second Language Writing* (Manchón & de Haan, 2008), and as reflected in the choice of theme for this volume. This lack can perhaps explain why EFL practitioners have tended to adopt the solutions presented by ESL writing research wholesale, or to adapt them *ad hoc*. Before introducing the principles I have adopted and adapted in my practice of teaching EFL writing, I would like to refer to two of the differences, as I see them: they concern motivation and exposure.

The motivation for learning to write in the institutional setting described above is mostly extrinsic and non-integrative. The learning needs are prompted by the institution, and the goals are defined by institutional requirements: e.g., an English language summary of the research is required to be submitted together with a PhD thesis; professors urge their students to publish with them in order to advance their respective careers; the university demands international dissemination of their work through conference presentations and publications; and, due to lack of sufficient university or personal financial support for their research, students need to write elaborate applications to international agencies for funding. All of these tasks require a circumscribed use of English, albeit a very expert one. In addition, some students are truly motivated by none of these goals at all, but rather by the urgency of passing the course, for their record. In view of the role of motivation in language learning (e.g., Dörnyei, 2001; Spolsky, 1990), the need for English targeted toward immediate and urgent tasks is a crucial factor in pedagogical choices and lesson planning.

Another vital difference is exposure. Most students of English in Israel at all levels have limited exposure to sources of acquisition of English before, during, and after writing instruction time, compared to their counterparts in ESL. Even though Israelis in general are exposed to English through the media and tourism, and in spite of a relatively high standard school program, placement test results of incoming students administered at Bar-Ilan University, for example, tend to show large deficiencies in both reading and writing ability. At all universities, reading comprehension is the focus of English language instruction, as defined by criteria agreed upon by UTELI (the association of University Teachers of English Language in Israel). Therefore, instruction is based on intensive and extensive exposure to the printed written text, for which little or no writing practice is demanded. Outside of the reading comprehension courses, even exposure to texts in English for content courses can be limited, depending on the field, as the use of translations, both professional and amateur, is rampant. Thus, when students enroll in the PhD writing course, not only has their writing experience been scarce, but also the input they have received in English is limited in many cases to extensive reading for their research, sometimes in translation, and to some time spent in an English classroom many years previously. Finally, there is not much hope for the continuation of guided, systematic development in English writing after the course: thus this is a *now-or-never* opportunity, which, unlike in the case in ESL contexts, both students and teachers must grab and make the most of.

These two differences, translated into practice, lead me to build into the syllabus a maximum of motivational strategies and exposure to linguistic input. In the next section I review briefly the principles that underlie the teaching of this course to these particular students.

Underlying Principles of the Teaching of Academic Writing to PhD Candidates

I start from the premise that the learners in this course possess characteristics of many different learner groups, which justifies an eclectic and flexible approach to teaching them: they are first of all acquirers of a foreign language; they are also peripheral participants in an academic discourse community, some of them already among the respected specialists in their field; they are already writers in their own language, possibly very competent, creative ones; and they are also students in higher education, who come with a heritage of past schooling, including English language learning and learning to write, which may be either cumbersome or favorable to their further development. Therefore, the principles that guide my own guidance of them, which are reviewed below, are inspired by, if not faithfully adopted from the many different domains and subdomains of the related fields within which they play these roles and I play mine.

Second Language Acquisition (SLA): English as a foreign language writers are essentially language acquirers. In this connection, the concept of writing research oriented specifically toward SLA (Ortega & Carson, 2010) confirms the need for strongly SLA-oriented writing teaching practice (Matsuda, 2003; Silva et al., 1997). Specifically, the practice described here draws on the following SLA principles, among others: language is acquired both cognitively and affectively (Schuman, 1998; Spolsky, 1990), and through interaction with input (Spada & Lightbown, 2000); the interface of conscious and unconscious knowledge is essential (Schmidt, 1990, 1994); opportunities for learning are sometimes more valuable for acquisition than the planned teaching points (Allwright, 2005; Breen, 1987, 1989); and finally, not every EFL learner needs to aim at native proficiency (Byrnes, 2002; Ringbom, 1998).

Studies in Writing Processes, the Process Approach: the main teaching principle I draw from this subdomain can be generalized as focusing on the writer and the writing, as opposed to focusing on the written text (Raimes, 1991); this is translated mainly into the practice of assigning multiple drafts, and conducting a dialogic process between the writer and the facilitator through feedback and revisions

(Perpignan, 2001). Demonstration of interest in the content, another principle of the process approach, is a prominent feature of the feedback, as is fostering a creative process moving from the generation of ideas to that of a whole text, with later focus on paragraph structure and sentence accuracy, rather than vice-versa. If this emphasis on the process seems to come into conflict with the product-oriented goals and expectations set by the institution or by the students themselves, i.e., being able to produce well-structured, cohesive, *error-free* text on demand in real-life *ad hoc* tasks, I allow this teaching principle to override these expectations. The debate over whether to encourage writing from the sentence first, avoiding error and aiming at accuracy, or from the whole text, with a higher risk of error and postponing attention to accuracy, is still not totally resolved (Matsuda, 2006). But in the case of these students, who already have a most personal agenda for writing, in the form of papers, grant proposals, or PhD summaries and reports, formulating and communicating their in the new language is the most motivating task. Making their passive vocabulary become active and writing cohesively and coherently are most urgent and meaningful immediate goals. Issues of accuracy can then be attended to through focused instruction and teacher feedback.

English for Academic Purposes and Genre Studies: According to the proponents of the social construction of knowledge (Berkenkotter & Huckin, 1995; Myers, 1985), many students in this course have already entered their respective discourse communities in their first language (MacDonald, 1994). However, most of them are merely standing at the threshold of the corresponding international community. To pave their way, a thoughtful examination of the genres in which they are expected to write is used as the foundation of teaching and learning tasks (e.g., Dudley-Evans, 1994; Hopkins & Dudley-Evans, 1988; Johns 1995; Lewin & Fine, 1996; Lewin, Fine, & Young, 2001; Swales, 1990; Swales & Feak, 1994, 2003; Motta-Roth, 1998). Learning points are induced from collective examination of academic texts, no longer exclusively for their research value but for their informational content and its linguistic representation. By examining, discussing, and comparing all together texts from the various disciplines represented in any given mixed group, the students are made aware of the exclusive characteristics of the genres in their respective disciplines, as well as the commonalities across disciplines (Hyland, 2006).

Composition and Rhetoric Studies: Neither of the more contemporary Composition Studies approaches, the expressivist and that of critical/cultural studies (Fulkerson, 2005), has made its way into my classroom. However, I owe a debt to the more traditional rhetorical approach, which is at the basis of the teaching of writing conventions and style. As for conventions of form, I do refer to principles of *good writing* as laid out decades ago by the classical writing experts (e.g., Strunk, 2000), such as "avoid a succession of loose sentences" (p. 25) or "express coordinate ideas in similar form" (p. 26). Even though addressed to writers in English as L1, they still are valuable and useful advice to learners who have reached a degree of fluency and accuracy that can be improved by attention to rhetorical qualities such as elegance, effectiveness, and economy. The last two principles on this list are connected to the way I see my role as facilitator.

Higher Education: It was once believed that the lecturer's role in higher education was to impart knowledge and skills; more recently it has become recognized that higher education is education, in all senses of the word, including the imparting of values and life-long habits of knowledge-seeking and personal improvement (Frye, 2000; Kress, 1995). Adopting this perspective, I have allowed myself to become more involved with the learner as a writer-as-person, in the hope that attention to the person will develop by-products of the writing process other than the writing itself (Katznelson et al., 2001; Perpignan et al, 2007).

At the same time, I am aware that my affiliation with an institution of higher education imbues me with a researcher's responsibility. In my role as teacher-as-researcher I have tried to better understand students' attitudes, behaviors, and performance as a function of the approaches, methods, and materials I use. In this task, I have been greatly assisted by one particular stream of classroom research, exploratory practice (EP). (Allwright, 2003; Allwright & Hanks, 2008; Perpignan, 2003). EP suggests that by searching together for understandings of the components of teaching and learning, and by articulating these understandings to each other, teachers and learners "are developing an enriched *classroom awareness* by which the nature of the experience of classroom life becomes qualitatively enhanced" (Gieve & Miller, 2006, p. 41). This view allows classroom research involving teachers and learners to contribute directly to the learning, and to be sustainable over time.

This rather personal overview of principles and their sources will hopefully help to justify the pedagogical decisions I have made concerning the practices described below.

Practices of the Teaching of Academic Writing for PhD Candidates

The design of the course is based on two interwoven and interdependent strands of activity. One is an individual semester project that consists of completing a written text, ranging from a few introductory paragraphs or a tentative exploration of bibliographical sources to a full-length article for publication. The exact content and length of the project is negotiated with the students at an individual meeting, according to factors such as the stage of advancement they have reached in their PhD research and their immediate practical needs, as well as their English proficiency (Frodeson, 1995). Each student receives individualized instructional feedback on this writing, which is used as the basis for revisions, and which has the potential for carryover to further writing (Hanaoka, 2007). The other strand consists of classroom instruction in the basic components of academic writing through analysis of authentic models, combined with the study of a limited number of grammatical issues chosen to meet the specific needs of these academic writers. This instruction is mostly inductive, through group or individual tasks, with opportunities for discussion and critique. In what follows I will describe briefly some of the ways in which these two organizational principles are translated into teaching and learning practices.

Semester Project: On the very first day of class the students are informed that their semester writing project has already begun: the thinking and planning begins at that very moment, without delay. This is how it is described to the students:

> [It] consists of a piece of writing of approximately 2000 words, which will correspond to one aspect of the students' academic writing needs. The finished project will be the result of careful planning, drafting, writing, revising and editing, with close supervision of the teacher *throughout the semester,* with the exception of the last installment, which will be the result of independent work.

Students submit a tentative outline and are encouraged to start writing immediately. Drafts are returned, revised, and resubmitted throughout the duration of the course, so that the first part written may go through about four revisions, time allowing, but the successive parts fewer and fewer, as the time left in the semester gets shorter.

The feedback is mostly written, since individual meetings, attended on a voluntary basis, are few or non-existent. Rather than review the guidelines for feedback available in the literature, which are often biased either toward error correction when dealing with L2 writing (e.g., Ferris, 2002) or toward content and communication when dealing with L1 writing (e.g., Procter, 2008), I will address two aspects of integrated instructional feedback that guide my practices, its underlying philosophy, and its strategy.

First, the power of written feedback both to facilitate the writing process and to improve learning outcomes cannot be sufficiently emphasized (Lee & Schallert, 2008; Lee, 2008; Hyland & Hyland, 2006). My own research consisting of a "systematic report of learner perspectives on the feedback: their predisposition before reception, their tendencies toward judgments and behaviors upon reception, and their reactions after reception" outlined this strength, when administered in the conditions described (Perpignan, 2001, p. 338). In a case study of seven learners of academic writing in EFL, data showed a great diversity in self-perceived needs and preferences for feedback, as well as in revision strategies. This leads to the conclusion that diversity in teacher response is highly desirable in mode (e.g., phrasing the comment as a replacement, as a restatement, or as a question), in content (e.g., commenting on text structure, on a lexical item, or on verb tense), and in orientation toward revision (e.g., requesting replacement of a discrete item, suggesting consultation in a dictionary or internet resource, or asking the writer to locate independently the missing link in an argument). Even more importantly, the data also showed that understanding each feedback unit was not the most essential road to successful revising and learning. Rather, it is the very existence of a written feedback dialogue, based on mutual understanding of intentions, which seemed to lead to most positive results (Perpignan, 2003).

Therefore, in my practice of feedback-giving, I invest great effort in coming to understandings (e.g., understanding of student intention in writing, understanding of student needs and preferences for feedback, understanding of the student's revision efforts). Reciprocally, I try to make my feedback practices transparent to the students in order to facilitate their interpretations of my responses. This strategy includes revealing my own difficulties in writing the feedback clearly and explicitly, and encouraging students to challenge it when it is unclear or seems unjustified. Several elements are built into the design of the course in order to promote mutual understanding and trust, e.g., periodically asking the students to make special requests for feedback; holding a *handing-in ceremony* for new drafts, during which they are asked to read their drafts with a focus on a specific problem and/or to write questions or special requests; returning papers at an early stage of a lesson, in order to allow class time for questions and requests for clarification.

The second issue in my feedback-providing strategy is connected to the debate over response to content first or to language first. In academic writing in a foreign language the issues of the message and the language are inextricably and sometimes desperately intertwined, as Turner reminds us (2004). I therefore do not see postponement of one issue in favor of the other as an option. In this writing context, the content is very much the domain of someone else, the academic advisor, whose territory I must take care not to invade. The general text structure is equally off-limits for me, since it is established by academic or publication demands. Therefore my priority goes to organization and structure of limited sections of a larger work, and to the writers' use of language. In fact, elements of learner interlanguage, as they are presented in their drafts, constitute an invaluable source of materials for classroom instruction, forming the bridge between individual writing and classroom teaching. They also provide training ground for self-monitoring: learners who are made aware of their weaknesses and who are given tools for revision can be reminded to look out for them themselves, anticipating teacher feedback. Therefore, to postpone dealing with issues of language would mean missing numerous learning and teaching opportunities.

Still, over time, my feedback strategy undergoes changes, with different tactics deployed as the students gain understanding of the issues, and as my understanding of their expectations grows. At the start of the course, first priority is given to comprehensibility of the message, i.e., general coherence and cohesion, both at the whole text and at the sentence level, along with the basic morphological and lexical choices. Later the focus is on syntactic structures: sentence construction and internal cohesion. Finally, attention is given to stylistic improvement and refinement. This is the general strategy employed with a group of average learners. However, at either extreme, the most expert and the least, the individual focus sequence might progress faster or slower, or the order of priorities may be changed. Above all, what I strive to achieve is an approach that strongly integrates feedback and classroom instruction.

Classroom Instruction: Indeed, while students and their teacher are working on their individual projects, the course must go on: there must be substantive teaching points presented according to some organizational principle. In this course, the choice and sequence of teaching points for the group is generated by two main sources of input: published texts and the students' own texts. Published texts can conveniently stand as input for two pedagogical concerns: text organization and elements of grammar. In addition to models of academic texts of general interest brought in by the teacher, students are encouraged to find their own models among their readings in their respective fields, and to analyze them in parts, using a simplified method of genre analysis: this is for them a process of discovery, both of informational content and of the linguistic manifestations of this content (Swales & Feak, 1994, 2003; Weissberg & Buker, 1990). For instance, literature reviews are a rich source of observation of verb tenses, definitions of words often yield relative clauses, and both literature reviews and discussions can reveal various facets of the language of hedging. This process of analysis is the springboard for teaching the production of informational content and its linguistic components simultaneously.

To illustrate, the following is the prototype of a sequence of teaching/learning activities: (1) awareness-raising of informational and linguistic components in authentic environments; (2) description of these informational and linguistic components as they occur in these environments; (3) practice of recognition and use of these elements in non-authentic contexts, including traditional transformation or fill-in exercises; (4) use of these elements in semi-authentic writing tasks; (5) follow-up through awareness-raising in subsequent individual semester project drafts. (Appendix A contains a more detailed description of such a sequence of activities, whose target text is a simple introductory paragraph within the genre of research reporting in the social sciences.)

However, this exercise in discovery based on genre analysis of published texts does not generate material to fill all the learners' linguistic needs. An examination of students' drafts, as the semester progresses, as well as error analysis resulting from experience with previous groups of students, points to additional problem areas that need to be addressed directly. This is where the opportunity for interaction between student writing and course design presents itself again. Being open to this opportunity has led me to design a sequence of teaching/learning events that use learner production as input combined with more traditional sources, and feed into new drafts.

A typical sequence of such events is as follows: (1) while preparing to give feedback, the teacher notices a pattern of irregular usage among several student texts (e.g., relative clauses with relative pronouns); (2) the teacher collects samples of these students' usage, both correct and incorrect, in a file; (3) the teacher draws attention to the item type in the following lesson, during the general feedback session; (4) the students are exposed to collected, typed, and photocopied anonymous samples from their own texts (see Appendix B); (6) the students are called upon collaboratively to improve on the items that need improvement. To complete the cycle, when the subsequent semester project draft is submitted, time is given during the *handing-in ceremony* for proofreading with a focus on this particular item.

One additional ingredient of the course is a limited number of classroom tasks that I like to call *lab experiments* since they are contrived, sometimes collaborative, not always authentic, but experiential and experimental in spirit. They consist of a sequence of activities providing controlled practice. These experiments, while admittedly violating the principle of authenticity in task assignment, nevertheless form a firm basis for further development and expansion and can eventually be incorporated into the students' individual semester project. (See again Appendix A, for a full description of a teaching unit incorporating such a task.) The possibilities for invention of target texts and ways to experiment with them are limited only by a teacher's imagination.

I hope to have shown that the design of this course is based on a movement back and forth between focus on published text and focus on student text, between authenticity and controlled activity, between learner writing and teacher-written feedback. The driving force is student-generated, but the means to achieve the goals are foreseeable and controllable.

Conclusion

The goals of this course are to bring a group of adults who are highly qualified in their respective fields of research to write as members of an international academic community whose language is mainly English, in an EFL context. These learners' limited exposure to the English language and their circumscribed motivation have led to certain compensating practices, such as exclusive use of English in the classroom and focus on authenticity in choice of writing tasks. In view of the extreme diversity of areas of interest, stages of advancement in PhD research, and incoming proficiency levels, there is great concern for seeking definitions of individual writing projects geared to individual interests and for applicability of the learning to real-life demands. In a situation where the proficiency level is sometimes desperately low and the communicative ambitions very high, there is a very wide gap to fill, in which the learner is prone to feeling belittled and inadequate at the start.

One example of the gap filled is found by following up on Eva, whose first piece of writing for the course appears at the head of this chapter. She had not only been limited in writing ability, she had been too inhibited to answer the simple question put to her on the first day of class: "What is your field of study?" She had eventually stuttered, barely audibly, the one word: "Literature." However, by the end of the course, she had not only completed the script of a presentation to be given at an international conference on contemporary art, she had successfully rehearsed its spoken version in front of her peers during our last class together. Others have written for publication, completed ten-page summaries in English to submit along with their dissertations in Hebrew, written proposals for funding for their research, or composed PowerPoint presentations of their original research for the benefit of visitors from abroad.

Eva's success story and student course feedback reports show that the first tangible learner achievement is to have overcome an enormous resistance to writing in English. It is difficult for students who have been at the top of Honors lists all their lives to be obliged to suddenly discover and reveal their ineptitude in this new area of expression; their ideas and their ability to express them are so far apart that it takes enormous courage and a certain degree of humility for that initial leap to be made. The second is the satisfaction that whatever writing project was negotiated by each individual has been completed. In fact, the only condition for passing the course is to submit a last draft, together with all the previous drafts and their comments. Thus, the very act of submitting such a portfolio gives closure to a process of which students can feel proud after all.

If the question about goals is posed as: Do all students who pass the course show the ability to write *error-free* academic texts independently? The short answer, disappointing to some students and staff, is "no," and from what we know about writing development, we can expect that writing will continue to progress only if continued, sustained efforts are made over the years. However, if one can judge by student feedback and by the growing demand for the course, one must believe that other, less measurable, positive outcomes are to be considered in the evaluation of the results.

Substantively, students at all incoming proficiency levels have become acquainted with the specific components of written English, and the relation between form and content in academic English. Particularly outstanding is their acquisition of a sense of academic register. The most-used lexical items in their field and in their particular research, which were passively known from their reading, have become active, as they have used them in context, built them into syntactic structures, spelled and even pronounced them. These are indeed concrete achievements, even though learners are not consistently able to apply all of the knowledge they have acquired.

Procedural outcomes seem even more considerable: students have learned about the writing process, painful and time-consuming as it is, and ultimately rewarding. They have specifically learned about their own writing process, having reflected on the relative usefulness of various tools and procedures, and experimented with them. They have come to recognize and discriminate among their diverse strengths and weaknesses within their use of the English language. They have also learned that collaborative writing (in this case with the teacher) can be fruitful, and they will perhaps be inspired to seek partners in writing for future projects, rather than translators. In addition, however these outcomes were achieved, and to whatever extent they are to be useful to their careers in the end, they have contributed to building a new identity for themselves as participants in an academic community no longer restricted to their national and linguistic borders (Ivanič, 1997), as well as to their own life-long personal development, one of the recognized goals of higher education (Kress, 1995).

Acknowledgments

I am deeply indebted to my many students over the years whose response to the course described here has been a valuable source of information for my teaching, and especially to the anonymous student whose first step in writing in English is quoted at the beginning of this chapter. I also wish to thank Iris Elisha-Primo of Bar-Ilan University for her request for clarification when reading parts of this text, and Bella Rubin of Tel Aviv University for her answer to my questions on the history of academic writing in Israel. I am also grateful to Beverly Lewin of Tel Aviv University for saving this chapter from total gloom.

References

Allwright, D. (2003). Exploratory practice: Rethinking practitioner research in language teaching. *Language Teaching Research, 7*(2), 113–142.

Allwright, D. (2005). From teaching points to learning opportunities and beyond. *TESOL Quarterly, 39*(1), 9–31.

Allwright, D., & Hanks, J. (2008). *The developing language learner.* Hampshire, UK: Palgrave Macmillan

Berkenkotter, C., & Huckin, T. N. (1995). *Genre knowledge in disciplinary communication.* Hillsdale, NJ: Lawrence Erlbaum.

Breen, M. (1987). Learner contributions to task design. In C. Candlin & D. Murphy (Eds.), *Language learning tasks* (pp. 23–46). Englewood Cliffs, N. J.: Prentice Hall.

Breen, M. (1989). The evaluation cycle for language learning tasks. In R. K. Johnson (Ed.), *The second language curriculum* (pp. 187–206). Cambridge: Cambridge University Press.

Byrnes, H. (2002). Toward academic-level foreign language abilities: Reconsidering foundational assumptions, expanding pedagogical options. In B. L. Leaver & B. Shekhtman (Eds.), *Developing professional-level language proficiency* (pp. 34–58). Cambridge: Cambridge University Press.

Dörnyei, Z. (2001). *Teaching and researching motivation.* Harlow, UK: Longman.

Dudley-Evans, T. (1994). Genre-analysis: An approach to text analysis for ESP. In M. Coulthard (Ed.), *Advances in written text analysis* (pp. 219–228). London: Routledge.

Ferris, D. R. (2002). *Treatment of error.* Ann Arbor: University of Michigan Press.

Frodeson, J. (1995). Negotiating the syllabus: A learning-centered interactive approach to ESL graduate writing course design. In D. Belcher & G. Brain (Eds.), *Academic writing in a second language* (pp. 331–350). Norwood, NJ: Ablex.

Frye, R. (2000). *Assessment, accountability and student learning outcomes.* Retrievd from http://www.ac.wwu.edu/~dialogue/issue2.html.

Fulkerson, R. (2005). Composition at the turn of the twenty-first century. *College Composition and Communication, 56*(4), 654–687.

Gieve, S., & Miller, I. K. (2006). *Understanding the language classroom.* Hampshire, UK: Palgrave Macmillan.

Hanaoka, O. (2007). Output, noticing, and learning: An investigation into the role of spontaneous attention to form in a four-stage writing task. *Language Teaching Research, 11*(4), 459–479.

Hopkins, A., & Dudley-Evans, T. (1988). A genre-based investigation of the discussion sections in articles and dissertations. *English for Specific Purposes, 7,* 113–121.

Hyland, K. (2006). Disciplinary differences: Language variation in academic discourses. In K. Hyland & M. Bondi (Eds.), *Academic discourses across disciplines* (pp. 17–45). Bern: Peter Lang.

Hyland, K., & Hyland, F. (2006). Interpersonal aspects of response: Constructing and interpreting teacher written feedback. In K. Hyland & F. Hyland (Eds.), *Feedback in second language writing: Contexts and issues* (pp. 206–224). New York: Cambridge University Press, 2006.

Ivanič, R. (1997). *Writing and identity: The discoursal construction of identity in academic writing.* Amsterdam/Philadelphia: John Benjamins.

Johns, A. (1994). L1 composition theories: implications for developing theories of L2 composition. In B. Kroll (Ed.), *Second language writing: Research insights for the classroom* (pp. 24–36). New York: Cambridge University Press.

Johns, A. (1995). Teaching classroom and authentic genres: Initiating students into academic cultures and discourses. In D. Belcher & G. Brain (Eds.), *Academic writing in a second language* (pp. 277–291). Norwood, NJ: Ablex.

Katznelson, H., Perpignan, H., & Rubin, B. (2001). What develops *along with* the development of second language writing? Exploring the by-products. *Journal of Second Language Writing, 10,* 141–159.

Kress, G. (1995). *Writing the future: English and the making of a culture of innovation.* Sheffield, England: National Association for the Teaching of English. Publishing Company.

Lee, G., & Schallert, D. L. (2008). Meeting in the margins: Effects of the teacher-student relationship on revision processes of EFL college students taking a composition course. *Journal of Second Language Writing, 17,* 165–182.

Lee, I. (2008). Student reactions to teacher feedback in two Hong Kong secondary classrooms. *Journal of Second Language Writing, 17,* 144–164.

Lewin, B., & Fine, J. (1996). The writing of research texts: Genre analysis and its applications. In G. Rijlaarsdam, H. van den Berg, & M. Couzijn

(Eds.), *Theories, models and methodology in writing research* (pp. 423–443). Amsterdam: Amsterdam University Press.

Lewin, B. A., Fine, J., & Young, L. (2001). *Expository discourse: A genre-based approach to social science research texts.* London and New York: Continuum.

MacDonald, S. P. (1994). *Professional academic writing in the humanities and social sciences.* Carbondale: Southern Illinois University Press.

Manchón, R. M. & de Haan, P. (2008). Writing in foreign language contexts: An introduction. *Journal of Second Language Writing, 17,* 1–6.

Matsuda, P. K. (2003). Second language writing in the twentieth century: A situated historical perspective. In B. Kroll (Ed.), *Exploring the dynamics of second language writing* (pp. 15–34). Cambridg: Cambridge University Press.

Matsuda, P. K. (2006). Second-language writing in the twentieth century: A situated historical perspective. In P. K. Matsuda, M. Cox, J. Jordan, & C. Ortmeier-Hooper (Eds.), *Second-language writing in the composition classroom: A critical sourcebook* (pp. 14–30). Boston, MA: Bedford/St. Martin's.

Motta-Roth, D. (1998). Discourse analysis and academic book reviews: A study of text and disciplinary cultures. In I. Fortanet, S. Posteguillo, J. C. Palmer, & J. F. Coll (Eds.), *Genre studies in English for academic purposes,* (pp. 29–58). Castelló de la Plana: Publicacions de la Universitat Jaume.

Myers, G. (1985). Texts as knowledge claims: The social construction of two biology articles. *Social Studies of Science, 15,* 593–63.

Ortega, L., & Carson, J. (2010). Multicompetence, social context, and L2 writing research praxis. In T. Silva & P. K. Matsuda (Eds.), *Practicing theory in second language writing* (pp. 48-71). Mahwah, NJ: Lawrence Erlbaum.

Perpignan, H. (2001). Teacher written feedback to language learners: Promoting a dialogue for understanding. Unpublished doctoral dissertation. Department of Linguistics and Modern English Language, Lancaster University.

Perpignan, H. (2003). Exploring the writing feedback dialogue: a research, learning and teaching practice. *Journal of English Teaching Research, 7*(2), 259–276.

Perpignan, H., Rubin, B., & Katznelson, H. (2007): "By-products": The added value of academic writing instruction for higher education. *Journal of English for Academic Purposes. 6,* 163–181.

Procter, M. (2008). Responding to student papers effectively and efficiently. Retrieved from http://www.utoronto.ca/writing/comm.html.

Raimes, A. (1991). Out of the woods: Emerging traditions in the teaching of writing. *TESOL Quarterly, 25*(3), 407–430.

Ringbom, H. (1998). Near-native proficiency in writing. In D. Albrechtsen, B. Henriksen, I. M. Mees, & E. Poulsen (Eds.), *Perspectives on foreign and second language pedagogy* (pp. 149–159). Gylling, Denmark: Odensee University Press.

Schmidt, R. (1990). The role of consciousness in second language acquisition. *Applied Linguistics, 11*(2), 129–158.

Schmidt, R. (1994). Deconstructing consciousness in search of useful definitions for applied linguistics. *AILA Review, 11,* 11-26.

Schuman, J. H. (1998). The neurobiology of affect in learning. *Language Learning Supplement* (pp. 237–255). University of Michigan: Blackwell Publishers.

Silva, T. (1993). Toward an understanding of the distinct nature of L2 writing: The ESL research and its implications. *TESOL Quarterly, 27*(4), 657–675.

Silva,T., Leki, I., & Carson, J. (1997). Broadening the perspective of mainstream Composition Studies, some thoughts from the disciplinary margins. *Written Communication, 14,* 398–428.

Spada, N., & Lightbown, P. M. (2000). *How languages are learned* (3rd ed.). Oxford: Oxford University Press.

Spolsky, B. (1990). *Conditions for second language learning.* Oxford: Oxford University Press.

Strunk Jr., W. (2000) *The elements of style* (4th ed.). New York: Longman.

Swales, J. (1990). *Genre analysis. English in academic and research settings.* Cambridge: Cambridge University Press.

Swales, J. M., & Feak, C. B. (1994). *Academic writing for graduate students: A course for nonnative speakers of English.* Ann Arbor: University of Michigan Press.

Swales, J. M., & Feak, C. B. (2003). *English in today's research world: A writing guide.* Ann Arbor: University of Michigan Press.

Turner, J. (2004). Language as academic purpose. *Journal of English for Academic Purposes, 3,* 95–109.

Weissberg, R., & Buker, S. (1990). *Writing up research: Experimental report writing for students of English.* Englewood Cliffs, NJ: Prentice Hall Regents.

Zamel, V. (1995). Strangers in academia: The experiences of faculty and ESL students across the curriculum. *College Composition and Communication, 46*(4), 506–521.

Zuckerman, T., & Rubin, B. (2007). Academic writing in Israel: Birth and development. Paper presented at the *Historical Roots of National Writing Cultures Symposium* at the 4th Biennial Conference of the European Association for the Teaching of Academic Writing (EATAW), Ruhr University Bochum, June 29—July 2, Bochum, Germany.

Appendix A

1. Elicit from students the informational components of an introduction to a research article.

2. Raise the students' awareness of informational content (moves) and linguistic markers in introductions of published texts chosen as models by the teacher. Awareness is raised by asking questions, such as "What information is given?" and "What linguistic (lexical and grammatical) clues tell you what kind of information it is?"

3. Show a graphic model of the information in an introduction (e.g., the Weissberg & Buker [1990] 5five-move model).

4. Elicit from students comparable information yielded by the articles from their respective field that they have brought to class; discuss differences and similarities within and across disciplines, obligatory and non-obligatory moves, sequence and length of moves.

5. During the same process, encourage students to make note of linguistic markers of different moves, grammatical and graphic features (such as verb tense and dates) as well as typical lexical items for each move.

6. Present a series of decontextualized sentences asking students to identify the moves according to content, linguistic and lexical, and discuss the ambiguities.

7. Assign and guide students through a five-sentence sequence of information for an introduction to their own research; they are to make use of all the previous material collected, informational and linguistic, focusing on each information unit and with no attention to cohesiveness yet.

8. Assign an expansion of this five-sentence sequence, including cohesion devices.

The outcome of this activity is a prototype of an introduction to their own research, which is not an authentic text, but the basis for one, which they can build into their project.

Appendix B

Relative clauses

1. They all worked in an era where some of the great events of our time took place.
2. There are many ways in which one can define the term *Jewish Identity*.
3. I will focus on the second option, by that I will examine the way A., B., and T. view their own national identity.
4. The case will stay open until new information can shed new light on the case, and then another estimation will be performed.
5. Effective and advanced management in the health system is a critical way to save a life more than advanced technology, which has the ability to give hospitals, organization of health maintenance and medical clinic autonomy.
6. A child who uses the net all over the world is exposed to violence and aggressiveness against people. This child's world is still shaping and forming.
7. The conceptualization of internal control as a process has roots in the question has so far been incompletely answered in relation to employees.

The different cases of successful use, avoidance of use, and faulty use are discussed in pairs and improvements are solicited. Improvements are to be restricted to the topic of relative clause structure and use of relative pronouns only.

9 Foreign Language Writing Instruction: A Principled Eclectic Approach in Taiwan

Hui-Tzu Min

INTRODUCTION

There has been a surge in interest in EFL writing recently, given the ever-increasing pressure to publish internationally among graduate students and academics as well as the universal desire to participate in commerce in the globalized world (Leki, 2002). In response to this growing demand on writing in English, both academically and professionally, EFL writing instructors have embarked on a search for the most efficient and effective approach to enhancing student writing. Although few still employed a single approach (Liu, 2008), most proposed a balanced or integrated EFL writing pedagogy, combining the process and genre approaches to form the process genre approach (Deng, 2007; Gao, 2007; Kim & Kim, 2005). Although the synthesis of process and genre approaches reflects EFL writing instructors' careful reflection on the inadequacy of current writing pedagogies in various local EFL contexts, it lacks a critical examination of English language literacy practices in the West that underpin the mainstream writing pedagogies. In addition, such a synergic approach fails to foreground local writing pedagogies by only incorporating ideas from the English center countries into local contexts. Given the foregoing critique, I propose a principled eclectic approach to EFL writing pedagogy that both adapts imported mainstream instructional approaches to local needs and highlights creations of local practices. Moreover, this approach features a critical reflection on and evaluation of mainstream writing practices and pedagogies. This principled eclectic approach to EFL writing is premised on the three parameters of Kumaravadivelu's macrostrategic framework of post-method pedagogy: particularity, practicality, and possibility (Kumaravadivelu, 2006, p. 69). In what follows, I briefly outline the current development of the post-method era in English language teaching (ELT) and the post-process movement (Atkinson, 2003, Casanave, 2003; Kent, 1999; Matsuda, 2003; Trimbur, 1994) in second language writing instruction. Then I discuss the theoretical framework of the proposed principled eclectic approach to teaching EFL writing. Finally, I illustrate how I use this principled eclectic approach to teaching essay writing to a group of sophomore English majors of Foreign Languages and Literature Department at a comprehensive university in Taiwan.

Principled Eclecticism in Post-Method Pedagogy

In a review article on TESOL methods, Kumaravadivelu (2006) aptly points out three major changes in English language teaching to non-native speakers, "from communicative language teaching to task-based language teaching, from method-based pedagogy to postmethod [sic] pedagogy, and from systemic discovery to critical discourse" (p. 60). Underlying these shifts is a general recognition among non-native ELT teachers that subscribing to any single centered-based method or approach fails to completely address local exigencies, given that reproduction of centered-based pedagogy can not create "the cultural forms and interested knowledge that give meaning to the lived experiences of teachers and learners" (p. 70). A call for a pluralistic and principled eclectic approach (Larsen-Freeman, 2000) is thus needed.

Principled eclecticism is the "desirable, coherent, and pluralistic" approach that entails diverse learning activities depending on learner needs (Mellow, 2002). It has been used interchangeably with "disciplined eclecticism" (Rodgers, 2001, p. 4), "informed eclecticism" (Larsen-Freeman, 2000), and "enlightened eclecticism" (Brown, 1994, p. 74), among other names. Rodgers (2001) predicts that this synergistic approach is "likely to shape the teaching of second languages in the next decades of the new millennium" (p. 4). Reid (2001) also echoes this viewpoint when discussing L2 writing pedagogy. Given that most L2 writing instructional approaches address only a certain aspect of L2/EFL writing (e.g., language, text, composing skills, reader expectations), commitment to any single approach can lead to a skewed perspective on the issues encountered by ESL/EFL students (Silva, 1990). Since "one size does not fit all, the use of a variety of approaches that permits teachers to extend their repertoire" becomes essential (Reid, 2001, p. 32).

Although Reid points out that principled eclecticism is essential to teaching second/foreign language writing to speakers of other languages, recent literature on second language writing approaches does not appear to uniformly reflect this conceptualization. As revealed in a special issue of the *Journal of Second Language Writing* on L2 writing in the post-process era (2003), scholarly opinions diverge in the interpretation of an upcoming post-process era. Some construe this era as a herald of genre approach, a social turn from the process approach (Hyland, 2003b), others deem this emerging paradigm as a refusal of "the dominance of process at the expense of other aspects of writing and writing instruction" (Matsuda, 2003, pp. 78–79). Still others (Casanave, 2003; Leki, 2003) consider it an optimal time to critique the mainstream second language writing pedagogy.

While there are still debates and controversies over the real meaning of a post-process approach in the post-process movement, many non-native EFL writing instructors in Asian countries have followed Reid's advice by advocating an eclectic approach. Many of them have combined practices from process and genre approaches to form a process genre approach (Gao, 2007; Kim & Kim, 2005) or "process-based approach imbued with product and genre based features" (Deng, 2007, p. 16). Although this synergistic approach reflects EFL writing instructors' attempt to best support effective EFL student writing, it lacks a scrutiny of the underlying assumptions of Anglophone written communication and their accompanying practices. Neither does this principled eclectic approach reflect genuine local practices. At its best, it is a combination or adaptation of mainstream L2 writing approaches, which does not include any contingent responsive approach when those prefabricated combinations and adaptations fail our students in class.

Principles of Macrostrategic Framework

Given the diverse needs of local EFL students that cannot be fully satisfied by any single centered-based pedagogy, Kumaravadivelu (1992) thus proposes that non-native ELT teachers need to equip themselves with "situation-specific ideas within a general framework" that is aligned with "current pedagogical and theoretical knowledge" (p. 41). This framework, premised on principles of particularity, practicality, and possibility, encompasses ten macrostrategies: "maximize learning opportunities, facilitate negotiated interaction, minimize perceptual mismatches, activate intuitive heuristics, foster language awareness, contextualize linguistic input, integrate language skills, promote learner autonomy, ensure social relevance, and raise cultural consciousness" (Kumaravadivelu, 2006, p. 69).

Although Kumaravadivelu's macrostrategic framework deals with English language teaching in general, it can apply to EFL writing pedagogy as well. Drawing on the three guiding principles—particularity, practicality, possibility—of his macrostrategic framework (2006, p. 69), I propose a principled eclectic pedagogy to EFL writing instruction. This principled eclectic pedagogy not only strikes a balance among various mainstream L2 writing approaches (e.g., product, process, genre, critical), but also between imported mainstream approaches and local modifications "based on a true understanding of local linguistic, social, cultural, and political particularities" (Kumaravadivelu, 2006, p. 69). It also seeks to foreground local practices, encouraging "a personal theory of practice" (Kumaravadivelu, 2003, p. 544) among local EFL writing instructors whose theorized practices can not only validate but also inform mainstream writing teaching theory. In other words, the principle of practicality aims to challenge the stereotypical role relationship between mainstream knowledge-transmitting theorizers and local knowledge-receiving practitioners. Finally, this principled eclectic EFL writing pedagogy seeks to cultivate among EFL students both a critical and pragmatic perspective on Anglophone writing practices and conventions and their own so they can make informed choices in their writing that reflect who they are, and who they want to be (the principle of possibility). In the remainder of this chapter, I showcase how I apply this principled eclectic approach to teaching essay writing in an EFL writing class in Taiwan.

Particularity

The principle of particularity emphasizes an active understanding of local exigencies, an area in which non-native writing instructors of English assume more authority than native speakers of English. In what follows is a description of a local secondary school context where English is learned as a foreign language—the specific writing context where I teach—students' needs analysis, and my personal beliefs in EFL writing.

An Overview of Local Exigency. English is deemed a prestigious foreign language in Taiwan, given the country's heavy reliance on foreign trade. Having recognized the increasing importance of English in global business transactions, high-tech industry, and higher education, the Taiwanese Ministry of Education has mandated that the original junior English language education be extended to middle graders at the elementary school since 2005 in the hope that students will gain a competitive advantage due to this early head start. Under the foregoing mandate, students have to study English for at least seven years (an average of ninety minutes per week for four years in elementary school, an average of 150–200 minutes per week for three years in junior high school). For those who attend senior high school, they continue learning English for another three years (an average of 200–250 minutes per week).

The focus of the English language class in elementary and secondary schools is principally on vocabulary and grammar instruction, with reading the main skill being taught and tested, followed by speaking and listening skills. Writing is rarely taught except for grammar practice in sentence construction in junior high and sentence combination and translation exercises in senior high school, despite the respective writing goals promulgated by the Ministry of Education in its Curriculum Guidelines (Ministry of Education, 2006; 2008) to cultivate junior high school students' ability to compose short paragraphs on prompts and to develop senior high school students' capability to write coherent essays on various topics in different genres without prompts.

It is not until the second year of senior high that most English teachers start preparing students for writing, given the English writing composition test on the university entrance examinations in the following year. Yet many of these English teachers, untrained as EFL writers and writing instructors, simply "design, assign, and evaluate [student] writing" (Reid, 1993, p. 23). Their assessment mostly focuses on language choice and grammar accuracy and rarely on idea development and organization. With such language-based writing training, it is not uncommon that most Taiwanese students equate writing in English with sentence construction, combination, and translation. To them, writing in English is a combination of all three exercises beyond the sentence level. Anglophone writing conventions and audience expectations, idea development and organization, as well as revising seldom occur to them because they are not explicitly taught about these notions.

Writing Curriculum and Student Profile of the Study. The English writing courses I offered for the last six years were to English majors in the Department of Foreign Languages and Literature (FLLD) at the second largest comprehensive university in Taiwan. Students of FLLD are required to take three hours of writing each semester for three consecutive years. Upon entering FLLD, they are assigned to one of the four concurrent writing sessions of writing I, with each class size less than twenty students. At the beginning of their second school year, they can choose a writing section of writing III taught by an instructor they like.

Unlike its counterparts in most North American and European universities, FLLD does not have explicit departmental curricular requirements for the writing courses, which gives whoever teaches writing (from I to VI) absolute freedom to design their own syllabus. Facing such a constraint-free teaching environment, I did not feel much relief but more responsibility when I was first assigned to teach writing III and IV. As I embarked on outlining the course objectives, I principally considered two criteria: what students want to learn and what I know about L2 writing. With regard to the first criterion, I followed Hyland's advice by performing some "present situation analysis" (Hyland, 2007, p. 155). I conducted an informal survey during the first class, asking students to tell me what they learned during the previous semester and what they expected to learn in my class. The following four excerpts provided me with knowledge of the varied writing experiences students had during the previous semester:

> Student A: The professor taught us how to write a procedure paragraph. We had to explain how to do something.
> Student B: The professor taught us to write letters to ask for application materials for graduate programs. She also asked us to present what we received from the university once we got their replies.

Student C: The professor taught us how to write beautiful sentences in English. She said that "diction" is very important. She also taught us how to combine short sentences into long ones.

Student D: The teacher asked us to keep journals, and she always encouraged me with compliments. But I want to improve my grammar.

Researchers, when examining EFL writers, tend to perceive them as a homogeneous group because they share the same culture and thus receive the same kind of writing training (e.g., Nelson & Carson, 2006). Yet the previous student responses reveal very little homogeneity, if not heterogeneity, with respect to their writing experiences.

Regarding their expectations of the writing class, most aspired to improve their writing ability and some desired to better their grammar. None had specific ideas of what they really wanted to learn, which is not surprising due to their much less experience in writing than in other skills in their secondary schools. Their responses to the question of future career, however, gave me more directions on designing my course. Most replied that they would continue further studies in graduate school or become English teachers at the secondary level. Given this information, I decided to introduce essay writing to them in writing III and source writing in writing IV. In writing III, students mainly draw on their personal experiences and knowledge to compose essays. In writing IV, they are required to cite credible sources to support their opinions and arguments.

While I made this decision on essay and source writing mostly on pragmatic and instrumental grounds due to student career aspirations, it is also a reflection of my previous training and subjective preconceptions of these two types of writing as a precursor to academic writing in higher educational context. I believe teaching students essay and source writing and providing with them opportunities to practice in class can both meet the immediate needs of these English majors, who are required to write term papers for their linguistics and literature courses in their third year, and better prepare them for their further studies and future careers. Secondary school English teachers in Taiwan, as mandated by the Curriculum Guidelines provided by the Ministry of Education (2006, 2008), are responsible for assisting their students in paragraph and short essay writing.

Teacher's Belief and Training. In addition to addressing student needs, I also follow Casanave's advice (2004, pp. 10–21) by examining my own beliefs and former academic training when planning course objectives and deciding on the principled eclectic pedagogy to teaching writing. Having learned to write in English for more than two decades, and given my constant wrestling with appropriate expressions and correct grammar to convey my thoughts, I deeply believe that learning to write in English is a developmental process requiring mastery of the English language. My academic training, on the other hand, helps me understand that learning to write in English entails knowledge of and skills in cognitive strategies and sociocultural conventions. For example, writers employ certain cognitive strategies that transcend language (Flower & Haynes, 1981) during the composing process to discover, construct, express, and share personal meanings (Zamel, 1976, 1980). I also realize distinctive features in the writing of ESL writers (Silva, 1993) and possible contributory sources, including developmental factors, L2 proficiency (Mohan & Lo, 1985), and rhetoric conventions in students' L1 writing (Connor, 1996; Hinds, 1987, 1990).

The foregoing writing experience and academic training cement my belief that writing in English is a linguistic, cognitive, expressive, social, cultural, and developmental process, necessitating a multidimensional approach (Kucer & Silva, 2006) to achieve the following three objectives:

Students will understand that

1. Effective written communication takes various lengths of time, depending on their current level of English language proficiency (linguistic, developmental).

2. Writing is a recursive process wherein writers plan, compose, and revise constantly (cognitive).

3. They will compose reader-based prose to meet the expectations of a certain discourse community (sociocultural) and write about their reflections on this learning process in journals (expressive).

The foregoing objectives obviously defy the employment of any single mainstream writing instruction approach. Silva (1990) cautions against staunch support on the one hand, or, on the other, premature abandonment of any mainstream approach without critical evaluation and deliberation (p. 18). Others challenge the adequacy and appropriateness of centered-based pedagogy (Casanave, 2004; Kumaravadivelu, 2006; Leki, 2002) and advise EFL writing teachers to exercise their "sense of plausibility" (Prabhu, 1990, p. 172) to devise a writing pedagogy that fits local exigencies. Bearing in mind their advice, I choose to employ a "pluralistic" perspective (Larsen-Freeman, 2000, p. 182) on L2 writing pedagogy. Relying on my own "sense of plausibility" and "personal conceptualization of how teaching leads to desired learning" (Prabhu, 1990, p. 172), I select and adapt teaching techniques from available mainstream writing approaches in the proactive stage (before students start to compose their drafts) and devise a proceduralized instruction to accommodate student needs in the reactive stage (during their composing process), practicing "principled eclecticism" to achieve the foregoing curriculum goals.

Practicality (Personal Theory of Practice)

This principled eclectic pedagogy not only integrates various mainstream L2 writing approaches (e.g., product, process, genre, critical) but also foregrounds local pedagogy, which remedies the situation where mainstream approaches fail to make sense to students (i.e., proceduralized instruction). The basic purpose of utilizing techniques from various mainstream writing approaches is to equip students with the prerequisite knowledge of the sociocultural conventions of the discourse community in Anglophone countries so that they can successfully participate in the academic writing community during their undergraduate and graduate studies and possess the qualifications for their future English language teaching career at the secondary school level. These techniques, mainly used in the proactive stage of writing instruction, involve a wide array of reading and writing activities from interactive reading approaches such as reading like an observant writer, and writing like a reflective reader, to current-traditional approaches such as introducing topic sentences (thesis statements), to analysis of the pragmatic functions of some rhetorical moves in the genre approach.

The creation of a proceduralized instruction in the reactive stage of writing instruction involves addressing student learning difficulty by offering them step-by-step instruction on how to incorporate their newly acquired declarative genre knowledge into their own writing. This tailor-made instruction is drawn on an understanding of the underlying causes of student problems revealed in their journals and teacher-student conferences.

To some, the integration of techniques from mainstream pedagogies appears to perpetuate established power hierarchies of the dominant culture of the academic discourse community. As a foreign language writer and writing teacher, I view this practice as "a hegemonic diffusion of the communication style judged desirable in the globalized world, rather than a direct imposition of someone else's language" (Cameron, 2002, in Kubota & Shi, 2005, p. 102). Like the Japanese teacher in Cumming's study (2003, p. 87), I consider learning and teaching the written communicative practices in the academic discourse community mainly from a pragmatic perspective, as a way to get my students to the wider world. I wish my own writing instructors had explicitly taught me the rhetorical conventions in my undergraduate study so that I could have spent less time struggling with them and more time exploiting and critiquing them. I concur with Williams (2005, p.15) that part of a writing teacher's responsibility is to "introduce students to the practical reality of the discourse community" they aspire to join, to initiate them into the Anglophone discourse community so that they do not spend an unduly lengthy period of time attempting to approximate prestigious forms without success (Johns, 1997).

Although I am of the opinion EFL writing teachers should explicitly apprentice their students into the Anglophone discourse community, I do not suggest EFL writers and students need to conform to patterns of communication of that discourse community after they have mastered the conventionalized modes. After reaching "a sufficient level of proficiency in academic discourse" (Santos, 2001, p. 184), they can judiciously incorporate their L1 writing strategies into their L2 writing to create a "third discursive discourse" (Matsuda et al., 2003; Kramsh, 2000; Li, 1999). But such a "transposition" (Matsuda et al., 2003, p. 159) must be premised on knowledge and mastery of the literacy practices of the Anglophone discourse community. Like Bakhtin's apt argument, EFL writers need to "command the genres they use before they can exploit them" (1986, p. 80, cited in Hyland, 2003b, p. 25). Until then, few readers in that discourse community would heed a critical EFL outsider's linguistically unsophisticated and rhetorically unconventional messages.

In what follows, I highlight some modified teaching techniques of mainstream writing pedagogies in the proactive stage and exemplify the proceduralized instruction with discussion of the rhetorical structure of the thesis statement in the reactive stage. I also discuss students' initial challenge to this rhetorical structure, and evaluate its pragmatic function and subsequent conditional acceptance to illustrate how students decide to accommodate it in the process of learning to become part of the Anglophone discourse community.

The Writing Class

As previously stated, the writing class is for second year English majors, the focus of which is on essay and source writing. I use *Mosaic One: A Content-Based Writing Book* (Blass & Pike-Baky, 2000), given its balanced coverage of reading and writing, process and product, ideas and language, writers and readers, which perfectly matches the curriculum goals and my pluralistic view of writing approaches. Through the past few years, I have adopted a modified "writing cycle" (Tsui & Ng, 2000) in class. The whole cycle is sequenced as follows (Figure 1):

Reading (Proactive Stage)
↓
Brainstorming (ideas for writing)
↓
First draft
↓
Peer review
↓
Second draft
↓
Oral presentation and Peer response
↓
Teacher-student conference on the second draft (Reactive Stage)
↓
Third draft

↓

Teacher comments (only written feedback) on the third draft

↓

Final draft

Figure 1: The writing cycle.

Proactive Stage. Each writing class starts with reading. I explicitly explain the four major purposes of reading assignments—language learning, reading comprehension, idea generation, and rhetorical analysis—to students before they begin to compose (Kroll, 1993). Close reading for language learning and general reading comprehension may seem unnecessary for and irrelevant to some native speakers, but is necessary for most ESL/EFL student writers who are in the process of acquiring the linguistic and content schema that experienced native writers expect them to have. Without first knowing the kind of language experienced writers use to convey ideas, it is less likely that EFL students can fully comprehend the author's messages or express similar ideas in their own writing, given the close relationship between reading and writing (Kroll, 1993). Despite the importance of reading for acquiring language and comprehending content, these two purposes are only means to the latter two ends—idea generation and rhetorical analysis—with which my students are not familiar. I always contextualize the purpose of including reading in the writing task students are going to perform. The following instruction is an illustration of this contextualization:

> You are to write about certain aspects of a new culture that are challenging/interesting to you and explain why (or some aspects of Taiwanese culture that might be challenging/interesting to foreigners). The reading assignment will give you some ideas. You are supposed to talk about what you have learned from this reading in class. Then we will discuss and analyze how the writer informed his friend of his new challenges.

When we meet the following week, I lead the students to read rhetorically by drawing their attention to "particular stylistic choices, grammatical features, methods of development" (Kroll, 1991, p. 254) to help them grasp the author's plan and purpose. An illustration is presented as follows. The letter is a reading piece from *Mosaic I: A Content-Based Writing Book* (Blass & Pike-Baky, 2000).

September 30

Dear Alex,

Thanks for your card. Sorry I haven't written sooner. I've spent all my free time wandering around Tokyo and learning about Japanese customs. It is very interesting here because everything is so different.

You asked me to write about some of the things I've noticed that are new to me. The most striking thing is the huge crowds. There are many, many people everywhere, but everyone is very orderly and polite. People at home would not be so orderly in such crowds. Another new thing for me is the way restaurants display food in restaurant windows. They arrange it beautifully on lacquer trays in simple, clean designs. The Japanese seem to value the appearance of food more than the taste. In my opinion, the sushi here is more delicious than at home. (But the wasabi was so strong I couldn't eat it!)

There are a few problems that I've had since I arrived. Everything is written in Japanese, and even though your mother taught me a few Japanese characters before I left, I can't read a thing. Since I can't read signs, it is difficult to travel around. Most people are friendly, but they can't help me much because they don't speak English. Another problem is the Japanese public restrooms. Nobody warned me that the toilets are not like our Western ones-That has been very hard to adjust to!

Well, that's about all for now. I hope I'll understand more Japanese when I write you next time. I think

things will get easier when I start teaching. Please
give my regards to your family. Write back soon.

    Take care,
    David

In order to encourage students to read like a writer, I prompt them to discuss whether David is going to talk about positive or negative differences when they finish the first paragraph. To introduce the notion of cohesion, I ask students to attend to the use of "but" in the second paragraph and its function. Then I lead them to discuss David's assumptions about huge crowds and possible sources of such assumptions. With regard to the notion of tone, I alert students to David's use of hedging to express his uncertainty and discuss with them other expressions that can denote the same meaning. When reading the third paragraph, we discuss its connection to the previous paragraph and relevance to the main idea in the letter. We also talk about the notion of audience when reading the description of Japanese public restrooms and discuss what information David would have included in the letter had he written to a person who has never been to Japan.

After discussing the previous questions, I outline the development and organization of the author's ideas in Figure 2. This information becomes the basis for writing, discussion, and follow-up questions. For example, we discuss aspects other than people's manner, food, languages, and toilets that can become interesting topics to readers, such as transportation and weather. In the meantime, I also review notions students learned in the previous year, such as topic sentence and paragraph, and demonstrate how to turn a simple paragraph into an essay.

The previous analysis is similar to the second stage of Feez's (1998, p. 28) teaching-learning cycle—modeling and deconstructing the text, the purpose of which is to model to students how to become observant readers who "read like a writer in order to write like a writer" (Smith, 1983, p. 562). Most Taiwanese students do not have this kind of reading for writing experience because they usually read for grammatical analysis of particular sentence structures. As pointed out by proponents of genre research (Feez, 1998; Hyland, 2007), we need to engage our students in this kind of conscious reading to prompt them to notice ways of reading that they might not otherwise engage in so that they can deliberately practice this skill on their own whenever

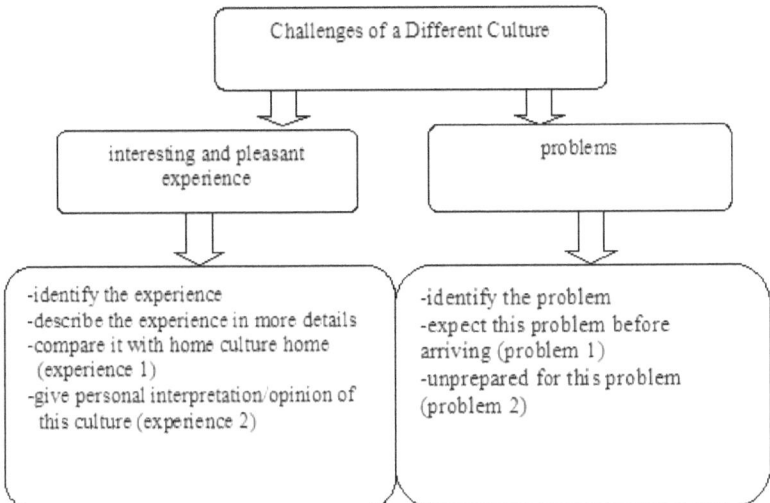

Figure 2: Analysis of idea development.

they compose, and ultimately turn this explicit knowledge into implicit knowledge and be able to draw on it automatically.

Students find such an approach to reading novel, which visually helps them understand that ideas in a paragraph should be organized, and requires them to consider their audience when explaining their ideas. The following is a student's reflection on this approach in her first journal entry (grammar and word choice are original):

> Well, I never know that a paragraph can be analyzed in such way. In the past, I always writed down what I thought immediately and almost never thought about to arrange a paragraph. For me, writed down a paragraph is simple. But after taking this course, I knew that a paragraph would contain many ideas, but this ideas must be organized! Now this is hard to me for I didn't used to organize a paragraph well although I have learn it in my first year. . . .

Through a semester's practice, she gradually adapts to the idea of organization, as disclosed in her last journal entry (grammar and word choice are original), in this class, I have learned about how to organize a article. I am getting used to focus on the topic and what I am going to say.

Of course, "learning" and "getting used to" the idea of paragraph organization do not guarantee flawless writing because possessing rhetorical knowledge (knowing what) and using that knowledge (knowing how) are different things. Students may have the declarative knowledge but lack the procedural knowledge. Through repeated teacher demonstration and explanation, most students understand the importance of presenting a thesis statement but experience difficulty when applying this knowledge to their own writing, as revealed in most students' verbal response, "Oh," to my enquiry about the whereabouts of their thesis statement. In nowhere is the lack of procedural knowledge more evident than in Miguel's confession during a student-teacher conference, "I knew that you would ask me about it but I did not know how to come up with one."

Reactive Stage. The fact that most students found stating their main ideas in the form of a sentence difficult is understandable given that they are not accustomed to the requirement of putting their main points in a "preview statement that forecasts the content and organization of the supporting details" (Kubota & Shi, 2005, p. 97), although they know they are supposed to express *zhongxinsixiang* (a central idea) clearly and in an organized way. The realization of students' lack of procedural knowledge prompts me to take reactive actions by employing a proceduralized instruction involving three intervention techniques—checking students' declarative knowledge, asking students to reread their essays and identify main ideas, and providing templates, if necessary.

When students experience problems with generating a thesis statement, I first ensure that they have the declarative knowledge by asking them the essential components of a thesis statement, to which most would reply "topic and main ideas." After ascertaining their declarative knowledge, I ask them to reread their essays and if possible, identify the main ideas in their own writing. Writing on the topic "New Culture," a student named Dennis discusses why traffic in the city where the university is located (Tainan) is worse than that in his hometown (Taipei). His thesis statement does not clearly indicate his purpose and the second main idea is vague. During our individual teacher-student conference, I asked him to reread his essay and discuss with me his intention (grammar and word choice are original).

2ⁿᵈ draft

The traffic in Tainan is worse than that in Taipei. I came to Tainan last summer and I found the intersections in Tainan are more confusing than those in Taipei. Most of the drivers and riders don't obey the traffic rules. For example, they usually run through the red light, drive or ride after driving, and so on. What stroke me most was that I've once seen a drunken driver lost his life when he drove through a red light and collide with a bus. Actually, the traffic accident in Tainan is more usual than that in Taipei because there are too many law-breakers here. Maybe the police should perform the traffic rules more strictly. Maybe the government should improve the problem of routing vehicular traffic into and out of Tainan. And more importantly, we should remind ourselves of obeying the traffic rules everywhere.

After rereading his own writing, Dennis expressed that his topic was traffic in Tainan, and the main idea was "worse." When I probed whether his purpose was mainly to describe the worse traffic situation in Tainan, explain why Tainan's traffic was worse, or provide solutions to the traffic situation in Tainan, he realized his intention was the middle. Then we discussed possible ways to make his intention more explicit by using a more precise thesis statement.

During our discussion, I also asked him to reflect on the main ideas. Dennis expressed that the third sentence was the first main idea because he had a lot to talk about, including a terrifying personal experience of witnessing a car accident. But when I asked him what he meant by "the intersections in Tainan are more confusing those in Taipei" in this draft, and the problem of the incurableness "of routing vehicular traffic into and out of any large city" he mentioned in his first draft, he explained in Mandarin how the roundabouts and complicated traffic signs confused him. I encouraged him to expand discussion on this idea because it could be another contributing factor to the worse traffic situation in Tainan. The following is the third draft he turned in a week later (grammar and word choice are original):

3rd draft

> The traffic in Tainan is worse than that in Taipei because of its road design and drivers who do not obey traffic laws. When I cam to Tainan first time, I found that the intersections here are more confusing than that in Taipei. One of the reasons is that there are many roads intercrossed in one intersection. Oppositely, there are only four roads at most in Taipei. In addition, what confused me most was I can hardly be sure which traffic light in the intersection I should abide by.
>
> Another reason is that most of the drivers and riders don't obey the traffic rules. For example, they usually run through the red light, like speeding and drive after drinking. However, the drivers and riders in Taipei pay more attention on following traffic rules. It seems that faulty traffic routing design and incorrect driving attitude are the traffic killers in Tainan.

I did not provide Dennis with any template to form his thesis statement because his language command is good. For less proficient writers who have difficulty putting the topic and main ideas together in a thesis statement, I offer them templates. Two templates for the topic of "New Culture" are as follows:

1. There are _____ (number) aspects about this culture that _____ (verb) me: its _____ (noun), _____ (noun), and _____ (noun).

2. _____ (number of things) that made me _____ (adjective) are its _____ (noun) and _____ (noun).

Two students using the previous templates generated the following two thesis statements respectively:

1. There are three aspects about this culture that attract me: its friendly people, delicious foods, and interesting customs.

    2. Two things about Thailand that made me uncomfortable are its food and traffic.

The provision of these templates is not to limit students but to provide interim scaffold. Once students become more experienced with producing thesis statements, they can dispense with the templates and have greater autonomy for generating their own.

Possibility

The principle of possibility is to give students guidance on making informed choices in their writing (i.e., conforming to or challenging extant academic norms) that reflect who they are, and who they want to be. In addition to directing students with proceduralized instruction to turn their declarative knowledge into procedural knowledge by following the checking, rereading, and identifying techniques, I also lead a class discussion on and examination of the merits and demerits of the thesis statement in response to some students' complaints about the constriction of this rhetorical convention on their ideas and the challenge of the necessity of a thesis statement in an essay. This student challenge is not premised on sociopolitical ideology as often seen in critical pedagogy but on pragmatics. Those students think a thesis statement is prescriptive, stifling their creativity both in ideas and forms. To them, a thesis statement is redundant. They do not understand why they need to pre-tell readers in a sentence about what follows in subsequent paragraphs where they will reveal their intentions in evolving examples. At this juncture, I brought up the notion of audience and asked them to reflect on who read their L1 writing. To this question, the unanimous answer was their Chinese writing teacher. Then I asked them to picture a different audience that expected a thesis to guide them through the text. Such an expectation, I told them, is derived from a cultural literacy practice that places more responsibilities on the writer in written communication (Hinds, 1987, 1990).

    The mentioning of audience in our discussion prompts some students to think about the functions of a thesis statement from the reader's perspective. Some are able to see that such a rhetorical device is reader-friendly, assisting readers in identifying writers' ideas so that they can start to evaluate subsequent information, explanation, and arguments in the essay. In addition to reader-friendliness, one student writer also mentioned that she often used the thesis statement to check the appropriateness and relevancy of her explanations and arguments in the essay. After listing the enabling and limiting functions on the white board, I asked students to weigh the pros and cons on the necessity of a thesis statement in an essay. The students reached a consensus that a thesis statement is necessary in this stage given their developing language proficiency, occasionally underdeveloped ideas, and developmental organizing skills. They decided that an early and explicit introduction of one's thesis imposes a less cognitive burden on the reader's part than an evolving point embedded in examples and metaphors and thus is more strategically appropriate.

The preceding critical examination and thoughtful adoption of a thesis statement in their essays signal student writers' active understanding of this rhetorical convention rather than an unavoidable cultural "tipping to the opposite that results from excesses, regardless of human intention" (Li, 2008, p. 17). This active understanding is a result of collective critical analysis rather than a teacher's self-initiated agenda. It shows that some EFL students do not "question the status quo" (Benesch, 2001, p. 167) and others do. The writing instructor's task is to equip all with necessary knowledge and skills they need in their academic settings and provide them with pragmatic analytical tools to question and challenge literacy standards and approaches, in case they wish to do so.

Conclusion

I have briefly outlined and demonstrated a principled eclectic approach to teaching writing in English as a foreign language. This principled eclectic approach is premised on the three guiding principles—particularity, practicality, and possibility—of Kumaravadivelu's (2006) macrostrategic framework of post-method pedagogy. The principle of particularity emphasizes an active understanding of local exigencies, an area in which non-native writing instructors of English assume more authority than native speakers of English. The principle of practicality encourages EFL writing instructors to rely on their understanding of local students' needs to create and tailor their own pedagogy to remedy the situation where mainstream approaches fail. In this case, it is the explicit and proceduralized instruction. The principle of possibility is to give students guidance on making informed choices in their writing (i.e., conforming to or challenging extant academic norms) that reflect who they are, and who they want to be.

It is known that a single writing approach is inadequate to cope with the diversified needs of EFL students in a writing class, be it linguistic, rhetorical, cognitive, social, cultural, and political. A principled eclectic approach appears a feasible solution, and the one proposed here is an example. EFL writing instructors need to take themselves, the writer, the reader, the text, the context, and the interaction of all these elements into account to devise their own principled eclectic approach.

A similar version has been published in Min, H. T. (2009). A principled eclectic approach to teaching EFL writing in Taiwan. Bulletin of Educational Research, 55(1), 63- 95.

References

Atkinson, D. (2003). L2 writing in the post-process era: Introduction. *Journal of Second Language Writing, 12*(1), 3–15.

Bakhtin, M. (1986). *Speech genres and other late essays.* Austin: University of Texas Press.

Benesch, S. (2001). Critical pragmatism: A politics of L2 composition. In T. Silva & P. K. Matsuda (Eds.), *On second language writing* (pp. 161–172). Mahwah, NJ: Lawrence Erlbaum.

Blass, L., & Pike-Baky, M. (2000). *Mosaic one: A content-based writing book.* New York: The McGraw-Hill.

Brown, H. D. (1994). *Teaching by principle: An interactive approach to language pedagogy.* Englewood Cliffs, N. J.: Prentice Hall Regents.

Cameron, D. (2002). Globalization and the teaching of 'communication skills.' In D. Block & D. Cameron (Eds.), *Globalization and language teaching* (pp. 67–82). London: Routledge.

Casanave, C. P. (2003). Looking ahead to more sociopolitically-oriented case study research in L2 writing scholarship (But should it be called "post-process"?). *Journal of Second Language Writing, 12,* 85–102.

Casanave, C. P. (2004). *Controversies in second language writing: Dilemmas and decisions in research and instruction.* Ann Arbor: The University of Michigan Press.

Connor, U. (1996). *Contrastive rhetoric: Cross-cultural aspects of second-language writing.* New York: Cambridge University Press.

Cumming, A. (2003). Experienced ESL/EFL writing instructors' conceptualizations of their teaching: Curriculum options and implications. In B. Kroll (Ed.), *Exploring the dynamics of second language writing* (pp. 71–92). Cambridge: Cambridge University Press.

Deng, X. (2007). A pedagogical response to the different approaches to the teaching of ESL/EFL essay writing. *STETS Language & Communication Review, 6*(1), 15–20.

Feez, S. (1998). *Text-based syllabus design*. Sydney: McQuarie University/AMES.

Flower, L. S., & Hayes, J. R. (1981). A cognitive process theory of writing. *College Composition and Communication, 32*(4), 365–387.

Gao, J. (2007). Teaching writing in Chinese universities: Finding an eclectic approach. *Asian EFL Journal: Professional Teaching Articles, 20*, A-2. Retrieved from http://asian-efl-journal.com/pta-May-07-jg.php.

Hinds, J. (1987). Reader versus writer responsibility: A new typology. In U. Connor & R. Kaplan (Eds.), *Writing across language: Analysis of L2 text* (pp. 141–152). Menlo Park, CA: Addison-Wesley.

Hinds, J. (1990). Inductive, deductive, quasi-inductive: Expository writing in Japanese, Korean, Chinese, and Thai. In U. Connor & A. M. Johns (Eds.), *Coherence in writing: Research and pedagogical perspectives* (pp. 87–109). Alexandria, VA: TESOL.

Hyland, K. (2003a). *Second language writing*. Cambridge: Cambridge University Press.

Hyland, K. (2003b). Genre-based pedagogies: A social response to process. *Journal of Second Language Writing, 12*, 1–29.

Hyland, K. (2007). Genre pedagogy: Language, literacy and L2 writing instruction. *Journal of Second Language Writing, 16*, 148–164.

Johns, A. M. (1997). *Text, role and context: Developing academic literacies*. Cambridge: Cambridge University Press.

Kent, T. (Ed.). (1999). *Post-process theory: Beyond the writing process paradigm*. Carbondale: Southern Illinois University Press.

Kim, Y., & Kim, J. (2005). Teaching Korean university writing class: Balancing the process and the genre approach. *Asian EFL Journal, 7*(2), A-5. Retrieved March 21, 2008 from http://asian-efl-journal.com/june_05_yk&jk.pdf.

Kramsch, C. (2000, March). *Linguistic identities at the boundaries*. Paper presented at the annual convention of American Association for Applied Linguistics, Vancouver, Canada.

Kroll, B. (1991). Teaching writing in the ESL context. In M. Celce-Murcia (Ed.), *Teaching English as a second or foreign language* (2nd ed., pp. 243–263). New York: Newbury House.

Kroll, B. (1993). Teaching writing is teaching reading: Training the new teacher of ESL composition. In J. Carson, & I. Leki (Eds.), *Reading in the composition classroom* (pp. 61–81). Boston, MA: Heinle & Heinle.

Kubota, R., & Shi, L. (2005). Instruction and reading samples for opinion writing in L1 junior high school textbooks in China and Japan. *Journal of Asian Pacific Communication, 15*(1), 97–127.

Kucer, S. B., & Silva, C. (2006). *Teaching the dimensions of literacy.* Mahwah, NJ: Lawrence Erlbaum.
Kumaravadivelu, B. (1992). Macrostrategies for the second/foreign language teacher. *The Modern Language Journal, 76,* 41–49.
Kumaravadivelu, B. (2003). Critical language pedagogy: A postmethod perspective on English language teaching. *World Englishes, 22*(4), 539–550.
Kumaravadivelu, B. (2006). TESOL methods: Changing tracks, challenging trends. *TESOL Quarterly, 40*(1), 59–81.
Larsen-Freeman, D. (2000). *Techniques and principles in language teaching.* Oxford: Oxford University Press.
Leki, I. (2002). Teaching L2 writing at the turn of the century and new perspectives. In R. Manchón (Ed.), *Special issue of International Journal of English Studies: Writing in the L2 classroom: In pedagogy and research* (pp. 197–209).
Leki, I. (2003). Coda: Pushing L2 writing research. *Journal of Second Language Writing, 12,* 103–105.
Li, X. (1999). Writing from the vantage point of an outsider/insider. In G. Braine (Ed.), *Non-native educators in English language teaching* (pp. 43–56). Mahwah, NJ: Lawrence Erlbaum.
Li, X. (2008). From contrastive rhetoric to intercultural rhetoric: A search for collective identity. In U. Connor, E. Nagelhout, & W. V. Rozycki (Eds.), *Contrastive rhetoric: Reaching to intercultural rhetoric* (pp. 1–24). Philadelphia: John Benjamins.
Liu, Y. (2008). Taiwanese students' negotiations with academic writing: Becoming "playwrights and film directors." *Journal of Second Language Writing, 17,* 86–101.
Matsuda, P. K. (2003). Process and post-process: A discursive history. *Journal of Second Language Writing, 12,* 65–83.
Matsuda, P. K., Canagarajah, A. S., Harklau, L., Hyland, K., & Warschauer, M. (2003). Changing currents in second language writing research: A colloquium. *Journal of Second Language Writing, 12,* 151–179.
Mellow, J. D. (2002). Towards principled eclecticism in language teaching: The two-dimensional model and the centering principle. *TESL-EJ, 5*(4), A-1. Retrieved http://iteslj.org/Techniques/Noonan-noticing.html.
Ministry of Education (2006). *Curriculum guidelines for English at senior high school.* Taipei: National Academy for Educational Research.
Ministry of Education (2008). *Curriculum guidelines for English at senior high school.* Taiepi: National Academy for Educational Research.
Mohan, B. A., & Lo, W. A.Y. (1985). Academic writing and Chinese students: Transfer and development factors. *TESOL Quarterly, 19*(3), 515–533.
Nelson, G., & Carson, J. (2006). Cultural issues in peer response: Revisiting "culture." In K. Hyland & F. Hyland (Eds.), *Feedback in second language*

writing: Contexts and issues (pp.42-59). New York: Cambridge University Press.

Prabhu, N.S. (1990). There is no best method. Why? *TESOL Quarterly, 24,* 161–176.

Reid, J. (1993). *Teaching ESL writing.* New Jersey: Prentice Hall Regents.

Reid, J. (2001). Writing. In R. Carter, & D. Nunan (Eds.), *The Cambridge guide to teaching English to speakers of other languages* (pp. 28–34). Cambridge: Cambridge University Press.

Rodgers, T. G. (2001). *Language teaching methodology* (ERIC Issue Paper). Washington, DC: ERIC Clearinghouse on Languages and Linguistics.

Santos, T. (2001). The place of politics in second language writing. In T. Silva & P. K. Matsuda (Eds.), *On second language writing* (pp. 173–190). Mahwah, NJ: Lawrence Erlbaum.

Silva, T. (1990). Second language composition instruction: Developments, issues, and directions in ESL. In B. Kroll (Ed.), *Second language writing: Research insights for the classroom* (pp. 11–23). Cambridge: Cambridge University Press.

Silva, T. (1993). Toward an understanding of the distinct nature of L2 writing: The ESL research and its implications. *TESOL Quarterly, 27*(4), 657–675.

Smith, F. (1983). Reading like a writer. *Language Arts, 60,* 558-567.

Trimbur, J. (1994). Taking the social turn: Teaching writing post-process. *College Composition and Communication, 45,* 108–118.

Tsui A. B. M., & Ng, M. (2000). Do secondary L2 writers benefit from peer comments? *Journal of Second Language Writing, 9*(2), 147–170.

Williams, J. (2005). *Teaching writing in second and foreign language classrooms.* Burr Ridge, IL: McGraw-Hill.

Zamel, V. (1976). Teaching composition in the ESL classroom: What we can learn from research in he teaching of English. *TESOL Quarterly, 10,* 67–76.

Zamel, V. (1980). Re-evaluating sentence-combining practice. *TESOL Quarterly, 14*(1), 81–90.

10 Teaching English Writing in Ukraine: Principles and Practices

Oleg Tarnopolsky

INTRODUCTION

This chapter deals with the basic issues of teaching writing in English as a foreign language (EFL) to tertiary students in Ukraine, a typical post-Communist country with all the peculiarities of EFL teaching and learning characteristic of that specific context.

For decades, teaching writing in English was the most neglected field in EFL teaching both in Ukraine and all over the former Soviet Union. The reason was simple—the Communist regime did not want people to establish across-the-border contacts with the outer world. As a result, after the downfall of Communism, such newly independent states as Ukraine found themselves in a situation where, on the one hand, there was a growing need for people who had a high, or at least sufficient, level of expertise in English writing to help the country develop, strengthen, and expand its contacts and ties with the West. On the other hand, that need could not be adequately met because of the lack of developed and efficient methods of teaching EFL writing, the lack of appropriate textbooks and other teaching materials, and even the lack of EFL teachers qualified to teach their students English writing skills. It was soon discovered that the problem could not be solved by simply borrowing those approaches to teaching writing skills that had been developed in the US and the UK or by borrowing writing textbooks published in those countries. Such approaches and textbooks, which did not (and naturally, could not) take into account the Ukrainian students' and teachers' mentality, background, the local conditions, and other similar factors, often failed to achieve the expected results when used in practical teaching. Therefore, the need arose for developing Ukraine-specific approaches and methods for teaching EFL writing and creating corresponding textbooks for such teaching (Tarnopolsky, 2000).

This chapter reports some theoretical and practical results of studies carried out by its author and directed at developing such a specific "Ukrainian" approach to teaching EFL writing to tertiary students. The underlying idea of the studies was to make an attempt to logically and organically combine the most progressive western approaches to teaching writing skills with strict account of the conditions of learning and teaching, the students, the teachers, and other local peculiarities.

The theoretical, practical, and experimental studies, whose results and conclusions are summarized in this chapter, were conducted in the period of 2003–2007 at Dnipropetrovsk University of Economics and Law. The studies mostly involved students of the linguistic department of that university who were trained as translators and interpreters of English. The theory underlying the approach was also developed in the US, at Portland State University, during the author's work there as a visiting Fulbright Scholar in 2005.

When developing the specifically Ukrainian approach to teaching EFL writing, two major subdivisions underlying such teaching were postulated. The first was the difference in the principal goals—*teaching writing techniques* versus *teaching writing skills*. The second subdivision was the direction of teaching—whether the teaching was directed at *writing for practical purposes* or whether the teaching was directed at developing students' *academic writing* skills. What is meant by these two subdivisions is discussed below.

Teaching Writing Techniques Versus Teaching Writing Skills

In the context of the studies being reported, *writing techniques* were postulated as those basic techniques that underlie all writing skills and make writing in the target language *technically possible*. There are different kinds of writing techniques. For instance, if a student punctuates his or her text, he/she may be said to have acquired English punctuation techniques. To choose appropriate words and spell them correctly when writing, vocabulary and spelling techniques are required. In general, it may be asserted that the full list of basic writing techniques includes:

1. *Graphic techniques*—in EFL teaching/learning such techniques should be acquired by students from those cultures where the Latin alphabet is not used, for example, in Ukraine and Russia where the alphabet is Cyrillic.

2. *Spelling techniques*—very difficult for acquisition by Ukrainian- or Russian-speaking students due to the peculiarities of English spelling.

3. *Vocabulary techniques*—correct and appropriate choice of words, word combinations, set expressions, and phraseology.

4. *Grammar/syntax* technique—correct and appropriate selection of grammatical/syntactical forms to be used in the text being written.

5. *Punctuation techniques*—properly punctuating and capitalizing the text being written.

6. *Stylistic techniques*—using the relevant style and register features of the text being written (it is a debatable point whether this is a technique or a more sophisticated skill but there are grounds for considering it a technique because the choice of style and register is and should be done, often unconsciously, even before starting to write a certain text).

If techniques are something that make writing both technically possible and technically appropriate from the point of view of linguistic, social, and cultural norms existing in a given speech community, *writing skills* are those that enable the writer to achieve his/her *communicative goals* when communicating in writing within the target culture. In the studies under discussion two principal writing skills were postulated.

The first and the most important of them are *the skills of expressing one's ideas in writing in the manner acceptable for the given target speech community.* There are differences in manners of expressing ideas when writing in Ukrainian or Russian, on the one hand, and in English, on the other hand. Early contrastive rhetoric as discussed in the well-known work by Kaplan (2001) demonstrated that quite clearly. (Kaplan did not analyze Ukrainian in that respect, but since the ways of expressing ideas in Russian and Ukrainian are practically identical, what was said in Kaplan's work about Russian can be applied to

Ukrainian too.) For instance, for an academic essay in English a thesis statement in the introductory paragraph and topic sentences followed by supporting statements in every paragraph of the body are typical (Reid, 2000) and sometimes even considered as practically obligatory. An academic essay in Ukrainian or Russian is much more amorphous and Ukrainian students are not required to follow such strict rules when writing academic essays in their mother tongue. So, from this point of view, to learn how to achieve their communicative goals when writing in English, such students have to master alternative ways of expressing their ideas. This is a long and complicated process of forming radically new skills that may be in conflict with the habitual way of writing in students' L1.

Certainly, findings in early contrastive rhetoric discussed in the above-mentioned work by Kaplan cannot be used uncritically in view of more recent research. But on the other hand, the dynamic model of L2 writing (Matsuda, 1997) shows that such writing is strongly influenced by the ESL/EFL writer's background (L1, culture, education). Without special training, this background stimulates ESL/EFL students to express their ideas in L2 writing in the same way they do when writing in their L1. To avoid that, learners should be encouraged to "think about, discuss, and write about how they perceive the ways in which they write—or not—in their first language and critically bring their perceptions to bear on the work of composing texts in another language (here, English) as a second language" (Kubota & Lehner, 2004, p. 21). Such a requirement is widely recognized now (see Connor, 2005) and it means nothing else but the necessity for learners to compare the ways of expressing ideas in writing in their mother tongue and in the target language for the purpose of making texts written in the L2 acceptable for the target speech community readership.

The second in importance among the postulated writing skills are *formatting skills* that are also substantially different when writing in Ukrainian/Russian and in English (see the argument above). For instance, the format of an English business letter requires stating the purpose of writing in the first paragraph, indicating the addressee's position above the text of the letter and addressing him/her by the last name with the title or as *To Whom It May Concern* (more common in the US) or *Dear Sir/Madam* (more common in the UK) if the name and sex of the addressee is unknown. In Ukrainian/Russian business correspondence formatting requirements do not necessitate statement of purpose in the first paragraph (the purpose may be implied but not stated explicitly), there is no indication of the addressee's position above the text of the letter, and he/she may be addressed by his/her position as *Respected Mr./Ms. Manager*. Such formatting peculiarities concern practically every genre of written documents; they make a lot of difficulties for Ukrainian-/Russian-speaking students and demand a lot of effort to be acquired.

The difference between writing techniques and writing skills lies not only in the above-mentioned fact that the former make the foundation for the latter. It also lies in different approaches to teaching them and in the results of such teaching. Learning writing techniques may require a lot of *formal exercises*. For instance, to learn punctuation techniques, formal exercises such as punctuating and capitalizing a text with no punctuation marks and capital letters are hardly avoidable. But if sufficient practice in using different writing techniques is provided, they could become more or less automatic and even writers whose L1 is not English can start unconsciously and effortlessly using correct grammatical forms, spelling, and vocabulary well-known to them when writing in English.

Developing writing skills could mostly rely on *communicative learning activities*. Expressing ideas in academic essays in the manner acceptable for English-speaking cultures can hardly be learned if such essays or, at least, complete paragraphs with appropriate topic sentences and supporting statements are not regularly written. Formatting a CV in a way that is appropriate in the US or the UK naturally requires practice in writing complete CVs. These are all communicative activities. But such communicative activities, even if they are very numerous, will rarely lead to fully automating and making unconscious the skills in question. For a writer to whom English is a foreign language, switching from his/her L1 manner of expressing ideas and formatting written documents to the manner proper for L2 will always require a conscious effort, and such conscious efforts will have to be made all through the process of writing not to deviate and return to the habitual and ingrained manner of expression.

It is due to such differences that teaching writing techniques and writing skills should be considered as interconnected and interdependent but also as *different teaching goals* requiring *different teaching approaches*.

Teaching Writing for Practical Purposes Versus Teaching Academic Writing

Writing for practical purposes and academic writing may be distinguished on the basis of learners' needs, i.e., their needs in English writing after they finish their English course. Writing for practical purposes (further called practical writing for short) is the kind of writing the absolute majority of students of English will most actively use in their future professional and personal life to achieve practical professional and personal goals. The needs analysis conducted in Ukraine (cf. Tarnopolsky & Kozhushko, 2008) demonstrated that teaching practical writing should include instruction in writing such documents as

1. business and personal letters,

2. CVs and letters of application when job hunting,

3. summaries and abstracts of professional literature read,

4. business contracts and agreements,

5. technical instructions.

Not all students need to learn to write all these types of documents (e.g., students of English for science and technology need to learn writing technical instructions but they do not need business contracts and agreements, and for business and law students it is vice versa). But the types of written documents above are practically important for very broad categories of student population (some types like business letters, CVs, and letters of application are required by all students with no exceptions).

Unlike practical writing, what is called academic writing in this chapter is needed by the minority of students, only those of them who plan academic/scholarly careers. Academic writing includes:

1. writing academic essays and compositions,

2. writing articles,

3. writing reports,

4. writing summaries and abstracts of one's own articles,

5. writing notes and full texts of presentations to be later orally delivered by the writer.

Practical writing and academic writing are different not only because teaching them differs *directionally*—they are taught with two almost opposite orientations in mind, orientation toward practical day-to-day professional and personal activities or orientation toward academic/scholarly work. Teaching them also has to be organized quite differently.

Practical writing skills are much simpler to teach due to the highly standardized nature of the majority of written documents belonging to this category. For instance, some research data show that business letter writing can be taught with the aid of computers and with little or no involvement of the teacher (Storozhuk, 2004). In fact, practical writing may be effectively taught using the traditional *textual approach*, i.e., when students mostly imitate in their own writing the format, structure, and modes of expressing ideas in sample texts given to them.

Academic writing is hard to teach and learn because the level of standardization of texts to be written is much lower than in the written documents produced when practicing practical writing. It is so because academic writing is naturally *creative*. It requires the most subtle and non-standard use of the language and deep understanding of its expressive possibilities. Writing business letters or CVs (practical writing), students cannot learn to write (or think) creatively because they have to write strictly following the existing standards and samples of similar documents that were used in teaching in order to demonstrate those standards. But when writing an essay in English, learners are supposed to express their own original ideas and find the most suitable language means for achieving this goal. Students obtain opportunities for creative and productive self-expression by means of the target language. This necessitates quite a different approach in teaching, the *process approach* (Tribble, 1996; White & Arndt, 1991), since only using the process approach gives students opportunities of becoming creative and original.

On the other hand, efficient teaching of both practical and academic writing presupposes the use of *genre analysis* and *genre approach* (Swales, 1990). First, deciding what to teach requires selecting specific genres of, for instance, business letters or academic essays in English that students should acquire for further use in their future careers and/or personal life. It is an important part of learners' needs analysis and when selecting specific genres in the studies being reported, such genres were identified for practical writing (cf. Tarnopolsky & Kozhushko, 2008). For instance, research done in those studies has argued that for teaching business correspondence to Ukrainian students, the specific genres of business letters to be taught comprised *letters of inquiry* (asking for information), *responding to inquiries* (supplying information), *letters of complaint, responding to complaints, letters of apology, letters of thanks, formal invitation letters, responding to formal invitations*, and no others. The genres of academic essays to be taught could not be identified through students' needs analysis because in the Ukrainian context students were not sure what they really wanted or needed in that respect. That is why traditional (for most American or British textbooks) genres were selected as the ones that form the basis of academic writing in general. Those genres were *description*—person or place description as well as process description*, narration, classification, comparison and contrast, cause and effect, definition, persuasion*, and no others.

Second, to learn to write properly different kinds of texts belonging to different genres within practical writing and academic writing categories, students need to have very clear understanding of how a written document of a definite genre should be structured and how ideas should be expressed in it so as to meet the specific genre requirements and achieve the writer's communicative goals in the most satisfactory manner. This, in its turn, necessitates the analysis of genre peculiarities of different sample texts of different genres to define the regular ways of achieving writers' communicative purposes that depend on genre-specific characteristics of the documents being written. And that means teachers should practice genre analysis with their students when teaching them both practical and academic writing.

It should be pointed out that the division into practical writing and academic writing helps clarify what types of EFL writing need to be taught to different categories of Ukrainian students. If speaking about university students, it is obvious that practical writing should be focused on when medical and law students, students of business and economics, and students of technology are taught English. Academic writing is much more required by students of history, philosophy, and linguistics. Those students who have chosen English as their major and prepare for future careers of EFL teachers, translators, and interpreters equally need both practical and academic writing.

Summarizing everything said above, it should be emphasized that the division into writing techniques versus writing skills and practical writing versus academic writing helps to determine

1. What the contents of teaching/learning EFL writing should be for different categories of Ukrainian students;
2. What the general directions in organizing and conducting teaching/learning of such writing are.

This, in its turn, created grounds for developing the principles of teaching EFL writing to Ukrainian students, as well as the ways of implementing those principles in teaching practice. The principles developed were divided into two categories: those referring to teaching both writing techniques and writing skills (irrespective of the division into practical writing and academic writing) and those referring to teaching writing skills only (where the difference between practical writing and academic writing is taken into account).

Principles for Teaching Both Writing Techniques and Writing Skills

The first principle was postulated on the basis of works by a number of authors (cf., for instance, Byrne, 1987; Oxford, 2001). It is the principle of *integrating teaching writing with teaching other communication skills: speaking, listening, and reading*. The necessity of following this principle when developing writing techniques is due to the fact that these techniques concern not only teaching writing. Vocabulary and grammar/syntax techniques pervade all communication, and graphic, spelling, and stylistic techniques are almost as important for reading as for writing. And this means the requirement to develop such techniques in an *integrated* manner by using learning activities focusing both on oral and written communication.

For developing writing skills, the integration is even more important than for developing writing techniques. To learn to express one's ideas in writing and to format one's written texts in the manner acceptable for the given target speech community, it is indispensable to see and analyze a lot of examples of how it is done in that community (reading), to discuss with the teacher and other students the best ways of doing it both before and after writing (speaking), taking into account the arguments of those who take part in the discussion (listening). This is why teaching writing should have a 'built-in mechanism' ensuring organic transitions from writing itself to speaking, reading, and listening (Byrne, 1987, p. 109).

The principle under consideration has some specific importance for the EFL teaching context in Ukraine. In that country, as it has already been noted, teaching EFL writing has not been very widespread until recently, so both teachers and students often consider developing speaking, listening, and reading skills as their primary goals. If developing such skills is integrated with acquiring writing techniques and skills, the latter ones are included more organically and naturally into the teaching/learning process.

In teaching practice, the integration may be achieved through devoting the *prewriting* stage to reading about what has to be written in each particular case and discussing in class how it should best be written (speaking and listening). *Writing* itself can mostly be done by students out of class, while the next *post-writing* class is devoted to discussing what has been written with the view of improving it (cf. Tarnopolsky, Kozhushko, & Rudakova, 2006).

The second principle formulated was *the principle of parallel development of writing techniques and writing skills*. It means that there is no development of writing techniques *prior* to starting the development of communicative writing skills. They are both developed in parallel, so that only those writing techniques that are required for a definite piece of writing are focused on in each case, with passing on to new techniques when they are required for further written communication.

The specificity and necessity of applying this principle to the Ukrainian context is due to the vestiges of grammar-translation and other obsolete methods still abounding in teaching practice. A good number of teachers are inclined to develop all writing techniques first and only after that start developing communicative writing skills. As a result, learners do a lot of formal exercises in grammar, vocabulary, punctuation, etc. without really practicing writing as a communicative activity.

The third principle was formulated due to the already mentioned fact that formal exercises are frequently required for teaching writing techniques while communicative activities may mostly help in developing writing skills. It indicates the *necessity of using both communicative and formal learning activities in teaching writing and finding proper places for each type of activity according to its usefulness*. That is the essence of the third principle, which allows using formal exercises when teaching writing techniques but demands concentration on communication when teaching writing skills. The significance of introducing this principle in the context under discussion can be explained by the same reasoning as for the second principle: the inclination of Ukrainian teachers to rely on formal exercises more than on communicative activities.

The fourth principle is the *principle of gradation of guidance in learning activities for teaching writing*. Writing techniques are mostly taught using guided exercises and activities where students get sufficient support for doing them correctly. Such almost total guidance is also characteristic of teaching writing skills at early stages. But with students' advance, the degree of guidance gets gradually reduced until practically unguided communicative writing activities are reached at later stages. This principle is not Ukraine-specific, but follows Reid's (2000) assertion that for teaching writing skills we do not need to guide and strictly control students' work, but just to steer it in the desired direction. That is why the principle in question regulates the gradual reduction of guidance and control in organizing learners' writing activities.

The last, fifth, principle for teaching both writing techniques and writing skills is the *principle of broadly using information/computer technologies in teaching writing*. In practice, this means not only students doing their writing assignments on the computer. It presupposes: (1) the use of computerized teaching programs for developing writing techniques; (2) students' use of the wealth of Internet resources when collecting materials for writing essays, articles, reports, business letters, contracts, etc.; (3) the use of the Web for publishing students' written works, for instance, on the website of the university or on the department's webpages; (4) the use of those sites and webpages by the students to peer review and peer assess each other's written works, etc. It is known that information/computer technologies greatly improve the results and intensify the process of learning to write (Slaouti, 2000). So, when teaching writing in English as a foreign language, i.e., without students' staying in the target language environment, such important support cannot be missed. The specificity of this principle for Ukraine is due to the fact of insufficient use of information/computer technologies in teaching EFL writing there and the necessity of stimulating such use in teaching practice.

Principles for Teaching Skills of Practical Writing and Academic Writing

The first of such principles is self-evident for Ukraine because of the above-mentioned considerable differences in the manner of formatting or expressing one's ideas when writing in English as compared to Ukrainian or Russian. Students have to clearly realize and understand those differences, which require the implementation of the *principle of supplying learners with detailed information and explanations concerning the format of different written texts in English, their structure, composition, component parts, ways of expressing ideas, and means of providing unity, coherence, and cohesion of those ideas and the text as a whole*. These explanations should be designed so as to make students compare the ways of formatting and expressing ideas in English written texts and in Ukrainian/Russian ones.

The next principle is also self-evident. Its necessity is caused by the problems students face when generating ideas for their written works and ensuring the logical sequencing of these ideas. The principle in question may be formulated as the *principle of using various learning strategies to help students generate ideas for their writing and logically unite those ideas in the framework of the text to be written*. The learning strategies in question are well-known. They are *brainstorming, freewriting, listing, grouping, looping, clustering, and outlining*. First, using such strategies is extremely important when teaching academic writing to Ukrainian students because of the already mentioned differences in the ways of expressing and uniting ideas in written texts in English and in Ukrainian/Russian (cf. the work by Kaplan, 2001). Second, purposeful teaching of those strategies is especially important for Ukrainian tertiary schools in view of the fact that in Ukrainian secondary schools students are practically not taught at all the strategies for generating ideas and ensuring their unity, cohesion, and coherence. Thus, the implementation of the principle in question when teaching EFL academic writing to university students in Ukraine helps to fill a rather wide, and otherwise unfilled, gap in their academic training.

On the other hand, the learning strategies under discussion are much less important for teaching practical writing because when doing practical writing tasks, students usually have the ideas to be expressed in the text formulated in the assignment. Also, in practical writing, thanks to its standardized character (see above), the ways of sequencing the ideas, of ensuring their unity, coherence, and cohesion are totally predetermined by the specific genre of the text to be written; students can simply follow the rules and samples given. This is why the principle being considered concerns mostly the teaching of academic writing skills.

The same concerns the next principle, called *the principle of combining cooperative* (Kessler, 1992) *and individual learning when acquiring writing skills*. Assignments in practical writing are mostly designed for individual learners' work due to the highly standardized and even algorithmic nature of such writing. On the contrary, more creative academic writing, because of its complexity, often requires learners' joint efforts when brainstorming, grouping, looping, clustering, and outlining, as well as when peer reviewing and commenting. That creates conditions not only for learners' mutual help but also for their acquiring information and skills from each other. But cooperative learning should be combined with individual writing of different drafts—otherwise, individual learning will not happen. From individual writing of drafts transition again can be made to discussions in pairs or teams of three/four students with the aim of improving the written drafts, etc. In the Ukrainian teaching practice, this approach to teaching academic writing has proved to bring the best results (cf. Tarnopolsky & Kozhushko, 2008) as compared to students' working on their essays only individually. This is caused by the fact that Ukrainian students are not used to fully independent work on their writing tasks. Initially, cooperative learning substantially facilitates doing such tasks for them while individual drafting gradually leads to total independence in essay writing.

Unlike the preceding two principles, the next, fourth, principle equally relates to practical and academic writing. It is the *principle of using the task-based approach* (Prabhu, 1987; Skehan, 2002) *in teaching both practical and academic writing skills*. Every writing assignment should be designed as a problem-solving task (e.g., writing a letter of complaint to make the request for a refund justified or writing an essay on ecological problems in students' hometowns with suggestions of realistic ways of solving those problems, etc.). Otherwise, the genuine communicative nature of such assignments may become less prominent because in real life writing (whether practical or academic) is done to solve some extra-linguistic problems and not to have practice in writing. If genuine extra-linguistic tasks are not included in the process of developing writing skills, such skills may never develop as tools to serve genuine written communication.

The need for the fifth principle is the result of students' not infrequent negative attitudes toward learning EFL writing. Such attitudes were emphasized by White and Arndt (1991, p. 11): "For many students writing is a chore to be got through for a grade, and to many others, not only is it a chore, but a boring one at that." The negative learners' attitude requires special measures to overcome it, and they may be regulated by the *principle of introducing specific learning activities aimed at enhancing learners' EFL writing motivation and creativity in EFL writing*. Those activities were developed specifically for Ukraine, and they include: *writing for fun, journal writing about oneself,* and *creative writing*. The scope of this chapter does not permit to dwell in detail on the essence and use of these learning activities, all the more so that they have already been thoroughly discussed in professional publications in the US and Canada (Tarnopolsky, 2000, 2004, 2005; Tarnopolsky & Kozhushko, 2007). The experimental results reported in those publications demonstrated the activities' great potential in enhancing learners' EFL writing motivation, as well as their great potential in accelerating the development of students' creative approach to EFL writing, development of their EFL writing skills and even writing techniques. But it should be noted that such activities (and the principle itself) mostly find their application when teaching academic writing, especially to tertiary students with English as their major. It is so because they are designed not for attaining practical goals but for developing students' creativity when writing in English and that corresponds to the creative nature of academic writing as distinct from practical writing. That is why the activities in question made an important part of the textbook *Writing Academically* (Tarnopolsky, Kozhushko, & Rudakova, 2006) developed for Ukrainian students with English as their major—those students who really need to develop a creative approach to EFL writing. Besides, though the experimental data proved that writing for fun could also be successfully used with non-linguistic students (Tarnopolsky, 2000), the length and scope of their courses of English may not give opportunities for introducing it.

The last two principles are interconnected and equally relate to teaching both practical and academic writing. They are the *principle of using different approaches to teaching writing skills (the textual, the process, and the genre approaches)* and the *principle of taking strict ac-*

count of the genre peculiarities of all kinds of texts that students are taught to write. The application of these two principles was discussed before when analyzing the differences between practical writing and academic writing. The first of them shows that practical writing should mostly be taught following the textual approach while academic writing requires the process approach. But both types of writing require using genre analysis and genre approach to be effectively taught (and this fact unites both principles under discussion). That is why practical writing should be taught following the combined *textual-genre approach*, while teaching academic writing stands in need of the combined *process-genre approach*. This follows Tribble's (1996) suggestion to combine approaches in all cases of teaching writing skills. All the 12 principles of teaching EFL writing to Ukrainian students were most fully embodied in the above-mentioned textbook *Writing Academically* (Tarnopolsky, Kozhushko, and Rudakova, 2006).

A special experimental study, with its results already reported in Ukrainian professional literature (Tarnopolsky & Kozhushko, 2008), has been conducted to determine the practical efficiency of the approach developed. In that study conducted in 2007 at Dnipropetrovsk University of Economics and Law six groups of first and second year students (seventy-two persons) majoring in English and acquiring academic writing skills with the help of the textbook *Writing Academically* were compared to five other (control) equalized groups of first and second year students (fifty-nine persons). In the control groups the students were working on their academic writing tasks using a British textbook *Upstream Intermediate* (Evans & Dooley, 2002).

A 100-point scale of ten criteria was developed to assess students' written academic essays both before and after their one-semester-long course on academic writing (thirty-six academic hours). Before the course, the students from both the experimental and the control groups demonstrated practically equal results when writing an academic essay on the topic *The Dreams of my Life*. The mean scores for the experimental groups were 57.5 points out of 100, and 55.7 points out of 100 for the control groups. After a one-semester-long course, when writing an essay on the topic *The Childhood of My Parents as Compared to My Own*, the mean scores for the experimental groups were 77.0 points out of 100, and 62.5 points out of 100 for the control groups. This means that while in the experimental groups the students' progress in developing their academic writing skills was quite considerable, in the control groups learners progressed at a much slower pace and were unable to achieve comparable results. Thus, the study showed that the approach suggested in this chapter really ensured the achievement of the pre-set teaching goals—and to a greater extent than when a British textbook was used.

Conclusion

An approach to teaching EFL writing to tertiary students of English in Ukraine has been discussed in this chapter. The differences between teaching writing techniques and writing skills were outlined, as well as the differences between teaching writing for practical purposes (practical writing) and teaching academic writing. Twelve strategic principles for organizing teaching EFL writing to Ukrainian tertiary students were suggested and discussed. Those twelve principles should not be considered as universal but rather as Ukraine-specific since the goal of formulating them was creating the foundation for developing a Ukraine-specific approach and methods for teaching EFL writing and developing textbooks and other materials for such teaching. The studies reported in this chapter have shown that teaching EFL writing in Ukraine may really be regulated by the suggested twelve principles since, on the one hand, they are based on the latest worldwide trends and, on the other hand, they take full account of local peculiarities and conditions.

It should be noted that the results of the studies reported in the chapter suggest future directions for research. The first of such directions is the experimental study of teaching practical EFL writing to Ukrainian tertiary students of English (both majoring in English and majoring in other fields) on the basis of the suggested approach. This can and should lead to developing a Ukraine-specific textbook for teaching practical EFL writing along the lines that the textbook for teaching academic EFL writing (*Writing Academically*) has been developed. The second direction is conducting a more detailed students' needs analysis for determining what genres of EFL writing should be taught at specific types of Ukrainian tertiary schools: medical schools as distinct from law schools, business schools as distinct from technical schools, etc. The third, and probably the most important direction is developing the approach to and methods of teaching EFL writing in Ukrainian secondary schools (especially high schools) where such writing is hardly taught at all in regular classes of English. That creates serious problems for teaching EFL writing on the tertiary level since students lack the basic writing techniques and skills that have to be developed in the university English course though they should have been developed much earlier in the secondary school course.

Successful solving of the problems outlined above may be instrumental in raising the standard of teaching EFL writing in Ukraine to the level required by the role of English as the language of international communication.

References

Byrne, D. (1987). Integrating skills. In K. Johnson and K. Morrow (Eds.), *Communication in the classroom. Applications and methods for the communicative approach* (pp. 108–114). Essex, UK: Longman.

Connor, U. (2005). Comments by Ulla Connor. *Journal of Second Language Writing, 14,* 132–136.

Evans, V., & Dooley, J. (2002). *Upstream intermediate B2: Student's book.* Berkshire, UK: Express Publishing.

Kaplan, R. B. (2001). Cultural thought pattern in inter-cultural education. In T. Silva & P. K. Matsuda (Eds.), *Landmark essays on ESL writing* (pp. 11–25). Mahwah, NJ: Hermagoras Press.

Kessler, C. (Ed.). (1992). *Cooperative language learning: A teacher's resource book.* Englewood Cliffs, NJ: Prentice Hall Regents.

Kubota, R., & Lehner, A. (2004). Toward critical contrastive rhetoric. *Journal of Second Language Writing, 13,* 7–27.

Matsuda, P. K. (1997). Contrastive rhetoric in context: A dynamic model of L2 writing. *Journal of Second Language Writing,* 6(1), 45–60.

Oxford, R. (2001). Integrated skills in the ESL/EFL classroom. *ESL Magazine,* 4(1), 18–20.

Prabhu, N. S. (1987). *Second language pedagogy.* Oxford: Oxford University Press.

Reid, J. M. (2000). *The process of composition* (3rd ed.). White Plains, NY: Pearson Education.

Skehan, P. (2002). Plenary: task-based instruction: Theory, research, practice. In A. Pulverness (Ed.). *IATEFL 2002. York conference selections* (pp. 90–99). Kent, UK: IATEFL.

Slaouti, D. (2000). Computers and writing in the second language classroom. In P. Brett & G. Motteram (Eds.), *A special interest in computers: Learning and teaching with information and communications technologies* (pp. 9–30). Kent, UK: IATEFL.

Storozhuk, S. (2004). Computer-aided teaching of business correspondence in English in Ukraine. *Business Issues, 2,* 14–17.

Swales, J. (1990). *Genre analysis: English in academic and research settings.* Cambridge: Cambridge University Press.

Tarnopolsky, O. (2000). Writing English as a foreign language: A report from Ukraine. *Journal of Second Language Writing, 9*(3), 209–226.

Tarnopolsky, O. (2004). Promoting EFL literacy via promoting motivation: A case for writing skills development. *TESL Reporter, 37*(1), 8–16.

Tarnopolsky, O. (2005). Creative EFL writing as a means of intensifying English writing skill acquisition: A Ukrainian experience. *TESL Canada Journal, 23*(1), 76–88.

Tarnopolsky, O., & Kozhushko, S. (2007). Teaching academic writing in English to tertiary students in Ukraine. In *Proceedings of the Third International Online Conference on Second and Foreign Language Teaching and Research* (pp. 45–50). Retrieved from http://www.readingmatrix.com/conference/pp/proceedings2007/ tarnopolsky_kozhushko.pdf.

Tarnopolsky, O., & Kozhushko, S. (2008). *Methods of teaching English writing to students of tertiary educational institutions.* Vynnytsya: Nova Knyha Publishers.

Tarnopolsky, O., Kozhushko, S., & Rudakova, M. (2006). *Writing academically. A coursebook for teaching academic writing in English to students of linguistic tertiary educational institutions.* Kyiv, Ukraine: INKOS.

Tribble, C. (1996). *Writing.* Oxford: Oxford University Press.

White, R., & Arndt, V. (1991). *Process writing.* Harlow: Longman.

11 Developing Spanish FL Writing Skills at a Netherlands University: In Search of Balance

Marly Nas and Kees van Esch

INTRODUCTION

A student of foreign language (FL) writing can be compared with a circus performer who is balancing plates on poles: seeking a balance between content, text organization and language in order to put up a good performance. Learning to write in the FL is a real challenge for the students: they have to acquire a complete new vocabulary and grammatical rules and put them into practice to be able to write a good letter, a well organized expository text or a convincing argumentative essay. Seeking the balance between content, structure and language will not be easy, and many plates will smash to pieces before the student dominates writing in the FL.

THE CONTEXT OF SPANISH LANGUAGE WRITING INSTRUCTION IN NIJMEGEN

The Radboud University in Nijmegen, situated in the southeast of the oldest city in the Netherlands near the border with Germany, has nine faculties and enrolls over 17,500 students in 107 study programs. Its Roman Languages and Cultures department offers students a broad perspective on both French and Spanish, focusing on their shared origin, history, culture and literature. After completing their studies our students, Spanish majors, usually find work in education, translation, journalism, tourism, investigation or at public institutions in the Netherlands or in Spanish-speaking countries. Especially the oral and written proficiency of Spanish acquired during their bachelor and master courses will be of use in these future professions, for example in teaching Spanish, communicating with other authorities, translating from Dutch to Spanish and vice versa, or publishing essays and articles on Spanish or Spanish American language, literature or culture.

When starting their academic career of Roman Languages, our students usually have no knowledge of Spanish since it is not a compulsory subject in secondary education. English is, and students may choose French and German, or other languages when offered.

What are the problems that have to be faced by students of FL writing, in our case of writing in Spanish? Firstly, learning the FL does not mean automatically that students also can write in that FL, especially when there is no great tradition in teaching writing in a FL, as is the case in Dutch secondary education where the focus is on reading, listening and speaking. If writing is practised, it is mostly limited to writing simple letters and not other text genres, such as argumentative essays. Furthermore, a writing class generally does not include multiple drafts or peer review. The result is that students are relatively poorly skilled in FL writing when they enter university. Even university FL writing courses are frequently focussed on linguistic aspects of writing, such as grammatical and lexical accuracy, spelling, and punctuation, while far less attention is given to structure and quality of argumentation.

Secondly, there are essential differences between writing in L1 and in L2 and FL. The FL writing skill entails both general FL proficiency and general writing skills and it cannot simply be taken for granted that a proper command of these two individually will automatically lead to a proper FL writing skill. It has been shown in the past that many FL students are adequate writers in their native language (L1), and are fairly competent in the FL, but that this does not guarantee success in FL writing (Silva, 1993). This is partly due to the teaching programme, which may concentrate primarily on improving general FL proficiency (and may take an implicit improvement of writing for granted), and partly to students' inability to realise the special demands FL writing makes on their FL repertoire, which may sometimes be very different from general proficiency. Naturally, there are a number of general criteria that apply to a text written in either L1 or FL. Taking for example writing argumentative texts in an academic context like ours, these texts have to meet general criteria like structure of the content, and the quality of the argument. Irrespective of quality of the language that is used, in terms of lexical sophistication or syntactic complexity, any argumentative text should enable a reader to follow the writer's line of argumentation. This can only be achieved if the writer can present the central idea of the text, is clear about the logical connection between the various arguments, and is able to draw a conclusion that is the logical consequence of the arguments presented.

The genre of argumentative texts is indispensable for academic students of a FL, in view of the many texts of this type they have to write during their study and the master thesis at the end of their academic education. But writing a good argumentative text requires knowledge of argumentation theory, in order to be able to convince the readers of the text. Hence, we developed for our second year students of Spanish as a FL an argumentative writing program based on theories of writing in L2 and FL and on argumentation. We will describe first the theoretical background of this program, and more specifically (development in) writing in L2 and FL, argumentation, revision and feedback. Then, we will explain the Spanish as a FL writing program: the context, the pedagogical and didactical approaches and the content. We will end with a short evaluation of the program.

Theoretical Background

In earlier articles, e.g. Van Esch, de Haan, and Nas (2004) have given an outline of what is involved in writing. They follow Connor and Mbaye (2002) who propose to use Canale and Swain's (1980) communicative competence model, and adapt it for writing. Connor and Mbaye (2002) distinguish four competences in writing: grammatical competence, the knowledge of grammar, vocabulary, spelling and punctuation; discourse competence, the way the text is structured, especially with reference to how coherence and cohesion are established; sociolinguistic competence, the appropriateness of the genre, register and tone of the writing; and strategic competence, the ability to assess the intended readership, to address the reader in the appropriate manner, and to present convincing arguments. We try to train all these competences during our Spanish FL writing course, as we will show in the next section. But how can we accomplish that students actually develop their writing skills and enhance their written proficiency?

According to Polio (2001) assessing the development of L2 or FL writers is very difficult:

> If we can show how written language develops over time, we can use that information, for example, to compare how groups of writers progress after a specific intervention. This is not an easy task. (p. 97)

Since our goal is developing the students' skills in writing FL argumentative texts, our intervention is focussed particularly on enhancing students' argumentative writing, as a part of their discourse competence.

Two other essential aspects of our Spanish FL writing course are revision and feedback. According to Fathman and Whalley (1990) revision effectively is a vital tool in the development of writing skills. However, several studies show that students, having received teacher feedback, usually do not revise the first draft if this is not required explicitly (Cohen, 1987; Cohen & Cavalcanti, 1990).

Teachers are not the only useful feedback source; peer response possibly also contributes to the development of writing skills. Lockhart and Ng (1993) have found seven positive effects of peer feedback in multiple studies: the audience for which students write texts becomes larger; students adapt both the roles of writer and of reader; students gain more insight in writing and revision processes; peer feedback may be more informative than teacher feedback, since peers have a similar level of development and interest; the discussions between peers make students discover what they actually wanted the text to say and how this meaning could be expressed in an improved way; and finally, peer feedback sessions can stimulate the student's attitude towards the writing process and increase the motivation to write and revise, as well as lessen possible writer's blocks. The authors mention, lastly, that the teacher can use the feedback sessions to save time, seeing that he or she does not necessarily need to read and comment on all drafts of a text (Lockhart & Ng, 1993).

We invite students to read their peers' first drafts and comment on them, keeping in mind a limited number of feedback categories within the four competences involved in writing, as suggested by Connor and Mbaye (2002). The teacher also comments the first draft, thus enabling all students to benefit not only from peer feedback but also from expert feedback. When revising the first draft in order to write the final version of a text, students can compare all comments given and adapt their texts accordingly as they see fit.

We will now examine our writing course in greater detail.

THE NIJMEGEN SPANISH AS A FL WRITING COURSE

Context and Aim of the Program

The students are (mostly 10–20) second year Dutch-speaking students that follow the writing course as a part of their academic education of Spanish. Since most of them have not learned Spanish at secondary school (Spanish not being a compulsory subject), they enter university without any knowledge of the language. Therefore, the first year language acquisition program is primarily dedicated to learn the vocabulary and grammar of Spanish. In the freshman writing classes the students practise reading proficiency by reading texts about, for example, family, health and racism. Important words and expressions of these texts are used to enhance their vocabulary and are the starting point for writing tasks related to the central theme, such as a letter, a column, or a *carta al director* (letter to the editor). The teacher's feedback focuses mainly on language use, and to a lesser extent aspects of text organization and content, underscoring errors and marking them with a code in order to make students themselves revise the errors.

In the subsequent year, the teacher focuses more on content and text organization while students have to meet increasingly stringent requirements of language, content and text organization. Despite the teacher's focus, students principally emphasize the development of their linguistic competence. The result is that students might not develop the other competences, particularly text organization and argumentation, as they could do. That is why one of the major aims of our second year writing program is to develop these competences by designing adequate tasks and enabling them to evaluate their peers' texts.

Pedagogical Approaches

In the writing programme for the second year students of Spanish at Radboud University Nijmegen, an important goal is gradually shifting the responsibility for learning from the teacher to the (individual) student(s) according to principles of learner autonomy. Van Esch and

St. John (2003) believe that learner autonomy can be realised as teacher control and management is progressively relinquished and transferred in cooperation with the learner. Development can only be sustained through a process in which control over and responsibility for the learning situation is gradually shifted from teacher to learner. This transfer implies a widening scope for learners to take charge of their own progress. Although far from a neat and automatic operation, this process can be achieved through a co-operative teacher-learner venture that might be illustrated by the figure below (Figure 1):

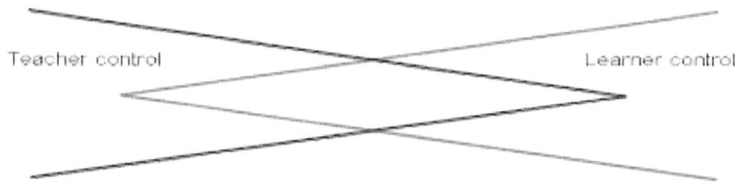

Figure 1: Teacher and learner control in learner autonomy (Van Esch & St. John, 2003, p. 17).

An example of how we try to enhance learner autonomy in learning to write argumentative texts is the increasing responsibility of students in commenting texts of others students in peer feedback sessions.

Another important approach of our writing program is exploring and expanding the Zone of Proximal Development (ZPD), a metaphor originated by Vygotsky, which reflects the difference between what a novice is capable of doing when acting alone and what he or she is able to do when acting under the guidance of a more experienced peer or adult or in collaboration with more capable peers (Lantolf, 2004; Vygotsky, 1978). Van Lier (1996) explains the ZPD as follows:

> At any point in a given time, there are things a person can do confidently in his or her own. This we might call the area of self-regulation. Beyond that there is a range of knowledge and skills which the person can only access with someone's assistance. In the case of performance of some complex action, then the person can perform the action if someone more capable is available to help. In the case of some piece of knowledge, this becomes available because it can be linked

to existing knowledge or experiences, again, perhaps with someone else's guidance. This material, which one might say is within reach, constitutes the ZPD. Anything outside the circle of proximal development is simply beyond reach and not available for learning. (Van Lier, 1996, pp. 190–191)

As the concept of ZPD suggests that learning is effective if learners can carry out tasks of writing that are within their reach, we try to give challenging but not too difficult tasks. All second year language acquisition courses for Spanish have an identical thematic context per seven week period, which we elaborate more on below. Reading several texts on the topic and discussing one's opinion about it are activities preceding all writing tasks, thus guaranteeing input. Moreover, the writing topics chosen relate to the students' perceptions of their environment and/or are current affairs dominating the news.

Content of the Writing Program

The second year programme covers four periods of seven weeks, each with a different central theme: Spanish society, young people, Spanish America, and immigration. During the various periods students are introduced to certain aspects of writing, and are encouraged to practice what they have learnt, writing one (first period) or two (remaining periods) argumentative texts of two drafts each, on a topic related to the central theme. The length requirement for the final draft is at least four hundred words, without specifying a maximum. All the texts produced by the students are published in Blackboard, the digital study environment that all students have access to. At the end of each period they are made to write an essay, without any reference works or other tools, in which they have to show that they master the subject matters and are able to put them into practice. These exams are all conducted under similar conditions: students dedicate the entire time available (105 minutes) to writing the essay, which should always count at least four hundred words.

As for the feedback on the writing tasks, the students are instructed to provide peer feedback relating to the relevant subject matters of that period and those studied before, and to ignore the mechanics. In their first year of studying Spanish students already practise how to give and receive feedback: feedback should be formulated using expressions like

"I think . . ." or "I feel . . ." instead of the more aggressive "You should not . . ." or "You always . . ." Furthermore it needs to address particular aspects of writing, in our case, and offer concrete advice or suggestions on how one could revise a text. In receiving feedback, students should try to appreciate the comments given and to ask more questions to make sure they fully understand the feedback. It is essential that students do not try to feel offended or attacked by the comments given. The teacher provides feedback about all aspects relevant to writing argumentative texts, focusing on the topics studied by the students, but also including grammar, vocabulary, spelling, and punctuation.

During the first period of seven weeks, the students study text structure (Cestero, 2001), introduction and conclusion (Serafini, 1996), and the organisation of argumentation (Goethals & Delbecque, 2001a). They practise these topics by reading texts about Spanish society, writing introductory and concluding paragraphs for existing texts, and writing an entirely new argumentative text (at least two drafts).

In the second period, the students read texts on young people. Students study general argumentation aspects and the Toulmin model (Toulmin, 1958; Schellens & Verhoeven, 1994), specific elements of Spanish argumentative texts (Onieva Morales, 1995), thematic coherence (Goethals & Delbecque, 2001b), and the way in which the writer and the reader can or must be present in the text (Goethals & Delbecque, 2001c). Whereas the general comments on argumentation could also be applied in argumentative texts written in other languages, the observations made regarding to thematic coherence do specify characteristics of the Spanish language context. In contrast to the Dutch language, the native tongue of the students in the Netherlands, Spanish syntax allows the writer to omit the grammatical subject, because the conjugated verb already clearly indicates the active person. Excessive presence of an explicit subject in Spanish written texts therefore indicates poor level of linguistic competence. Another characteristic of Spanish academic texts is the absence of the author in the body of the article. The use of the first person singular is rather uncommon in Spanish academic texts: Spanish conventions stipulate that to strengthen the idea of objectivity the first person plural is more adequate (Goethals & Delbecque, 2001b, 2001c). Students practise these subjects by analysing texts on the central theme, and by writing two argumentative texts, for example, one on adolescents and violence (two versions), and the other on adolescents and alcohol (again, two versions). Toward the end of this period they revise (parts of) the exam text they wrote at the end of period one, incorporating the newly acquired knowledge.

The theme for period three, Spanish America, presents the students with an opportunity to write argumentative texts about how the dictatorial past is coped with in countries like Argentina and Chile, and about Spanish America-US relations. The instructions for these writing assignments are far less concrete than in the earlier periods, allowing the students a greater amount of freedom in determining what they find relevant and interesting, within the domain of the context. Below, we will discuss the approach and content of this period more in detail.

Period four, which has immigration for a central theme, is a period for rehearsal of all subject matters taught and discussed so far, and the introduction of techniques for reformulation (cf. Laca, 2001c), to convince students of the importance of rewording in argumentative texts' (intermediate) conclusions, since this shows an improved level of linguistic competence.

An Example: The Third Period

We will now focus on the third period because in our opinion it clearly demonstrates the pedagogical approach. In Appendix A we give an overview of this period in Spanish. The grammar exercises indicated in the overview are meant as self-education and will not be mentioned in our discussion of writing activities below.

After having evaluated the exam of the periods one and two before this period starts, students study in week one of period three a chapter called *Matizaciones, modalizaciones y comentarios evaluativos*, about expressions (hedges), modal qualifiers and evaluative comments that may enable writers to formulate claims in a less definite way so to increase chances of convincing the audience (Laca, 2001a). They apply what they have read to the exam of the period before, marking hedges they used and/or adapting the text including hedges, modal qualifiers and evaluative comments when convenient, and read two texts about the political, economic and cultural development of Spanish America. In week 2 they discuss the reading comprehension tasks, thus receiving the input they need for the writing assignment they have to make at home: task 3.1 *Hispanoamérica: lo pasado, pasado,* which is about whether or not prosecuting inhabitants of Chile, Argentina and so on for crimes committed during the dictatorial past of these countries is still adamant.

They publish their texts on Blackboard, make a print of the texts of the members of their group and prepare the peer feedback to these texts. In the third week they orally explain their feedback to their peers, exchanging annotated documents and the specially prepared feedback forms that indicate the evaluation criteria for the task at hand. This feedback form is used by both the teacher and the students. Appendix B contains an example of the feedback form, pointing out the topics relevant for discussion regarding text structure, argumentation and language. The form can be printed out and written on, or used digitally. The students should not comment on grammar or spelling, but topics such as thematic coherence, presence of author and hedges do need to be commented on when applicable. The form offers enough space for the students and teacher to explain whatever feedback they like to give. Furthermore, on the back (or: page two) of the form we offer an evaluation guide for argumentative texts (in Spanish) made by Onieva Morales (1995), which contains control questions on important aspects of argumentative texts, such as thesis, reasoning, structure and order, connection between ideas, conclusion and the vocabulary and tone used. Comments can be added by means of symbols that indicate that certain aspects are done well (+), averagely (±) or not at all (-), and further explained in words if necessary. During class, students work in groups of three to four students, explaining their feedback in Dutch (L1), since this will enable them to explain more precisely what they mean by certain comments. After the group discussions, the teacher gives feedback to each student individually on the same feedback form and to the group as a whole, highlighting aspects that need to be revised in general, explaining grammar, structure, or argumentation topics when needed.

The next step is that the students have to revise task 3.1 with help of the comments of their peers and the teacher and to publish the final version on Blackboard. Furthermore, they have to read another text *Una América sin Monroe,* to study a part of chapter seven of Vázquez (2001) about discourse markers (*relaciones retóricas y conectores*): rhetorical link words (addition, opposition, cause, effect, condition) that aim at better cohesion between paragraphs (Laca, 2001b). In week four students receive only teacher feedback to the final version of task 3.1. The teacher compares the first and second draft to see what students have done with the feedback they received, and grades the essays weighing structure for 20%, and argumentation and language each for 40% language, resulting in a note ranging from 1 (bad) to 10 (excellent).

Students study the second part of Laca (2001b), read the text *Las 'putas tristes' de Fidel,* written by the well-known Peruvian author Vargas Llosa, and make the corresponding reading comprehension and vocabulary exercises. In week five until week seven included, the same procedure is repeated: writing a draft version, this time about the relationship between the United States and Latin America as a continent, or the relationship between the US and a specific Spanish American country, chosen by the students themselves. The students subsequently give feedback to their peers and use this feedback and that of the teacher to write a final version with use of all topics studied so far.

Appendix C shows the revision Roos, one of the students of academic year 2007–2008, made based on her first draft, after having received both teacher and peer feedback. We have made all revisions visible, by indicating in underlined text fragments newly introduced clauses, and showing at the same time removed parts in the balloons in the right text margin.

Appendix D contains transcriptions of peer feedback discussions about the writing tasks of one particular student, Marisa, in academic year 2004–2005.

Evaluation of the Program

The most essential question about our Spanish as a FL writing program is "Does it work?" To answer this question, we need a further analysis of important aspects of our program, for instance, of the texts written by the students, both the draft versions and the exams of each period, the feedback forms and the peer feedback sessions. Aspects to analyse include whether the quality of argumentation and organization of the texts have improved, and whether students have corrected language aspects, such as correctness and adequacy. An interesting question is to see to which extent the feedback influences the overall text quality. We are carrying out these analyses and will publish the results in a few years (Nas, forthcoming). For the moment, we would like to share some provisional impressions based on the classes and feedback sessions so far.

Referring to important aspects such as motivation and attitude towards the program: students indicate in their evaluations that they like the current writing program, especially writing one or two draft versions and the possibility to improve these draft version(s) to a final version. Revision was not obligatory in the first academic year: texts were immediately graded; improved versions were only handed in when students failed.

As for the teacher feedback, this seems to lead to better texts, not only for the language aspects but also in particular for the quality of argumentation and of organization of the text. Revisions are not superficial; Roos's final draft differs to a great extent from her first. It still is not error free, but she has definitely extended her content, probably at least partly because of the teacher feedback given by means of the feedback form (see Appendix B, second page, first question on development of argumentation):

> Question: Have you considered other points of view and have you refuted those that contradict your opinion?
>
> Feedback: You do try, but the body of the text is still too short to really convince readers. You have worked out Chile reasonably, but it could be even better. As far as Argentina is concerned, I do not see how people should "just continue with their lives." (Question originally in Spanish, feedback in Dutch. Feedback by Marly Nas on first draft Lo pasado, pasado by Roos, Feb. 25, 2008.)

Roos effectively rewrote most of the paragraph on Argentina, as we can see in Appendix C.

Peer feedback also plays an important role in the process of improving texts. Students declare that they are encouraged by the peer feedback sessions, because they feel more valued by the support and comments of other students. Students like reading their peers' texts: not only because of the (partially) different content, but it also invites them to discuss topics further and to learn form each other how to improve argumentation and organization of their texts. It is encouraging to see that development not only takes place in writing skills, but also in more affective ways: there is a shift in self confidence. If we consider the case of Marisa (Appendix D) we see how insecure she reacts to feedback of her peers. She hesitates, laughs quietly, and tries to defend herself by apologizing ("I was still working on that one"). In the next session, however, she seems to be more confident, proud of her solution, thanking her peers. In the first session of the second period, Marisa is guiding her peers towards concrete solutions for her text by asking questions. She does not seem to accept all comments as necessary improvements, a contrast with the first period fragments. It even leads one of her peers, Carolina, into saying "You don't necessarily have to do something with this [feedback], do you?"

As for the pedagogical approach we opted for, i.e. the Zone of Proximal Development and the increasing responsibility of students: we notice that a gradual shift in expertise does take place: the further along the program, the teacher (Marly Nas) notices that the feedback she has written on the feedback form still to hand over to the students, is already addressed in the peer feedback discussions. Most of Lockhart and Ng's (1993) advantages of peer feedback sessions are valid, save the last one: the teacher has not felt comfortable yet to skip her feedback on the first draft. It may save a lot of time, and in the interest of shifting responsibility and control to the students it will be an important, ultimate step. However, the students who, due to missing the deadline, handed in their final draft without having benefited from teacher feedback, made sure they did not miss the next deadline: it seemed that, although they valued their peers' comments, they really wanted the teacher's input as well.

There are so many things to consider when writing a text. We feel that with our writing program we are offering students the means to find a balance between L1 and L2/FL writing, between content and form, between reason and emotion. And, to finish this first evaluation, we see that students have learnt to write better argumentative texts in Spanish as a FL, and that is what it is all about.

References

Canale, M., & Swain, M. (1980). Theoretical bases of communicative approaches to second language teaching and testing. *Applied Linguistics, 1,* 1–47.

Cestero, A. M. (2001). Organización del texto. In Vázquez, G. (Ed.), *Guía didáctica del discurso académico escrito ¿Cómo se escribe una monografía?* (pp. 17–39). Madrid: Edinumen.

Cohen, A. (1987). Student processing of feedback on their compositions. In A. Wenden & J. Rubin (Eds.), *Learner strategies in language learning* (pp. 57–69). Englewood Cliffs, NJ: Prentice Hall.

Cohen, A. D., & Cavalcanti, M. C. (1990). Feedback on compositions: teacher and student verbal reports. In B. Kroll (Ed.). *Second language writing: Research insights for in the classroom* (pp. 155–177). New York: Cambridge University Press.

Connor, U., & Mbaye, A. (2002). Discourse approaches to writing assessment. *Annual Review of Applied Linguistics, 22,* 263–278.

Fathman, A. K., & Whalley, E. (1990). Teacher response to student writing: Focus on form versus content. In B. Kroll (Ed.), *Second language writing: Research insights for the classroom* (pp. 178–190). Cambridge: Cambridge University Press.

Goethals, P., & Delbecque, N. (2001a). La construcción de la argumentación y de la exposición. In Vázquez, G. (Ed.), *Guía didáctica del discurso académico escrito ¿Cómo se escribe una monografía?* (pp. 41–53). Madrid: Edinumen.

Goethals, P., & Delbecque, N. (2001b). La coherencia temática. In Vázquez, G. (Ed.), *Guía didáctica del discurso académico escrito ¿Cómo se escribe una monografía?* (pp. 54–66). Madrid: Edinumen.

Goethals, P., & Delbecque, N. (2001c). Personas del discurso y 'despersonalización.' In Vázquez, G. (Ed.), *Guía didáctica del discurso académico escrito ¿Cómo se escribe una monografía?* (pp. 67–73). Madrid: Edinumen.

Laca, B. (2001a). Matizaciones, modalizaciones, comentarios. In Vázquez, G. (Ed.), *Guía didáctica del discurso académico escrito ¿Cómo se escribe una monografía?* (pp. 95–105). Madrid: Edinumen.

Laca, B. (2001b). Relaciones retóricas y conectores. In Vázquez, G. (Ed.), *Guía didáctica del discurso académico escrito ¿Cómo se escribe una monografía?* (pp. 107–148). Madrid: Edinumen.

Laca, B. (2001c). Las reformulaciones. In Vázquez, G. (Ed.), *Guía didáctica del discurso académico escrito ¿Cómo se escribe una monografía?* (pp. 149–163). Madrid: Edinumen.

Lantolf, J. (2004). An overview of sociocultural theory. In Van Esch, K. & St. John, O. (Eds.), *New insights into foreign language learning and teaching* (pp. 13–34). Frankfurt: Peter Lang.

Lockhart, C., & Ng, P. (1993). How useful is peer response? *Perspectives, 5*(1), 17–30. Retrieved from http://sunzi1.lib.hku.hk/hkjo/ view/10/1000051.pdf.

Nas, M. S. (forthcoming). *The effects of feedback on the development of Spanish FL writing skills.* Nijmegen: PhD thesis.

Onieva Morales, J. L. (1995). *Curso superior de redacción.* Madrid: Verbum.

Polio, C. (2001). Research methodology in second language writing research: The case of text-based studies. In T. Silva & P. K. Matsuda (Eds.), *On second language writing* (pp. 91–115). Mahwah, NJ: Lawrence Erlbaum.

Schellens, P. J., & Verhoeven, G. (1994). *Argument en tegenargument. Analyse en beoordeling van betogende teksten.* Groningen: Martinus Nijhoff.

Serafini, M. T. (1996). *Cómo se escribe.* Barcelona: Ediciones Paidós.

Silva, T. (1993). Toward an understanding of the distinct nature of L2 writing: The ESL research and its implications. *TESOL Quarterly, 27*(4), 657–677.

Toulmin, S. (1958). *The uses of argument.* Cambridge: Cambridge University Press.

Van Esch, K., de Haan, P., & Nas, M. (2004). El desarrollo de la escritura en inglés y español como lenguas extranjeras. *Estudios de Lingüística Aplicada, 22*(39), 53–79.

Van Esch, K., & St. John, O. (Eds.). (2003). *A framework for freedom: Learner autonomy in foreign language teacher education.* Frankfurt am Main: Peter Lang.

Van Lier, L. (1996). Interaction in the language curriculum. *Awareness, autonomy, and Authenticity.* London/New York: Longman.

Vázquez, G. (Ed.) (2001). *Guía didáctica del discurso académico escrito ¿Cómo se escribe una monografía?.* Madrid: Edinumen.

Vygotsky, L. S. (1978). *Mind in society. The development of higher psychological processes.* Cambridge, MA: Harvard University Press.

Appendix A: Period 3 *Hispanoamérica*

Table 1. Activities in the Third Period: What Students Do Before, During, and after Class.

Sem	Actividades del curso *Destrezas escritas* B2	
	En clase	**Después: en casa/ en grupos**
	• Evaluar el examen del 1er periodo según Onieva (versión digital de las (see tareas en BB) • Practicar Toulmin: hacer modelo Toulmin del mismo examen • Hacer ejercicios de gramática sem 1	
1	• Introducción periodo 3: explicar programa y objetivos • Feedback sobre el examen de periodo 2 • Repetición de teoría periodo 2 • Evaluación del examen de periodo 1, en grupos: Toulmin (preparado antes) y Vázquez Cap.3 y 4 (en clase) • Gramática semana 1: selección	• Hacer versión digital del examen de periodo 2; publicar tanto en carpeta del grupo (3a/b/c/d) como individual; • Estudiar Vázquez Cap.6: *Matizaciones, modalizaciones, comentarios*, p.95-105 • Marcar en examen de periodo 2 las matizaciones/modalizaciones/comentarios (Vázquez Cap.6) • Leer *América Latina: de la complacencia a la demencia* y *Los siete pecados capitales de América Latina* y hacer las tareas correspondientes • Hacer ejercicios de gramática sem 2
2	• Discutir presencia Vázquez 6 en examen, en grupos • Tratar *América Latina: de la complacencia a la demencia* y *Los siete pecados capitales de América Latina* • Dar tarea de redacción: *tarea 3.1* • Gramática semana 2: selección	• Poner tarea 3.1 versión 1 en BB • Imprimir textos del grupo • Dar feedback según los puntos de evaluación determinados • Releer Onieva Morales: *El texto argumentativo*, p.184-193 • Hacer ejercicios de gramática sem 3
3	• Discutir feedback con las compañeras del grupo • Feedback de la profesora: en general e individualmente • Gramática semana 3: selección	• Revisar tarea 3.1 a base de los comentarios y publicar esta versión definitiva en Blackboard • Estudiar Vázquez Cap.7: *Relaciones retóricas y conectores*, hasta § 7.6 inclusive, p.107-129 • Leer *Una América sin Monroe* y hacer las tareas correspondientes • Hacer ejercicios de gramática sem 4
4	• Feedback de la profesora en tarea 3.1 • Tratar *Una América sin Monroe* • Tratar Vázquez Cap. 7 y explicar esquema de nexos • Gramática semana 4: selección	• Estudiar Vázquez Cap.7: *Relaciones retóricas y conectores*, § 7.7 hasta §7.9 inclusive, p.129-149 • Leer *Las "putas tristes" de Fidel* y hacer las tareas correspondientes • Hacer ejercicios de gramática sem 5
5	• Tratar *Las "putas tristes" de Fidel* • Dar tarea de redacción: *tarea 3.2* • Gramática semana 5: selección	• Poner tarea 3.2 versión 1 en BB • Imprimir textos del grupo • Dar feedback según los puntos de evaluación determinados • Hacer ejercicios de gramática sem 6

6	• Hablar del feedback en textos de miembros del grupo
	• Feedback de la profesora: en general e individualmente
	• Practicar Vázquez Cap.7 en 1ª versión de 3.2
	• Gramática semana 6: selección
		• Revisar tarea 3.2 a base de los comentarios la nueva teoría y publicar esta versión definitiva en Blackboard
		• Evaluar el examen del 2° periodo (versión digital de las tareas en BB)
		   o apuntar puntos fuertes y flojos según la teoría de Vázquez (cap. 6 y 7).
		   o Comentar el texto con la lista de Onieva
		• Hacer ejercicios de gramática sem 7

7	• Feedback de la profesora en tarea 3.2 • Discutir los resultados de la evaluación según Onieva y del análisis basado en Vázquez: las consecuencias para textos futuros • Gramática semana 7: selección	• Prepararse para el examen
Ex	• Examen 3	

Appendix B: Example Feedback Form, Third Period (Dutch parts translated)

Table 2. Feedback Form Part I: Focus on Particular Items, Room for Open Comments.

Feedback by Marly Nas Task: El pasado, pasado versión 1 Student: Roos	25 February 2008
Points of interest:	<ul><li>Text structure: introduction, body, conclusion (Vázquez Ch1) & types of introductions and conclusions (Serafini)</li><li>Argumentation:<ul><li>Claim; Strategies (Vázquez Ch2); Logical order</li><li>Toulminmodel of the text (Schellens & Verhoeven)</li><li>Evaluation according to Onieva Morales</li></ul></li><li>Language:<ul><li>Vocabulary and grammar</li><li>Thematic coherence</li><li>Presence of author</li><li>Hedges, modal qualifiers and evaluative comments</li></ul></li></ul>

Interesting start: the parallel with Cuba is quite nice. There may be an objection, though: to what extent do your readers consider Cuba a dictatorship? And where there as many victims during Castro's regime? You might want to reconsider this; perhaps you could attenuate your words a bit with the help of Vázquez' chapter 6.

In your conclusion you say nothing about Cuba! The content of the text does not appear sufficiently in it; try to explain how the relationship with the past should be, what "living the right way" means → it sounds idealistic, and that is okay, as long as you crystallize your ideas, which you do not do adequately.

Language: mind:
- *Se Construction with reflexive verbs: make the grammatical subject explicite;*
- *Prepositions → a-personal, compound prepositions;*
- *Subjunctive;*
- *Concordance in verb tenses*

- *Good luck!*

Table 3. Feedback Form Part II: Feedback on Argumentation (Onieva Morales,1995, pp. 193–4).

GUÍA PARA LA EVALUACIÓN DE TEXTOS ARGUMENTATIVOS (ONIEVA)

+ = bien   ± = regular   - = no se hace

Tesis "One has to try to find a relationship with the past & punishing is less important"   • ¿Expresa la tesis su opinión sobre un tema serio, susceptible de discusión? +   • ¿Está redactada de forma clara y concisa? ± It is rather vague ... what exactly is a relationship with the past?   • ¿Aparece la tesis en la introducción? +
Desarrollo de la argumentación   • ¿Ha aducido por lo menos tres razones que confirmen su opinión? ± 2: Chile & Argentina   • ¿Cada razón o argumento está suficientemente apoyada por evidencias (datos, ejemplos, experiencias personales, argumento de autoridad...)? ±   • ¿Ha considerado los puntos de vista contrarios y ha refutado las opiniones que se oponen a sus tesis? ± You do try, but the body of the text is still too short to really convince readers. You have worked out Chile reasonably, but it could be even better. As far as Argentina is concerned, I do not see how people should "just continue with their lives".
Unidad   • ¿Está relacionado directamente cada párrafo con la opinión expresada en la tesis? +   • ¿Hay alguna razón o argumento que se aparte del tema? -
Conexión entre ideas   • ¿Se puede seguir con facilidad el hilo de argumentación? ±   • ¿Ha usado las referencias directas y los conectores lógicos adecuados para enlazar las oraciones y párrafos entre sí? +
Ordenación   • ¿Ha ordenado las razones según su importancia? ¿? Same level
Conclusión very short: see p.1 of the feedback   • ¿La conclusión resume su opinión sobre el tema y se infiere de las razones aducidas? -   • ¿Apunta la conclusión una solución al tema planteado? +
Vocabulario   • ¿Ha empleado un vocabulario apropiado a los destinatarios? +
Tono   • ¿Es lo suficientemente serio y objetivo el tono de la argumentación? +   • ¿Se ha dejado llevar por sus sentimientos acerca del tema? -

Appendix C: Revision Process Task *Lo Pasado, Pasado:* Roos' Final Version

Figure 2. Final draft of "Lo Pasado, Pasado" by Roos: revisions made visible.

Llevamos con nosotros el pasado y el El 20 de febrero de 2008 Fidel Castro renunció su poder de la isla que gobernó hace muchos años. Hay algunas conjeturas acerca de lo que pasará en el país que fue aislado por tanto tiempo del resto del mundo. ¿Cómo cambiará la vida cubana? Durante el largo periodo en que gobernó Castro, los cubanos vivieron en un carcel encerrado por el agua. Otros países hispanoamericanos como Chile y Argentina han precedido en el proceso de recuperar de una dictadura. Es un proceso complicado en que el pueblo debe acostumbrarse a una nueva manera de vivir pero al mismo tiempo comprobar su relación con el pasado. Es decir, encontrar una manera de manejar el pasado, a lo mejor usarlo para formar un futuro estable. Los países tienen que manejar el problema de la responsabilidad, borrar los hechos o punir a los culpables. Pero cómo comprobar quién es y quién no, resultará ser difícil. No es objeto de volver a escribir la historia, sino usarla para tomar posición en el presente y para contraer el futuro. Se debe intentar encontrar una relación con el pasado o sea usarlo para dar forma a la vida, en este proceso el castigo de los culpables es de menos importancia. El pasado de que trata es uno que lleva un trauma consigo: lo de una dictadura. Vivir en esto significa sobre todo que uno no vive en libertad y esto significa que hay ellos que controlan y ellos que son controlados. El grupo que tiene el poder puede imponerlo a través de violencia directa como sucedió en las juntas militares de Argentina y Chile pero también por una manera que se puede llamar más amenazadora, como se instaló en Chile después de los primeros meses de violencia, una violencia de saber que los paredes tienen ojos y orejas. Y que no se puede confiar en nadie. ¿Este ambiente es ahogante pero cómo es posible comprobar quién será culpable para hacer la vida así? En general se busca maneras para punir al grupo que representa el regimen, pero en este proceso habrá el problema de distinguir culpables de complices y complices de inocentes. ¿Dónde está la linea entre los grupos? El problema de la culpabilidad es demasiado complicado para punir todos, por eso la gente debe encontrar una manera de manejar su pasado en otro manera en todos casos no ser dependiente de la castigación de los culpables.

En Chile por mucho tiempo se ha intentado enjuiciar al antiguo dictador Augusto Pinochet que gobernó el país con mano duro por 16 años después de un golpe de estado en que murió el presidente socialista Salvador Allende. Pero por una construcción de leyes que hizo Pinochet antes de transpasar el poder, no lograron en presentarle ante un tribunal. Hasta su muerte en 2006 diferentes grupos de interés intentaban de hacerlo bajo la atención de la media mundial. ¿Hubiera sido mejor la transición chilena con un juicio legal de Pinochet o es un juicio que puede hacer cada persona para si misma, sin la necesidad confirmación de un instancia público? La

APPENDIX D: EXCERPTS OF FEEDBACK TRANSCRIPTION

Group: Carolina, Marisa, & Madeline

first period, week 5, first discussion of peer feedback on task *Mendigos* (first draft)

> Carolina: Er, let's see. I think the text organization is okay, er . . . I think I would've set the content in a different order, er . . . I find it hard to explain this. I think the paragraphs are quite short, and they skip from one subject to another, like. Er . . . it is like . . . every paragraph has a completely different subject. You are discussing, er . . . for example the ideas of the beggars and the mayors, and then you move to the causes, and then to er . . . what er . . . the beggars want, I thought it was quite, well, maybe I would've just changed it a bit, to make the transition smoother. But of course that can be personal. . . .
>
> Marisa: So first . . . Yes. For example first mention the causes and afterwards . . .
>
> Carolina: Yes because her you say for example that er . . . well that er. . that there are people who think it is simply the beggars' fault, well then that's something you could go into, like "this often is not the case because there are causes that . . ." then it would be more fluent . . . but, well that can be personal, maybe you thought it was ok, but this was my feedback on that aspect. Furthermore, the content is very well, er. . yes, only the conclusion, but that probable has to do with my Spanish, (laughs) I didn't really understand what you were trying to say.
>
> Marisa: Er . . . ok. Yes, I was still working on that one.
>
> Carolina: Yes, I saw that.
>
> Marisa: I have to er . . . elaborate more on that.
>
> Carolina: Yes. .
>
> (a few minutes later)
>
> Madeline: (. . .) Let's see, er . . . I think the er . . . conclusion on the content . . . I think, well, the example, you know, a bit . . . weak compared to the text of the . . .

of the central part of the text, like. Er . . . let's see . . . I didn't think it was an attractive combination with the rest of the text.

Marisa: No, I was er I am still . . . how I can like connect it with the, with the conclusion . . . with the rest of the text.

Madeline: Yes. Because in itself it's a good example, because . . . to indicate . . . it's just the way I see it now, reading the text at this moment I didn't think the transition was very, er . . . beautiful actually, not very beautiful.

Marisa: No, that's right, er . . . I'm still working on it (Laughs quietly)

first period, week 7, first discussion of peer feedback on task *Mendigos* (last draft)

Carolina: Let's see. I don't have that much because I really think your revision was quite well, like. So er . . . we had some feedback and I found that you had . . . that you really have done something with it. (. . .) Er . . . you've changed your conclusion completely, I think?

Marisa: Correct.

Carolina: Well, I think it is, better and clearer, a better connection to the text. I thought that was really good. Er . . . argumentation . . . yes, also very good. The text organization is good, the order is logical, and the arguments are good. You, er . . . you really explain your point of view. (. . .)

Marisa: Thank you. I actually adjusted the point of view a bit. I immediately changed er . . . the title and from that point on I er . . . went in a different direction, actually. I'm glad that, er . . . yes, that it's better now.

second period, week 3, 1st first discussion of peer feedback on task *Jóvenes y violencia* (first draft)

Carolina: Er . . . the title was not really good. Er . . . but, well, that's also very personal, it does indicate clearly what the text is about. But, hey, I didn't think like, o wow that text I'll (read) . . . it's not . . . well how can I put this? That you think wow, what would that be (about) oh, I'm gonna read this, you know. It's very,

very clear and all what it is about, but, well, I don't know, I didn't think it was very strong. But it's only a detail.

(five minutes later)

Madeline: Yes. And er . . . about the title, well, I didn't think too much of it either, but then again, my title wasn't too good either.

Marisa: (laughs)

Madeline: No, but er . . .

Marisa: No, you're right. Carolina said that too . . . I mean, how could I change that? Yes, I think it's very hard to find a title for this . . .

Madeline: Maybe you just need another word for "busca," I think

Carolina: Yes.

Madeline: Er . . . I don't know if, when you would translate it, if you, I fit would be in Dutch like, one demands, like, I don't know, it would be tougher than "busca."

Carolina: Yes, but anyhow. . . . I think anyhow that whole piece of "se busca" isn't quite good, but well . . .

Marisa: To me it was like the idea of an add, you know.

Carolina: Yes, yes, that's what I thought. (. . . . .)

Marisa: Yes, these always begin with "se busca," right?

Carolina: Yes, one is looking for, yes, "se busca."

Madeline: Yes, but I don't know if I would . . . yes in any case I would try to find something different for "busca" . . . but of course if that's what you want . . .

Carolina: No, because then her idea is gone.

Madeline: Then it's gone, maybe a different title.

Marisa: Yes, I'll think about it.

Carolina: It's very personal, of course.

Marisa: Yes, it is. (. . .)

Carolina: In itself it's a nice idea to do it this way, but, well.

Marisa: But you say something is missing?

Carolina: I think it doesn't quite fit the text, like. I don't know, the idea of an add. But well.

Marisa: Yes, I think it actually was . . . well . . .

Carolina: (But) if you like it.

Marisa: Yes, I thought it did fit like, well, this is the case and we are still looking for how we can improve, how we can solve this.
Carolina: Yes.
Madeline: Yes, but it's about your best solution is that people discuss about it, maybe that's what you need to er . . .
Marisa: That (should be) more . . .
Madeline: . . . link with the title.
Marisa: Yes.
Madeline: If you, with a discussion you find a solution but you're not looking like, well, I don't know. I just don't like it this way.
Marisa: Yes.
Madeline: I think.
Marisa: Well, yes, ok. I will er . . . think about it in any case.
Carolina: You don't necessarily have to do something with this (feedback), do you?
Madeline: No.
Carolina: If you like it, then er . . .
Marisa: Anyway. Er . . . shall we move on to the next text?

12 The Quest for Grammatical Accuracy: Writing Instruction among Foreign and Heritage Language Educators

Natalie Lefkowitz

Background

My colleague, John Hedgcock, and I have for some time been interested in the social dynamics of the foreign language (FL) classroom (Hedgcock & Lefkowitz, 2000; Lefkowitz & Hedgcock, 2002, 2006, 2011). Most recently, we have been drawn to contrasting language socialization processes of traditional FL and heritage language (HL) students of Spanish at the university level in the US (Lefkowitz & Hedgcock, 2007, 2008, 2009; Hedgcock & Lefkowitz, in press). According to Valdés (2000a), a HL speaker is someone who has been "raised in a home where a non-English language is spoken, who speaks or merely understands the heritage language and who is to some degree bilingual in English and the heritage language" (p. 1).

Roca and Colombi (2003) noted that "multicultural classrooms are the norm in our schools today" (p. 3), yet Spanish language instruction—frequently geared toward monolingual, Anglophone students—does not uniformly address the unique educational needs of diverse populations of HL students (Bucholtz, 2007; Chevalier, 2004; Colombi, 2003; Colombi & Roca, 2003; Hidalgo, 1993; Mar-Molinero, 1997, 2000; Roca, 1997, 2001; Valdés, 2000b, 2001; Zentella, 2007). Valdés, Fishman, Chávez, and Pérez (2006), have called for a deeper understanding of bilingualism, language contact, and the need to develop appropriate language and literacy instruction.

Nevertheless, Duff (2004) observed that research has just begun "to study heritage-language learners in comparison with non-heritage students, especially in terms of their ultimate attainment [and] identity issues" (p. 3). Few studies have systematically compared HL and FL students' learning patterns, particularly in classroom contexts where the two populations are intermingled (Campbell & Rosenthal, 2005; Lynch, 2003a, 2003b). My recent work with John Hedgcock has examined how linguistic attitudes expressed by FL educators in US university writing classrooms influence the self-perceptions, identity (re)construction processes, language learning, and literacy development patterns of FL and HL students. As a further step, this chapter explores how a group of FL instructors' beliefs about writing may inadvertently affect their instructional approaches, their attitudes toward FL and HL students, and perhaps ultimately, those students' opinions about themselves.

Not unlike many FL departments in the US, the one considered in the present study offers Spanish, Japanese, French, German, Russian, Chinese, Latin, and ASL. With the exception of Spanish, the other language programs are considerably smaller, and are staffed by only one professor with occasional adjunct assistance or help from other professors with sufficient proficiency in an additional language. It is reasonable to say that the students in these courses receive the majority of their first three years of FL input from the same instructor. Because of limited offerings, many students are required to finish their FL majors by supplementing their courses with study abroad programs. Spanish, however, is taught by seven professors and one to two adjuncts, depending on demand. The most highly enrolled languages are Spanish and ASL, lending credence to the folk myths that Spanish is easy and that ASL is even easier because of the absence of a writing system. For this chapter, ASL and Latin have been excluded, largely due to the absence of composition in their programs.

The context I have described is perhaps familiar to many. A diverse group of overworked individuals resides under the same roof, working diligently to teach everything they know about Spanish, Japanese, French, Chinese, Russian, and German, with the goal of imparting their considerable passions for these languages to oversized classes of both willing and not-so-willing students. Until recently, these learners were mostly monolingual Anglo-Americans, but that situation has changed due to the influx of HL speakers of Spanish. In this environment, many professors share long-established views about writing instruction. Some faculty members admitted to having inherited these professional beliefs from their predecessors, at times carrying on traditions that they themselves might have scorned in the past. All approach their teaching with good intentions and the conviction that their practices will serve the best interests of the department. Although these instructors inhabit the same space, they vary in terms of language background, native-speaker (NS) versus non-native speaker (NNS) status, formal training (literature versus linguistics), age, gender, and educational philosophy. Despite these differences, they are united by the quest for accuracy. This pursuit often takes priority over other factors, particularly when it comes to teaching and evaluating FL and HL students' writing.

While extensive research has focused on second language (L2) writing in ESL and EFL contexts, comparatively fewer studies have addressed L2 writing in FL settings until recently. This lacuna in the field may indirectly contribute to the proliferation of traditional practices in the teaching of writing in FL education. Oversized classes, heavy teaching loads, multiple preparations, budget cuts, understaffing, and consequent limited time result in further impediments to these instructors' abilities to access resources available for their professional growth.

Method and Guiding Questions

This study is part of an ongoing, exploratory investigation of the language and literacy socialization patterns of HL and FL students in university settings (Lefkowitz & Hedgcock, 2007, 2008, 2009, 2011). The approach taken to data collection and analysis is heuristic, reiterative, and action-oriented (Brown & Rodgers, 2002; Creswell, 2007; McKay, 2006; Nunan, 1992; Patton, 1990; Richards, 2003). The mixed methods design reflects a concurrent triangulation approach in which "the researcher collects both quantitative and qualitative data concurrently and then compares the two data bases to determine if there is convergence, differences, or some combination" (Creswell, 2009, p. 213). Quantitative data consist of written responses to a survey administered to students and oral responses to questions posed to instructors during structured interview segments. Qualitative data consist of selected instructor and student responses to semi-structured interview prompts. The three questions that guide this work address pedagogical practices employed in L2 writing instruction geared toward FL and HL student writers:

1. What beliefs about writing instruction are predominant among FL educators?

2. How do instructors' perceptions influence pedagogical practices geared toward FL and HL students?

3. How might FL and HL learners be affected by their language teachers' attitudes and instructional approaches?

Participants

Participants in this study included thirty third year Anglophone FL students (seven male, twenty-three female), ranging in age from 19–34 years enrolled in Spanish language and literature courses at a comprehensive, regional university in the western United States; 73% of FL students (22 of 30) reported having taken Spanish courses alongside HL students. Also included were twenty-four Spanish HL learners (Spanish-English bilinguals) enrolled in Spanish language and literature courses. Eleven were male and thirteen female with an age range of 19–52. In addition to surveying students, we solicited data from fourteen FL instructors currently teaching at the same tertiary institution as the student participants, eight who teach Spanish, and two who teach Chinese. Remaining participants include one French instructor, one German instructor, one Japanese instructor, and one Russian instructor.

The number of native speaker (NS) instructors in this group includes two in Spanish, one in Russian, one in Japanese, two in Chinese, and one in German. Eight of the instructors were female and six were male. Twelve had received their degrees in literature and two in linguistics. With the exception of three adjuncts with MA degrees, all writing instructors have PhDs. The educators who participated in interviews included two novice adjuncts among seasoned lecturers and professors with 5–40 years of experience. These instructors were chosen because they have taught the first or second term of the third year FL writing course, Composition and Grammar, or its HL equivalent, Spanish for Heritage Speakers.

Materials

Following the initial phase of this research, John Hedgcock and I administered an adapted version of the Valdés et al. (2006) survey to HL and FL students; we followed a semi-structured protocol for ethnographic interviews conducted with the HL student group (Creswell, 2007; Johnson & Christensen, 2008). Interviews with fourteen FL instructors involved a highly structured segment (which supplied quantitative and qualitative responses), as well as a semi-structured segment (which supplied open-ended qualitative responses). Interviews were audio recorded, with selected portions transcribed and analyzed (Creswell, 2009). The extracts below are drawn mainly from interviews with eight Spanish language professors, though data from interviews with FL instructors who teach other languages are also included. Guiding questions focused on participants': (1) demographics and prior training, (2) impressions of students, instructional aims, and course content, (3) beliefs and practices regarding error treatment, and 4) views on academic literacy. The complete interview protocol appears in the Appendix.

Analyses and Results

Formal teacher training. When asked about their formal knowledge regarding the teaching of writing, only half of the FL instructors reported having received any training, often a short unit on writing instruction in the methods course they had taken as graduate students. The other half reported having undergone no training in composition teaching. In fact, the novice instructors repeatedly described their approach in FL writing courses as "flying by the seat of my pants," and "trial and error." None of the HL writing instructors interviewed reported having received any formal training in teaching their target language (TL) to heritage students, a finding consistent with Valdés (2000b). Schwartz (2001) pointed out that "few teacher preparation programs include training in heritage language issues, and those that do find little to guide them in the development of instructional methods and curricula" (p. 229). She further observed that "most teachers of heritage language classes are trained as foreign language teachers, or they are native speakers of the language with little or no training in language instruction" (p. 230). Gutiérrez (1997) agreed: "Teacher training programs pay little to no attention to preparing future educators to meet the needs of heritage speakers" (p. 34).

Teachers' comfort level. Table 1 displays responses to a question regarding instructors' comfort level teaching HL learners. Results indicate that all participants reported feeling somewhat to very comfortable. Nevertheless, details contradicting these claims emerged in participant interviews.

Table 1: Comfort level teaching HL students (Q 4).

Very comfortable	7
Somewhat comfortable	4
Neither comfortable nor uncomfortable	0
Somewhat uncomfortable	0
Very uncomfortable	0
Not reported	3

The issue of comfort is particularly striking in the responses of inexperienced professors teaching FL writing courses and NNS professors teaching HL writing courses. For instance, one novice FL writing instructor stated, "Frankly, I don't know what I am doing in there." Several NNS instructors teaching HL learners shared their experiences. After reporting feeling "very comfortable" teaching writing to HL students, one professor mentioned feeling uncomfortable about having disagreed with an HL student about adjective placement. "I try to value [HL students' linguistic varieties], but I don't know if it is standard or not. I am not quite sure of expressions, turns of phrases, prepositions (*entrar a* versus *entrar en*). There is discomfort when I am right and they are not." A novice NNS adjunct teaching a course serving both HL and FL students noted, "I feel more intimidated and less experienced with HL students. They question your authority. With non-native speakers you can appear as an unqualified expert and won't be questioned." This uneasiness was shared by a NS instructor teaching HL writing who claimed, "You feel they are challenging your authority and you don't really want this as a teacher."

Earlier research reflects this awkwardness among FL educators. In line with Kramsch (1997), Edstrom (2005) addressed the question of native versus nonnative speakership regarding Edstrom's own teaching:

> I wrestled with the question of my legitimacy and my abilities as a nonnative and worried about a variety of possible scenarios. For example, would I commit grammatical errors as I conducted class? Or would students ask me about vocabulary I did not know? Time and experience gradually convinced me that my personal insights and empathy as a language learner outweighed my gaps in L2 vocabulary or lapses in grammatical accuracy. (pp. 27–28)

Reagan and Olson (2002) echoed these sentiments:

> In some school districts, [FL] teachers replace guidance counselors in the context of placement advisor with respect to foreign language classes, and have been known to use this power to guide native speakers (and heritage language learners as well) into independent study courses, thus isolating the student and protecting the teacher from any challenge to linguistic authority in the classroom. (p. 10)

Level of enjoyment as teachers of composition. When asked to rate their level of enjoyment as composition teachers, more than half of the instructors queried indicated that it was moderate to high; one reported neither high nor low, three said low, and one said very low. A salient feature emerging here is that levels of enjoyment were often associated in some way with grammar and error correction as illustrated by the following comments:

- "I really enjoy teaching grammar" (High);
- "I am looking at language rather than content" (Moderate);
- "It's mostly grammar" (Neither high nor low);
- "Labor intensiveness and torture of reading student compositions because of linguistic difficulties, lack of ideas and uninteresting content" (Low);
- "90% of the class is not prepared. They don't understand grammar" (Very low);

- "The students have very poor performance in spite of correction" (Very low).

These responses reveal a striking pattern throughout the interviews: the equation of FL composition instruction with grammar instruction and error prevention. One cannot help but speculate whether their quest for accuracy may somehow influence FL instructors' perceptions of their students and their language abilities.

Instructor perceptions and beliefs about students' language abilities. We asked professors to assess their FL and HL students' strengths and weaknesses in sub-skill areas. Table 2 reports the frequency of those ratings, which are not dissimilar to HL students' own perceptions of their stronger and weaker competencies.

Table 2. Instructors' perceptions and beliefs about FL and HL students' strengths and weaknesses (Qs 18–21).

	L	S	R	W	G
Q18. FL Strongest	8	3	3	2	3
Q19. HL Strongest	6	3	0	0	0
Q20. FL Weakest	1	6	2	7	2
Q21. HL Weakest	1	1	2	7	3

L = Listening; S = Speaking; R = Reading; W = Writing; G = Grammar

Interestingly, when asked to elaborate upon their numeric ratings of students' abilities, instructors evinced contradictory attitudes, providing qualitative responses that differed from quantitative responses. The instructors' opinions about FL learners were equally discouraging to those they held of HL students, but for different reasons. We analyzed the interviews of selected Spanish instructors for evidence of their beliefs about, and attitudes toward, HL students and their linguistic strengths and weaknesses, as well as toward FL learners of Spanish. When providing examples of students' typical errors, instructors expressed the view that HL learners displayed intuitive but uninformed grammatical knowledge and strong oral and aural skills. In contrast, instructors felt that HL students exhibited limited reading skills, which negatively affected their writing performance, specifically in areas such as spelling, punctuation, mood, and constituent structure (e.g., *lacasa*, rather than *la casa*). Instructors further observed interlingual transfer between Spanish and English (also referred to as *Spanglish*), lexical errors, problems with register, and lack of metalinguistic knowledge. These characteristics parallel those discussed in the HL literature (Carreira, 2007; Hidalgo, 1990; Lipski, 2006; Martínez, 2006; Potowski, 2002; Potowski & Cameron, 2007; Roca & Lipski, 1993: Schwarzer & Petrón, 2005; Valdés, 1995, 2000a, 2001).

Common FL errors were seen by instructors to result from direct translation, ineffectual bilingual dictionary use, poor syntax, and errors involving verb tenses, gender, articles, agreement, mood, aspect, prepositions, and limited vocabulary. In languages other than Spanish, both Russian and German instructors discussed the challenging nature of case systems, the Japanese teacher mentioned particles, and the French professor pointed to spelling and accents, referring to the lack of grapheme-phoneme correspondence in French. Interview data again reveal a strong concern among instructors about students' deficient grammar and poor reading habits.

- " . . . Their reading habits are not good. They are only motivated to read to pass the exam";
- "The ones that need the most help won't seek it out";
- "Their language skills need lots of improvement."

Spanish instructor attitudes about HL writing. Holmes (1992) asserted that " . . . students who speak stigmatized varieties are not disadvantaged by inadequate language. They are disadvantaged by the negative attitudes toward their speech—attitudes that derive from their relatively low social status and its associations in people's (teachers') minds" (p. 356). When asked in their interviews to share their attitudes about HL students' writing, teachers expressed attitudes reflecting a subtractive rather than additive view of linguistic diversity, a trait often discussed in the literature (Edstrom, 2005; Pérez-Leroux & Glass, 2000; Valdés, 2006; Villa, 1996, 2002).

- HL students "recognize their literacy skills are not what they could be. They need to get a good foundation";
- HL students' "language skills need lots of improvement. They feel that there are lots of gaps, which there are . . .";

- HL students' writing "reflects their oral practice—it is not appropriate for a literature paper";
- "That's a good word to use with friends or at home, but not in more formal environments."

Driven by good intentions and a quest for accuracy, some instructors failed to report any connection between their own attitudes toward HL students and their possible effect on students' linguistic self-esteem. As a Spanish professor observed, HL students "feel failure . . . don't know grammar because they did not learn it in first and second year. They haven't been coached." This tendency to shift blame to beginning level classes is a common practice (Byrnes, 1998; Reichelt, 1999).

One Spanish professor of HL students, when asked to discuss the value of maintaining HL students' varieties, replied, "I never thought of maintaining what most people would consider substandard." A less experienced Spanish adjunct added that "Teaching [HL students] is like teaching illiterate adults how to become writers." Such comments confirm findings by Reagan and Olson (2002) regarding "which language varieties are deemed by the society (or some subset of the society) to be legitimate, and which are not." They further added that the issue of linguistic legitimacy " . . . touches on issues of social class, ethnicity, and culture, and is embedded in relations of dominance and power" (p. 34).

Impressions of HL students by NS instructors of FLs other than Spanish. Although most of this discussion has been confined to the Spanish as a foreign language context, it is worth noting that NS FL instructor attitudes toward HL students and their language proficiency is apparently not unique to Spanish. The following observations shared by instructors of German, Chinese, Russian, and Japanese refer to the same mismatches between high-prestige registers and home dialects and to the same perception that HL students' knowledge exhibits weak grammatical control and a low degree of language awareness.

- "HL students are not grammatically correct . . . they are incorrect. They learn spoken language, use family language (mixture), and it's not appropriate or useful in formal situations";

- "I try to get them to break their bad habits and attitudes. They take the language because it is easy. They feel that their language is much higher than it is. Some of them are not familiar with the characters";
- "HL students have prior exposure to incorrect language. 'My mother said this.' Their language is a mix. At home they speak both and that it is a no-no";
- "HL students can speak but they can't write. Their style tends to be casual—the way we speak in the house. I try not to belittle them, but they need to know, 'Maybe you are not aware how this sounds to other people—it can be viewed as offensive.'"

It seems fair to assume that instructors' opinions do not go unnoticed by students. Given the similarities between the instructors' perceptions of their students' abilities and their students' self-perceptions, one at times wonders if these opinions may, at some level, contribute to students' low linguistic self-esteem. Although both student groups strongly valued high proficiency in Spanish, the HL students consistently expressed a high level of insecurity when it came to writing, as these comments illustrate:

- "Sometimes I don't know if what I'm saying in my dialect is correct according to where [teachers] learned it";
- "I use colloquial—I want to make it more standard . . . now I'm aware that I was poor in Spanish and need to improve it . . . I know that I'm limited to some parts of my language";
- " . . . I had no notion of [writing]. I made lots of mistakes as far as writing goes . . . I might be at a higher level as far as conversating and speaking";
- "My writing is not professional."

In addition to making comments that exposed their negative linguistic identities, HL students expressed the view that they were being held to different and unrealistic standards compared to their FL counterparts.

Differing expectations of HL and FL students. In their discussion on double standards for FL and HL students, Reagan and Olson (2002) emphasized that "the kind of proficiency downplayed in bilingual education programs as inadequate would be seen in a foreign language context as quite impressive" (p. 6). Comparably contradictory expectations were expressed by instructors in the present study. For example, although some individuals reported expecting fewer linguistic difficulties from HL students, thus allowing them to focus more on content and ideas, others found HL student writing to lack imagination, much like that of FL student writing. One instructor said that she held HL students to higher standards; another mentioned that he expected them to grasp the material more quickly. Similar to findings by Carreira (2004, 2007) and Potowski (2002), HL students in this study were acutely aware of these divergent standards:

- [One native Spanish speaker] professor " . . . was always making negative comments and that made me feel bad . . . My vocabulary was not the one the professor was expecting. The professor was constantly correcting my vocabulary and said you should say this instead of that";
- Spanish teachers "[perceive] me as a native speaker and then hold me to a higher standard than other students. They expect me to succeed more because I am a native speaker. It's bad to have different expectations";
- Professors "always expect the native speakers to know everything";
- Professors sometimes "expect natives to know everything" and say that HL students do not speak Spanish well. A standard variety of Spanish should be taught, "but that doesn't mean that other countries don't speak good Spanish."

Instructional aims. Recurring themes emerge in surveying the interview data, including a persistent concern for grammatical accuracy and awareness, as well as traditional academic literacy skills associated with a literature-based curriculum. These views are reflected in pedagogical practices. When asked about their most important goals for FL and HL students taking writing courses, instructors consistently referenced grammar as a top priority. Teachers expressed a desire for their students to "perfect their grammar," "review it," "acquire it at a more sophisticated level," "master and solidify grammar, analyze grammar, use grammar correctly," and be able to use "basic parts of speech." One instructor hoped that his students would attain "some proficiency at

The Quest for Grammatical Accuracy

writing business and personal letters," but was unable to define what he meant by "proficiency." Secondary objectives included the ability to:

- express, narrate, and describe ideas and events with a degree of linguistic sophistication;
- translate;
- speak only the TL;
- watch films in their original versions;
- converse on a topic of medium difficulty;
- develop a broader understanding of rhetorical modes;
- engage in critical thinking;
- learn how use the dictionary efficiently;
- communicate effectively in the TL without translation.

When asked how they would achieve these goals, instructors suggested practicing grammar, providing more exposure to written materials for reading and writing, studying model texts, and applying textbook activities to new contexts.

Materials, syllabi, and course content. In terms of materials, syllabi, and course content, the majority of FL courses were driven by grammar textbooks and supplemented by authentic documents and writing exercises. Fewer professors incorporated a multimedia component to their classes, but several expressed a desire to do so. Four Spanish professors and the Russian professor wrote their syllabi in the TL. The rest used English to ensure adequate understanding. Culture was clearly viewed as important, but only if there were enough time. The general consensus was that cultural topics are addressed "as they come up" in assigned texts or by sharing personal experiences, customs, and cultural tidbits.

Sociolinguistic awareness. When questions of sociolinguistic awareness and sensitivity were raised, several instructors requested clarification about the meaning of the term. Teachers of Asian languages expressed the importance of teaching honorifics, politeness, and formality norms. Professors of HL speakers of Spanish mentioned that register comes up all the time and emphasized developing a response to students who say, "We always say that." In reference to non-academic registers, a NNS Spanish instructor said, "They are all valid, they are just different styles and registers. We are trying to increase the more formal register—the way we speak is different from the way we write." However, when talking about providing HL students with sensitive feedback on their writing, the same professor reported,

> I have no time for that crap. Sure it doesn't build a lot of self-esteem, but comments like 'This could be better' don't work. Instead of saying 'I think your title could be improved, or 'It doesn't capture my attention.' I now say things like 'To be brutally honest, your title is boring and meaningless.'

It is evident here that "instructors may not be aware of the messages they are sending when they correct heritage Spanish speaking students' language, a sensitivity that might be developed" (Potowski, 2002, p. 39). Carreira (2007) and Gutiérrez (1997) made similar observations. Along the same lines, van Lier (1995) wrote that "[l]anguage awareness must involve a conscious effort to put correctness in its proper place: It is a social phenomenon, on par with dress codes and table manners" (p. 82).

Also consistent in several instructor responses is an implicit—and sometimes explicit—view that HL students' home and community dialects are incompatible with, and less prestigious than the pedagogical standard. As one NS Spanish professor reflected,

> I tolerate all [HL students' varieties]. I accept. I'm not against. It's fine. Very colorful . . . the sintaxis (sic) and grammar is not always correct . . . [a] very colloquial dialect—to live day by day and talk about simple things, not good for abstract thinking or sophisticated ways of thinking. I don't think it is high prestige . . . In many cases, they feel ashamed, but they don't want to express it.

This perspective, similar to those expressed earlier, coincides with Valdés's (2006) observation that native-speaking educators of the same language background as their HL students may view these learners "with contempt" (p. 126).

Error treatment. Teachers were also asked to comment on their approaches to correction, as well as the types of assignments they preferred, the ways in which they assessed them, and the feedback they provided. A preoccupation with grammar was pervasive among their responses. An abundance of research is available on L2 writing feedback and error treatment in the ESL context (Chandler, 2003; Fathman & Whalley, 1990; Ferris, 2002, 2003, 2004; Goldstein, 2005; Hyland & Hyland, 2001, 2006; Truscott, 2007). However, when asked to give reasons for their correction strategies, FL instructors justified their actions based on having learned it that way as graduate students and added that they did not feel a strong conviction about some of their practices. Table 3 suggests a range of approaches to correction. Instructors were permitted to check more than one option. Most reported using implicit approaches, such as symbols, codes, and underlining, but explicit correction, editing, marginal comments and endnotes were also popular choices.

Table 3. Error treatment strategies (Q 25).

Symbols	8
Underlining	8
Color coding	1
Explicit correction/editing	4
Marginal comments	3
Endnotes	8

Instructors' views toward the importance of students knowing metalinguistic terminology. In a question regarding the importance of students knowing metalinguistic terminology (e.g., noun, pronoun, subjunctive, indicative, and so on), the majority of instructors responded with a resounding "Yes!" This approval parallels findings by Reichelt (1999), and is consistent with the tendency throughout the interviews for FL instructors to equate writing with grammar. When asked to give reasons for this view, they offered a range of comments:

- "It's the only way to communicate. It's like a mathematical formula."
- "I like it so I force it on my students. Screw it if they don't like it."

- "Since they have no idea about English grammar, it helps them understand better. It is essential for comparative grammar."
- "So they can understand my explanations and analyze sentences."
- "If they are going to be teachers, they need to be able to explain grammar."

Number of assignments, favored tasks, and goals. In FL and HL writing courses, the number of compositions assigned ranged from one to five, with three being the average. In general, composing assignments were somewhat guided, relied on models, or were designed to elicit specific grammatical features (Scott, 1996). Russian and Japanese instructors felt that their students were not capable of writing freely and consequently assigned translation tasks. When asked to share their favorite assignments, several professors had difficulty remembering any. Others pointed to creative narration, literary analysis, and grammar identification exercises. In fact, once again, writing and grammar were viewed as synonymous in these responses. The least favorite assignments included portfolios. Respondents appeared overwhelmed by the task and showed a lack of understanding of the purpose of a portfolio as indicated by observations such as, "It's a pain in the ass. What's the point?" and "What does that mean, they put the compositions in a folder?"

Multiple-drafting. All participants reported using a multiple-drafting approach in teaching writing, with two professors requiring two drafts and the others three. The required length of compositions ranged from 250 to 450 words. Reasons given for length choice included: "It's a fairly easy length to write and long enough for me to see their skills"; "They can't ramble on forever and it forces them to get to the point;" and "It's long enough to develop an argument, but short enough to prevent multiple mistakes." The eradication of errors appears to be a recurring theme among these educators' pedagogical choices.

Rhetorical modes and genres. 50% of the instructors taught rhetorical modes, with narration the most popular choice. The most common genre employed was the expository essay, although creative fiction, poetry and verse, and business correspondence were also addressed. In the interviews, these topics were mentioned less often than the desire for grammatical accuracy.

Classroom activities. Teachers were also asked to identify their preferred classroom procedures and task types and to provide reasons for their beliefs. Their choices and responses are listed in Table 4.

Table 4. Procedures/task types (Q 43)*.

Literary analysis	4
Analysis of student writing	10
Peer response	5
Grammar presentation/explanation	8
Oral grammar practice	4
Intensive reading	3
Extensive reading	2
Vocabulary practice	8
Dictation	4
Language awareness activities	3

*Multiple responses were permitted.

As already noted, instructors' beliefs about writing strongly influenced their procedures and preferences. Of all the tasks listed in Table 4, answers clustered around grammar-driven activities, such as grammar presentation and explanation and oral grammar practice. According to some interviews, even analysis of student writing, dictation, and language awareness activities centered on discrete grammatical features. Peer response, as will be seen later, was unpopular due to instructors' perceptions that their students' language skills were too poor for the procedure to be effective. After form-focused tasks, vocabulary instruction received the second most attention, with reading at the bottom.

When teachers were asked to justify these choices, similar patterns emerged. In addition to giving "familiarity" as a reason for choosing these activities, other explanations included the reinforcement of grammatical knowledge and idiomatic language. German, French, and Spanish professors offered the following form-focused comments:

- "Once the groove is made, the needle will pick it up."
- "They reinforce the purpose of the class—grammar."
- "These tasks are most effective for grammar and writing."

The phonograph metaphor in the first comment mirrors the traditional principles guiding some of these pedagogical choices. It was also not unusual for professors to express the belief that grammar should be taught in English.

Assessment and feedback. Assessment and feedback approaches varied. Although some professors claimed to use a multi-draft approach in order to pay attention to content, organization, and the writing process, other interview responses revealed a more product-oriented perspective, emphasizing the correction of linguistic errors. By focusing on their students' written shortcomings, instructors aimed to help them:

- "Rewrite flawlessly."
- "Revisit their mistakes and try to figure them out."
- "Make their students do their best work from the start."
- "Figure out their problems, decipher and figure out how to fix it."

Written comments. With one exception, all instructors reported providing their students with written comments. Professors wrote comments in both the TL and English. Regarding writing comments in English, one NNS instructor said, "It takes less time, and I can express myself better. The whole point is to give them feedback, and it doesn't matter what language it is. They can process English better." A Spanish professor stressed never using red, while a Chinese colleague stated, "In Chinese, it's rude to write in red because it is more highlighted.

Chinese teachers always use red so I got used to it. I am the teacher so I can be rude."

Peer response. As noted above, peer response was less widely employed. Six professors reported never using it because they were concerned with protecting students' privacy and avoiding embarrassment. Paradoxically, the very same instructors were not opposed to revealing their students' grammatical mistakes in class. One reason for avoiding peer response was that "[students'] grammar was so bad [that] they were reinforcing each others' mistakes, and it didn't work." Instructors who used peer response felt the peer review process was successful because it gave students a sense of what their peers were doing, was less intimidating and teacher-centered, gave them a chance to discuss their mistakes, and broke classroom monotony. During the interviews, when pressed to describe specific practices, most instructors indicated that they offered very little coaching on the peer review process. They consistently directed their students to focus more on grammatical and mechanical accuracy than on text content and rhetorical structure.

Instructors' views about academic literacy development and the time required to achieve it. Instructors' views of their students' academic literacy skills reiterated the trend toward grammar instruction and error elimination. To illustrate, a professor said that students "need to be really strong in grammar. That is what the whole language is about." One professor referred to the goal of "improvement in problematic grammar issues and better knowledge of basic grammar," while another described students' academic literacy as "deficient." A professor concurred, saying, "They are not going to get there." Providing a more extensive characterization of instructional goals, another professor insisted that "[students] need to read, write and speak at an intermediate level in a grammatical, syntactic and comprehensible way." Less grammatically focused portrayals of academic literacy goals included the ability to "express oneself appropriately across a wide variety of contexts" and "perform at the minimum standard to function and communicate in an academically acceptable way." To achieve these objectives, instructors felt students needed to take their studies more seriously, be more challenged in the first two years, learn more grammar, get lots of input and practice, and study abroad.

A range of expectations was expressed regarding the amount of time necessary to achieve academic literacy in a writing course. Among the Spanish professors, only one thought it was unreasonable to expect students to acquire academic literacy during their time in school and thought it would take them at least ten more years, an opinion shared by Cummins (1981). Another believed it was possible in three years, but blamed inadequate instruction in the first two for upper level students' weaknesses. Byrnes (1998) addressed this problem: "An expectation of target-like norms during the learning experience only aggravates this situation, contributing to an air of unreality" (p. 289).

Reading-writing connections, the value of writing for academic and professional success, and reading habits. Although reading received a low rating in Table 4, all of the FL instructors believed in a strong connection between reading and writing, emphasizing the necessity of writing for success in academic and professional endeavors: "The more I read, the better I write" and "Great readers can recognize great writing." They agreed that the ability to write is essential for students to be taken seriously, to have their ideas validated, and to avoid being seen as stupid, uneducated, or illiterate.

Several Spanish professors reiterated the observation that their students were not readers, that they did not like to read, and that they were visual learners who prefer movies to books.

- FL students "are not big readers. I don't think they read a great deal at home. They are unaware of the canon in American and English literature";
- "They are not used to read much. HL students' reading proficiency in Spanish is equivalent to middle school level."

Preliminary Conclusions

This project is still a work in progress, although we believe that the perceptions and beliefs gathered from FL educators and two distinct samples of classroom language learners point toward consistent trends in our small but growing pool of data. These tendencies are similar to observations made by Hyland and Hyland (2006) regarding pedagogical choices:

Whether teachers decide to focus on form or content, look to praise or criticize student writing, establish an equal or hierarchical affiliation, or adopt an involved or remote stance, they are at least partly influenced by the dominant ideologies of their institutions and the beliefs acquired as a result of their cultural backgrounds and educational experiences. (p. 11)

In response to our questions, we found the following patterns: first, instructors' quest for accuracy is a predominant goal of FL writing instruction, one that potentially interferes with sociolinguistic sensitivity, realistic expectations, and professional enjoyment. Second, the underlying principle guiding writing instruction geared toward FL and HL students is that grammar is the equivalent of writing. Third, these pedagogical practices may affect HL students' claims to linguistic legitimacy and self-esteem. We observed a rather consistent alignment between Spanish language instructor attitudes and HL students' perceptions of themselves, their language varieties and skills, and their biliterate development.

References

Brown, J. D., & Rodgers, T. S. (2002). *Doing second language research*. Oxford: Oxford University Press.

Bucholtz, M. (2007, April). *Becoming Latino through language: Americanization and its limits in a migrant classroom*. Paper presented at the Annual Meeting of the American Association for Applied Linguistics, Costa Mesa, CA.

Byrnes, H. (Ed.). (1998). *Learning foreign and second languages: Perspectives in research and scholarship*. New York: Modern Language Association.

Campbell, R. N., & Rosenthal, J. W. (2005). Heritage languages. In J. W. Rosenthal (Ed.), *Handbook of undergraduate second language education* (pp. 165–184). Mahwah, NJ: Lawrence Erlbaum.

Carreira, M. (2004). Seeking explanatory adequacy: A dual approach to understanding the term "heritage language learner." *Heritage Language Journal, 2*. Retrieved from http://www.heritagelanguages.org.

Carreira, M. (2007). Teaching Spanish in the US: Beyond the one-size-fits-all paradigm. In K. Potowski & R. Cameron (Eds.), *Spanish in contact: Policy, social and linguistic inquiries* (pp. 61–79). Amsterdam: John Benjamins.

Chandler, J. (2003). The efficacy of various kinds of error feedback for improvement in the accuracy and fluency of L2 student writing. *Journal of Second Language Writing, 12*, 267–296.

Chevalier, J. F. (2004). Heritage language literacy: Theory and practice. *Heritage Language Journal, 2*. Retrieved from http://www.heritagelanguages.org.

Colombi, M. C. (2003). Un enfoque funcional para la enseñanza del ensayo expositivo. In A. Roca & M. C. Colombi (Eds.), *Mi lengua: Spanish as a heritage language in the United States* (pp. 78–95). Washington, DC: Georgetown University Press.

Colombi, M. C., & Roca, A. (2003). Insights from research and practice in Spanish as a heritage language. In A. Roca & M. C. Colombi (Eds.), *Mi lengua: Spanish as a heritage language in the United States* (pp. 1–21). Washington, DC: Georgetown University Press.

Creswell, J. W. (2007). *Qualitative inquiry and research design: Choosing among five approaches.* Thousand Oaks, CA: Sage.

Creswell, J. W. (2009). *Research design: Qualitative, quantitative, and mixed methods approaches.* Los Angeles, CA: Sage.

Cummins, J. (1981). The role of primary language development in promoting educational success for language minority students. In *Schooling as language minority students: A theoretical framework* (pp. 3–49). Los Angeles: California State University, National Evaluation, Dissemination and Assessment Center.

Duff, P. (2004). Foreign language policies, research, and educational possibilities: A Western perspective. Paper presented at the APEC Educational Summit, Beijing. Retrieved from http://www.apecknowledgebank.org/knowledgebank/index.cfm?action=dsp_content_detail&document_id=744.

Edstrom, A. (2005). "A gringa is going to teach me Spanish!": A nonnative teacher reflects and responds. *ADFL Bulletin 36,* 27–31.

Fathman, A., & Whalley, E. (1990). Teacher response to student writing: Focus on form versus content. In B. Kroll (Ed.), *Second language writing: Research insights for the classroom* (pp. 178–191). Cambridge: Cambridge University Press.

Ferris, D. R. (2002). *Treatment of error in L2 student writing.* Ann Arbor: University of Michigan Press.

Ferris, D. R. (2003). *Response to student writing: Implications for second language students.* Mahwah, NJ: Lawrence Erlbaum.

Ferris, D. R. (2004). The "Grammar Correction Debate in L2 Writing: Where are we, and where do we go from here? (and what to do in the meantime . . . ?). *Journal of Second Language Writing, 13,* 1–14.

Goldstein, L. M. (2005). *Teacher written commentary in second language writing classes.* Ann Arbor: University of Michigan Press.

Gutiérrez, J. R. (1997). Teaching Spanish as a heritage language: A case for language awareness. *ADFL Bulletin 29,* 33–36.

Hedgcock, J., & Lefkowitz, N. (2000). Overt and covert prestige in the French language classroom: When is it good to sound bad? *Applied Language Learning, 11,* 75–97.

Hedgcock, J., & Lefkowitz, N. (in press). Exploring the learning potential of writing development in heritage language education. In R. Manchón (Ed.), *Learning to write and writing to learn in an additional language.* Amsterdam: John Benjamins.

Hidalgo, M., (Ed.). (1990). On the question of "standard" versus "dialect": Implications for teaching Hispanic college students. In J. Bergen (Ed.), *Spanish in the United States: Sociolinguistic issues* (pp. 110–126). Washington, DC: Georgetown University Press.

Hidalgo, M. (1993). The teaching of Spanish to bilingual Spanish speakers: A problem of inequality. In B. Merino, H. T. Trueba, & F. A. Samaniego, (Eds.), *Language and culture in learning: Teaching Spanish to native speakers of Spanish* (pp. 82–93). London: Falmer.

Holmes, J. (1992). *An introduction to sociolinguistics.* London: Longman.

Hyland, F., & Hyland, K. (2001). Sugaring the pill: Praise and criticism in written feedback. *Journal of Second Language Writing, 10,* 185–212.

Hyland, K., & Hyland, F. (Eds.). (2006). *Feedback in second language writing.* Cambridge: Cambridge University Press.

Johnson, B., & Christensen, L. (2008). *Educational research: Quantitative, qualitative, and mixed approaches* (3rd ed.). Los Angeles, CA: Sage.

Kramsch, C. (1997). The privilege of the nonnative speaker. *PMLA, 1122,* 359–369.

Lefkowitz, N., & Hedgcock, J. (2002). Sound barriers: Influences of social prestige, peer pressure and teacher (dis)approval on FL oral performance. *Language Teaching Research 6,* 223–244.

Lefkowitz, N., & Hedgcock, J. S. (2006). Sound effects: Social pressure and identity negotiation in the Spanish language classroom. *Applied Language Learning, 16,* 1–21.

Lefkowitz, N., & Hedgcock, J. (2007, April). *Heritage vs. foreign language learners: Foreign in the home language—Not at home in the foreign language.* Paper presented at the Annual Meeting of the American Association for Applied Linguistics, Costa Mesa, CA.

Lefkowitz, N., & Hedgcock, J. (2008, April). *Inheriting more than just Spanish: Heritage and foreign language learners' internalization of instructor attitudes.* Paper presented at the Annual Meeting of the American Association for Applied Linguistics, Washington, DC.

Lefkowitz, N., & Hedgcock, J. (2009, March). *Writing to learn vs. learning to write.* Paper presented at the Annual Meeting of the American Association for Applied Linguistics, Denver, CO.

Lefkowitz, N., & Hedgcock, J. (2011, March). *Handle with care: Understanding the fragile linguistic identities of FL and HL learners.* Paper presented at the Annual Meeting of the American Association for Applied Linguistics, Chicago, IL.

Lipski, J. M. (2006). *El español de América* (3rd ed.). Madrid: Catedra.

Lynch, A. (2003a). The relationship between second and heritage language acquisition: Notes on research and theory building. *Heritage Language Journal, 1*. Retrieved from http://www.heritagelanguages.org.

Lynch, A. (2003b). Toward a theory of heritage language acquisition. In A. Roca & M. C. Colombi (Eds.), *Mi lengua: Spanish as a heritage language in the United States* (pp. 25–50). Washington, DC: Georgetown University Press.

Mar-Molinero, C. (1997). *The Spanish speaking world: A practical introduction to sociolinguistic issues.* London: Routledge.

Mar-Molinero, C. (2000). *The Spanish speaking world: From colonization to globalization.* London: Routledge.

Martínez, G. (2006). *Mexican Americans and language: Del dicho al hecho.* Tucson: University of Arizona Press.

McKay, S. L. (2006). *Researching second language classrooms.* Mahwah, NJ: Lawrence Erlbaum.

Nunan, D. (1992). *Research methods in language learning.* Cambridge: Cambridge University Press.

Patton, M. Q. (1990). *Qualitative evaluation and research methods.* Newbury Park, CA: Sage.

Pérez-Leroux, A., & Glass, W. (2000). Linguistic diversity and inclusion in the foreign language classroom. *Foreign Language Annals, 33,* 58–62.

Potowski, K. (2002) Experiences of Spanish heritage speakers in university foreign language courses and implications for teacher training. *ADFL Bulletin, 33*(3), 35–42.

Potowski, K., & Cameron, R. (Eds.). (2007). *Spanish in contact: Policy, social, and linguistic inquiries.* Amsterdam: John Benjamins.

Reagan, T., & Olson, T. (2002). *The foreign language educator in society: Toward a critical pedagogy.* Mahwah, NJ: Lawrence Erlbaum.

Reichelt, M. (1999). Toward a more comprehensive view of L2 writing: Foreign language writing in the US *Journal of Second Language Writing, 8,* 181–204.

Richards, K. (2003). *Qualitative inquiry in TESOL.* New York: Palgrave MacMillan.

Roca, A. (1997). Retrospectives, advances, and current needs in the teaching of Spanish to United States Hispanic bilingual students. *ADFL Bulletin, 29,* 37–43.

Roca, A. (2001). Heritage language maintenance and development: An agenda for action. In J. K. Peyton, D. Ranard, & S. McGinnis (Eds.), *Heritage languages in America: Preserving a national resource* (pp. 307–316). McHenry, IL: Delta.

Roca, A., & Colombi, M. C. (Eds.). (2003). *Mi lengua: Spanish as a heritage language in the United States*. Washington, DC: Georgetown University Press.

Roca, A., & Lipski, J. (Eds). (1993). *Spanish in the United States*. London: Routledge.

Schwartz, A. (2001). Preparing teachers to work with heritage language learners. In J. K. Peyton, D. Ranard & S. McGinnis (Eds.), *Heritage languages in America: Preserving a national resource* (pp. 229–254). McHenry, IL: Delta.

Schwarzer, D. & Petrón, M. (2005). Heritage language instruction at the college level: Reality and possibilities. *Foreign Language Annals 38*, 568–578.

Scott, V. (1996). *Rethinking foreign language writing*. Boston, MA: Heinle.

Truscott, J. (2007). The effect of error correction on learners' ability to write accurately. *Journal of Second Language Writing, 16*, 255–272.

Valdés, G. (1995). The teaching of minority languages as academic subjects: Pedagogical and theoretical challenges. *The Modern Language Journal, 79*, 299–328.

Valdés, G. (2000a). Introduction. In *Spanish for native speakers, Vol. 1* (pp. 1–20). New York: Harcourt.

Valdés, G. (2000b). The ACTFL-Hunter College FIPSE Project and its contributions to the profession. In J. B. Webb & B. L. Miller (Eds.), *Teaching heritage language learners: Voices from the classroom* (pp. 235–251). Yonkers, NY: American Council on the Teaching of Foreign Languages.

Valdés, G. (2001). Heritage language students: Profiles and possibilities. In J. K. Peyton, D. Ranard, & S. McGinnis (Eds.), *Heritage languages in America: Preserving a national resource* (pp. 37–77). McHenry, IL: Delta.

Valdés, G. (2006). The foreign language teaching profession and the challenges of developing language resources. In G. Valdés, J.A. Fishman, R. Chávez, & W. Pérez, *Developing minority language resources: The case of Spanish in California* (pp. 108-139). Clevedon, UK: Multilingual Matters.

Valdés, G., Fishman, J.A., Chávez, R. & Pérez, W. (2006). *Developing minority language resources: The case of Spanish in California*. Clevedon, UK: Multilingual Matters.

van Lier, L. (1995). *Introducing language awareness*. London: Penguin.

Villa, D. (1996). Choosing a "standard" variety of Spanish for the instruction of native Spanish speakers in the US *Foreign Language Annals 29*, 191–200.

Villa, D. (2002). The sanitizing of US Spanish in academia. *Foreign Language Annals 35*, 222–30.

Zentella, A. C. (2007, April). *With friends like these, who needs enemies? Strange bedfellows on the Spanglish bandwagon*. Paper presented at the Annual Meeting of the American Association for Applied Linguistics, Costa Mesa, CA.

Appendix: Foreign/Heritage Language Instructor Interview Protocol

Table 5.

Foreign/Heritage Language Instructor Interview Protocol

Participant ID: _____

Participant Demographics

#	Question	Response Options
1.	What is your primary language?	☐ English ☐ Spanish ☐ French ☐ German ☐ Japanese ☐ Chinese ☐ Russian ☐ Other ☐ Other: _____
2.	What language(s) do you teach?	☐ English ☐ Spanish ☐ French ☐ German ☐ Japanese ☐ Chinese ☐ Russian ☐ Other ☐ Other: _____
3.	Are you a native speaker (NS) of that language?	☐ Yes ☐ No
4.	How comfortable are you teaching students who are NSs of your target language (heritage students)?	☐ Very comfortable ☐ Somewhat comfortable ☐ Neither comfortable nor uncomfortable ☐ Somewhat uncomfortable ☐ Very uncomfortable
5.	What is your educational background?	☐ Literature ☐ Linguistics ☐ Other: _____
6.	Have you had any formal training in teaching composition (other than on-the-job training)?	☐ Yes ☐ No

Impressions of Students, Instructional Aims, + Course Content

7.	How would you describe your impression of FL students? HL students?	☐ Highly favorable ☐ Favorable ☐ Neither favorable nor unfavorable ☐ Unfavorable ☐ Highly unfavorable
8.	At what point do you think your FL students are ready to begin writing?	☐ First year ☐ Second year ☐ Third year ☐ Fourth year ☐ Other: _____
9.	How would you rate your level of enjoyment as a teacher of composition?	☐ High ☐ Moderate ☐ Neither high nor low ☐ Low ☐ Very low
10.	Do your expectations of FL students differ from those of heritage students (HSs)?	☐ Yes ☐ No If yes, how?

11. In what ways is the experience of teaching FL students similar to/different from your experience teaching HSs?	
12. What are your top 3-5 goals for students in the 341-342/301 course?	a. b. c. d. e.
13. What steps do you take to help students achieve these goals?	a. b. c. d. e.
14. What materials do you use in your syllabus? Check and list all that apply.	☐ Textbook(s):_____ ☐ Authentic Texts: _____ ☐ Multimedia, including film: _____
15. How does the 341/342/301 course address culture?	
16. How does your 341/342/301 course address sociolinguistic awareness and competence (appropriateness), if at all?	
17. What would you describe as typical linguistic tendencies of these learners?	Sp VT P Ag Gender
18. What are your FL students' strongest skill areas?	☐ Listening ☐ Speaking ☐ Reading ☐ Writing ☐ Grammar
19. What are your HL students' strongest skill areas?	☐ Listening ☐ Speaking ☐ Reading ☐ Writing ☐ Grammar
20. What are your FL students' weakest skill areas?	☐ Listening ☐ Speaking ☐ Reading ☐ Writing ☐ Grammar
21. What are your HL students' weakest skill areas?	☐ Listening ☐ Speaking ☐ Reading ☐ Writing ☐ Grammar
22. Overall, how would you rate your FL students' proficiency levels?	☐ Excellent ☐ Above Average ☐ Average ☐ Below Average ☐ Poor
23. Overall, how would you rate your HL students' proficiency levels?	☐ Excellent ☐ Above Average ☐ Average ☐ Below Average ☐ Poor
Error Treatment Beliefs + Practices	
24. What are the 3-5 most common formal errors that you notice in your	a. b.

students' writing? Of these errors, which are the most significant and require your intervention?	c. _____ d. _____ e. _____	
25. What types of error treatment strategies work best for you? Mark all that apply.	☐ Symbols ☐ Underlining or circling ☐ Color coding ☐ Explicit correction/editing ☐ Marginal comments ☐ End comments	
26. Do you believe it is important for your students to know and use metalinguistic terminology? Why?	☐ Yes ☐ No _____	
27. How many essays or compositions do you assign in 341/342/301?	☐ 5 ☐ 4 ☐ 3 ☐ 2 ☐ 1	
28. What are your favorite assignments? Why?		
29. What are your least favorite assignments? Why?		
30. Do you use a multi-drafting method? If so, how many drafts do you typically require per essay/composition?	☐ Yes ☐ No ☐ 3 drafts ☐ 2 drafts	
31. About how long do you require students' drafts to be? Why?	____ paragraphs ____ pages ____ words	
32. Why do you require/not require your students to compose multiple drafts?		
33. If you use a multi-draft approach, how do you respond to each draft, if at all? (focus and grade)	Draft 1: _____ Draft 2: _____ Draft 3: _____	
34. What are your reasons for responding to these drafts as you do?		
35. Do you also provide students with written comments on their writing, e.g., during conferences?	☐ Often ☐ Sometimes ☐ Never	
36. Do you require peer editing/response in the drafting and revision process? If so, when does it occur, and how does it work?	☐ Often ☐ Sometimes ☐ Never	
37. What are your reasons for incorporating/not incorporating peer		

38. What features do you instruct students to focus on when they respond to their peers' drafts? Check all that apply.	☐ Text content ☐ Text organization ☐ Grammatical and mechanical accuracy ☐ Other: _____
39. If you incorporate peer editing/response, how do you feel it benefits students?	
40. Would you describe your approach to teaching writing as based on rhetorical modes? That is, do assignments aim to help students produce narrative, expository, argumentative texts, and so on?	☐ Yes ☐ No
41. If so, what modes does your syllabus typically target?	☐ Narrative ☐ Descriptive writing ☐ Expository writing ☐ Argumentation and persuasion ☐ Other: _____
42. What genres do you teach and require your students to write?	☐ Formal essays and compositions ☐ Creative fiction/narrative ☐ Journalistic writing (e.g., news reports, editorials, etc.) ☐ Poetry and verse ☐ Other: _____
43. What instructional procedures and task types would you describe as most typical of your approach to teaching 341/342/301? Check all that apply, then rank-order from most to least frequent.	☐ Literary analysis ☐ Analysis of student writing ☐ Peer response ☐ Grammar presentation/explanation ☐ Oral grammar practice ☐ Intensive reading ☐ Extensive reading ☐ Vocabulary practice ☐ Dictation ☐ Portfolio/*Archivo* ☐ Language awareness activities (e.g., comparison of register, stylistic choices, vocabulary, etc. in written texts)
44. Why do you assign these tasks?	

Views of Academic Literacy Development

45.	How would you define academic literacy?
46.	What do you think your students need to achieve academic literacy in their target language?
47.	How reasonable is it to expect students to achieve academic literacy during or after your course?
48.	In what ways do you think reading and writing are connected?
49.	Do you use writing as a means of teaching other skill areas?
50.	What purposes do you think writing instruction and practice serve?
51.	In what ways does developing writing skills benefit L2 students?
52.	In what ways is learning to write necessary for academic and professional success?
53.	In what ways does learning to write contribute to students' communicative competence, self-esteem, and confidence levels as bilingual and biliterate individuals?
54.	How would you describe your students' reading habits and strategies, their oral language use, and their vocabularies?
55.	If you have heritage students (native speakers of your target language) in your courses, in what ways do you adjust your teaching, if at all?

13 Student Perceptions of Writing as a Tool for Increasing Oral Proficiency in German

Helga Thorson

A typical foreign language curricular model at many institutions of higher education in the US and Canada begins with a language program that is divided into a first year beginning language sequence (elementary foreign language), a second year language sequence (intermediate foreign language), followed by courses focusing on specific skills or modalities (e.g., conversation, composition, advanced grammar) or a combination thereof. Titles such as Composition and Syntax, Advanced Conversation, Advanced Grammar, or Composition and Conversation I and II are common at this level. Third year language courses often function as a bridge to upper level content courses in cultural studies[1], especially if these courses are taught in the target language. Many colleges and universities also offer some, if not all, of the cultural studies courses in English, allowing students the opportunity to take these courses in conjunction with their language courses (see Figure 1). Of course, this is a simplified model and every department has its own unique course listings.

In recent years, a number of language programs have made significant changes to their second year curriculum, often including a content- or skills-based course in the fourth semester. This has come about mainly because many institutions have chosen to use one textbook over three semesters, thus "freeing up" the fourth semester for something new and different. Since most foreign language textbooks are not only lengthy but also costly, a number of departments have decided against adopting a textbook in the fourth semester and are put-

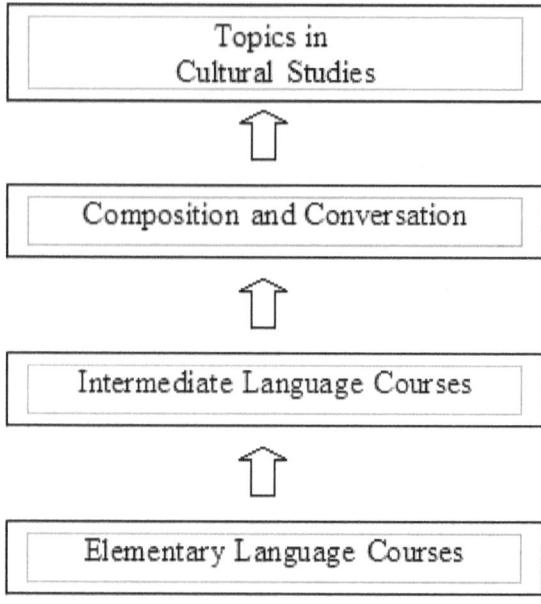

Figure 1. Typical model of foreign language curriculum in post-secondary institutions in the US and Canada.

ting together their own course packs and curricular material for their fourth semester course.

In the German language program in the Department of Germanic and Slavic Studies at the University of Victoria, a mid-sized public university in British Columbia, Canada, the language courses follow the basic model outlined above, with the fourth semester course concentrating on conversational German. The third year sequence consists of Advanced Grammar and Stylistics I in the fall, followed by Advanced Oral German I in the spring semester (see Figure 2)[2]. During the spring semester of 2008, I had the opportunity to teach both of the courses focusing on oral production (i.e., Conversational German and Advanced Oral German I). Because of my experience with teaching foreign language conversation courses, I have become increasingly interested in the interconnections between foreign language writing and speaking, especially writing as a tool for enhancing oral proficiency.

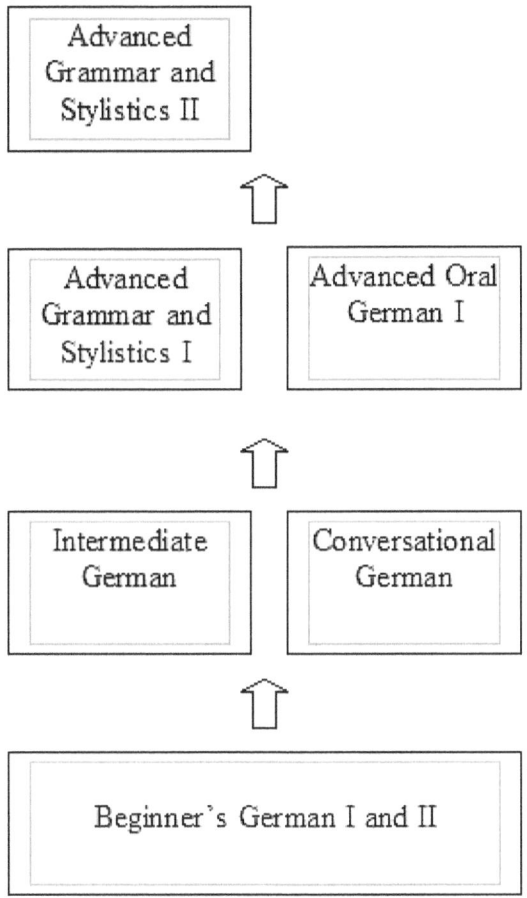

Figure 2. German language courses at the University of Victoria in 2008.

Guiding Principles in FL Teaching

In what follows, I outline some of the basic principles that inform my pedagogy—particularly those principles that address the speaking/writing connection. I do not consider speaking and writing to be two completely different modalities that stand in total opposition to one other, but tend to view them as dynamically interrelated. Both written and oral language contain a range of styles, from a more spontaneous style on the one hand to a more careful and well-thought out style on the other hand (Chafe, 1982; Halliday, 1987) and, as Robert Weissberg (2006) contends, writing and speaking are social acts that exist in dialog with one other. I believe that fostering the dialog between speaking and writing (whether in courses designed for writing instruction or those designed for oral production) can prove quite helpful in the foreign language classroom—not only because mixed-modality tasks can help students transfer their skills from one modality to another (Weissberg, 2006) but also because the speaking/writing connection is part of how students interact with language in their everyday lives.

To begin with, I define speaking and writing quite broadly to include any utterance that is either spoken or written down/typed respectively. These could include anything from repeating or transcribing a word or sentence, to singing or doodling with words on paper, to sharing or presenting ideas orally or in writing. It is important to note that the distinctions between speaking and writing are not always clearly defined. Advances in speech-recognition software or, conversely, text to speech software that allows students with speaking disabilities to actively participate in class have served to erase traditional demarcations separating language modalities. Due to these technological advances as well as several emergent "genres" such as chat sessions or email that tend to blur the boundaries between speaking and writing, it may be helpful to abandon the notion of four distinct language modalities and begin to think more in terms of language input (Krashen, 1985) and output (Swain, 1985; Swain & Lapkin, 1995). Yet even these categories overlap to a certain degree since language output can also simultaneously be a form of input—for example, when a learner hears the language as s/he is speaking or reads the text as it is being composed.

In what follows, I summarize five basic principles that underlie my FL teaching philosophy. Since it is impossible to include every aspect that comes into play when designing and implementing a FL course, I have chosen to list five main beliefs I hold that pertain to the speaking/writing connection in a post-secondary FL program.

1. Students should "write from the start" (Scott, 1992) as well as speak from the start. Although proponents of the natural approach to language teaching advocate holding off on language output until there has been significant L2 or FL input, thus simulating the L1 acquisition process (Krashen & Terrell, 1983), I believe postponing language output is an "unnatural approach" given that literate adult learners function quite well as speakers and writers in their everyday lives.

2. Both speaking and writing are powerful tools for learning. Students often use speaking and writing in various ways in both their L1 and FL courses to help them learn course material and organize their thoughts. Speaking to learn, for example, often takes the form of singing (such as the use of Strauss's "The Blue Danube" waltz to learn the German dative prepositions), practicing a speech, discussing course content, or repeating words or phrases out loud. Writing to learn may include such things as mind mapping, note taking, writing out vocabulary or grammar exercises, or summarizing readings and lecture notes. In this sense, writing and speaking often complement and support one another, as when students read sentences out loud while composing in order to find the right word or phrase, or when they write an outline for an oral presentation to help them organize and remember their main points.

3. Language input and output are intricately intertwined and necessary for achieving overall FL proficiency. Although the emphasis in conversational courses is on speaking, speaking cannot—and should not—occur in a vacuum. Comprehensible input (Krashen, 1985) is necessary for language learners to acquire language and to experience grammar and vocabulary in context. Without input, students would not be able to make progress in their language abilities. Even so, enough class time needs to be reserved for language output. Once texts, films, or other forms of input are assigned, significant class time is often spent focusing on listening or reading comprehension. Reading texts and listening clips need to be carefully chosen so that they stimulate, rather than suppress, discussions.

4. It is important to include a variety of tasks and assignments that lead to FL output, both spontaneous and planned. In terms of writing, for example, I believe it is important to include both extensive and intensive writing (Homstad & Thorson, 2000). A good example of extensive writing is a dialog journal in which students write about a topic every week and then enter a dialog about what they had written with either another classmate or the teacher either orally or in writing. Extensive writing could also take the form of threaded discussions, blogs,

or chat sessions that take place regularly over the semester. Intensive writing focuses on the quality rather than quantity of writing and includes short writing assignments in which accuracy, audience, and style play a significant role. In terms of speaking, plenty of opportunities should be given for spontaneous discussions and role plays as well as planned speaking activities. Variety, in my opinion, is essential because it not only provides students with different learning styles the opportunity to engage in the material in a way that is particularly helpful to them individually, but the various tasks also emphasize different dimensions of language output, such as comprehensibility, register, spontaneity, fluency, and/or accuracy.

5. Languages are vehicles that facilitate interaction with other people and the cultures and societies in which they live. Therefore, language teaching is not just about teaching the target language, but more importantly about building multiple cultural literacies (Swaffar & Arens, 2005) through observation, interaction, and discovery. Providing students with the opportunities and skills to effectively negotiate between languages and cultures is a major goal of my teaching. Moving away from the objective that the superior language learner is the one who is able to "pass" as a native speaker, a more beneficial aim is to provide students with the trans-linguistic and trans-cultural skills they need to function across languages and cultures (MLA Ad Hoc Committee on Foreign Languages, 2007). Therefore, learning the language is just a part of what happens in the FL classroom. It is one of many skills that students need as they learn to interact with the world around them. Students are not expected to become native speakers or to take on the "identity" of a native speaker in their speaking or writing, but rather to gain the skills they need to effectively function across cultures and languages.

Implementing Writing in FL Conversation Courses

These five principles are at the heart of my teaching philosophy and inform my curricular planning—whether I am designing a lower level language course, a composition course, a conversation course, or a cultural studies seminar. The two oral production courses I discuss in this study meet three times a week for fifty minutes over twelve weeks. In these courses I make a conscious effort to include opportunities for input as well as output. Both courses are conducted in the target language and attempt to provide opportunities for students to come into contact with other German speakers (both in and outside of class). In the second year conversation course, I assign an online cultural reader (Lazda & Thorson, 2005), which the students can either listen to or read (or they can choose to do both at the same time). In the third year conversation course, one day a week is spent focusing on the 1929 German youth novel *Emil und die Detektive* by Erich Kästner, as well as two films based on the story (Gerhard Lamprecht's 1931 film adaptation and Franziska Buch's 2001 version). I use the language input that these texts and films provide as a springboard for language output, whether in the form of skits, role plays, or discussions.

Both courses offer a variety of tasks and assignments that lead to FL output, both spontaneous and planned. I assign extensive writing in the form of dialogue journals and intensive writing in the form of short writing assignments (in the second year course) and projects (in the third year course). My goal in each course is to have every single student speak every single day. In the third year oral German course, I reserve one day a week for practicing oral language functions such as description, storytelling, arguing a point, stating an opinion, and debating a topic. The midterm and final exams in each course consist of fifteen-minute individual interviews with me during which the student spends part of the time presenting a topic and the rest of the time discussing course content.

In the third year oral production course, students work on three projects, each containing an oral and a written component. For the first project, students interview a native speaker and present the person to the class. This is accompanied by a written report about the person, containing at least three quotes from the actual interview. The second project involves setting up a "German city" in a classroom on campus and inviting the second year conversation students to visit the city. The students in the third year course discuss and negotiate what the city should look like and what they want the visiting students to do during their time in the city[3]. After the event takes place, the students in the third year course have to submit a written description of their day in the city and the people they met who visited their city. The third project is open and it is completely up to the students to brainstorm ideas and implement the project[4].

In the courses above, I try to work on skills that the students need to effectively function across languages and cultures. Therefore, learning the language is only a part of what happens in the FL classroom. In the second year conversation course, students read an online cultural reader, *Neuer Wein und Zwiebelkuchen* (Lazda & Thorson, 2005), about an American exchange student who spends a year in Freiburg, Germany. Through the story itself as well as the accompanying Internet and discussion activities, students "virtually" travel to Germany with the protagonist of the text and help make decisions for her along the way. They observe how she interacts in her new cultural setting and are invited to discover, negotiate, and reflect upon the new "space" she encounters. In the final weeks of the semester, students work in groups to write and perform their own ending to the story—often drawing on linguistic and cultural topics that have come up during the semester. The third year students focus on obtaining cultural literacies through their interactions with native speakers (project 1), through historical research (such as their chosen focus on East German culture and society for project 2), through the various cultural artifacts we analyzed—including objects, texts, and films discussed in class, and through their own trans-cultural storytelling (project 3).

The two courses described here stem not only from the five principles I have previously outlined, but also from my interest in the ways writing can be used as a tool for enhancing oral proficiency. Although there has been a fair amount of research in recent years on L2 writing (see, for example, the overview by Leki, Cumming, & Silva, 2008), there has been much less research on foreign language writing and even less on the speaking/writing connection and ways in which writing can positively affect speaking.

The Speaking/Writing Connection

Cross-modality research, which has been defined as research in areas where two or more modalities intersect and interact with one another, has become a new, and I believe important, area of investigation. Research on the dynamic relationship between speaking and writing has been conducted in L1 research and the extent to which speaking and writing are similar to or differ from each other continues to be negotiated and discussed (see Sperling, 1996 for an overview of the major debates). On the one hand, it has been pointed out that both writing and speaking are acts of communication and conversation—comprised of interlocutors (whether through spoken words or words on a page) in dialog with one another. On the other hand, the expectations for written and spoken discourses are often quite different and depend on the context of the specific situation. Writing in an educational or academic setting, for example, is often expected to be quite different from spoken language. As Melanie Sperling (1996) has illustrated, many researchers claim that bad writers are the ones who "compose 'under the influence' of their oral language habits" (p. 60).

The relationship between second language (L2) or foreign language (FL) speaking and writing is even more complex because of the added element of language proficiency. Do the ACTFL proficiency guidelines in speaking and writing provide clear indicators of how students actually progress from one proficiency level to the next or do they fail to recognize that many adult learners bring their own knowledge and experience in literacy, composition, and conversation to the foreign language environment? Valdés, Haro, and Echevarriarza (1992), for example, challenged assumptions made in the ACTFL writing guidelines suggesting that organizational skills or extended discourse skills emerge only at higher proficiency levels and argued that some FL writers transfer these skills from their L1 into the FL writing context. There has been emerging research in the past two decades on the extent to which L2 or FL writers transfer their L1 writing strategies and skills into the new language they are learning (see Cumming, 1989; Silva, 1993; and Thorson, 2000 for a sampling of early studies in L2 and FL writing).

Cross-modality research on speaking and writing has tended to focus on two distinct areas that benefit the writing researcher: the extent to which oral language proficiency can be used as an indicator for writing success (Cumming, 1989) and ways in which learners can use speaking as a means of describing, clarifying, and negotiating the writing process through such techniques as interviews, peer discussion groups, or think aloud protocols (Weissberg, 2005, 2006). Analyzing the writing performance of twenty-three young adult Francophone ESL learners in three different tasks, Alister Cumming focused on the role of writing expertise and oral L2 proficiency on both the writing process and the writing product. Although both writing expertise and L2 proficiency affected the type of problem-solving strategies used during the writing process and the quality of the final compositions, Cumming concluded that they each did so in very distinct ways. A higher second language proficiency did not necessarily affect the participant's decision making strategies during the composition process, but did enhance the overall quality of the final written product. Robert Weissberg (2005) has brought attention to the social context of writing and its connection to oral language, focusing on what researchers can gain from a type of sociocultural research that looks specifically at the intersections of speaking and writing, but that is still mindful of the context of the L2 writing environment. Weissberg (2006) has provided examples of ways to use purposeful talk to enhance the process of writing, illustrating that "[t]he most effective writing classrooms are not always quiet places" (p. 1).

Another area of investigation that has become increasingly popular in recent years has focused on new, emergent "genres" such as dialog journals, instant text messaging, email, and chat sessions and ways in which the communication environment or medium affects language production (Chun, 1994; Kern, 1995; Payne & Whitney, 2002; Thorne & Reinhardt, 2008; Warschauer, 1996). Both dialog journals and computer-mediated communication (CMC) have tended to blur the boundaries between oral and written communication and, to a certain extent, have challenged the notion that there are indeed four distinct language modalities. In fact, as Weissberg (2000) has pointed out, it is often "cross-over" genres such as the dialog journal that exhibit examples of some of the best-written language production in a second language. Discussing the use of dialog journals in a study he conducted with five literate adult second language learners, Weissberg maintains that the journals were "the site for some of their most expressive and accurate writing" (p. 51). Similarly, studies on L2 chat room use have argued that learners use more complex language in chat rooms than they do in face-to-face conversation (Kern, 1995; Warschauer, 1996).

The question remains whether writing can in fact enhance L2 or FL oral proficiency and, if so, whether learners gain and express proficiency in different ways when producing written and spoken discourse. In the above-mentioned study, Weissberg (2000) analyzed the writing of five native Spanish-speakers learning English along with oral speech samples and found that, although there were individual differences, these learners tended to exhibit morpho-syntactic innovation more often in their writing than in their speaking. In addition, Weissberg noted that different types of innovation emerged in each modality. A study by Payne and Whitney (2002) has suggested that synchronous CMC may positively affect oral production. These researchers analyzed pre- and post-speaking tests of fifty-eight postsecondary students in their third semester of Spanish instruction and found that the experimental groups (those learners who spent two out of the four instructional hours in a synchronous online environment) outperformed the control groups in oral proficiency development. These two cross-modality studies will hopefully pave the way for further investigations into the complex and dynamic interconnections between speaking and writing.

Similar to Linda Harklau (2002), I believe that more focus needs to be given to "how students learn a second language through writing" (p. 329) and how, in particular, writing affects overall L2 and FL proficiency. Whereas Harklau laments the fact that "scholarship in applied linguistics—particularly the sub-field of classroom second language acquisition—has evolved in ways that implicitly privilege face-to-face interaction over learning through written modalities" (p. 330), I believe that spoken language (particularly in academic settings) is often combined with writing (whether it be brainstorming, note-taking, script-writing, or reporting) and that writing can (and does) play a role in spoken academic discourse. FL and L2 language instructors need to better understand the complex dynamics between speaking and writing so that they can design their courses to include writing techniques that prove useful in fostering oral proficiency. Although there has been some attention paid to ways in which speaking can be used to facilitate the composition process (Weissberg, 2006), there has been little focus on ways in which writing can be used to facilitate the speaking process. My study serves as an introductory investigation into this area.

Students' Perceptions on the Speaking/Writing Connection

Since the winter of 2006, I have been regularly teaching the fourth semester conversational German course at the University of Victoria. In 2008, I was also asked to teach the sixth semester conversation course (Advanced Oral German I) as well. Since the focus of these two courses is on oral communication, I realized I was in a good position to begin examining ways in which writing can be used to enhance oral proficiency. The focus of my study is not on whether (or how) writing increases oral proficiency in a foreign language but rather on students' perceptions, practices, and opinions on the speaking/writing connection. In the spring semester of 2008, I surveyed students in my two conversation courses in order to determine whether they believe writing could be used to augment oral production. An initial survey was administered during the second full week of classes and a follow-up survey addressing the same questions was given in the second-to-last week of the semester (see Appendix). By administering two surveys in two different classes, I hoped to determine whether students' opinions changed over time, i.e., whether their experiences in the conversation class changed their initials views on the speaking/writing connection and also whether the language level (second year versus third year conversation course) made a difference in their perceptions.

The surveys investigate three main topics: (1) the modality the FL learner believes has the greatest impact on increasing oral proficiency, (2) the extent to which students use writing to prepare for both formal and informal speaking activities in their L1 and in their FL classes, and (3) the writing activities they find the most helpful for improving oral proficiency. Surveys were administered during class time at the beginning and end of the semester and only the answers from students who filled out both surveys were included in the study. Although the two surveys addressed the same topic areas, the specific wording differed slightly (see Appendix). The first survey asked participants to hypothesize on what they would do in certain situations (see questions 4 & 6), whereas the second survey, taken at the end of the semester, encouraged participants to reflect on what they had actually done in the course that semester (see questions 4, 6, 7, & 8). In the end, twenty-four sets of surveys (out of twenty-seven students in the class) were analyzed from the second year conversation course and fifteen sets (out of seventeen students) from the third year course. I decided to analyze the results of the two courses separately in order to see whether there were differences between course levels.

When asked which activity (listening, reading, speaking, or writing) serves to increase oral proficiency the most, students in the second year conversation class ranked speaking the highest, followed by listening, writing, and reading in both their first and second surveys. Even though the question is in itself quite simplistic since none of these activities occur in a vacuum, it does give an indication as to students' perceptions on how they can improve their oral proficiency. The survey results for the third year students were quite similar, although these students tended to rank reading higher than writing in both surveys. Students in the second year conversation course would not have had much exposure to FL reading beyond isolated textbook pages in their first three semesters of language study if they were continuing students in our language program. In terms of writing, students in our program completed several short essays in their previous three semesters of German—but the fourth semester conversation course was their first exposure to any sort of extensive writing. This could explain why the answers between the second year and third year students differed at the outset, but not at the end, of the course. Students in the third year course did not necessarily read more in their particular course than the second year students—although they did have one more year of reading under their belts if they had previously taken the intermediate course sequence.

Table 1. Second year course: Conversational German (n=24).

Survey Question: I believe the best way to increase my oral proficiency is to:

	Survey 1		Survey 2	
	Mode	Mean (SE)	Mode	Mean (SE)
listen to German as often as I can	2	2.23 (.130)	2	2.43 (.197)
read German texts as often as I can	4	3.48 (.152)	4	3.43 (.164)
speak German as often as I can	1	1.04 (.043)	1	1.25 (.109)
write German as often as I can	3	3.14 (.165)	3	2.87 (.181)

Table 2. Third year course: Advanced Oral German I (n=15).

Survey Question: I believe the best way to increase my oral proficiency is to:

	Survey 1		Survey 2	
	Mode	Mean (SE)	Mode	Mean (SE)
listen to German as often as I can	2	2.40 (.214)	2	1.93 (.206)
read German texts as often as I can	3	2.87 (.256)	3	3.07 (.228)
speak German as often as I can	1	1.33 (.187)	1	1.53 (.192)
write German as often as I can	4	3.40 (.214)	4	3.47 (.215)

Tables 1 and 2 show the results in terms of mode (the number that comes up most frequently in the ranking) as well as mean (the average of the individual rankings) for each of the two courses. Since one is the top ranking, a lower mean signifies a higher ranking. The standard error of the mean is listed in parentheses after the mean as well. The Tables show little or no change in terms of mode and mean from one survey to the next.

Since the surveys also track individual students' rankings over time, it may be helpful to see how individual students' answers changed from the beginning to the end of the semester. Table 3 shows the number of rankings that stayed the same from one survey to the next for each of the two courses. Two survey pairs in the second year course were not filled in properly (the students used check marks instead of actual rankings), so there is an extra column in the second year course results pertaining to the number of surveys that were not considered. Whereas the majority of the third year students' rankings did not change over the course of the semester, the second year students' rankings varied considerably over time, especially in the way they ranked listening and writing. Overall, students' rankings of speaking did not change. Eighteen out of twenty-four (75%) of the second year students and ten out of fifteen (66.7%) of the third year students gave speaking the same ranking in the first and second surveys. The rankings of reading also stayed fairly stable. Eleven out of twenty-four students (45.8%) in the second year course and eleven out of fifteen (73.3%) ranked reading

Writing as a Tool for Increasing Oral Proficiency in German 269

the same in the two surveys. Opinions on the ranking of listening and writing, however, changed more frequently over the course of the semester. Eight out of twenty-four (33.3%) of the second year students and eight out of fifteen (53.3%) of the third year students kept the same ranking for listening and six out of twenty-four (25%) students in the second year course and eight out of fifteen (53.3%) kept the same ranking for writing.

Table 3. Number of rankings that did not change over time for the second year and third year courses.

Survey Question: I believe the best way to increase my oral proficiency is to:

	Second Year Course			Third Year Course	
	No Change	% of n (n=24)	No Answer	No Change	% of n (n=15)
listen to German as often as I can	8	33.3%	2	8	53.3%
read German texts as often as I can	11	45.8%	1	11	73.3%
speak German as often as I can	18	75.0%	1	10	66.7%
write German as often as I can	6	25.0%	2	8	53.3%

Since perceptions seemed to have changed on the importance of writing as a tool for increasing oral proficiency from the beginning of the semester to the end of the semester (especially in the second year conversation course), the next question that arises is how students' opinions changed. Of the students who changed their rankings for writing, how many ranked writing higher in the second survey? Tables 4 and 5 show that ten (out of sixteen) individuals in the second year course and three (out of seven) in the third year course ranked writing higher in the second survey (shown by a positive number in the difference column). Of the ten students in the second year course who gave writing a higher ranking at the end of the semester, seven students raised their ranking of writing by one level and three students raised their ranking two levels. Four students changed from a rank of 4 for writing in the first survey to a rank of 3 in the second, three students moved from a rank of 3 to a rank of 2, two students jumped from a rank of 4 to a rank of 2, and one student jumped from 3 to 1. Three of the students in the third year course ranked writing higher in the second survey—two of whom changed from a ranking of 4 to 3 and one of whom changed from 2 to 1. Whereas nobody gave writing a top ranking at the beginning of the semester, by the time they filled out the second survey two students (one in each class) believed that the best way to increase their oral proficiency was to write as often as they could in German. In general, the overall rankings for writing increased in the second year course by the end of the semester, but not in the third year course.

The second topic addressed in the survey is the extent to which students use writing to prepare for both formal and informal speaking activities in their L1 and in their FL classes. The survey results are found in Tables 6 and 7. All students claim that they use writing to a certain extent to prepare for oral presentations in both their L1 and German courses (except for one student who claimed in the second survey not to use writing to prepare for oral presentations in German). According to the results of the second year conversation course, students tend to do more scripting (either writing out the full script or writing out the full script plus taking notes, outlining their talk, or brainstorming ideas (labeled as "scripting plus") to prepare for oral presentations in German than for their L1 oral presentations. Students in the third year course did not report differences between the amount they script FL and L1 presentations. Furthermore, all students reported doing less scripting in the second survey (in both L1 and FL presentations) compared to the first. This could reflect differences in their expectations at the beginning of the semester with their actual practices by the end of the semester. Whereas students may have planned to put a lot of time into preparing for their L1 and FL oral presentations, the work they actually did preparing for these presentations may have been significantly less than they had planned.

It is interesting to note that the majority of students claim to use writing to prepare for informal class discussions in L1 and FL courses—except for the students completing the second survey in the third year oral German course. Eleven out of fifteen of these students (73.3%) claim that they did not use writing to prepare for informal class discussions that semester. In both courses, students' expectations at the beginning of the semester for using writing to prepare for informal

Table 4. Individual ranking for writing in Survey 1 and Survey 2 in the second year course (Conversational German).

Student	Survey 1	Survey 2	Difference
1	3	3	0
2	4	3	1
3	2	3	-1
4	3	1	2
5	3	2	1
6	4	2	2
7	2	3	-1
8	4	2	2
9	4	3	1
10	4	4	0
11	4	4	0
12	3	4	-1
13	3	2	1
14	2	2	0
15	2	3	-1
16	3	4	-1
17	3	2	1
18	2	2	0
19	3	3	0
20	3	4	-1
21	4	3	1
22	4	3	1

*The highlighted rows show a higher ranking for writing in the second survey. The lighter highlight shows a higher ranking for writing by one level in the second survey and the darker highlight shows a two-level jump in rankings.

Table 5. Individual ranking for writing in Survey 1 and Survey 2 in the third year course (Advanced Oral German I).

Student	Survey 1	Survey 2	Difference
1	4	4	0
2	3	3	0
3	4	4	0
4	3	4	-1
5	4	3	1
6	2	1	1
7	4	3	1
8	3	4	-1
9	4	4	0
10	2	3	-1
11	2	3	-1
12	4	4	0
13	4	4	0
14	4	4	0
15	4	4	0

*The highlighted rows shows a higher ranking for writing by one level in the second survey.

class discussions were higher (100% in the second year course and 60% in the third year course) than the actual practices they reported on the final surveys (75% in the second year course and 26.7% in the third year course).

Writing as a Tool for Increasing Oral Proficiency in German 273

Table 6. The extent to which students claim they use writing to prepare for formal and informal oral activities in their L1 and L2 (second year course: n=24).

		No Writing	Some Writing	Full Script	Full Script Plus
FORMAL PRESENTATIONS	L1 Writing (Survey 1)	0	10 (41.7%)	6 (25.0%)	8 (33.3%)
	FL Writing (Survey 1)	0	3 (12.5%)	18 (75.0%)	3 (12.5%)
	L1 Writing (Survey 2)	0	16 (66.7%)	4 (16.7%)	4 (16.7%)
	FL Writing (Survey 2)	0	8 (33.3%)	12 (50%)	4 (16.7%)
INFORMAL CLASS DISCUSSIONS	L1 Writing (Survey 1)	9 (37.5%)	15 (62.5%)		
	FL Writing (Survey 1)	0	24 (100%)		
	L1 Writing (Survey 2)	10 (41.7%)	14 (58/3%)		
	FL Writing (Survey 2)	6 (25.0%)	18 (75.0%)		

Finally, students were asked to rank four writing activities that they believe help increase their oral proficiency in German: essay writing, free writing (writing without stopping for five minutes without worrying about accuracy), group writing projects, and journal writing. Tables 8 and 9 summarize these results, where the mode describes the ranking that was most frequent and the mean is composed of the average of the rankings. The standard error for the mean is listed in parentheses. In terms of the second year conversation class, high rankings (evidenced by lower numbers) occur for both free writing and journal writing—activities that tend to concentrate on getting thoughts down on paper rather than on the actual quality of the writing. This is similar in the first survey of the third year course, but by the end of the semester there do not appear to be great differences in the average

Table 7. The extent to which students claim they use writing to prepare for formal and informal oral activities in their L1 and L2 (third year course: n=15).

		No Writing	Some Writing	Full Script	Full Script Plus
FORMAL PRESENTATIONS	L1 Writing (Survey 1)	0	6 (40.0%)	1 (6.7%)	8 (53.3%)
	FL Writing (Survey 1)	0	5 (33.3%)	5 (33.3%)	5 (33.3%)
	L1 Writing (Survey 2)	0	10 (66.7%)	3 (20.0%)	2 (13.3%)
	FL Writing (Survey 2)	1 (6.7%)	9 (60%)	4 (26.7%)	1 (6.7%)
INFORMAL CLASS DISCUSSIONS	L1 Writing (Survey 1)	4 (26.7%)	11 (73.3%)		
	FL Writing (Survey 1)	6 (40.0%)	9 (60.0%)		
	L1 Writing (Survey 2)	5 (33.3%)	10 (66.7%)		
	FL Writing (Survey 2)	11 (73.3%)	4 (26.7%)		

rankings of the four writing activities. The actual rankings of the writing activities in the two surveys in the second year course (see Table 10) reveal that more students ranked journal writing higher at the end of the semester—after writing in their journals for ten weeks. Whereas seven students ranked journal writing the highest at the beginning of the semester, eleven of them gave journal writing a number one ranking at the end of the semester. Twenty students (out of twenty-three students—since one survey was not filled out correctly) gave journal writing a ranking of either 1 or 2 at the beginning of the semester, and twenty-three (out of twenty-four students) ranked journal writing first or second at the end of the semester. By the end of the third year, however, the mean ranking for all writing activities was fairly similar. These students did not perceive that any particular writing activity

Writing as a Tool for Increasing Oral Proficiency in German 275

seemed to greatly enhance oral proficiency over any of the other writing activities listed in the survey.

Table 8. Second year course: Conversational German (n=24).

Survey Question: Rank the following writing activities in terms of the extent to which you believe they could serve to enhance your oral proficiency in German:

	Survey 1		Survey 2	
	Mode	Mean (SE)	Mode	Mean (SE)
essay writing	3	3.00 (.166)	3	2.74 (.180)
freewriting	1	1.96 (.237)	1	2.39 (.249)
group writing projects	4	3.30 (.222)	4	3.21 (.225)
journal writing	2	1.83 (.136)	2	1.58 (.119)

Table 9. Third year course: Advanced Oral German I (n=15).

Survey Question: Rank the following writing activities in terms of the extent to which you believe they could serve to enhance your oral proficiency in German:

	Survey 1		Survey 2	
	Mode	Mean (SE)	Mode	Mean (SE)
essay writing	4	2.73 (.300)	1	2.47 (.350)
freewriting	1	1.93 (.300)	1	2.47 (.307)
group writing projects	4	3.20 (.262)	2	2.87 (.256)
journal writing	2	2.13 (.192)	2	2.20 (.243)

Table 10: Rankings for writing activities for the second year course in both surveys (n=24).

		#1	#2	#3	#4	No Answer
Survey 1	essay writing	1	4	12	6	1
	freewriting	12	5	3	4	0
	group writing projects	3	1	5	14	1
	journal writing	7	13	3	0	1
Survey 2	essay writing	2	6	11	4	1
	freewriting	8	3	7	5	1
	group writing projects	3	3	4	14	0
	journal writing	11	12	1	0	0

CONCLUSIONS

The results of these surveys need to be viewed in connection with the way the two courses were planned and implemented as well as with students' overall satisfaction with the courses. Future studies might consider taking course evaluations into account as well in order to get a sense of whether students felt motivated, challenged, overwhelmed, or disappointed with the course by the end of the semester. Nonetheless, the surveys provide interesting information about students' expectations, opinions, practices, and perceptions on the use of writing as a tool for increasing oral proficiency in German.

In general, there seemed to be some significant differences between how the second year and third year students answered the surveys. Although students in each of the two courses completed the same type of writing activities (dialogue journal, two short written assignments, and a group writing assignment), the students in the second year course also had to write four in-class quizzes on the story we were discussing as well. This added exposure to writing may have affected the survey results. In terms of which modality they believed could help increase their oral proficiency in German, the third year students did not vary their answers from one survey to the next to the same extent as the second year students. It is also interesting to note that 75% of the students in the second year course (including the two who filled out the survey incorrectly) changed their rankings of writing—with writing ranking higher in the second survey. When asked which writing activity best enhanced oral proficiency, the students in the second year conversation course ranked both free writing and journal writing very high—with journal writing receiving the lowest mean score (signifying a high ranking) at the end of the semester. These results would suggest that students in the second year course believed that overall the extensive writing they did during the semester—their first encounter with this type of writing in a German language course (if they were a continuing student in our program)—was particularly helpful in enhancing their oral proficiency. Journal writing also received the lowest mean score in the final surveys in the third year course, but overall the differences between the rankings of writing activities were much less pronounced at the end of the semester in the third year course than at the beginning of the course. This could either imply that, by the end of their oral German course, the third year students believed that each of the writing activities listed was beneficial for increasing oral proficiency or that their perceptions on how to most effectively use writing to increase oral proficiency varied greatly on the individual level.

In terms of expectations (Survey 1) and actual practices throughout the semester (Survey 2), the students in the third year course claimed to do less writing to prepare for informal class discussions and less scripting of formal presentations than the students in the second year course. Whether this change has to do with language proficiency levels, course expectations, learner motivation, time management issues, or comfort level remains unclear. Furthermore, the extent to which this should be seen as a positive development (students are more comfortable speaking freely with notes rather than relying on a full script) or a negative development (students are putting less time into the language learning process) is also not clear.

The surveys provide a first glimpse into how students perceive writing as a tool for increasing oral production. Given the small sample size as well as the fact that the surveys were tied to two particular courses, one would want to use caution applying the results to other courses, languages, or institutional contexts. The surveys suggest that students often use writing as a way to prepare for both formal and informal speaking in both their L1 and FL courses. Although much of the speaking and writing that happens over a semester is assigned, there is also a lot that goes on behind the scenes. Students are not only learning to speak and write in their language courses, but they often use speaking and writing as a way to process and learn course content. Understanding the extent to which students bring these learning practices into the FL classroom environment will help instructors ascertain whether it would be beneficial for these tools to be explicitly taught as part of the language-learning process. Much more research needs to be conducted on how language-learning techniques can serve to increase language proficiency as well as the learning of course content.

The survey results also suggest that students appreciate opportunities for free writing and journal writing. Writing activities that promote fluency rather than accuracy seem to be perceived by these students as particularly helpful for gaining oral proficiency and preparing for in-class speaking activities. It would be interesting to have students rank a longer list of writing activities (including chatting, threaded-discussions, email exchanges, etc.) and to state which aspects of the activities they like the best (the interaction, the language environment, the content, etc.).

The speaking/writing connection is important in a world in which technology is changing our everyday means of communication. It is also important in FL learning. In the words of one student who took the survey[5], "Writing . . . is most effective when combined with an oral component. Writing, combined with discussion and conversation, improves oral proficiency much more than writing or speaking alone." It is clear that much more research needs to take place before we understand the intricate relationship between speaking and writing and how both forms of output (taken separately as well as combined) can increase overall language proficiency.

Notes

1. I use the term "cultural studies" loosely to include any course that could be listed as part of the curriculum in a language, literature, or cultural studies program. These typically include courses on literature, film, linguistics, and foreign language teaching methodology and may include interdisciplinary course content focusing on anthropology, art history, business, economics, gender studies, history, literary or cinematic theory, media studies, museum studies, philosophy, political science, sociolinguistics, and sociology.

2. Curricular design is ever changing. At the moment the Department of Germanic and Slavic Studies at the University of Victoria is planning to undergo a major curricular change at all levels in order to achieve a cohesive

and integrated program that focuses on language and cultural studies at all levels of the curriculum.

3. In spring 2008, the students decided to call the city "Deutschburg," a city in the German Democratic Republic. Using the target language to discuss the project, they decided that the city would have a border control, a bakery, a movie theater, a soccer stadium, an opera house, a restaurant, a walk-in medical clinic, a disco, and a bookstore and that the visitors should take on the identity of some famous German-speaking person. After crossing the border with their passports, the visitors were greeted with a speech from the mayor who invited them to experience the city and informed them of the rules and restrictions (such as the consequences of what would happen if one was caught speaking English). After roaming around the city, watching previews of films at the movie theater, eating at the restaurant, buying tickets to the opera, and other activities, the visitors were treated to an opera performance of music by Hanns Eisler (by a music student in the third year course) and were invited to participate in a rap-off in the disco.

4. For this final project, the students in the spring of 2008 chose to do a photo-treasure hunt. Working in groups, students wrote a list of five items that could be found on campus. Later that week, the groups exchanged their lists and had to photograph the five items on the new list they had received and then email their five pictures to another group. Each group had to then write a story based on the five photographs they had received. The stories were presented orally to the class and handed in to me in writing. The entire project was created and planned by the students.

5. The comment was written on the second survey by a student in the second year German conversation course.

References

Buch, F. (Director). (2001). *Emil und die Detektive* [Motion Picture]. Germany: Bavaria Filmverleih- und Produktions GmbH.

Chafe, W. (1982). Integration and involvement in speaking, writing and oral literature. In D. Tannen (Ed.), *Spoken and written language: Exploring orality and literacy* (pp. 35–54). Norwood, NJ: Ablex.

Chun, D. M. (1994). Using computer networking to facilitate the acquisition of interactive competence. *System, 22*(1), 17–31.

Cumming, A. (1989). Writing expertise and second-language proficiency. *Language Learning, 39,* 81–141.

Halliday, M. (1987). Spoken and written modes of meaning. In R. Horowitz & S. Samuels (Eds.), *Comprehending oral and written language* (pp. 55–82). San Diego: Academic Press.

Harklau, L. (2002). The role of writing in classroom second language acquisition. *Journal of Second Language Writing, 11,* 329–350.

Homstad, T., & Thorson, H. (2000). Quantity versus quality? Using extensive and intensive writing in the FL classroom. In G. Bräuer (Ed.), *Writing across languages* (pp. 141–152). Stamford, CT: Ablex.

Kästner, E. (1997). *Emil und die Detektive.* Easy Reader Series. Copenhagen: Aschehoug.

Kern, R. (1995). Restructuring classroom interaction with networked computers: Effects on quality and characteristics of language production. *The Modern Language Journal, 79,* 457–476.

Krashen, S. D. (1985). *The input hypothesis: Issues and implications.* London: Longman.

Krashen, S. D., & Terrell, T. D. (1983). *The natural approach: Language acquisition in the classroom.* Hayward, CA: Alemany Press.

Lamprecht, G. (Director). (1931). *Emil und die Detektive* [Motion picture]. Germany: Universum Film (UFA).

Lazda, R., & Thorson, H. (2005). *Neuer Wein und Zwiebelkuchen: A cultural reader.* New York: McGraw-Hill.

Leki, I., Cumming, A., & Silva, T. (2008). *A synthesis of research on second language writing in English.* New York: Routledge.

MLA Ad Hoc Committee on Foreign Languages. (2007). Foreign languages and higher education: New structures for a changed world. *Profession, 2007,* 234–245.

Payne, J. S., & Whitney, P. J. (2002). Developing L2 oral proficiency through synchronous CMC: Output, working memory, and interlanguage development. *CALICO Journal, 20*(1), 7–32.

Scott, V. M. (1992). Write from the start: A task-oriented developmental writing program for foreign language students. In R. M. Terry (Ed.), *Dimension: Language* (pp. 1–15). Valdosta, GA: Southern Conference on Language Teaching.

Silva, T. (1993). Toward an understanding of the distinct nature of L2 writing: The ESL research and its implications. *TESOL Quarterly, 27*(4), 657–677.

Sperling, M. (1996). Revisiting the writing-speaking connection: Challenges for research on writing and writing instruction. *Review of Educational Research, 66*(1), 53–86.

Swaffar, J., & Arens, K. (2005). *Re-mapping the foreign language curriculum: An approach through multiple literacies.* New York: Modern Language Association.

Swain, M. (1985). Communicative competence: Some roles of comprehensible input and comprehensible output in its development. In S. M. Gass & C. G. Madden (Eds.), *Input in second language acquisition* (pp. 235–256). Rowley, MA: Newbury House.

Swain, M., & Lapkin, S. (1995). Problems in output and the cognitive processes they generate: A step towards second language learning. *Applied Linguistics, 16*(3), 371–391.

Thorne, S. & Reinhardt, J. (2008). "Bridging activities," new media literacies, and advanced foreign language proficiency. *CALICO Journal, 25*(3), 558–572.

Thorson, H. (2000). Using the computer to compare foreign and native language writing processes: A statistical and case study approach. *The Modern Language Journal, 84,* 155–169.

Valdés, G., Haro, P., & Echevarriarza, M. P. E. (1992). The development of writing abilities in a foreign language: Contributions toward a general theory of L2 writing. *The Modern Language Journal, 76,* 333–352.

Warschauer, M. (1996). Comparing face-to-face and electronic discussion in the second language classroom. *CALICO Journal, 13*(2), 7–26.

Weissberg, B. (2000). Developmental relationships in the acquisition of English syntax: Writing vs. speech. *Learning and Instruction, 10,* 37–53.

Weissberg, R. (2005). Talking about writing: Cross-modality research and second language speaking/writing connections. In P. K. Matsuda & T. Silva (Eds.), *Second language writing research. Perspectives on the process of knowledge construction* (pp. 93–104). Mahwah, NJ: Lawrence Erlbaum.

Weissberg, R. (2006). *Connecting speaking & writing in second language writing instruction.* Ann Arbor: University of Michigan Press.

Appendix

Student Survey #1

1. I am currently enrolled in (check one):

__German 252

__German 352

2. Please rank the following activities in terms of the extent to which you believe they could serve to enhance your oral proficiency in German. (Rank your top three choices from the list below by supplying a #1, #2, and #3 in the blanks in front of your top three responses.)

I believe that the best way to increase my oral proficiency is to:

_____ listen to German as often as I can.

_____ read German texts as often as I can.

_____ speak German as often as I can.

_____ write in German as often as I can.

3. When you are giving a formal speech or presentation in your native language, how do you prepare for it? To what extent does writing play a role in your preparations (e.g., taking notes, writing out the full script, etc.)? (Please explain in the space below.)

4. If you were to give a formal speech or presentation in German, would you follow the same procedure as outlined in #3 above? To what extent would you prepare for the German presentation differently? How do you envision the role of writing in your preparations for giving a speech or presentation in German? (Please explain in the space below.)

5. When attending classes in your native language, do you ever use writing to prepare for informal class discussions (e.g., notes on the readings, articulating or organizing your thoughts, etc.)? (Please explain in the space below.)

6. In what ways do you envision using writing to prepare for informal class discussions in a German conversation course? In what ways is it similar to how you prepare for discussions in courses taught in your native language? How does it differ? (Please explain in the space below.)

7. Please rank the following writing activities in terms of the extent to which you believe they could serve to enhance your oral proficiency in German. (Rank your top three choices from the list below by supplying a #1, #2, and #3 in the blanks in front of your top three responses.)

_____ essay writing

_____ freewriting (writing without stopping for 5 minutes without worrying about accuracy; getting thoughts down on paper)

_____ group writing projects

_____ journal writing

8. Please discuss your beliefs on how writing can best be used as a tool to increase oral proficiency. (Please explain in the space below.)

Student Survey #2

1. I am currently enrolled in (check one):

__German 252

___ German 352

2. Please rank the following activities in terms of the extent to which you believe they could serve to enhance your oral proficiency in German. (Rank your top three choices from the list below by supplying a #1, #2, and #3 in the blanks in front of your top three responses.)

I believe that the best way to increase my oral proficiency is to:

_____ listen to German as often as I can.

_____ read German texts as often as I can.

_____ speak German as often as I can.

_____ write in German as often as I can.

3. When you are giving a formal speech or presentation in your native language, how do you prepare for it? To what extent does writing play a role in your preparations (e.g., taking notes, writing out the full script, etc.)? (Please explain in the space below.)

4. Did you follow the same procedure as outlined in #3 above when preparing for your German presentations this semester? To what extent did you prepare differently? What role did writing play in your preparations for giving a speech or presentation in German this semester? (Please explain in the space below.)

5. When attending classes in your native language, do you ever use writing to prepare for informal class discussions (e.g., notes on the readings, articulating or organizing your thoughts, etc.)? (Please explain in the space below.)

6. In what ways did you use writing to prepare for informal class discussions in this German course this semester? In what ways was it similar to how you prepare for discussions in courses taught in your native language? How did it differ? (Please explain in the space below.)

7. Please rank the following writing activities in terms of the extent to which you believe they served to enhance your oral proficiency in German this semester. (Rank your top three choices from the list below by supplying a #1, #2, and #3 in the blanks in front of your top three responses.)

_____ essay writing

_____ freewriting (writing without stopping for 5 minutes without worrying about accuracy; getting thoughts down on paper)

_____ group writing projects

_____ journal writing

8. Please discuss your beliefs on how writing can best be used as a tool to increase oral proficiency. What writing activities did you find most helpful this semester? (Please explain in the space below.)

14 Teaching Academic Writing to Advanced EFL Learners in China: Principles and Challenges

Wenyu Wang

> *Writing is hard work. A clear sentence is no accident. Very few sentences come out right the first time, or even the third time. Remember this in moments of despair. If you find that writing is hard, it's because it is hard. It's one of the hardest things people do.*

These words are not mine. They were uttered by William Zinsser (1994), a craftsman in both writing and the teaching of writing, in his best-selling book, *On Writing Well* (p.12). If I had read these words eighteen years ago, I could not have agreed more. At that time, I was a freshman English major in college in China, overwhelmed by disorientation in a new world of academia. Part of the disorientation related to being (forced to be) a new member of an academic discourse community that requires heavy reading and writing. Reading was fine, as I grew up with books. But writing was killing me, as I believed I had no aptitude for writing. To make it worse, all the writing was not in my mother tongue but a foreign language I was (and still am) grappling with. Today, I can still recall those moments of despair on sleepless nights, usually as a writing assignment due date drew near. Writing, no doubt, is one of the hardest things people do.

It was not until nine years later—after I finally survived all my college and graduate course papers as well as degree theses and became a teacher of EFL (English as a foreign language) writing—that I came to realize: writing is *not* the hardest thing; teaching writing *is*. (How ironic that my career involves teaching of writing, considering that

I myself often "hate" writing.) I became a teacher of writing largely because my PhD thesis centered on second language (L2) writing and naturally I was assumed to know how to teach writing—which I did not. Desperately, I turned to all those L2 writing books and articles and practiced things advocated by product-, process-, and later genre-based pedagogies (Grabe & Kaplan, 1996; Leki, 1992; Reichelt, 2001; Reid, 1993; Hyland, 2003a); some proved successful, others not. I also reflected on how my own writing instructors conducted class and applied their strategies; again, some proved successful, others not.

With trials and successes and failures over the years, I am growing into a less desperate, more confident teacher, though sometimes still plagued by a feeling of incompetence, especially when faced with new obstacles arising from the classroom I thought I knew so well. In this chapter, I introduce the principles I follow and the challenges I meet in my writing classroom to those who also happen to consider teaching of writing as "one of the hardest things." By putting our heads together, we may be able to make it less hard.

Background

The institution where I teach is a large research university located in Nanjing, the capital of east China's Jiangsu Province, one of the most developed areas in the nation. Rated as a first class university in China, it houses a number of programs granted the title of "National Key Discipline" by the Chinese Education Ministry, the nation's highest appraisal of education at post-secondary levels[1]. One of its national key disciplines is the English major program, comprising undergraduate and graduate divisions[2]. Since this chapter focuses on the teaching of an undergraduate English composition course, the information below pertains to the undergraduate program only.

English Major Curriculum

The curriculum for the four-year undergraduate English major program aims at cultivating English language skills, cultural, linguistic, and literary knowledge, as well as knowledge about related fields such as international business[3]. Training in language skills is conducted in a variety of courses: speaking and listening courses are offered during the first two years, translation and oral interpreting are introduced in the second and third years, and reading and writing are required throughout all four years. Cultural courses (e.g., Introduction to British/ American Culture and Society, Cross-cultural Communication) start from the second year, linguistics and literature courses (e.g., British/ American Literature, General Linguistics) from the third. Courses on related subjects (e.g., International Trade) are also available from the third year.

Writing Instruction

Writing courses in my department are required throughout the four years, with two class hours per week[4]. Courses during the first two years develop general, fundamental writing skills: The first year writing course begins with sentences, paragraphs, and simple texts like description and narration, and the second year writing proceeds with such expository texts as process and procedures, comparison and contrast. The third and fourth year courses deal exclusively with discourse needed in academic settings: argumentative writing is taught in the third year, research paper and thesis writing in the fourth year. Instructors of these courses are both Chinese- and English-speaking expatriate teachers. Though instructors are encouraged to be creative in their teaching, they are required to use the textbooks assigned by the department[5].

The sizes of these writing classes normally range from twenty-five to thirty. Most of the students, before entering this program, have not received systematic training in English writing, despite the fact that they have studied English for seven to nine years in primary and secondary schools, with two to four hours per week of classroom instruction that often emphasized grammar and reading.

PRINCIPLES

The writing courses I have been undertaking include both third and fourth year writing courses. The principles and challenges of teaching that I present below, however, surround the third year argumentative writing course[6]. These principles show features of product-, process- and genre-based approaches to L2 writing instruction, as use of one approach does not necessarily exclude the use of another (Matsuda, 2003).

Knowing Students' Needs

Before I begin to teach the writing course, or any other course, I like to analyze my students' needs, which include their goals, abilities, prior knowledge, and preferences for teaching approaches (Hyland, 2003b). For my students, the goal of taking my writing course is obvious: to learn basic academic discourse skills so they can fulfill writing tasks in their subject matter courses such as linguistics and literature. It is also not difficult for me to know about their prior knowledge of writing no matter who taught them in the previous year because the same textbook was assigned, and by analyzing the textbook I can gain a glimpse of their previous learning. Of course, talking with former writing instructors can reveal more details about students' prior knowledge of writing as well as their writing abilities.

Information drawn from these channels, however, may not be sufficient to paint a clear picture of what students really need. Therefore, I consider it a necessity to approach my students directly. In the first class, I usually ask students to respond in written form to questions related to their needs, especially their difficulties in writing ("Do you have any difficulties in writing in English? If so, what are they?"), their expectations for the course ("What do you want from this writing course?"), and their preferences for classroom activities ("What classroom activities do you think should be included in this writing course? What do you think should not be included? Why?"). Students' responses to these questions can give me a better picture of their needs.

According to their responses, my students experience immense difficulties in writing in English. Table 1 presents a summary of reports on writing problems by thirty students in one of my writing classes. They mentioned altogether seventy-two difficulty points, which may occur at all levels of writing (content, organization, language use, and style). For me, this is by no means surprising, not only because research consistently shows the laborious nature of L2 writing (Silva, 1993), but also because as an L2 writer myself, I share their feelings and experiences. (Some of these difficulties may also be shared by L1 writers—if Zinsser, as a seasoned writer, was not exaggerating in saying writing is hard.) The second time I meet my class, I show them the summary of their reported difficulties. I think it important to let students know each other's difficulties so that they know they are not alone; students, when they know others share their problems, tend to feel less frustrated.

Table 1: Summary of writing difficulties reported by thirty students.

Content (20)	I usually don't have much to write about the assigned topic, especially if it's not familiar or interesting (5)
	My writing lacks interesting and original ideas (5)
	I can't find sufficient support for my point (3)
	I can't find good examples to support my point (3)
	My writing lacks depth (3)
	I don't know how to state the main idea (1)
Organization (14)	My writing lacks logic (4)
	My writing lacks good transitions between paragraphs (3)
	I don't know how to arrange paragraphs (3)
	I don't know how to begin an essay (2)
	My writing lacks an effective ending (2)
Language (30)	I can't find the exact words to accurately express my ideas (10)
	My vocabulary is not large enough to express my ideas (6)
	The language of my writing lacks variety (5)
	My language is not vivid (4)
	I have to literally translate my ideas from Chinese into English because I do not know the English expressions (2)
	My language is not idiomatic (2)
	I can't write long sentences (1)
Others (8)	I can't think in an English way when writing English essays (4)
	I'm not familiar with English writing conventions (3)
	I can't write enough to meet the length requirement (1)

Note: Numbers in parentheses indicate times each difficulty was mentioned in students' reports.

In addition to analyzing students' difficulties in writing, I also look into their expectations for my course and their preferences for classroom activities. Over the years, most of my students have expressed their desires to "improve their writing skills" and "be able to write well" in the course. In order to improve, they hope I can show them "good models" and point out the "good things" in them. They hope I can help them find "interesting ideas" and develop "deep thinking." Though they do not resent reading and responding to each other's works and admit they sometimes find their peers' responses helpful, they still hope I can "meticulously read" their writing, "appreciate" their ideas, but "ruthlessly" point out their problems and "catch all the language mistakes." Again, I bring the summary of these responses to my class and explain how I will incorporate their needs into my teaching.

Informed of students' writing difficulties, learning expectations, and teaching preferences, I feel more confident in deciding what should be carried out in the classroom. Indeed, the following practices and principles of my teaching are, to a large extent, based on my students' needs.

Connecting Reading and Writing

One important principle guiding my teaching of writing is to use reading as the basis for writing. As Carson and Leki (1993) have claimed, "reading can be, and in academic settings nearly always is, the basis for writing" (p. 1). For one thing, students in academic settings often write about materials they have read; for another, reading provides a vital source of linguistic and rhetorical input for writing (Hirvela, 2004). Therefore, I value the use of reading in the writing classroom, and reading, in my view, may serve multiple functions: as the writing prompt, the model for students to follow, and the source from which students generate ideas.

Reading is used, first of all, as the prompt for writing. Most of the writing tasks in my class are based on reading, and this meets my students' needs because the vast majority of writing tasks they need to fulfill in other content courses are reading-based. Secondly, reading is provided as the model for students to emulate in their own works. This, again, responds to my students' request for "good models," and personally I too believe in the role of modeling in the writing classroom. As Hirvela (2004) points out, by reading and analyzing model texts, students can learn about rhetorical patterns (e.g., location of thesis statements and topic sentences), study linguistic features (e.g., transitional words and phrases), and examine lexical as well as stylistic characteristics of writing (e.g., the use of formal vocabulary). Moreover, reading can also serve as the source for ideas. Since many of my students report they often experience writer's block or their writing lacks interesting and original ideas, I provide them with or urge them to search for readings associated with a certain topic, from which they may get inspiration.

The writing textbook I use contains a generous pool of readings that can be used for different purposes. For example, in teaching how to respond to an argument, several readings are available for use. The first reading, "The Commencement Speech You'll Never Hear" by Jacob Neusner[7], puts forward the controversial view that college fails to prepare students for the real world. Using the reading as a prompt, students are required to write an essay responding to Neusner's argument. The reading of this text is guided with questions that engage students in a critical analysis of the argument construction in the text (see Table 2). Such an analysis helps lead students to a substantive response to the original argument. However, even with thoughts in their minds, students still may not be ready to write. Another reading—an essay titled "College: An All-Forgiving World?" by Ida Timothee, an American college student who disagreed with Neusner—is provided as a model. By engaging in a teacher-led analysis of how the writer responds to Neusner's view and builds up her argument, students gain a glimpse of how to construct their own arguments. To further facilitate their argument construction, two more readings on college education ("A Proposal to Abolish Grading" by Paul Goodman and "What True Education Should Do" by Sydney Harris) are provided for students to read. They may then use these two texts as additional models of good argumentation or as sources for ideas to support their own viewpoints. I also encourage students to search for and read more papers on college education in order to enrich their ideas.

Among the various functions reading serves in the writing classroom, modeling is undoubtedly an essential one (Cumming, 1995; Swales, 1990). One thing worth noting, in my view, is that teachers should select a variety of writing models that show different levels of sophistication. Since models ought to be good, L2 writing instructors tend to choose sophisticated works of native speakers, in many cases works by great writers. I agree with the value of reading such great works. However, I also think it important to read less sophisticated but

Questions	Purpose: Guiding students to
Q1: What is the author trying to prove?	Find the main idea.
Q2: What evidence does the author use to prove it?	Find the gist of the argument.
Q3: Does the evidence prove the author's point? a) Is the evidence sufficient? b) Is the evidence relevant? c) Are the examples representative? d) Are the facts accurate? e) Are the opinions cited given by qualified sources?	Critically evaluate the argument.
Q4: What points do you agree or disagree with?	React to the argument.
Q5: Why do you agree or disagree?	
Q6: What do you want to prove?	Look for supporting evidence. Bring thoughts to a focus.

Table 2: Reading questions for "The Commencement Speech You'll Never Hear."

still good works by student writers, especially L2 students. Whereas the sophisticated L1 sample texts set a high standard for L2 students, the L2 student samples stand for a more accessible (and realistic) goal that students may find easier to reach. I have shown my students samples written by novice L2 student writers as well as skillful native English speakers, and they have found both types of models helpful.

Explicating Discourse Structures

Modeling is one way to provide students with input about rhetorical and linguistic knowledge. Explicit teaching of genre knowledge is another (Hyland, 2004, 2007). In my class, I explicitly teach conventions for organizing a typical English argumentative essay, including:

- The opening paragraph must contain a thesis statement;
- The thesis should be supported by examples or statements of evidence;
- Each of the statements should be presented in separate paragraphs, introduced by a topic sentence;
- All material in individual paragraphs should relate to the topic sentence;
- The final paragraph should be the conclusion, in which the thesis is stated in a somewhat different way. (See Williams, 2005.)

Following the explicit teaching of conventions and rules, model texts are analyzed. Discourse patterns at the paragraph level are taught in the same way. In teaching how to write an introduction, for instance, I illustrate the rules (e.g., "An introduction may have four components: background, topic, opinion, and elaboration" and "The opinion is obligatory and has to be made clear in the beginning") with analysis of samples (see Table 3).

Table 3: Analysis of a sample introduction.

Sample	Analysis
	The writer
[1] For people growing up in the Information Age, it is hard to imagine a world without computers and the Internet. [2] Due to its incredible growth, claims about the Internet revolutionizing our lives are now commonplace. [3] This revolution, in my view, has had important implications for our educational system. [4] The world of education is experiencing some major changes: people have more opportunities for education, more access to quality teaching and more flexibility in learning.	[1] Begins by introducing background; [2] Brings up the topic; [3] States his or her own opinion; and [4] Summarizes the elaboration of this opinion. [3] + [4]: Thesis statement

In addition to explicating discourse patterns at both overall and paragraph levels, I also bring students' attention to culturally-specific discourse features. As Hyland (2003b) says, "what is seen as logical, engaging, relevant, or well-organized in writing, what counts as proof, conciseness, and evidence, all differ across cultures" (p. 45), and such cultural differences ought to be explicitly taught (Connor, 2003; Ferris & Hedgcock, 2005). In my class, I use Kaplan's landmark work (1966), which has initiated great interest as well as controversy in the study of contrastive rhetoric, as a prompt for students to ponder on rhetorical difference. When I brought this work to my students the first time, I was very unsure about whether it would be too academic for them. Surprisingly, students appeared interested in Kaplan's "doodles" of the Anglo-European (English) rhetorical pattern being a straightforward line and the Oriental (Chinese) a spiral. Since then, Kaplan has remained in my teaching plan. After introducing his theory, I then summarize the support for and attacks on it (Connor, 1996, 2003) and ask students to discuss whether they agree with Kaplan or not by reflecting on their own L1 (Chinese) and L2 (English) literacy learning experiences. This discussion finally leads to a take-home writing assignment arguing for or against Kaplan's view by comparing Chinese and English expository texts.

Such discussion and writing about features of Chinese and English discourses help raise students' cultural and rhetorical awareness. Nevertheless, it does not prevent them from producing L1-like (Chinese) discourse features in their own L2 (English) compositions, the same features reported in literature about ESL writing by students of East Asian backgrounds (Connor, 1996; Fox, 1994; Leki, 1992). Such features include introductions without clear thesis statements (in some cases the thesis finally emerges in the last paragraph; in others, it never really shows up, though it may be inferred from the text), paragraphs without proper topic sentences, and conclusions that do not restate the thesis but rather state a point loosely related to the topic under discussion. These features seem to belong to an inductive, or quasi-inductive, approach to argument construction, which Hinds (1990) believes more typical in Chinese, Japanese, and Korean expository discourse. Although I have recently heard voices arguing for rhetorical plurality in academic discourse (Kubota & Lehner, 2004), I still want my students to write with conventions more typical of English rhetoric, so that someday when they need to participate in a western discourse community, they will not be misread or misunderstood. Therefore, I often collect and display examples of student writing with rhetorical problems. Students, too often, cannot detect the problem at first sight, but after I direct their attention to it (e.g., by asking the question "Can you find a clear thesis statement in this paragraph?"), they realize something *is* wrong.

Designing Communicative Writing Tasks

Teaching students rhetorical knowledge and exposing them to model texts does not necessarily make them good writers. In order to develop writing skills, students should be given ample chances to exercise their knowledge of writing (Hyland, 2003b; Williams, 2005). Meanwhile, how well students can make use of these practice opportunities to some extent depends on how well they are designed. In creating and implementing writing tasks, I believe one of the essential principles is communicativeness, because students write not simply to sharpen their writing skills but more importantly to engage in meaningful communication with an interested audience. Writing is, in essence, communication and the sharing of ideas.

One way to make writing tasks communicative is to find authentic audiences. In the traditional writing classroom, the instructor used to be the only reader of student writings. With the popularity of process pedagogy since the 1980s, teachers can arrange for real readers by having students share and comment on each other's works (Casanave, 2004; Liu & Hansen, 2002). In my classroom, I urge students to read each other's works; they read not only finished products but also outlines and preliminary thoughts at the planning stage. In addition, I implement the practice of interactive journal writing, in which students become "interested participants in ongoing conversations" (Casanave, 2004, p. 160). This takes the form of group reading diaries: three students form a group and together select a work (e.g., a short story) to read; after reading, one group member writes down his or her reaction to the work, the second person writes comments on both the original work and the first person's reaction, and the third responds to the work and all others' comments. In this way, writing is no longer a lonely process of self-discovery and expression, but a social, interactive event with communication purposes.

Sometimes audiences can be arranged outside of the writing class. One project I assign to my students involves writing opinion letters to newspaper editors. Students are required to read pieces in the opinion section of *China Daily,* the most widely circulated English newspaper in China, or of *21st Century,* an English newspaper in China targeting college students, and then write to editors about their reactions to these opinions. Since the final products can be sent out, this writing task enables students to write to a real audience for an authentic purpose[8].

Another important point in designing communicative writing tasks is to make sure students feel the need or even the impulse to communicate. And this communication need can either be spurred or suppressed by the topic of the writing task. My students report they do not want to write when they find the assigned topic unfamiliar or uninteresting. Most of the topics in my writing textbook are very likely to arouse interest from students because some of them are related to students' life experiences (e.g., "Do you think boys are better learners of the sciences whereas girls are better language learners?" or "How should universities improve teaching on the undergraduate level?") and others are important social issues students often hear and read about (e.g., "Do you think the Chinese government should levy heavy taxes on the purchase of cars?" or "Do you think women are underrepresented in public life? If so, what should we do about it?"). Even so, when giving writing assignments, I still urge students to explore their own topics, topics about which they have something to say and are eager to say it. This, I contend, is the premise for an earnest engagement in a meaningful writing event.

Scaffolding the Writing Process

Writing is fun, but at the same time, it is also a challenging, laborious process. This is especially true with writing in a second/foreign language. Studies comparing L1 and L2 composing processes have found the latter is much slower and more laborious (Silva, 1993), and L2 writers may experience a cognitive overload when they write (Williams, 2005). This explains why so many students, when faced with a writing assignment, suffer from anxiety and avoid the assignment until the last minute before it is due. As the writing instructor, I consider it my absolute obligation to assist students throughout the process of writing, to make it less painful but more fruitful.

The first step I take to assist students is to reduce their writing anxiety and fear of writing. I like to tell them it is perfectly normal to find English writing laborious and often unfulfilling; it is perfectly normal to sit before a computer for hours and produce virtually nothing—one may encounter writer's block when writing in one's mother tongue, not to mention writing in an unfamiliar language. I also like to tell them writing, especially academic writing, is not simply putting down words on paper; rather, it entails "gathering ideas and information, analyzing and organizing this information, and presenting it in a way that effectively communicates those ideas to the reader" (Williams, 2005, p.13). Going through this process may be painful, but once it is fulfilled, it is fruitful—it develops writing skills, improves overall English language ability, and at the same time sharpens the mind. In saying such things, I attempt to lower students' affective barriers to writing.

The second step I take to assist students' writing process is to help them generate ideas at the prewriting stage, since many students report their writing lacks interesting and original ideas or lacks support for their arguments. Investigations into the L2 composing process have shown that L2 writers plan less than native speakers do (Leki, 1992; Silva, 1993). Therefore, I always "force" my students to do extensive reading, thinking, discussing, and researching before they really put pen to paper. Various prewriting tasks are carried out in class, including individual brainstorming and more often pair, group, or full class discussions. As the writing topic tends to be a controversial issue, students are encouraged to think about both the pros and cons of the issue during their brainstorming and discussions. When students discuss in pairs or small groups, they are required to note the major points and then report to the whole class. Following the in-class discussion, students are then told to do more library research after class. Occasionally, prewriting activity takes the form of debating. In this case, students should do library research about the assigned topic (a controversial issue) beforehand. Then, in class, divided into different camps according to the position they take toward the issue, they engage in a free debate conducted in English. I find students more enthusiastic about the subsequent writing task after they have engaged in such a discussion or debate.

The third step to facilitate students' writing process is to adopt the multi-draft approach—at least three drafts for each writing assignment. One benefit of this approach is that students have chances to revise their writings based on suggestions from both their teacher and peers (this is discussed in greater detail in the next section). In fact, revision begins even at the prewriting stage. Students share their brainstorms or outlines with each other, ask each other for responses, and then modify their plans accordingly. With each revision, they can, hopefully, bring the argument to a newer and clearer stage. Another benefit I find of the multi-draft approach is that students can focus on a different aspect of writing in each draft. Research shows that our brains have a limited processing capacity and we can only pay attention to a limited number of things at once (Bereiter & Scardamalia, 1987). When students are concentrating on building up effective arguments, they may not be able to devote sufficient attention to language choices; conversely, if they are very concerned with lexical and syntactic choices, they may not be able to pay enough attention to idea development. In order to reduce the cognitive overload in composing, I urge students to concentrate on idea development and argument construction in the first and second drafts without worrying about sentence level accuracy; they can take care of language issues in later drafts when argument construction is finalized.

Maximizing the Effect of Response

As discussed above, a multi-draft approach makes possible chances for students to revise their ideas and wording. In order to help students revise, teachers need to consider how to respond to students' works effectively. While it is agreed that response to written work is essential for the development of writing skills, "there is less certainty about who should give this response, the form it should take, and whether it should focus more on ideas or forms" (Hyland, 2003b, p. 177). These questions are also my concerns in giving feedback and maximizing its effect on student revision.

The first question is who should respond. In the traditional writing classroom, the teacher used to be the only provider of feedback. In the 1980s, peer feedback was introduced into the L2 writing classroom (Zamel, 1985). Since then, there has been disagreement on the relative superiority of teacher versus peer feedback (Hedgcock & Lefkowitz, 1992; Zhang, 1995), but one thing researchers seem to agree on is that these two types of feedback are not exclusive (Ferris, 2003; Zhang, 1999). Indeed, I implement both in my classroom and find them complementary in effect. Students read each other's written works (including brainstorms and tentative outlines) and write down their comments; I then read and comment on both the student's written work and the peer comments on it. Since research has proven positive effects of peer feedback on student revision when students are trained and guided in how to give feedback (Berg, 1999; Min, 2006; Stanley, 1992), I provide my students with "peer review questions" to guide them[9]:

1. What do you think of the main idea of this draft? Is it clearly stated near the beginning? How should it be improved so that the reader can easily understand it?

2. Is the main point well supported with several major points? Are these points clear and logical? Do you agree? If you agree, what additional things can be said of it so as to strengthen the argument? If you disagree, give your reasons so as to persuade the writer to look at the issue differently.

3. Does each paragraph in the main body have a topic sentence with supporting details? Does each paragraph read coherently?

4. Is there a conclusion in the draft? Does it tie the ideas in the body back to the main idea? If not, how should it be improved?

These questions, on the one hand, focus students' attention on argument construction rather than surface language problems; they help students read critically, on the other, so that they will not be more concerned about maintaining group harmony than providing critical input on others' drafts—a tendency Nelson and Carson (1998) uncovered among Chinese-speaking ESL peer reviewers, which I also find true with some of my students. With such guidance, my students *are* able to produce critical comments, good complements to mine. In fact, I often find they understand each other better and can detect issues I have not noticed. By reading and commenting on each other's works, students learn how to write for an audience and how to improve their own writings, "to write like a reader" (Williams, 2005).

The second question is what form feedback should take. I give written commentary to students' work, comprising both marginal and end comments, probably the most common form of teacher feedback (Hyland, 2003b). In the end note, I state how the text appears to me as a reader, how successful I think it has been, and how it could be improved, by using the "*praise, criticism,* and *suggestions*" formula suggested in L2 writing literature (Hyland & Hyland, 2001). In the margins, I offer more immediate, text-specific comments, addressing a certain issue at the exact point where it occurs.

Written commentary is certainly not the only option. Another form of giving feedback I have adopted is conferencing (i.e., sitting down and talking to the student face-to-face). Conferencing has important advantages as it can supplement the limitations of one-way written feedback with opportunities for "the teacher and the student to negotiate the meaning of a text through dialogue" (McCarthey, 1992, p. 1). Despite its advantages, the time conferencing demands is excessive (Campbell, 1998), and I do find it impossible to have frequent face-to-face meetings with my students. However, I manage to make use of my office hours to arrange for at least one formal conference with each student during a semester, in addition to many mini-conferences during breaks between classes. For mini-conferences, my major concern is to clarify meaning and resolve ambiguities in students' texts and/or explain my comments. For formal conferences, my focus is not limited to discussion of the text; I also ask students about their reactions to my teaching, and their perceptions of their problems as well as progress in writing. Both my students and I enjoy and benefit from such conversations. Through exchanging ideas, students realize why I give certain suggestions and thus are more inclined to accept them; meanwhile, I come to understand their intended meaning and therefore know better how to help them communicate it more effectively. Moreover, better informed of my students' responses to my teaching, and of their problems and progress, I am able to keep my teaching tailored to their needs.

The third question about giving feedback is whether to focus more on ideas or forms. My students expect me to provide feedback on all aspects of writing including content, organization, language, style, and presentation. I should give them what they want; I have no choice. What I can choose is when to give what. Since my students write on a multi-draft basis, I do not have to cover every aspect on every draft. When reading and commenting on the first and second drafts, I focus more on idea development and argument construction, ignoring grammatical errors unless they make sentences unintelligible; these syntactic and lexical pitfalls will be taken care of in later drafts, as advocated by some L2 writing professionals (Campbell, 1998; Ferris & Hedgcock, 2005). When students are reading each other's works, I urge them to focus on ideas rather than form because for one thing, previous research has discovered that students tend to focus on "surface concerns" (Leki, 1990), ignoring larger revising issues; for another, my classroom experience shows students are more able to give constructive suggestions on content than they are on form, largely due to their limited English proficiency.

Challenges

The above principles have been guiding my teaching of EFL academic writing during the past years. Yet these guidelines by no means provide cure-all solutions to the writing classroom problems. In fact, I often feel challenged by new problems arising in the seemingly familiar classroom. (Practice does not always make perfect!) The following examines several major challenges I currently face in my writing class, in hopes of drawing attention to them and gaining insights from other L2 writing instructors and researchers.

Rhetorical Problems

As mentioned before, I explicitly teach English rhetorical patterns at both the overall and paragraph levels and highlight English discourse features that differ from Chinese rhetoric. In addition, I show and analyze inappropriate discourse samples to prevent students from committing similar mistakes. With these efforts, students do show some progress but their progress is not significant. Although they quickly learn the overall organizational pattern (i.e., the introduction-main body-conclusion structure), problems persist at other levels of writing such as argument construction and intersentential coherence.

One problem with argument construction lies in the thesis statement and topic sentences. At least one third of my students consistently fail to give a clear thesis at the beginning and/or topic sentences in middle paragraphs. When I explain to them why they should clearly state the thesis in the introduction and give a topic sentence for each paragraph in the main body, they nod their heads agreeably. But when they write for another assignment, the same problem reoccurs: there is simply no thesis statement or topic sentences. Or they produce the so-called "forced or false" thesis statement or topic sentences[10] (Shen, 1989), which I see as their struggling between deductive and inductive (or quasi-inductive) approaches to argument, as if they were struggling in a whirlpool with currents from opposite directions. It bothers me that I am unable to pull them out of the whirlpool.

Another problem quite a few students have with argument construction lies in taking their own positions. These students like to make contradictory statements such as, "On the one hand, I think X is important; on the other hand, I believe there are good reasons against it" or "X is both good and bad, because every coin has two sides." No matter how I have stressed that in English argumentation one needs to take a position, they still look puzzled at why "X is both good and bad" is not a position. This is a middle-of-the-road position, they say, and this is a "wise" position advocated by Confucianism. Yes, but now you are writing an English essay, so you should write according to English rhetorical rules. I hear myself saying these words while finding them not very powerful. Indeed when my students finally agree to take a position, they appear so unconvinced that I suspect they give in simply to avoid contradicting their teacher and to be obedient students—as advocated by Confucianism[11].

One more problem some students have in constructing argument lies in the use of supporting evidence. Students often make vague and general statements rather than using facts, statistics, and illustrations to support a point. When they do use concrete examples to make a point, they sometimes do not state the point or relate the examples to each other[12]. This might come from the Chinese rhetorical convention that the writer leaves it to the reader to make inferential bridges among the statements, a "reader-responsible style" (Hinds, 1987). Nevertheless, as Leki (1992) notes, "For the English reader accustomed to being shown how an example is linked to a generalization, this approach is perceived as failing to make an argument" (p. 96).

Rhetorical problems also occur at the sentence level: sentences go together without obvious links, which hampers the coherence of the writing. Encountering such sentences, I underline them and ask students to rewrite, to make them "flow." When the next draft comes, though those sentences have been rearranged, they still seem to me as disjointed as they were before. Reading these illogical sentences makes me wonder whether they are contrastive rhetorical problems, problems of low language proficiency, or problems of thinking. This question has been raised by other L2 writing instructors (Casanave, 2004; Fox, 1994). It might be related to rhetorical differences among languages: whereas English often makes use of formal ties or surface markers (such as connectors) to achieve coherence, coherence in Chinese writing is more subtle and implicit (Evensen, 1990; Hinds, 1987). Or is it because students, with limited L2 proficiency, are weak in using cohesive devices to connect sentences? Or is it simply a result of troubled thinking students may encounter when writing in both L1 and L2? So far there is no definite answer, and research is definitely needed to address this issue.

Plagiarism

Plagiarism, or use of unattributed sources, has long been observed in both L1 and L2 student papers (Bloch, 2001; Pecorari, 2003; Pennycook, 1996). I am also faced with this problem. In fact, I see two types of plagiarism in my classroom: unintentional and intentional.

By unintentional plagiarism, I refer to students using unattributed sources out of, to quote Deckert (1993), "an innocent and ingrained habit of giving back information exactly as they find it" (p. 133). Chinese literacy learning emphasizes memorization and imitation of authorities (Matalene, 1986). Chinese students are encouraged to memorize good writings of the ancient scholars and to use those "great words" in their own writing, without having to specify the source, as such ancient works are already shared knowledge for general readers. This literacy habit seems to exert an impact on my students writing practice in English. When they quote other people's words, they simply say "Someone once said" without specifying who said so and where this information was found. When they use statistics, they say "According to some survey," again without giving details about the survey. When they define a concept, they may use an existing definition, but the way they say it sounds as though they are defining it themselves. When I ask them to give the source, they think it ridiculous, because, to borrow their words, everybody knows this quote. As some L2 writing professionals have observed, L2 students may not know unattributed textual borrowing is considered an academic "crime" in western academic contexts (Casanave, 2004), and thus instruction is needed on how to incorporate the voices of others in one's own work (Berks & Watts, 2001; Leki, 1992; Swales & Feak, 1994). To prevent my innocent students from committing this "crime," I incorporate lectures about documentation and citation styles into my teaching.

Not all unattributed sources, or "borrowing others' words" to use Pennycook's term (1996), are unintentional. Quite a few students, having learned how to cite properly, still borrow others' words without proper acknowledgment. When reading their essays, my eyes occasionally catch patches of beautiful, well-constructed sentences embedded in the larger incoherent, grammatically-challenged text. Out of suspicion, I then look for them on Google, and my cop-like search often proves the writer a "thief" of others' words. Even when I fail to locate the origin of those beautiful sentences, I find it hard to push away the suspicion from my mind; I trust my judgment grounded in years of learning and teaching English writing. In these cases, I can hardly attribute such direct copying to cultural difference in textual borrowing practices; rather, I regard it as intentional plagiarism.

Students in this information age seem to have ample opportunity to plagiarize if they want to because the Internet provides them with easy access to an enormous amount of sources they can "borrow" for their own work (Casanave, 2004). Reasons for intentional plagiarism could be various. It may be developmental and compensatory strategies because of students' low language proficiency (Bloch & Chi, 1995; Currie, 1998; Spack, 1997) or, in other words, linguistic insecurity and a fear of making mistakes (Bloch, 2001), or resistance against writing tasks students consider meaningless (Pennycook, 1996). More research effort should go into exploring how students write from sources, why they plagiarize, and how they use this cut-paste strategy, so that as teachers, we will know how to help them integrate other's words and ideas into their own work, and still manage to be original. After all, in preventing plagiarism, proactive teaching may be more important than post facto punishment (Pecorari, 2003).

Error Treatment

In the L2 writing field, there has long been debate about the value of treating grammatical errors in students' writing (Chandler, 2004; Ferris, 1999; Ferris & Roberts, 2001; Truscott, 1996, 1999, 2004). Today, scholars and practitioners seem to agree on the necessity of error correction, considering, above all, that students strongly demand it and they believe it helps them (Casanave, 2004; Ferris & Hedgcock, 2005). For me, whether to treat errors is no longer a question, it is an important component of my feedback on students' writing (even though I do doubt its effects at times when I see corrected errors reoccurring). Still I find myself perplexed with other questions, such as whether I should treat all errors or focus on some, and whether my own correction is the most effective.

To the first question of whether to treat all or some of the errors in students' writing, responses from L2 writing professionals tend to be: correction of all errors is unnecessary and not very effective (Ferris, 2002; Ferris & Hedgcock, 2005). The task of assiduously addressing all errors is too daunting on the part of the teacher, and too overwhelming on the part of the student. I tend to accept this point of view. My students, however, do not. Instead, they expect me to point out all language problems for them because they believe this is the way they learn and improve (whether they attend to all the errors or not is another story). Their expectation puts me in a dilemma: whereas I know it is not necessary or effective to address all errors, I have to try to do so in order not to let my students down.

Even if I can convince my students of the view of selective error correction, then another question may pop up: what errors should I focus on? Scholars (Ferris, 2002; Hyland, 2003b) have suggested that teachers focus on errors that are global (interfering with the comprehensibility), frequent (relative to other error types), and stigmatizing (more typical of L2 than of L1 students). These suggestions, as appealing as they sound, are hard to apply. Analyzing and judging which errors interfere with comprehension of the text, which occur more frequently, and which characterize L2 writers requires much expertise and more time. Ferris (2002) admitted it took her, a veteran writing teacher and experienced researcher on error analysis, eleven hours to complete the task of identifying frequent errors in twenty-one student in-class compositions. Most of us would certainly use more time. It could be more daunting than treating all errors.

One more question I ask myself when treating students' errors is whether my correction itself is correct. As a NNES (non-native English-speaking) teacher, I often doubt my own corrective ability, since I am not endowed with the native English speaker's intuition. In general, I feel more confident and at ease dealing with syntactic errors (such as problems with sentence structure, tense, etc.) rather than lexical ones (like unidiomatic language use), and least confident in errors involving articles and prepositions. Such self-doubt is not uncommon; many of my Chinese colleagues share it. For us, the job of treating students' errors is far more laborious and far less effective than it is for our NES counterparts. This phenomenon, more prevalent in the FL context, has not received much attention from L2 writing research and pedagogy.

Conclusion

When I started to teach EFL writing, I turned to the L2 writing literature, hoping to find the best teaching approach, a ready-made recipe that would solve all the problems I might encounter in my classroom. The ensuing years of classroom practice have, however, taught me that there is no single best approach in the first place, no matter whether it is product-, process-, or genre-based. Indeed, the principles guiding my teaching are not limited to any single approach; instead, they show traces of all these pedagogies. Maybe the best principle of teaching is simple: use whatever works to make your own recipe. And if there is another rule, it may be: never stop looking for new ingredients for your recipe, as new obstacles and challenges always emerge in the classroom.

Notes

1. Such information is given not to boast but to specify the context of my teaching, which by no means represents an average institution of higher learning in China.

2. So far there are only four English programs granted the title of "National Key Discipline" among all Chinese universities.

3. This curriculum is in accordance with the nationally mandated *Teaching Syllabus for College English Majors* (2000), which regulates and supervises teaching in all English departments in Chinese colleges and universities.

4. The nationally mandated syllabus requires at least two years of training in writing: one year for training basic writing skills, the other year for academic writing.

5. The assigned textbooks, *College English Writing* (Ting, 1996) comprised of four volumes, are complied by a team of experienced writing instructors in my department.

6. I narrow down the focus not only due to the scope constraints of the chapter but also because the majority of English major programs in China offer only a one-year academic writing course, which is similar to my third year argumentative writing course.

7. Jacob Neusner was Professor at Brown University in Rhode Island, US. This speech was originally published in Brown University's campus newspaper, *Daily Herald*, on June 12, 1981.

8. Two years ago, I was very glad to read about a similar practice in a Japanese EFL writing classroom (see Casanave, 2004, p. 180).

9. For general strategies of giving feedback, these students have already received training in their Year One and Year Two writing courses.

10. As an ESL writer with a Chinese literacy background, Shen (1989) recalled "I had considerable difficulty writing (and in fact understanding) topic sentences. In what I deemed to be topic sentences, I grudgingly gave out themes. Today, those papers look to me like Chinese papers with forced or false English openings" (p. 463).

11. It is interesting to note that over the years one student did resist me by holding on to his middle-of-the-road position throughout his drafts, bravely ignoring my repeated criticism. Similar cases of resistance have been recorded by Fox (1994).

12. Similar problems have been recorded by Fox (1994) and Matalene (1985).

References

Bereiter, C., & Scardamalia, M. (1987). *The psychology of written composition.* Hillsdale, NJ: Lawrence Erlbaum.

Berg, C. E. (1999). The effects of trained peer response of ESL students' revision types and writing quality. *Journal of Second Language Writing, 8,* 215–237.

Berks, D., & Watts, P. (2001). Textual borrowing strategies for graduate-level ESL writers. In D. Belcher & A. Hirvela (Eds.), *Linking literacies: Perspectives on L2 reading-writing connections* (pp. 246–267). Ann Arbor: University of Michigan Press.

Bloch, J. (2001). Plagiarism and the ESL student: From printed to electronic texts. In D. Belcher & A. Hirvela (Eds.), *Linking literacies: Perspectives on L2 reading-writing connections* (pp. 209–228). Ann Arbor: University of Michigan Press.

Bloch, J. G., & Chi, L. (1995). A comparison of the use of citations in Chinese and English academic discourse. In D. Belcher & G. Braine (Eds.), *Academic writing in a second language: Essays on research and pedagogy* (pp. 231–274). Norwood, NJ: Ablex.

Campbell, C. (1998). *Teaching second-language writing: Interacting with text.* Boston, MA: Heinle & Heinle.

Carson, J. G., & Leki, I. (1993). Introduction. In J. G. Carson & I. Leki (Eds.), *Reading in the composition classroom: Second language perspectives* (pp. 1–7). Boston, MA: Heinle & Heinle.

Casanave, C. P. (2004). *Controversies in second language writing: Dilemmas and decisions in research and instruction.* Ann Arbor: University of Michigan Press.

Chandler, J. (2004). A response to Truscott. *Journal of Second Language Writing, 13,* 345–348.

Connor, U. (1996). *Contrastive rhetoric: Cross-cultural aspects of second-language writing.* Cambridge: Cambridge University Press.

Connor, U. (2003). Changing currents in contrastive rhetoric: Implications for teaching and research. In B. Kroll (Ed.), *Exploring the dynamics of second language writing* (pp. 218–241). Cambridge: Cambridge University Press.

Cumming, A. (1995). Fostering writing expertise in ESL composition instruction: Modeling and Evaluation. In D. Belcher & G. Braine (Eds.), *Academic writing in a second language: Essays on research and pedagogy* (pp. 375–397). Norwood, NJ: Ablex.

Currie, P. (1998). Staying out of trouble: Apparent plagiarism and academic survival. *Journal of Second Language Writing, 7,* 1–18.

Deckert, G. D. (1993). Perspectives on plagiarism from ESL students in Hong Kong. *Journal of Second Language Writing, 2,* 131–148.

Evensen, L. S. (1990). Pointers to superstructure in student writing. In U. Connor & A. M. John (Eds.), *Coherence in writing: Research and pedagogical perspectives* (pp. 169–183). Alexandria, VA: TESOL.

Ferris, D. R. (1999). The case for grammar correction in L2 writing classes: A response to Truscott (1996). *Journal of Second Language Writing, 8,* 1–10.

Ferris, D. R. (2002). *Treatment of error in second language student writing.* Ann Arbor: University of Michigan Press.

Ferris, D. R. (2003). *Response to student writing: Implications for second language students.* Mahwah, NJ: Lawrence Erlbaum.

Ferris, D. R., & Hedgcock, J. S. (2005). *Teaching ESL composition: Purpose, Process, and practice.* Mahwah, NJ: Lawrence Erlbaum.

Ferris, D. R., & Roberts, B. (2001). Error feedback in L2 writing classes: How explicit does it need to be? *Journal of Second Language Writing, 10,* 161–184.

Fox, H. (1994). *Listening to the world: Cultural issues in Academic Writing.* Urbana, IL: National Council of Teachers of English.

Gaodeng xuexiao yingyu zhuanye yingyu jiaoxue dagang [Teaching syllabus for college English majors]. (2000). Beijing: waiyu jiaoxue yu yanjiu chubanshe [Foreign Language Teaching and Research Press].

Grabe, W., & Kaplan, R. (1996). *Theory and practice of writing.* London: Longman.

Hedgcock, J., & Lefkowitz, N. (1992). Collaborative oral/aural revision in foreign language writing instruction. *Journal of Second Language Writing, 1,* 255–276.

Hinds, J. (1987). Reader vs. writer responsibility: A new typology. In U. Connor & R. Kaplan (Eds.), *Writing across languages: Analysis of L2 text* (pp. 141–152). Reading, MA: Addison-Wesley.

Hinds, J. (1990). Inductive, deductive, quasi-inductive: Expository writing in Japanese, Korean, Chinese, and Thai. In U. Connor & A. M. John (Eds.), *Coherence in writing: Research and pedagogical perspectives* (pp. 87–109). Alexandria, VA: TESOL.

Hirvela, A. (2004). *Connecting reading and writing in second language writing instruction.* Ann Arbor: University of Michigan Press.

Hyland, F., & Hyland, K. (2001). Sugaring the pill: Praise and criticism in written feedback. *Journal of Second Language Writing, 10,* 185–212.

Hyland, K. (2003a). Genre-based pedagogies: A social response to process. *Journal of Second Language Writing, 12,* 17–29.

Hyland, K. (2003b). *Second language writing.* New York: Cambridge University Press.

Hyland, K. (2004). *Genre and second language writing.* Ann Arbor: University of Michigan Press.

Hyland, K. (2007). Genre pedagogy: Language, literacy and L2 writing instruction. *Journal of Second Language Writing, 16,* 148–164.

Kaplan, R. (1966). Cultural thought patterns in intercultural education. *Language Learning, 16,* 1–20.

Kubota, R., & Lehner, A. (2004). Toward critical contrastive rhetoric. *Journal of Second Language Writing, 13,* 7–27.

Leki, I. (1990). Potential problems with peer responding in ESL writing classes. *CATESOL Journal, 3,* 5–19.

Leki, I. (1992). *Understanding ESL writers: A guide for teachers.* Portsmouth, NH: Boynton/Cook.

Liu, J., & Hansen, J. (2002). *Peer response in second language writing classrooms.* Ann Arbor: University of Michigan Press.

Matalene, C. (1985). Contrastive rhetoric: An American writing teacher in China. *College English, 47,* 789–808.

Matalene, C. (1986). Response to a comment on contrastive rhetoric: An American writing teacher in China. *College English, 48,* 846–848.

Matsuda, P. K. (2003). Second-language writing in the twentieth century: A situated historical perspective. In B. Kroll (Ed.), *Exploring the dynamics of second language writing* (pp. 15–34). Cambridge: Cambridge University Press.

McCarthey, S. J. (1992). The teacher, the author, and the test: variations in form and content of writing conferences. *Journal of Reading Behavior, 24,* 51–82.

Min, H. T. (2006). The effects of trained peer review on EFL students' revision types and writing quality. *Journal of Second Language Writing, 15,* 118–141.

Nelson, G. L., & Carson, J. G., (1998). ESL students' perceptions of effectiveness in peer response groups. *Journal of Second Language Writing, 7,* 113–132.

Pecorari, D. (2003). Good and original: Plagiarism and patchwriting in academic second-language writing. *Journal of Second Language Writing, 12,* 317–345.

Pennycook, A. (1996). Borrowing others' words: Text, ownership, memory, and plagiarism. *TESOL Quarterly, 30,* 201–230.

Reichelt, M. (2001). A critical review of foreign language writing research on pedagogical practices. *The Modern Language Journal, 85,* 578–598.

Reid, J. M. (1993). *Teaching ESL writing.* Englewood Cliffs, NJ: Regents/Prentice-Hall.

Shen, F. (1989). The classroom and the wider culture: Identity as a key to learning English composition. *College Composition and Communication, 40,* 459–466.

Silva, T. (1993). Toward an understanding of the distinct nature of L2 writing: The ESL research and its implications. *TESOL Quarterly, 27,* 657–677.

Spack, R. (1997). The acquisition of academic literacy in a second language: A longitudinal case study. *Written Communication, 14,* 3–62.

Stanley, J. (1992). Coaching student writers to be effective peer evaluators. *Journal of Second Language Writing, 1,* 217–233.

Swales, J. M. (1990). *Genre analysis: English in academic and research settings.* Cambridge: Cambridge University Press.

Swales, J. M., & Feak, C. B. (1994). *Academic writing for graduate students: Essential tasks and skills.* Ann Arbor: University of Michigan Press.

Ting, Y. R. (1996). *College English writing.* Nanjing: Nanjing University Press.

Truscott, J. (1996). The case against grammar correction in L2 writing classes. *Language Learning, 46,* 327–369.

Truscott, J. (1999). The case for "the case against grammar correction in L2 writing classes": A response to Ferris. *Journal of Second Language Writing, 8,* 111–122.

Truscott, J. (2004). Evidence and conjecture on the effects of correction: A response to Chandler. *Journal of Second Language Writing, 13,* 337–343.

Williams, J. (2005). *Teaching writing in second and foreign language classrooms.* Boston: McGraw-Hill.

Zamel, V. (1985). Responding to student writing. *TESOL Quarterly, 19,* 79–101.

Zhang, S. (1995). Reexamining the affective advantage of peer feedback in the ESL writing class. *Journal of Second Language Writing, 4,* 209–222.

Zhang, S. (1999). Thoughts on some recent evidence concerning the affective advantage of peer feedback. *Journal of Second Language Writing, 8,* 321–326.

Zinsser, W. (1994). *On writing well: An informal guide to writing nonfiction.* New York: HarperCollins.

Afterword

Collectively, this volume carries out a number of important functions. First, with chapters based on presentations made at the seventh Symposium on Second Language Writing in the summer of 2008, it represents the definitive textual record of that event, an important step in the ongoing evolution of the *Symposium*. Second, by including authors who are scholars from North America, Europe, East Asia, the Middle East, and North Africa, this volume arguably offers a more broadly international representation of FL writing scholarship than has been presented in any other available text. One of the distinguishing features of this volume is that it groups FL writing in English and other foreign languages together, thus highlighting the shared features of FL writing in a range of languages and contexts (and noting differences as well).

Third, and perhaps most importantly, this collection provides a picture of the contemporary state of FL writing studies—not a fully comprehensive picture, of course, since embodying the full diversity of the field would be nearly impossible, but one that is still instructive, hinting at the field as a whole, and hopefully inviting others to respond with their own perspectives. This view of the state of contemporary FL writing instruction around the world elucidates the relationship of FL writing scholarship to L2 writing studies as a whole, demonstrating how FL writing concerns overlap with and complement broader L2 writing concerns, and showing how FL writing scholarship adds something new to the understanding of writing in other languages.

In the preface to this volume, the editors address the importance of expanding the scope of L2 writing literature beyond writing in English as a second language in order to fully understand L2 writing as a whole. One major factor that distinguishes ESL writing from EFL and other FL writing is the *status* of the target language. The status of a target language resonates throughout the national or regional contexts in which it is studied, and downward through departmental and institutional responses, classroom level teaching and learning, one-on-one peer and teacher feedback, and individual writing processes and cognition as single writers relate to the language. In the bulk of recent English as a second language writing research, the dominant status of the English language goes unchallenged or unremarked. Since the majority of current L2 writing research is focused on ESL settings (a recent Google Scholar search of literature since 2000 produced 15,300 hits for "English as a second language writing," compared with 6,980 for "English as a foreign language writing"), there exists the possibility of taking for granted the influence on L2 writing instruction of national, regional, linguistic, cultural, historical, political, economic, and educational factors, marginalizing them in analyses. In contrast, FL writing work is compelled to deal more directly with language status and is therefore likely to be at the forefront of this important facet of L2 writing scholarship. Throughout this volume on FL writing, these contextual influences are brought front and center, where they can more powerfully inform both research and pedagogical practice. A number of authors in this collection expand upon the strand of EFL writing literature, which examines English language writing in contexts where English is enmeshed in complex relationships with home languages and other foreign languages, making it difficult to ignore explicit discussions of its status. Other authors in this volume address writing in FLs other than English (including Japanese, French, Spanish, and German), often noting how the status of those languages is impacted by their relationship with English and other languages.

The authors in this collection touch upon the following specific questions, which are of significance to FL writing:

In FL writing instruction, what should be the role of local educational values, practices, and rhetorics?

One of the most important themes among the chapters is the identification of aspects of pedagogy that do not align with local realities of FL teaching, learning, and usage. Perpignan, for instance, notes that English in Israel is very much an "extrinsic and non-integrative" concern, a language that is required by the national curriculum but one that has little basis in students' prior experiences or their future language use. Nevertheless, EFL writing, especially in higher education, is defined by goals that are more suited to intrinsic and integrative L1 and SL writing. In response, Perpignan calls for educational goals that better reflect students' immediate needs. Lee finds similar disconnects between pedagogy and meaningful EFL writing in Hong Kong, but these stem in part from the *dynamism* of English there, as it moves away from its SL colonial past and deeper into a FL role following the handover. Similarly, Elqobai highlights the importance of the role of the target language in FL writing, calling for changes in FL writing pedagogy in Morocco that take into consideration, among other things, the Moroccan sociolinguistic landscape. These authors point to the need to regularly renew understanding of the contexts of FL writing.

Differences between local rhetorical practices and those of the target language can also cause conflict in FL writing instruction. Reichelt describes two situations where this occurs; in both cases, the target language is English. She notes that in Italy, according to Hargan (1995), students' strategies of summarize-and-comment, which align with local practices, were devalued by their native English-speaking teachers, who criticized students' work as lacking in explicit argument structures, supporting evidence, originality, and point of view. Reichelt also reports Clachar's (2000) findings in Turkey, where local English teachers reported conflicting views of western writing pedagogy; some viewed it as a means of enriching their students' experience, while others felt that imposing western conventions for writing overshadowed students' own cultural writing styles. These cases demonstrate the need in curriculum design to take into consideration the fact that at least some rhetorical practices are culturally informed.

Despite these problems, it is important to note where and how pedagogy is getting it right and aligning successfully with local FL realities, partly to give due credit, but also to highlight actions that may be useful in addressing problems elsewhere. Reichelt describes ways in which EFL writing instruction in Germany draws on local educational values, including the valuing of close, critical reading of texts. Lee finds a balance between local educational practices and new developments from outside Hong Kong: while recognizing the importance of grammar-focused English writing instruction in a testing-oriented system, she advocates language-in-use and genre approaches that maintain an important role for grammar while making such work more meaningful for learners. Tarnopolsky overviews a writing curriculum developed with the specificities of the Ukrainian context in mind, one that takes into consideration students' previous education experiences, which focused on grammar-translation methods, de-emphasized writing, and required little or no independent composition. Finally, Wang and Min both detail practical responses to the demands of contexts in China and Taiwan, respectively, that can be enacted more immediately: knowing students' particular needs by relying more heavily on individual teacher and student input, identifying culturally-specific discourse features and not relying exclusively on ideas from English center countries, and creating writing opportunities that are communicatively meaningful to students.

Just as in contexts where English is not the primary language, local circumstances are important to FL writing instruction in English center countries. Hatasa discusses the evolution of Japanese as a FL in the US away from text-heavy, academically-oriented writing to more realistic and limited writing instruction that better mirrors American students' intention to primarily use spoken Japanese in less professional circumstances. These changes also reflect the relative difficulty for US students to learn Japanese, which includes the challenging orthography of the language and the unfamiliarity of *Ki-Sho-Ten-Ketsu* rhetorical patterns. Beyond students, this change can also be seen as a response to the limitations of *teachers* in composition training, with many L1 Japanese instructors having had little systematic writing courses at any level. Schultz also addresses FL writing in North America, arguing that, in response to globalization, fostering foreign language literacy in North America is particularly important because, among other things, it can help students develop critical and cultural awareness about themes such as identity, worldwide economic and cultural trends, and multilingualism. Similarly, Thorson notes the potential of FL writing in the North American context to promote the development of multiple cultural literacies.

Throughout this collection, nearly every author attends to context in some form: educational guidelines and practices, institutional practices, the relationship between target languages and the society in which pedagogy operates, students' interest in and practical use for FL writing, and in a few cases, contrastive rhetorical concerns. Despite the broad diversity of contexts encountered by the authors, one common message on the role of locality emerges: always remain responsive to it. The broad acceptance that this message finds among the scholars here suggests that future research, pedagogy, and even moves toward strengthening disciplinary ties are best served by keeping local context central.

How can FL writing research draw on related disciplines like SLA, ESL composition, and L1 composition without being limited or overly determined by them?

It is on this question that FL writing arguably finds both its greatest unifying force as a discipline and one of its most tenacious barriers. On the one hand, as exemplified by the chapters in this collection, FL scholarship is grounded in a shared pool of SLA, L1 composition, and SL composition literature. Manchón's survey identifies a strong two-way relationship between linguistic processes and FL writing and a mutually supportive role for both. Ruiz-Funes specifically grounds her work in Flower (1990) and others on the L1 composition side and from Carson (1993) and others on the ESL side, to conclude that FL writing is more closely linked to complex thinking and cognitive processes rather than language skills per se. Conversely, Perpignan argues for a strong role in FL writing on the part of SLA while still allowing for a lesser role for L1-based genre, process, and post-process perspectives, as do Min and Lee. That there is only an extremely small body of FL-specific literature makes this body of shared external resources more important, as in Hatasa's identification of studies of feedback and process in ESL as the only existing theoretical underpinnings for JFL writing research, and Lefkowitz's observation that FL and HL training does not have its own tradition to use in teacher training.

In her argument for the relevance of (non-English) FL writing in response to globalization, Schultz draws widely on a range of relevant literature, including literature related to Global Studies, FL studies, SL writing in general, and non-English FL writing. This latter body of literature (see, e.g., Kern & Schultz, 2005; Schultz, 2001, 2004), though quite small, reflects an important movement in FL writing in North America toward an emphasis on a FL literacy that includes a sociocultural and sociolinguistic awareness, also emphasized in Thorson's chapter.

Because there is at present only a small body of literature defining the unique issues of FL writing, contemporary FL writing research finds itself turning to many of the same external sources. It is this reliance that stands in the way of disciplinary divergence away from these other disciplines. At this point, though, only a few note this reliance on other disciplines—and the possibility of being limited or overly determined by them—as problems for future consideration. Perpignan notes that SL concerns obscure FL ones, in part due to an "ad hoc" approach to borrowing from the former. That SL writing literature comes from English center countries stands as a barrier to reliance on local contexts and needs, in Min's view.

If and when FL writing pedagogy borrows from SL writing, what sorts of modifications should be made so that they are more appropriate for FL settings and goals?

With local contexts looming large in FL writing, adaptations of SL writing to be more suitable are assumed to be necessary by many of the authors, although the specifics of those adaptations are by and large left to future scholarship. Min's principled eclectic approach, strongly informed by decision making authority granted to both instructors and students in pedagogical interactions, indicates one direction these adaptations may take. Regarding Morocco, Elqobai writes of the need to adapt the currently-advocated imported teaching methodologies to the realities of the local context, which include overcrowded classrooms and students' multilingual backgrounds. Continuing examination of educational contexts and the uses FL students have for writing will remain the foundation of these adaptations.

Are there any differences in the processes used by writers working in a foreign language and writers working in a second language?

As discussed above, many of the authors in this collection draw heavily from SLA, second language composition, and L1 composition, which may suggest that few differences are to be found between FL and SL writing processes. Nevertheless, Hatasa suggests that those differences exist and are created in large part by the circumstances of FL writing: "given the context of instruction, studies on L2 writing in Japanese cannot simply simulate English studies, thus requiring different types of research." Additionally, as Elqobai notes, FL writers may have fewer resources to draw upon (e.g., no writing centers) and may rely more on their L1(s) or other languages in writing, on-line translation websites, and/or plagiarism because of weakness in the target language, due perhaps in part to lack of target language exposure. Unique sociolinguistic, pedagogical, and practical circumstances have been most frequently noted by the authors in this collection, and it is possible that those externalities also translate into the ways writers compose and revise. Even if further investigations reveal few differences, though, it is those smaller differences that may play a significant role in students' response to FL writing, and the success of their written products.

What role should writing play in the overall FL curriculum, and how much time should be devoted to FL writing instruction? What constitute appropriate purposes for students writing in FLs, especially in contexts where students' real-life needs for FL writing are not immediately obvious?

While many of the authors in this collection look at FL writing separately from reading, speaking, and listening, many others outline a wide range of roles and purposes for FL writing within the FL curriculum. Many, including Elqobai, argue that writing can play a role in fostering acquisition of the target language: Thorson describes its role (and students' perceptions of its role) in enhancing oral proficiency, and Ruiz-Funes and Schultz discuss how FL writing plays a part in acquisition of a critical FL literacy. Similarly, Ruiz-Funes argues that FL writing instruction should involve complex reading-writing tasks that push students to read texts critically and write about them insightfully. Manchón takes this idea further, noting that in the literature, other researchers have repeatedly observed the type of linguistic processing in writing that occurs in other FL work. Because of this, writing is not only important in its own right, but functions together with other FL skills. Hatasa argues for relevance in FL writing, and notes a move toward a more realistic role for writing in US-based Japanese as a foreign language programs. However, she sees the relationship between writing and other language skills as limited, at least in Japanese, observing that Japanese writing lexicon is very different from spoken lexicon.

Other authors, including Thorson, advocate the role of writing in learning content knowledge. Reichelt describes the use of FL writing in Germany as a means of deepening students' understanding of the culture(s) of the target language, and Schultz advocates the use of a historically and politically grounded approach to the teaching of literature and literacy as a means of fostering awareness of many of the cultural and linguistic trends associated with the phenomenon of globalization. Schultz also notes the important positive transfer effect that FL literacy can have on L1 literacy skills.

Several authors also write about the role they believe writing should play in the FL classroom; for example, Elqobai advocates allotting more time to writing and devoting a higher percentage of students' course grade to writing. She also argues that students should be encouraged to produce more quantity and higher quality writing. Nas and van Esch argue for inclusion of writing tasks that are challenging but not too difficult, and for an emphasis on learner autonomy. Other roles for writing advocated include writing as a means of developing outside contacts (e.g., Tarnopolsky), as a means of passing exams and completing other academic requirements, such as papers and theses (e.g., Nas and van Esch), and fostering motivation, especially through creative writing (e.g., Tarnopolsky).

How should L2 teacher education programs prepare future teachers for teaching FL writing, and how can current FL writing preparation and teacher support be improved?

Lefkowitz directly addresses issues of foreign language (and heritage language) writing teacher development in this text as the best way of working with the gaps and limitations found in her study of instructors' beliefs and their effects on instructional approaches and students' opinions. She notes a strong correlation between the emphasis on SL writing (and EFL writing to a lesser extent) and a reliance on traditional and less well-regarded teaching practices in FL classrooms, numerous classroom and institutional difficulties that do not permit more up-to-date practices and, ultimately, a lack of FL- or HL-specific training for future instructors. Elqobai argues that it is crucial to provide the training, supervision, guidance, and appropriate equipment necessary for instructors to implement the FL writing pedagogies that are currently advocated by decision makers in Morocco, also noting the importance of rewarding teachers for their achievements. Wang's argument that no one *single* best approach exists, but that eclectic and locally responsive teaching is best, points to the need for diversity and flexibility in FL writing teacher education programs. Likewise, Lee suggests directions for such programs. By discussing the importance of building motivation and confidence in writing, de-emphasizing error correction, sharing responsibility with students through peer evaluation, and by assessing what is taught as strong practices, she suggests the content of the most successful future FL writing education programs. Regardless of program content, future teacher development is going to depend upon, and contribute to, the development of greater FL disciplinary identity.

Is it feasible for FL writing to be a unified discipline, given the fact that those interested in FL writing work in a range of geographical, institutional, and departmental environments, and publish in a broad range of venues?

The authors are generally quiet on issues of FL writing disciplinarity. The closest direct reference comes in Manchón's invocation of Ortega's (2009) warning to avoid an "undifferentiated, homogeneous contextual class of 'FL' or 'EFL.'" Along this line of thought, the strong acknowledgement of local differences and needs for FL writing throughout this text would seem to suggest difficulties in creating a strongly unified discipline. However, all the authors draw from a diverse but common body of knowledge from SLA, ESL composition, and L1 composition. This shared intellectual foundation can, like the diverse foundations of ESL composition before it (e.g., Silva & Leki, 2004), become the basis for a recognized discipline. Events such as the FL writing-based 2008 Symposium on Second Language Writing will undoubtedly contribute to solidifying ties among FL writing researchers and instructors.

How does use of electronic media influence FL writing?

The authors in this collection point to a number of important effects that the availability of online and offline electronic tools are having on FL writing pedagogy and practices. Wang warns against the increasing temptation of plagiarism in the online era. Turning once again to context, Lee discusses the importance of electronic media in the lives of students and teachers as a reason to incorporate such tools into FL pedagogy, making it more relevant to both. Hatasa points out that digital technology is an important component in JFL, but also stresses that differences in quantity of use exist between JFL and western languages, opening an avenue for future research into the *contextually* dependent dimensions of such technology. Specific digital formats such as blogs, wikis, and social networking sites are addressed in this book, as well as formats that are frequently multimodal—using still images, video, sound, and design options such as fonts and layout, along with the written word. Future FL writing research can benefit from investigations of how these non-linguistic modes interact with the written word, in both process and product.

In closing, it is important to note some questions that were not addressed in this collection, but which may be fruitful to cover in future FL writing literature:

- What can L2 writing scholarship, including ESL writing scholarship, learn from FL writing scholarship?
- What kinds of collaborations between FL and SL instructors and researchers will be most fruitful for both?
- If it is feasible for FL writing to establish itself as a discipline, what directions should FL writing research pursue: which issues should be investigated, which research methodologies are most appropriate, and how can the field of FL writing form a community to support an emerging research agenda?

It is our hope that scholars will take up these issues and concerns in future professional conferences and published works.

References

Carson, J. G. (1993). Reading for writing: Cognitive perspectives. In J. G. Carson, & I. Leki (Eds.), *Reading in the composition classroom* (pp. 85–104). Boston, MA: Heinle and Heinle.

Clachar, A. (2000). Opposition and accommodation: An examination of Turkish teachers' attitudes toward western approaches to the teaching of writing. *Research in the Teaching of English, 35,* 67–100.

Flower, L. (1990). The role of task representation in reading-to-rite. In L. Flower, V. Stein, J. Ackerman, M. J. Kantz, K. McCormick, & W. C. Peck, (Eds.), *Reading-to-write: Exploring a cognitive and social process* (pp. 35–75). New York: Oxford University Press.

Hargan, N. (1995). Misguided expectations: ESL teachers' attitudes towards Italian university students' written work. *Language and Education, 9,* 223–232.

Kern, R., and Schultz, J. M. (2005). Beyond orality: Investigating literacy and the literary in second and foreign language instruction. *The Modern Language Journal, 89,* 381–92.

Ortega, L. (2009). Studying writing across English as a foreign language contexts: Looking back and moving forward. In R. M. Manchón (Ed.), *Foreign language writing. Learning, teaching, and research* (pp. 232–255). Clevedon: Multilingual Matters.

Schultz, J. M. (2001). The Gordian knot: Language, literature, and critical thinking. In Virginia M. Scott & Holly Tucker (Eds.). *SLA and the literature classroom: Fostering dialogues* (pp. 3–31). Boston, MA: Heinle & Heinle.

Schultz, J. M. (2004). Toward a pedagogy of the francophone text in intermediate language courses. *The French Review 78,* 260–277.

Silva, T., & Leki, I. (2004). Family matters: The influence of applied linguistics and composition studies on second language writing studies: past, present, and future. *The Modern Language Journal, 88*(1), 1–13.

Contributors

Rachida Elqobai graduated from Marc Bloch University, France, and worked as a high school French teacher for many years in Morocco. In 2001, she moved to the US and earned her PhD at Purdue University. She has presented her work at many conferences in France, and at Purdue University, where she was a member of the local committee and a presenter at the Symposium on Second Language Writing, 2004–2008. She was also an Arabic translator for the *Journal of Second Language Writing*. She is currently teaching communication at Cadi Ayyad University, Marrakech, Morocco, where she coordinates French, English, and management courses. Her research area relates to foreign language acquisition, including second language writing, third language writing, and the effect of L1 on foreign languages writing.

Yukiko Abe Hatasa received her PhD in linguistics in 1992 from the University of Illinois at Urbana Champaign, US. She has taught all levels of Japanese since the early 1980s, and has worked on curriculum development and teacher training in five major institutions in the US and Australia. She is currently a professor at Hiroshima University, Japan. She has published articles in journals such as *The Modern Language Journal* and *Acquisition of Japanese as a Second Language*. Her books include *Invitations to Second Language Acquisition, Gaikokugo to shiteno nhonngo kyoiku: Takakuteki shiya ni motozuku kokoromi* (*Teaching Japanese as a Foreign Language: Attempts Based on Multilateral Perspectives*) and the first and second editions of *Nakama: Japanese Communication, Context, Culture*.

Icy Lee is an associate professor in the Faculty of Education at the Chinese University of Hong Kong, where she teaches English language education courses in the undergraduate and graduate programs. Her publications have appeared in a number of international journals, including the *Journal of Second Language Writing*, *Canadian*

Modern Language Review, *System*, and *ELT Journal*. She is president of the Hong Kong Association for Applied Linguistics, and was winner of the 1999 TESOL/Mary Finocchiaro Award for Excellence in the Development of Pedagogical Materials, and the 2008 *Journal of Second Language Writing* Award.

Natalie Lefkowitz is a distinguished professor of Spanish, French, and applied linguistics at Central Washington University, where she has taught courses in language, FL and TESOL methodology and practicum, sociolinguistics, and second language acquisition. Her work has been published in a variety of journals, including the *Journal of Second Language Writing, The Modern Language Journal, Foreign Language Annals, The French Review, Applied Language Learning,* and *Language Teaching Research*. She has also authored, co-authored, and contributed to several textbooks on ESL composition, contemporary French culture, the French language game *Verlan*, and Spanish language teaching. She is currently engaged in research on heritage and foreign language learners of Spanish.

Rosa Manchón is an associate professor of applied linguistics at the University of Murcia, Spain. Her research interests and publications focus on cognitive aspects of SLA and L2 writing. She has edited *Writing in Foreign Language Contexts* (Multilingual Matters, 2009), as well as co-editing several guest-edited issues on SLA and L2 writing for *IRAL* (2008), *Journal of Second Language Writing* (2008), and *International Journal of English Studies* (2001, 2007). She has published articles in leading journals, including *Learning and Instruction, The Modern Language Journal, Language Learning, Journal of Second Language Writing,* and *IRAL*. Together with Ilona Leki, she edits the *Journal of Second Language Writing*.

Hui-Tzu Min received her PhD in education at the University of Illinois at Urbana-Champaign, US. She is currently a professor of foreign languages and literature at National Cheng Kung University, where she is in charge of curriculum reform for freshman English, and teaches courses in TESOL and linguistics. She has published her work in the *Journal of Second Language Writing, Language Learning, English for Specific Purposes, Bulletin of Educational Research, Bulletin of Educational Psychology,* and *English Teaching & Learning*. She has presented her work at conferences such as TESOL, AAAL, and the Symposium on Second Language Writing.

Marly Nas completed her MA studies of Spanish and first-degree teacher training at Nijmegen University, the Netherlands. She taught Spanish in several institutions for higher professional education for tourism and international business and management studies. In 1999, she joined the Spanish department of Nijmegen University, where she is currently teaching Spanish writing courses and applied linguistics. She is also writing a PhD dissertation on the effects of peer and teacher feedback on Spanish FL writing development, and enjoying life with her husband Raymond and their three children Jonard (2002), Marit (2007), and Sybren (2009).

Hadara Perpignan held a PhD in linguistics from Lancaster University, UK. She was senior lecturer in the Department of English as a Foreign Language at Bar-Ilan University, Israel, where she taught courses in writing for academic purposes for doctoral students. Her previous experience had been in developing academic reading and writing programs in EFL through teaching, and as a coordinator at several tertiary level institutions in Israel and Brazil. Her research interests included teacher-written feedback to student writing, affective and social outcomes of writing instruction, and, more recently, genre analysis of literary criticism.

Melinda Reichelt graduated from Purdue University, US, with an MA in English (1991) and a PhD in English (1996). Currently, she is a professor of English at the University of Toledo, US, where she directs the ESL writing program and teaches courses in TESOL, ESL writing, and linguistics. She has published her work in the *Journal of Second Language Writing*, *World Englishes*, *Composition Studies*, *Issues in Writing*, the *ELT Journal*, *The Modern Language Journal*, the *International Journal of English Studies*, *College ESL*, *Foreign Language Annals*, the *WAC Journal*, *English Today*, and *International Education*. She has presented her work at conferences such as TESOL, CCCC, AAAL, and the Symposium on Second Language Writing. With Tony Silva and Colleen Brice, she is co-author of *Annotated Bibliography of Scholarship in Second Language Writing: 1993–1997* (1999), published by Ablex.

Marcela Ruiz-Funes received her PhD and MA degrees in Second Language Education from Virginia Tech, US, and her dual BA degrees in English and Translation from the Facultad de Lenguas, Universidad Nacional de Córdoba, Argentina. She is currently Associate Professor of Hispanic Studies and Coordinator of the Second Language Education Program at East Carolina University, US. Her research examines second/foreign language writing, including the cognition of reading to write, task representation, task complexity, and syntactic complexity measures, as well as second language and literacy development of children in two-way immersion programs. Ruiz-Funes is the author of *On Teaching Foreign Languages: Linking Theory to Practice* (2002); she has published in *Foreign Language Annals* and *Hispania*, among other journals, and has received grants for her research in foreign language pedagogy and two-way immersion. She has presented her work at conferences such as ACTFL, TESOL, AAAL, and the Symposium on Second Language Writing.

Jean Marie Schultz received her PhD in comparative literature from UC Berkeley, US, where she served as coordinator for the Intermediate French program from 1986 to 2002, before becoming the director of the Lower Division French program at UC Santa Barbara, US. In addition to the intermediate French textbook *Réseau* (2009), she has published widely in the areas of foreign language writing, the teaching of language through literature, issues of articulation, and multiculturalism in language teaching. Her publications have appeared in *The Modern Language Journal, The French Review, The AAUSC*, and various edited volumes. In 2004 she received the University of California Consortium for Language Learning and Teaching Award for Outstanding Contribution to Language Teaching.

Oleg Tarnopolsky, doctor of pedagogy and full professor, is the head of the Department of Applied Linguistics and Methods of Foreign Language Teaching at Dnipropetrovsk University of Economics and Law, Ukraine. His research interests lie in the area of EFL teaching in general, and particularly, in teaching EFL writing, business English, and cross-cultural training. He has thrice conducted his research in the US (in 1995, Fulbright Award, the State University of New York at Buffalo; in 1999, the Regional Scholar Exchange Program, the University of Pennsylvania; and in 2005, Fulbright Award, Portland State University). He is the author of more than two hundred and twenty research publications in Ukraine, Russia, the US, UK, Canada, France, Spain, the Czech Republic, and China. He has also delivered 128 presentations and talks at 126 professional conferences, symposia, and seminars in Ukraine, Russia, the US, the UK, France, Spain, Switzerland, Austria, Germany, Uzbekistan, Poland, Greece, the Netherlands, and Monaco.

Helga Thorson received her PhD in German literature at the University of Minnesota, US, and subsequently taught for nine years at the University of Arkansas at Little Rock, US. Currently she is an associate professor in the Department of Germanic and Slavic Studies at the University of Victoria in Canada. Her research concentrates on foreign language writing processes and the use of extensive writing in the foreign language classroom. Her current research focuses on the use of dialogue journals in the foreign language classroom as well as on peer-assisted and experiential learning. She also specializes in late nineteenth- and early twentieth-century German and Austrian literary and cultural studies.

Kees van Esch conducted his MA studies of Spanish at Nijmegen University, the Netherlands, and at the Universidad Nacional Autónoma and El Colegio de México. After a short professional career as a teacher of Spanish in secondary education, he worked from 1975 until mid 2008 at Nijmegen University in the areas of didactics, applied linguistics, and language acquisition of Spanish. He published articles, supervised dissertations, and contributed to books on reading comprehension, the teaching and learning of vocabulary, learning strategies, personality characteristics, and learner autonomy. In addition, he co-authored several course books for Spanish as a Foreign Language and organized conferences, lectures, workshops, and in-service training courses in Holland, Belgium, Spain, Germany, and the US. From 1998–2004 he coordinated two European projects on learner autonomy and action research in FL teacher training.

Wenyu Wang graduated from Nanjing University, China, with a BA in English language and literature (1995) and a PhD in applied linguistics (2000). She is currently an associate professor of English at Nanjing University, where she teaches EFL writing courses at both undergraduate and graduate levels. She has published her work on EFL writing in the *Journal of Second Language Writing* and *TESOL*

Quarterly, as well as various refereed Chinese journals including *Foreign Language Teaching and Research*, *Foreign Language World*, and *Foreign Language Teaching*.

Index

Abu-Rabia, S., 83, 95
academic text, 144, 149, 152, 208
academic writing, 15, 28, 36, 39, 43, 99, 116, 139, 140, 146–148, 153–156, 165, 167, 181, 184, 188–191, 194–198, 200, 297, 301, 306–308, 310
ACTFL, 37–38, 249, 263
Adams, R., 49, 53, 57, 59
administrators, vii, 87, 93, 94, 127
admission, 116, 120, 140
Africa, 5, 12, 19, 75, 311
African, 20, 75
Ahllal, M., 95
Akyel, A., 23–24, 39
Alegría de la Colina, A., 49, 53, 55, 59
Algeria, 76
Allwright, D., 143, 145, 153
Amazigh, 84
American, 3, 32, 69, 71, 76, 96, 98, 102, 104–106, 110, 115, 117, 136, 180, 190, 202, 211, 244–245, 247, 248, 249, 262, 287, 291, 309, 314
analysis, 7, 9, 23, 29, 34–35, 37, 40, 43, 45, 49, 53, 62, 78–79, 116, 146, 153–155, 164, 167, 172, 178, 211, 227, 240, 241, 291, 293; error, 150, 305; genre, 149–150, 153–154, 156, 189–190, 197, 200, 310, 325; literature, 5, 11; needs, 163, 188–190, 198; rhetorical, 170
Anglophone, xi, 16, 76, 161–162, 164, 167–169, 225, 228
apprentice, 168
Arabic, ix, 69, 76, 84–86, 92, 96, 99, 101, 140
Arabization, 85
Arens, K. M., 26, 42, 260, 280
argument, 14–15, 47, 89, 147, 168, 186, 202–203, 205, 208, 210–212, 215, 222, 240, 291, 294, 298–302, 313, 315, 318
argumentation, 14, 202–203, 205, 208, 210–212, 222, 291, 302; argumentative essay, 51, 78, 201–202, 292; argumentative texts, 111, 202- 204, 206–210, 213
Armengol-Castells, L., 6, 18
Arndt, V., 91, 95, 189, 196, 200
Asato, N., 98, 114
Asia, 5, 7, 122, 135, 311
Asian, 43, 98, 102, 135, 161, 180, 237, 294
ASL, 226
assessment, 11, 18, 39, 45, 70, 123–126, 128–130, 134–136, 154, 163, 214, 242, 246
assignments, 11, 13, 19, 32, 71, 74, 170, 193, 195, 209, 239–240, 259, 261, 276, 296
Atkinson, D., 160, 179
attitudes, ix, xi, 6, 9, 14, 18, 19, 69, 76, 136, 145, 196, 226, 228, 232–235, 245, 247, 320; linguistic, 226
audience, 24, 125–126, 130, 164,

329

172–173, 177, 204, 209, 260, 295–296, 299
audiolingual, 96, 98
aural, 232, 308
Australia, 3, 102
Australian, 135
authenticity, 68, 103–104, 110, 112–113, 146, 149–151, 154, 157, 237, 295–296

Badger, R., 13, 21, 130, 134
Bailey, N. H., 29, 40
Baker, L., 27, 39
Bakhtin, M., 168, 179
Barlow, L., 6, 18
Barnett, M. A., 25, 36–37, 39, 70, 81
Beile, W., 9, 18
Belcher, D., 39, 96, 131, 135, 153, 154, 307–308
beliefs, xi, 10, 27, 69, 136, 163, 166, 226–229, 232, 241, 244–245, 258, 282, 284, 318
Bellout, Z., 89, 95
Benati, A., 49, 59
benchmark, 123, 126–127
Benesch, S., 178–179
Benson, P., 94–95
Berber, ix, 84, 96
Bereiter, C., 298, 307
Berg, C. E., 154, 299, 307
Berkenkotter, C., 144, 153
Berks, D., 303, 307
Berman, R., 91, 95
Berns, M., 8, 18
Bianciotti, H., 73
biculturalism, 78
Bigelow, M., 49, 57, 61
bilingual, 21, 73, 75, 77, 79–80, 96, 116, 225, 233, 235, 247–248
bilingualism, 67, 73, 76, 78, 226
biliteracy, 81, 120, 122, 245, 254
Bitchener, J., 57, 59
Black, P., 130, 134

Blackboard, 207, 210
Blass, L., 169, 171, 179
Bliesener, U., 8–9, 18
Bloch, J. G., 303–304, 307
blogs, 122, 131, 259, 319
Bolton, K., 121, 134
Boukous, A., 85, 95
Bouziane, A., 90, 95
Braine, G., 181, 307–308
brainstorming, 23, 194–195, 262, 265, 270, 297
Bräuer, G., 11, 18, 280
Breen, M., 143, 153
Brock, M., 125, 134, 137
Brooks-Carson, A., 91, 96
Brown, A., 27, 39
Brown, H. D., 160, 179
Brown, J. D., 227, 245
Bryant, K., 5, 21
Buch, F., 261, 279
Bucholtz, M., 225, 245
Buckner, L., 85–86, 90, 95
Buker, S., 149, 156–157
Byrd, P., 129, 131, 134
Byrne, D., 191–192, 199
Byrnes, H., 11, 18–19, 26, 42, 70, 75, 81, 143, 153, 234, 244–245

Cameron, D., 168, 179
Cameron, R., 233, 245, 248
Campbell, C. C., 28, 39, 300, 307
Campbell, R. N., 226, 245
Canada, 3, 5, 95, 180, 196, 200, 255, 256
Canadian, 7, 61, 76, 97, 134, 136
Canagarajah, A. S., 6, 18, 181
Canale, M., 203, 213
Cantonese, 101, 120–121, 134
Carreira, M., 233, 236, 238, 245
Carrell, P. L., 25, 29, 39
Carson, J. G., 22, 28–29, 39–40, 44, 62, 143, 155–156, 165, 180–181, 290, 299, 307, 309, 315, 320

Casanave, C. P., 160–161, 166–167, 179, 295, 302–304, 307
Catalán, 6
Caucasian, 110
Cavalcanti, M. C., 204, 214
Cenoz, J., 92, 95
Cestero, A. M., 208, 213
Chafe, W., 257, 279
Chaibi, A., 87, 95–96
Chandler, J., 72, 81, 239, 245, 304, 308, 310
Chávez, R., 225, 249
Cheddoudi, A., 88, 94, 96
Chédid, A., 76
Chen, J., 127, 135
Cheng, Y.-S., 6, 18
Chevalier, J. F., 225, 246
Chi, L., 304, 307
Chikuma, Y., 97, 115
China, 4, 7, 12–13, 18, 21, 97, 102, 119, 120–121, 180, 285–286, 296, 306, 309, 314
Chinese, x, 3, 6, 12–13, 21, 43, 64, 97, 99, 101, 106, 109–110, 114, 117, 119, 120–122, 134, 177, 180, 181, 226, 228, 234, 242, 286–287, 294, 296, 299, 301–303, 305–307, 309
Christensen, L., 229, 247
Chun, D. M., 264, 279
Clachar, A., 14, 18, 313, 320
classroom activities, 288
classroom instruction, 146, 148–149, 287
cognate, 19, 96, 99, 115
cognition, ix, 22, 26, 29–30, 38, 42, 92, 312
cognitive, viii, 6, 19, 23, 36, 40, 42, 48, 50, 64, 74, 115, 125, 166, 178–180, 281, 296, 298, 315, 320
Cohen, A. D., 91, 96, 204, 214
coherence, 40, 47, 148, 160, 163, 194, 203, 208, 210, 301–302

cohesion, 106, 148, 157, 172, 194, 203, 210
cohesive, 106, 111, 144, 278, 303
Colby-Kelly, C., 131, 134
collaboration, 10, 49, 50, 53–56, 58–61, 63–64, 131, 137, 150, 152, 206
colloquial, 235, 238
Colombi, M. C., 225, 246, 248–249
colonial history, 3, 4, 7, 17, 67, 75, 77, 84–85, 248, 313
communicative, 10, 19, 42, 48, 61, 63, 70, 86, 90, 98–99, 151, 160, 168, 185–187, 190, 192–193, 195, 199, 203, 213, 280, 295, 296
communicative activities, 187, 192
communicative competence, 42, 203
communicative goals, 185–186, 190
communicative tasks, 10
communicative writing skills, 192
Communism, 14, 183
composing processes, 23–25, 29, 43, 82, 97, 114, 296
comprehensibility, 148, 260, 305
comprehensible input, 259
comprehension, 25–26, 28, 41, 139, 142, 170, 305
computers, 11, 12, 110, 189, 199, 280
Confucianism, 302
Connor, U., 23, 29, 32, 39, 166, 179–181, 186, 199, 203–204, 214, 294, 308–309
Conroy, P. V., 6, 12, 18
construction, viii, 19, 25, 75, 79–80, 82, 116, 144, 148, 154–155, 163, 226, 281, 291, 294, 298–302
context, vii-viii, x, 3–6, 8, 11, 13–14, 16–18, 25, 29, 31–32,

38, 46, 48, 61–62, 67, 69, 71, 73–75, 79, 83, 86–90, 94–95, 97, 109–110, 112–113, 119, 123, 126, 130, 132–133, 135, 138–139, 148, 151–152, 155, 162, 179–180, 183–184, 190, 192–193, 199, 201, 203, 205, 207–209, 226, 231, 234, 236, 239, 259, 263–264, 306, 312–314, 316, 319; educational, 84, 165, 316; historical, 37, 74; institutional, 139, 277; international, 86–87
contexts: local, ix, 17, 159, 316
contextualization, 162, 170
contrastive rhetoric, 181, 185–186, 199, 294, 302, 308–309, 314
convention, 177–178, 180, 302
Coombe, C., 6, 18
Cossé, L., 73, 81
Coulmas, F., 109, 114
coursebooks, 125
Coxhead, A., 129, 131, 134
creative writing, xii, 9, 11, 27, 73, 128–129, 143–144, 189, 195–196, 240, 287, 318
Creswell, J. W., 227, 229, 246
critical: critical discourse, 160; critical examination, 159, 178; critical pedagogy, 177, 248; critical reading, 21, 88, 311, 325; critical reflection, 159
critique, 21, 77, 146, 159, 161
critiques, 168
cultural consciousness, 162
cultural forms, 160
cultural identity, 33–34, 68
cultural literacy, 260, 262, 314
cultural materials, 111
cultural sensitivity, ix, 72
cultural topics, 237, 262
culture, 7, 11, 14, 17, 70, 76, 95, 98, 102–110, 112, 115–116, 135, 154, 165, 168, 170, 174, 176, 181, 185–186, 201, 234, 237, 247, 262, 287, 310, 317; assessment, 125, 127, 130; dominant, 79, 158; teaching, 65
Cumming, A., 23, 41, 49, 51–53, 56, 59–60, 91, 96, 168, 179, 262–263, 279–280, 291, 308
Cummins, J., 135, 244, 246
curricular design, 278
curriculum, vii, x, 7, 9, 12, 18–19, 22–23, 38, 70–72, 74–75, 87–88, 93–95, 102–103, 120, 125, 134–135, 153, 156, 163–165, 167, 169, 179, 181, 215, 236, 255–256, 278–280, 286, 306, 312–313, 317; national, 312
Curriculum Guidelines, 163, 165
Currie, P., 304, 308
Curtis, A., 125, 135
Cyrillic, 185

Davison, C., 125–126, 135
de Haan, P., 6, 18, 45, 61, 70, 72, 82, 136, 141, 155, 203, 215
Deckert, G. D., 303, 308
deconstructing, 172
decontextualized, 123, 157
DeKeyser, R., 46, 60
Delbecque, N., 208, 214
demographics, 229
Deng, X., 159, 161, 180
Denmark, 156
Dewaele, J., 96
diacritic, 107
dialect, 84, 92, 109, 120, 235, 238, 247
dialog journal, 11, 259, 264
dialogic, 53, 143
dialogue, 147, 154–155, 261, 276, 300; collaborative, 53, 61–64
diaries, 99, 295
Dib, M., 76
dictionary, 32, 110, 112, 147, 233, 237

Dimock, W. C., 68, 81
discourse, 30–32, 40–42, 89–90, 111, 125, 130, 143–144, 155, 203–204, 210, 263–265, 287–288, 301, 307; community, 42, 143, 166–169, 285; feature, 294, 301, 314
dissertation, 4, 21, 39, 42, 115, 155
diversity, vii, 95, 140, 147, 151, 233, 248, 311, 314, 318
Djebar, A., 76
Donato, R., 50, 53, 60
doodles, 294
Dooley, J., 197, 199
Dörnyei, Z., 104, 114, 142, 153
Doughty, C., 46, 48, 60, 62, 63
drafting, 146, 195, 240
drafts, 13, 125, 147–150, 152, 167, 195, 204, 207–208, 240, 297, 299–300, 307
Dudley-Evans, T., 144, 153–154
Duff, P., 226, 246
Dunmire, L., 89, 96
Dutch, 3, 6, 100, 202, 205, 208, 210, 212, 218, 223
Duval-Couetil, N., 97
Dvorak, T., 23, 40

Echevarriarza, M. P. E., 263, 281
eclecticism, x, 89, 143, 159, 160–162, 166–167, 178–181, 316, 318
Ecuador, 5, 21
Edelsky, C., 91, 96
editing, xii, 23, 29, 49, 55, 63, 115, 146, 239
Edstrom, A., 230, 233, 246
Edwards, J., 65, 71, 81
Eisterhold, J. C., 25, 39
elaborating when writing, 26, 29
Elqobai, R., ix, 4, 16–17, 83–84, 91–92, 96, 313, 316–318
email, 6, 12, 16, 99, 111–112, 258, 264, 278–279

empathy, 231
England, 21, 154
English, vii-x, 3–10, 12–13, 15–22, 28, 39–41, 59–62, 65–66, 68–69, 71–74, 76, 80–87, 89–97, 99–102, 104–106, 113, 115–124, 127, 129, 131–136, 138–146, 151–156, 159–160, 162–167, 169, 171, 178, 180–190, 193–194, 196–200, 202, 225, 228, 233, 237, 240, 242, 244, 255, 264, 279, 280–281, 285–288, 292, 294, 296–297, 301–316, 320
English as a foreign language (EFL), viii-x, 4–10, 12–15, 18, 20–21, 39, 41–43, 46, 51–52, 59–60, 62, 64, 82–83, 87–90, 93–97, 118–119, 123, 128, 130–133, 135–141, 143, 147, 151, 154, 159–163, 165, 167–168, 170, 178–180, 183–186, 190–194, 196–200, 227, 285, 301, 306–307, 309, 311–313, 318–320
English as a second language (ESL), vii-xi, 4, 12, 17–19, 21–22, 28–29, 32, 39, 41–43, 53, 60, 63–64, 66, 70, 80, 82, 96, 97, 99, 104, 114, 118–119, 133, 135–137, 141–142, 153, 156, 161, 166, 170, 179–180, 182, 186, 199, 215, 227, 239, 263, 280, 294, 299, 307–311, 315, 319, 320
English for Academic Purposes, 7, 144, 155, 156
error correction, 49, 127, 130, 147, 231, 249, 304, 305, 318
error treatment, 229, 239
essay, 6, 9, 13, 24, 37, 77–78, 111, 123, 126, 160, 162, 165, 169, 172, 175, 177, 180, 186, 189, 195, 197, 207, 240, 273,

275–276, 282–283, 291, 302
ethnicity, 234
ethnography, 14, 132, 229
Europe, 5, 10, 18, 94, 311
European, 10, 12, 67, 77, 102, 111, 156, 164, 294
European Union, 10, 12, 77
evaluation, 21, 23, 25, 41, 48, 51, 79, 126, 130, 152, 153, 159, 163, 166, 169, 177, 203, 205, 210, 213, 248, 318
Evans, S., 126, 135
Evans, V., 197, 199
Evensen, L. S., 303, 308
exam, 10, 90, 120, 123, 125–127, 134, 139, 209, 233; exit exam, 140
examination, 7, 18, 103, 105, 116, 144, 150, 177, 316, 320
Expanding Circle, 3
expatriate, 287
expository writing, 40, 111, 201, 240, 287, 294
extensive writing, 99, 259, 261, 267, 277

Facebook, 122, 131
Falvey, P., 118, 135
Fan, F. H. K., 124, 135
Farsi, 76, 100
Fathman, A., 72, 81, 204, 214, 239, 246
Feak, C. B., 144, 149, 156, 303, 310
Fearnow, S., 49, 61
feedback, 13, 19, 21, 48–49, 54–55, 63–64, 71, 92, 105, 129, 131, 135, 143, 146, 148, 151–152, 203, 205, 207, 214, 224, 238–239, 242, 245, 304, 307, 312, 315; accuracy vs. revision, 57–59; oral, 57, 169, 210, 259, 308; peer, 6, 10, 12, 20, 114–115, 169, 193, 195, 202, 204, 206–217, 210–213, 221–222, 243, 298–299, 309–310; written, 62, 124, 127, 136, 147, 150, 154–155, 170, 247, 300, 309
Feez, S., 172, 180
Ferris, D. R., 12, 18, 147, 153, 239, 246, 294, 298, 300, 304–305, 308, 310
film, 181, 261, 278
Fine, J., 144, 154–155
first language (L1), viii-ix, 6, 8, 12, 19–26, 30–32, 36, 38, 43, 64, 70, 72–73, 82, 84, 91, 95–97, 105, 114–116, 140–141, 144–145, 147, 154, 166, 168, 177, 180, 186–187, 202, 210, 213, 258–259, 262–263, 266, 270, 273, 277, 288, 292, 294, 296, 303, 305, 313–317, 319
Fishman, J. A., 225, 249
FL proficiency, 10, 202, 259, 265
Flahive, D. E., 29, 40
Flower, L. S., 22, 26, 30–31, 34, 40, 42, 166, 180, 315, 320
fluency, 45, 79, 129, 133, 145, 245, 260, 278
Focus on Form (FonF), 46
foreign language (FL), vii, 44, 104, 201, 225, 263
Fortune, A., 49, 53–55, 60
Fox, S., 131, 136, 294, 302, 307–308
France, 12, 77, 96
Francophone, 76, 82, 263
Frantzen, D., 72, 81
Freeman, I., 41
French, ix, 5–7, 12, 17–20, 40, 53, 61, 64, 75–80, 82, 84–86, 89, 91–92, 96, 100, 104, 119, 201–202, 226, 228, 233, 242, 247, 312, 321
Friedlander, A., 91, 96
Frodeson, J., 146, 153

Frye, R., 145, 154
Fujiwara, M., 49, 61
Fulkerson, R., 145, 154

Gajdusek, L., 29, 40
Gao, J., 159, 161, 180
García Mayo, M. P., 49, 53, 55, 59–60, 63
Gass, S. M., 63, 280
generic structure, 129
genre, 11, 13, 72, 74, 76, 78–79, 126, 128–130, 134, 149, 150, 154–155, 159, 161–162, 167, 172, 180, 187, 189–190, 195–196, 203, 240, 286, 287, 292, 306, 313, 315
genre approach, 129–130, 134, 159, 161, 167, 180, 189, 196, 313
German, xi, 5, 9, 11, 18, 20–21, 76, 80, 85, 100–101, 104, 119, 202, 226, 228, 233–234, 242, 255–257, 259, 261–262, 265, 267–270, 272–273, 275–276, 279, 281–283, 312
Germany, 4, 8–9, 18, 20, 156, 201, 262, 279–280, 313, 317
Gieve, S., 145, 154
Glass, W., 233, 248
global studies, 12, 65, 66, 80
globalization, viii-ix, 10, 21, 65–68, 70–75, 78–79, 81, 85–86, 90, 95, 159, 168, 179, 248, 314–315, 317
Goethals, P., 208, 214
Goldstein, L. M., 239, 246
Goodman, K. S., 25, 40
government, 10, 104, 120, 122, 124, 126–127, 175, 296
Grabe, W., 124, 135, 286, 308
grammar, 6, 10–11, 14, 20, 36–37, 40, 45, 55, 60–61, 63, 70, 72–73, 81, 90, 98, 103, 124–126, 128–131, 134, 136, 149, 163, 165–166, 173, 175–176, 185, 191–192, 203, 205, 208–210, 228, 231–234, 236–243, 245–246, 255–256, 259, 287, 308, 310, 313
grammar instruction, 6, 36, 130, 163, 232, 243
grammar translation, 70, 98, 103
grammatical competence, 203
grapheme, 109, 233
Greenblatt, S., 68, 79, 81
Gui, L., 7, 18
Gunn, G., 65, 81
Gutiérrez, J. R., 229, 238, 246

Hadley, A. O., 11, 12, 18
Hammadou, J., 25, 40
Hamp-Lyons, L., 125, 126–127, 135
Hanaoka, O., 49, 54, 60, 146, 154
handbook, 20, 62, 135
handwriting, 111
Haneda, M., 5, 18
Hanks, J., 145, 153
Hansen, J., 295, 309
Hargan, N., 15, 19, 313, 320
Harklau, L., 45, 60, 70, 81, 90, 96, 181, 265, 279
Haro, P., 263, 281
Harris, S., 291
Hatasa, Y. A., x, 6, 16–17, 19, 98, 102–103, 110, 114–115, 314–317, 319
Haus, G. J., 26, 41
Hayes, J. R., 52, 60, 180
Hebrew, 100, 139, 140–141, 151
Hedgcock, J. S., 5, 12, 18–19, 225–227, 229, 247, 294, 298, 300, 304–305, 308
Henning, S. D., 36–38, 40
heritage language (HL), xi, 12, 98, 225–238, 240, 244–249, 315, 318
Heron, A., 125, 135
heuristic, 227

Hidalgo, M., 225, 233, 247
Higgs, T., 99, 101, 115
Hinds, J., 166, 177, 180, 294, 302–303, 308–309
hiragana, 106–107, 109, 111
Hirose, K., 23–25, 40
Hirose, W., 114–115
Hirvela, A., 96, 124, 126, 131, 135–136, 290, 307, 309
Hispanic, 32, 68, 247–248
history, 9, 21, 76, 81, 84, 117, 153, 181, 190, 201, 278
Holmes, J., 233, 247
Holtwisch, H., 9, 19
homogeneity, 46, 165, 319
Homstad, T., 259, 280
Hong Kong, x, 4–5, 16–17, 19, 118–126, 128–137, 154, 308, 313
honorifics, 237
Hopkins, A., 144, 154
Hopper, P. J., 29, 40
Horowitz, R., 279
Huckin, T. N., 144, 153
Hunt, K. W., 35, 40
Huston, N., 73, 76, 79
Hyland, F., 123, 125, 136, 147, 154, 299, 309
Hyland, K., 79, 81, 129–130, 136, 144, 147, 154, 286, 288, 292, 294–295, 298–299, 305, 309

ideology, 177
Ikeda, R., 114–115
immigration, 67, 75, 207, 209
India, 4, 20
individual differences, 6, 54, 264
Indonesia, 102
Indonesian, 101
Inner Circle, 3
input, ix, x, 19, 47–49, 57–60, 63, 104, 142–143, 149–150, 162, 207, 209, 213, 226, 243, 258–259, 261, 280, 290, 292, 299, 314

institution, 82, 104, 105, 141, 144–145, 228, 286, 306
integrated literacy skills, 11
interference, 46, 92
interlanguage, 59, 96, 148, 280
Internet, 7, 69, 122, 136–137, 193, 262, 304
interview, 68, 227, 229, 233, 236, 242, 250, 261
interweave, 131
Iran, 5
Iranian, 77
Ishihara, C., 105, 115
Ishihara, T., 105, 115
Israel, x, 16, 138–140, 142, 153, 156, 312
Israeli, x, 139, 140
Itagaki, N., 53, 63
Italian, 6, 15, 19, 82, 85, 100, 320
Italy, 15, 313
Ivanič, R., 139, 152, 154
Izumi, S., 47–49, 57, 60–61

Japan, 4, 6, 17, 98–99, 101–102, 104–105, 115–116, 172, 180
Japanese, x, 5–6, 16–17, 40, 43, 73, 98–111, 113–117, 168, 171–172, 180, 226, 228, 233–234, 240, 294, 307, 309, 312, 314, 316–317
Japanese as a foreign language (JFL), 98–99, 102, 104, 106, 110, 113–114, 315, 317, 319
Japanese Language Proficiency Test (JLPT), 101–102, 112, 115
Jay, P., xii, 66, 81
Johns, A. M., 141, 144, 154, 168, 180
Johnson, B., 153, 199, 229, 247
Jorden, E. H., 99, 115
journal, 7–8, 18, 19–21, 39–43, 59–64, 70, 81–82, 95–97, 114–118, 132, 134–137, 141, 154–156, 161, 173, 179–182,

196, 199–200, 245–249, 264, 273–276, 278–282, 284, 295, 307–310, 320–321
Journal of Second Language Writing, 7–8, 19–21, 40, 42–43, 59–64, 70, 81–82, 96–97, 116, 118, 132, 134–137, 141, 154–155, 161, 179, 180–182, 199–200, 245–249, 279, 307–310

Kachru, B. B., 3, 4, 19
Kageyama, Y., 114–115
kanji, 101, 105–106, 108–109, 111–114, 116–117
Kantor, K. L., 28, 41
Kantz, M., 26, 30–31, 33, 40, 42, 320
Kaplan, R. B., 79, 124, 135, 180, 185–186, 194, 199, 286, 294, 308–309
Kästner, E., 261, 280
Katznelson, H., 145, 154–155
Kaufer, D., 89, 96
Kennedy, M. L., 26, 40
Kent, T., 160, 180, 199
Kenya, 4
Kern, R., 11, 19, 22, 40, 66, 70, 74, 77, 81, 264, 280, 315, 320
Kessler, C., 195, 199
Kim, J., 159, 161, 180
Kim, Y., 159, 161, 180
Kirby, D. R., 28, 41
Kobayashi, H., 6, 19, 23–24, 41, 73, 82, 91, 96, 105, 115–116
Koda, K., 113, 116
Kondo, K., 104, 116
Korea, 82, 102, 137
Korean, 99, 101, 110, 115, 117, 180, 294, 309
Kozhushko, S., 188, 190, 192, 195–197, 200
Kramer, M. G., 32, 39
Kramsch, C., 180, 230, 247

Krashen, S., 23–25, 38, 41, 258–259, 280
Kress, G., 145, 152, 154
Kroll, B., 21, 23, 39, 41, 81, 96–97, 136, 154–155, 170, 179–180, 182, 214, 246, 308–309
Krug, C., 12, 19
Kubota, R., 105, 116, 168, 174, 180, 186, 199, 294, 309
Kucer, S. B., 166, 181
Kuiken, F., 6, 19, 49, 53–55, 61, 72, 82
Kumaravadivelu, B., 160–162, 167, 178, 181

L1 writing instruction, 12
L2 proficiency, 23–25, 49, 51, 54, 166, 263, 303
Laca, B., 209–211, 214
Lalande, J. F., 35, 41
Lamprecht, G., 261, 280
Lantolf, J., 60, 64, 206, 214
Lapkin, S., 49, 52–54, 61–62, 64, 258, 281
Larsen-Freeman, D., 129, 136, 160, 167, 181
Latin, 185, 211, 226
Latino, 245
Law, E., 15, 126, 136, 184, 197
Lazda, R., 261–262, 280
Lee, G., 147, 154
Lee, I., x, 4, 16–17, 19, 118, 124–126, 131, 136, 147, 154
Lee, J. F., 12, 19, 26, 41, 45, 61
Lee, S.-Y., 23–25, 38, 41
Leeser, M. J., 49, 53–54, 61
Lefkowitz, N., xi, 5, 11–12, 19, 225, 227, 247, 298, 308, 315, 318
Lehner, A., 186, 199, 294, 309
Leibowitz, B., 5, 19–20
Leishman, S., 105, 116
Leki, I., 8, 20, 23, 29, 39, 40–41, 70, 72, 82, 89, 96, 132–133,

136, 156, 159, 161, 167, 180–181, 262, 280, 286, 290, 294, 297, 301–303, 307, 309, 319–321
Lenhart, A., 131, 136
letter to the editor, 205
Levine, M. G., 26, 41
Lewin, B. A., 144, 153–155
lexico-grammatical features, 129
lexicon, 6, 25–26, 39, 51, 92, 111, 114, 147–148, 152, 157, 202–203, 233, 291, 298, 300, 305; spoken, 106, 317; written, 106
Li, X., 13, 20, 168, 178, 181
Lightbown, P. M., 143, 156
Lin, A., 118, 136
Lindgren, E., 49, 61
lingua franca, ix, 69, 122
linguistic imperialism, 4, 18
linguistic processing, 49–50, 52–53, 55–56, 58–59, 317
linguistics, 7, 58, 63, 139, 156, 165, 190, 227–228, 265, 278, 287–288, 321
Lipski, J. M., 233, 248–249
listening, vii, 70, 110, 126, 163, 191–192, 202, 259, 266, 268, 286, 317
literacy, viii, 6, 8, 11, 14, 19, 28–29, 46, 66, 72, 74–75, 77, 81–82, 117, 131, 136, 159, 168, 177–178, 180–181, 200, 226, 227, 229, 233, 236, 243–244, 246, 263, 279, 294, 303, 307, 309, 310, 314, 315, 317, 320
Liu, J., 295, 309
Liu, Y., 159, 181
Lo, J., 123, 125, 136
Lo, W. A. Y., 166, 181, 212, 220
local exigencies, 160, 162, 167, 178, 312
local practices, 15, 159, 161–162, 313
Lockhart, C., 204, 213–214

Lorish, F. C., 117
Luke, K. K., 120, 136
Lynch, A., 226, 248
MacDonald, S. P., 144, 155
macrostrategies, x, 160, 162, 178
Makine, A., 73, 79
Manchón, R. M., ix, 17, 21, 44–45, 47, 49–50, 52, 61–62, 70, 72, 82, 118, 136, 141, 155, 181, 247, 315, 317, 319–320
Mandarin, 69, 101, 120, 175
Marín, J., 23, 41, 50, 62
Mar-Molinero, C., 225, 248
Martínez, G., 233, 248
Matalene, C., 303, 307, 309
Matsuda, P. K., xii, 62, 89, 96, 143–144, 155, 160–161, 168, 179, 181–182, 186, 199, 215, 281, 287, 309
Mbaye, A., 203–204, 214
McCarthey, S. J., 300, 309
McCormick, K., 40, 42, 320
McKay, S. L., 227, 248
Melendez, J. E., 26, 41
Mellow, J. D., 160, 181
Melouk, M., 83, 85, 97
Messaoudi, L, 86, 97
metalanguage, ix, 47–49, 53, 56–58, 60, 63, 233, 239
Middle East, 5, 311
Miller, I. K., 145, 154, 249
Mills, C., 35, 41
Milton, J., 131, 136–137
Min, H. T., x, 3, 6, 16, 17, 20, 159, 179, 299, 309, 314–316
Mo, R. P., 7, 19–21, 40–42, 61, 64, 81–82, 96–97, 114, 134, 136–137, 155, 181, 245, 249, 280–281, 310, 320–321
Mohan, B. A., 166, 181
Mok, J., 127, 135
monitoring, 26, 29, 39, 54, 148
Morimoto, T., 98, 116

Morishima, H., 105, 116
Morocco, ix, 16–17, 83–89, 93–95, 97, 313, 316, 318
mother tongue, 81, 84, 120, 124, 186, 285, 297
motivation, x, 10–11, 13, 31, 71, 86, 88, 94, 102, 104, 110, 114, 125, 126, 128, 131, 133, 136, 141, 151, 153, 196, 200, 204, 212, 233, 276–277, 318
Motta-Roth, D., 144, 155
multicultural, viii, 12, 18, 74, 76, 79, 122, 132, 225
multidimensional, 89, 166
multilingual, viii, 4, 12, 16, 18, 20, 76, 79, 84, 88–89, 94, 316
multilingualism, 67, 314
multimedia, 237
multiple drafts, 12, 143, 202
Murphy, L., 23, 41, 49–50, 52, 61–62, 153
Myers, G., 144, 155

Nas, M., xi, 3, 16, 201, 203, 211–215, 318
Nash, J. G., 52, 60
Nassaji, H., 49, 62
native speaker, 3, 28, 99, 104–105, 110, 162, 170, 178, 228–229, 231, 236, 247, 249, 260–262, 291, 297
Nazi party, 10
Nelson, G. L., 165, 181, 299, 309
Netherlands, xi, 3, 16, 201, 208
New Zealand, 3
Newell, A., 27, 41
Ng, M., 169, 182
Ng, P., 204, 213–214
Nishigaki, C., 105, 116
Noda, M., 117
nonnative, 3–4, 17, 20, 101, 156, 160–162, 178, 227, 230–231, 246–247, 305
Norris, J. M., 46, 56, 62

North America, 5, 102, 164, 311, 314–315
Noticing Hypothesis, 47
Nunan, D., 94–95, 182, 227, 248

Olson, T., 231, 234–235, 248
Omaggio, A., 90, 97
Onieva Morales, J. L., 208, 210, 214, 218
onomatopoeic, 107
oral language, xi, 257, 261, 263
oral skill, 11
Ortega, L., 44–46, 56, 62, 70, 80, 82, 118, 132–133, 137, 143, 155, 319–320
orthography, 16, 106–107, 110–111, 113, 114, 314
Outer Circle, 3, 4
output, ix, 19, 44–49, 51–52, 56, 58–61, 63–64, 82, 258–259, 261, 278, 280–281
Output Hypothesis, 47, 51
overcrowded classrooms, 316

Paesani, K., 6, 20
patchwriting, 310
Patton, M. Q., 227, 248
Pavlenko, A., 72, 74, 82
Payne, J. S., 264–265, 280
Pearson, P. D., 39, 199
Pecorari, D., 303–304, 310
peer feedback, 10, 12, 114–115, 204, 206–207, 210–213, 221–222, 298, 310
Pennington, M., 125, 137
Pennycook, A., 303–304, 310
perception, 11, 35, 118–119, 121, 123, 165, 186, 234, 236, 274, 277
Perera, H., 32, 41
Pérez, W., 225, 249
Pérez-Lerou, A., 233, 248
Perpignan, H., x, xii, 16, 138, 144–145, 147, 154–155, 312, 315–316

Petrón, M., 233, 249
Peyton, J. K., 11, 20, 248–249
PhD, x, 16, 18, 21, 138–144, 146, 151, 214, 286
PhD candidate, 138
PhD student, x, 16, 139–141
Phillips, J. K., 25, 41
Phillipson, R., 4, 20
Piepho, H., 9, 20
Pike-Baky, M., 169, 171, 179
plagiarism, 15, 93, 303–304, 307–308, 310, 316, 319; intentional, 304; unintentional, 303
planning, 12, 23–26, 29, 39, 60, 86–87, 99, 142, 146, 166, 260, 278, 295
Poland, 5, 10, 20, 97
policy, 12, 32, 69, 76, 78–79, 87, 120–121, 124, 134
policy brief, 76, 78–79
Polio, C., 49, 56, 62, 204, 215
Polish, 10, 100
politeness, 237
Pooser, C., 12, 20
portfolio, 6, 18, 20, 126, 152, 240
post-colonial, 4, 6, 119–122, 124
postgraduate, 43, 122
post-method, 160, 178
post-method pedagogy: particularity, 160, 162, 178; possibility, 37, 74, 77, 160, 162, 177–178, 212, 312, 316; practicality, 69, 160, 162, 178
post-process, x-xi, 160, 161, 179, 181, 182, 315
Potowski, K., 233, 236, 238, 245, 248
Prabhu, N. S., 167, 182, 195, 199
practical writing, 184, 198
pragmatism, 123, 162, 165, 167–169, 178–179
praxis, 62, 155
prewriting, 192, 297–298
prior knowledge, 25, 27, 40, 288

process writing, 10, 84, 89–90, 126, 135, 137, 161
Procter, M., 147, 155
proficiency, 11, 15, 17, 23–25, 32, 38, 40–41, 47, 51–52, 54, 59, 61, 64, 70, 90, 92, 94, 96–97, 99, 100–101, 104, 113–115, 122, 126, 135, 140–141, 146, 151–153, 155, 166, 168, 176, 178, 202–203, 205, 226, 234–236, 244, 301–302, 304, 317; native, 143, 155; oral, vi, 11, 255–257, 259, 261–271, 273, 275–284, 317
psycholinguistic, 56, 58, 61
psycholinguistic processes, 56, 58
public examination, 123
punctuation, 184, 187, 192, 202–203, 208, 233
Putonghua, 120, 134

Qi, D. S., 49, 53–54, 62, 91, 97
Qin, J., 49, 62

Raimes, A., 23–24, 41, 91, 97, 133, 137, 143, 155
Ramanathan, V., 6, 20
reading, ix, 6–7, 9, 11–12, 21–22, 25–26, 28–33, 36–42, 70, 76, 90, 95–96, 104, 109–112, 116–117, 124, 126, 130, 134–135, 137, 152–153, 163, 167, 169–173, 180, 182, 191–192, 202, 205, 207–209, 211–212, 222, 231–233, 237, 241–242, 266, 268, 285–287, 290–292, 295, 297, 299–300, 302, 304, 307–309, 313, 317, 320; comprehension, 11, 25, 28, 38, 39, 41, 95, 105, 117, 139, 142, 170, 209, 211, 259; habits, 233, 244, 254; strategy, 109
reading skill, 76, 104, 192, 232
reading-writing connections, 6–7,

9, 11–12, 26–27, 29, 36–40, 96, 110, 124, 135, 142, 167, 169–170, 237, 244, 285–286, 307, 309; reading to write tasks, 22, 26, 38
Reagan, T., 231, 234–235, 248
Reder, L. M. T., 25, 41
Reed, L., 11, 20
register, 130, 152, 185, 203, 233, 237, 260
Reichelt, M., viii, 3–4, 6, 10, 12, 20–21, 85, 97, 133, 137, 234, 239, 248, 286, 310, 313, 317
Reid, J. M., 160–161, 163, 182, 186, 193, 199, 286, 310
Reinhardt, J., 264, 281
relexification, 92
research methods, 7, 248
revision, 7, 12, 20, 23–25, 41, 51, 62, 147–148, 154, 203–204, 211, 222, 298–299, 307–309
rhetoric, viii, 14, 30, 32–33, 41, 73, 104–106, 116–117, 145, 166–170, 174, 177–179, 181, 199, 210, 237, 240, 243, 290, 292, 294–295, 301–302, 308–309, 313–314
rhetorical moves, 167
rhetorical organization, 111
rhetorical patterns, 290, 301, 314
rhetorical problems, 295, 302
Richards, J. C., 103, 117, 120, 136
Richards, K., 227, 248
Ringbom, H., 143, 155
Rinnert, C., 6, 19, 23–24, 41, 73, 82, 91, 96, 105, 116
Roberts, B., 304, 308
Robinson, B., 60, 62, 65, 82
Roca, A., 225, 233, 246, 248–249
Roca de Larios, J., 35, 37, 53, 59, 61–64, 73–74
Rodgers, T. S., 160, 182, 227, 245
Rogers, T., 103, 117
Rosenthal, J. W., 226, 245

Rubin, B., 140, 153–156, 214
Rudakova, M., 192, 196–197, 200
Ruiz-Funes, M., ix, 3, 5–6, 11, 21–22, 28–30, 32, 42, 315, 317
Russia, 185
Russian, 100, 140, 185–186, 194, 226, 228, 233–234, 237, 240

Sachs, R., 49, 56, 62
Sadiqi, F., 85–86, 97
Saito, M., 105, 115
Samimy, K. K., 104, 117
Santos, T., 168, 182
Sapp, D. A., 13, 21
Sasaki, M., 24–25, 40, 42
Sato, I., 104, 117
Satrapi, M., 76
Saudi Arabia, 4
scaffolding, 53–54, 58, 60, 177; collective, 53
Scardamalia, M., 298, 307
Schallert, D. L., 147, 154
Schellens, P. J., 208, 215
schema, 30–31, 41, 170
Schmidt, R. W., 47, 62, 143, 156
Schofer, P., 36–38, 42
Schultz, J. M., ix, 10–12, 19, 22, 36–38, 40, 42, 65–66, 70, 72, 74, 77, 80–82, 314–315, 317, 320–321
Schuman, J. H., 143, 156
Schwartz, A., 229, 249
Schwarzer, D., 233, 249
science, 59–60, 65, 92–93, 105, 116, 136–137, 155, 188, 278
Scott, V. M., 23, 42, 70, 72, 82, 131, 137, 240, 249, 258, 280, 321
second language acquisition (SLA), 19, 44–47, 56, 60–64, 81–82, 96, 115, 143, 156, 265, 279–280, 315–316, 319, 321
secondary level, 5, 6, 20, 89, 165, 286

Segalowitz, N., 46, 62
semibilingual, 116
Shehadeh, A., 45, 52, 56, 59, 63
Shen, F., 301, 307, 310
Shi, L., 168, 174, 180
Silva, C., 166, 181
Silva, T., xii, 12, 21, 23, 41, 62, 91, 94, 97, 141, 143, 155–156, 161, 166, 179, 182, 199, 202, 215, 262–263, 280–281, 288, 296–297, 310, 319, 321
Simon, H. A., 27, 41
Simpson, J. M., 5, 21
Singapore, 4, 133
Skehan, P., 195, 199
Skill Learning Theory, 46
skilled writers, 24
Slaouti, D., 193, 199
Slavic, 256, 278
Smith, F., 25, 42, 172, 182
Smith, M., 49, 53, 61
social science, 149, 155
sociocultural, ix-x, xii, 37, 50, 75, 89, 166–167, 214, 264, 315
socioeconomic, 15, 84, 86, 123
sociolinguistic awareness, 237, 315
sociolinguistic competence, 203
sociolinguistics, 134, 247, 278
sociology, 65, 97, 103, 278
sociopolitical, 74–75, 78–79, 127, 133, 177
Soeda, E., 6, 19, 110, 114–115
software, 7, 111, 131, 258
Sommers, N. I., 24, 42
Soviet Union, 14, 183
Spack, R., 29, 42, 304, 310
Spada, N., 143, 156
Spain, 21
Spanglish, 233, 249
Spanish, ix, xi, 3, 5–6, 12, 16, 18, 21, 29, 32, 42, 51, 57, 73, 80–81, 85, 100, 104, 119, 201–205, 207–214, 221, 225–226, 228–229, 232–233, 234–238, 242, 244–249, 264, 312

speaking, vii, 70, 82, 85, 101–102, 110, 115, 117, 121–122, 126, 163, 185, 187, 190–192, 202, 205, 232, 235, 238, 248, 257–260, 262–263, 265–266, 268, 270, 277–281, 286–287, 299, 305, 313, 317
speaking and writing connections, 257–258, 262, 266, 278, 281
speech, 48, 76, 111–113, 185–186, 191, 233, 236, 258–259, 264, 279, 281–283, 306
spelling, 14, 92, 123, 184–185, 187, 191, 202–203, 208, 210, 233
Sperling, M., 262, 280
Spolsky, B., 142–143, 156
Sri Lanka, 6
St. John, O., 206, 214–215
standardized exams, 13
Stanley, J., 299, 310
status of the target language, viii, 311
Stein, V., 26–27, 29, 40, 42, 320
Storch, N., 49, 50, 53–55, 63
Storozhuk, S., 189, 199
Stotsky, S., 124, 137
strategic competence strategies, 203
strategy, x, 6, 18, 19, 23–25, 30, 36, 41, 43, 62, 84, 91, 96, 109, 110, 113, 115, 124, 132, 142, 147–148, 168, 194, 198, 203, 214, 239, 263, 286, 304, 307, 313; cognitive, 23, 166; feedback, 148; writing, 92
structuring, 26, 29
Strunk Jr., W., 156
style, 9, 20, 27, 35, 145, 149, 156, 168, 170, 185, 191, 235, 257, 260, 288, 291, 300, 302
Sullivan, K. P. H., 49, 61
summaries, 9, 23, 26, 30, 33, 34–35, 45, 58, 74, 115, 118, 141, 144, 151, 188, 288–289, 290

surveys, 82, 266–269, 271–272, 274–277, 281–282
Suzuki, W., 49, 53, 63
Swaffar, J. K., 26, 42, 71, 82, 260, 280
Swain, M., ix, 47–50, 52–54, 61–64, 203, 213, 258, 280–281
Swales, J. M., 144, 149, 156, 189, 200, 291, 303, 310
syllabus, 13, 29, 89, 110, 112, 129, 140, 142, 153, 164, 180, 237, 306, 308
Symposium on Second Language Writing, xii, 4, 70, 96, 311, 319
syntactic complexity, 35–36, 203
syntax, 25, 72–73, 185, 191, 208, 233, 281
synthèse, 76
Sze, P., 131, 137

Tabuse, M., 104, 117
Taiwan, 3, 16, 102, 119, 159–160, 162–165, 179, 314
Taiwanese, 163, 170, 172, 181
Takagi, A., 105, 117
Tamil, 6
Tarnopolsky, O., xi, 13, 21, 183–184, 188, 190, 192, 195–197, 200, 313, 318
task representation, 11, 21–22, 28–32, 36, 38, 40, 42, 320
task-based writing, 11, 195
Tateoka, Y., 106, 117
Taylor, I., 109, 117
Taylor, M., 109, 117
teacher shortage, 183
teacher training, 229, 248, 315; lack of teacher training, 88
teaching context, 87, 94, 192
teaching materials, 10, 183
teaching methods: center imposed, 8; imported, 87, 93
teaching philosophy, 258, 260
technology, 12, 69, 84, 92, 131,

158, 188, 190, 193, 199, 278, 319; absence of support, 87; electronic media, 319
Terrell, T. D., 258, 280
TESOL, 7, 20, 39, 42–43, 61, 82, 96–97, 115, 137, 153, 155–156, 160, 180–182, 215, 248, 280, 308–310
testing, ix, 41, 47–49, 125–126, 133, 135, 213, 313
tests, 50, 127, 265
textbook, 196–198, 237, 255, 267, 288, 291, 296
Thailand, 177
theory, viii, xii, 6, 18, 20, 22, 26, 31, 38, 39, 41–42, 44–46, 52, 59–62, 64, 82, 132, 135, 140, 155, 160, 162, 167, 180, 184, 199, 203, 214, 246, 248–249, 278, 281, 294, 308, 315
thesis, 15, 106, 140–141, 167, 169, 174–178, 186, 203, 210, 214, 286–287, 290, 293–294, 301
thesis statement, 106, 167, 169, 174–178, 186, 290, 293–294, 301
think-aloud protocol, 7, 50, 51, 53
Thompson, S. A., 29, 40
Thorne, S., 264, 281
Thorp, D., 49, 53, 55, 60
Thorson, H., xi, 5, 11, 21, 255, 259, 261–263, 280–281, 314–315, 317
Ting, Y. R., 306, 310
Tocalli-Beller, A., 49, 53, 64
Tonkin, H., 65, 67, 69, 72, 82
topic sentence, 167, 172, 186–187, 290, 293–294, 299, 301, 307
topicalization, 109
Toulmin, S., 208, 215
transcultural, 75, 79
transfer: linguistic, 25, 73, 95, 116–117, 206, 233, 258, 263, 317; rhetorical, 73

translation, 25, 70, 92, 97, 142, 163, 192, 201, 223, 233, 237, 240, 286, 314, 316
triangulation, 227
Tribble, C., 189, 197, 200
trilingual, 122
Trimbur, J., 160, 182
Truscott, J., 81, 239, 249, 304, 308, 310
Tsui, A. B. M., 169, 182
Turkey, 14, 313
Turner, C. E., 131, 134
Turner, J., 148, 156

Ukraine, 13, 21, 183, 185, 188, 192–194, 196, 198–200
Ukrainian, xi, 14, 100, 183–186, 190–198, 200, 313
Unger, J. M., 99, 117
United States, ix, x, 3, 5, 10–12, 17, 20, 65–66, 68, 71, 74, 80–81, 94, 98–99, 101–103, 105, 110, 113–114, 117, 133, 183–184, 186–187, 196, 207, 209, 211, 225–226, 228, 245–249, 255–256, 306, 314, 317
University of Victoria, BC, 256–257, 265, 278
University Teachers of English Language in Israel (UTELI), 142
uptake, 54
utilitarian, 123–124

Valdés, G., 225, 229, 233, 238, 249, 263, 281
van Esch, K., xi, 3, 6, 16, 18, 201, 318
Van Lier, L., 206–207, 215
VanPatten, B., 12, 19, 44, 60–61, 64
Vázquez, G., 210, 213–215
Vedder, I., 6, 19, 49, 53–55, 61, 72, 82

Velez-Rendon, G., 97
Verhoeven, G., 208, 215
Victori, M., 24, 43
Villa, D., 233, 249
vocabulary, 10, 26, 76, 92, 105–106, 111–113, 124–125, 129, 131, 134, 144, 163, 184–185, 187, 191–192, 201, 203, 205, 208, 210–211, 231, 233, 236, 241–242, 259, 291
voice, 62, 76, 121
Vygotsky, L. S., 206, 215

Wada, Y., 117
Walton, A. R., 99, 115
Wang, L., 91, 97
Wang, W., xi, 6, 13, 17, 21, 23, 25, 43, 50, 64, 91, 97, 285, 314, 318–319
Warschauer, M., 181, 264, 281
Watanabe, Y., 49, 53–54, 64
Watts, P., 303, 307
Weissberg, R., 149, 156, 157, 257–258, 263–265, 281
Welles, E., 98, 117
Wen, Q., 6, 21, 23, 25, 43, 50, 64, 91, 97
Whalley, E., 72, 81, 204, 214, 239, 246
White, G., 130, 134
White, R., 189, 196, 199, 200
Whitney, P. J., 264, 265, 280
Wigglesworth, G., 49–50, 53, 55, 63–64
Wiliam, D., 130, 134
Williams, J., xii, 44, 46, 60, 63–64, 168, 182, 293, 295–297, 299, 310
Woodall, B., 91, 97
workplace, 122, 132
writing and speaking relationships, 256–257, 259, 263
writing process, 21–23, 25, 38, 41–42, 50, 55, 62, 91, 145, 147,

152, 180, 204, 242, 263, 281, 297, 312, 316
writing program, xi, 99, 125, 203, 205–206, 211–213, 280

Yamada, K., 109, 117
Yang, M., 13, 21
Yasuda, S., 23–24, 43
You, X., 12–13, 21, 83, 97, 170–171, 208, 212–213, 221–222, 224, 230, 291, 292
Young, L., 144, 155

Yu, Z., 13, 21
Yue, F., 125, 137

Zamel, V., 23–24, 43, 72, 82, 141, 156, 166, 182, 298, 310
Zentella, A. C., 225, 249
Zhang, S., 298, 310
Zinsser, W., 285, 288, 310
Zone of Proximal Development, 206–207
Zuckerman, T., 140, 156

About the Editors

Tony Cimasko is a visiting assistant professor in the Department of English at Miami University in Oxford, Ohio, USA, teaching undergraduate and graduate second language writing courses, helping to build the university's second language writing program, and conducting workshops on international students for faculty across the university curriculum. His work has been published in the *Journal of Second Language Writing, Computers and Composition, English for Specific Purposes*, and the online edition of *What Is College Writing? Volume 2*. He is currently conducting research on differences between "real-world" professional genres and the pedagogical versions of those genres, and is continuing research into ways in which second language writers can successfully use elements from their first language-based experiences.

Melinda Reichelt graduated from Purdue University with an MA in English (1991) and PhD in English (1996). She is currently Professor of English at the University of Toledo, where she directs the ESL writing program and teaches courses in TESOL. ESL writing, and linguistics. She has published her work in the *Journal of Second Language Writing, World Englishes, Composition Studies, Issues in Writing,* the *ELT Journal, Modern Language Journal,* the *International Journal of English Studies, College ESL, Foreign Language Annals,* the *WAC Journal, English Today,* and *International Education*. She has presented her work at conferences such as TESOL, CCCC's, AAAL, and the Symposium on Second Language Writing. She is co-author with Tony Silva and Colleen Brice of *Annotated Bibliography of Scholarship in Second Language Writing: 1993-1997* (1999), published by Ablex.

www.ingramcontent.com/pod-product-compliance
Lightning Source LLC
Chambersburg PA
CBHW020635230426
43665CB00008B/190